ROGUES

Dedication

For Felix and Bea. I've taught you all I can, now read this and learn from the best – oh, apart from the one about the guy who eats his victims, that's taking things a touch too far. Dad

Publisher's Note

The rogues' 'Lives' in this book were taken from *A General History of the Lives and Adventures of the Most Famous Highwaymen, Murderers, Street-Robbers, &c. To which is added, a genuine account of the voyages and plunders of the most notorious pyrates...*, published in 1734. To aid readability, modern styling has been applied to the use of italics and initial caps for nouns, but spellings and punctuation have generally been left as they appeared in the original volume for authenticity. This is an historical text and certain terms, for Africans who were transported across the Atlantic as slaves and which are now unacceptable racial slurs, have been changed in the chapter on Colonel Jack.

This edition first published in 2021 by
The British Library
96 Euston Road
London NW1 2DB

Text and illustrations © 2021 The British Library Board
Introductory text © 2021 Sam Willis

Cataloguing in Publication Data
A catalogue record for this publication is available from the British Library

ISBN 978 0 7123 5339 7

Design styling by Blok Graphic, London
Typesetting by IDSUK (DataConnection) Ltd
Printed and bound in the Czech Republic by Finidr

A General History of the Lives,
Murders and Adventures of the

Most Notorious
ROGUES

Captain Charles Johnson
Introduced by Sam Willis

CONTENTS

Colonel Jack Robbing Mrs Smith?

B. Cole sculp.

INTRODUCTION

The book you are holding is a box of historical treasures. This edited collection of rogues' lives comes from Captain Charles Johnson's

A General History of the Lives and Adventures of the Most Famous
Highwaymen, Murderers, Street-Robbers, &c. To which is added, a genuine account
of the voyages and plunders of the most notorious pyrates . . .

Printed in 1734, this is far more than a collection of fascinating stories about highwaymen, pirates and rogues, however; it is a volume that raises questions that go to the very heart of what we know about the past . . . and the present.

Captain Charles Johnson was something of a literary phenomenon in the first half of the eighteenth century. He first roared onto the London publishing scene in a cloud of gunsmoke and cursing a full decade before the 1734 edition was published, with the first-ever published collection of pirates' lives, *A General History of the Robberies and Murders of the most notorious Pyrates*, which came out in the spring of 1724. By the end of that summer – just three months later – he had issued a second, longer and more detailed edition. A third followed the subsequent year and then a fourth, now further extended and split into two volumes, in 1726. Although it is impossible to recreate sales figures for this period, it is generally considered that these volumes sold well, and we can say with confidence that, by 1734, both Johnson and his pirates were already famous.

Johnson did not create a market in criminal biography: in 1724 that market was already long-established. In the same year that Johnson made his first literary appearance, four other criminal biographies were published, each of them a life of Jack Sheppard (also spelled Shepherd, see page 265), a notorious thief who was executed that winter at Tyburn, the 600-year-old, central-London location for public hangings. Two biographies had been published the year before, one on the highwayman Rob Roy, and the other on John Stanley, a murderous 'Knight-Errant'; five had been published the preceding year and so on. In fact, the phenomenon of criminal biography can easily be traced back to the reign of the Tudor queen Elizabeth I: in 1592 five such biographies were published – that is, 132 years before Johnson published his collection of pirates' lives.

Throughout these centuries criminals were celebrities and these books gave the public a glimpse into their lives. Indeed, if you change the words in the title 'highwaymen, murderers, street-robbers' for 'celebrities' you have '*A General History of the Lives and Adventures of Celebrities*' – and *that* is something we can all relate to: it's the very essence of Instagram.

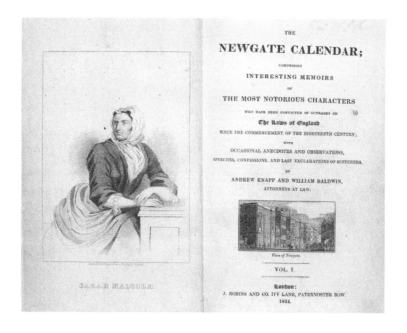

Johnson was also building on the publishing entrepreneurialism of another man, Captain Alexander Smith, who had already done what Johnson did with pirates, but with highwaymen. In 1713 Smith published

The History of the lives, of the most noted Highwaymen, foot-pads, shop-lifts and cheats of both sexes, in and about London and other places . . . for fifty years last past.

Just like Johnson's book, Smith's was very popular and two new editions had appeared by 1714. By 1734, therefore, not only were Johnson and his pirates famous, so too were Smith and his highwaymen. In that year Charles Johnson decided to combine these two literary sensations and create what we would describe today as a mash-up: in his new book Smith's highwaymen and rogues would sit alongside his pirates, but the book would be issued under his name alone.

Considering the fame of both Smith and Johnson, it is perhaps surprising that we don't know who either of these people were – though considerable effort has been made to unravel their identities. It has been assumed by all historians who have written on the subject that both are men, but there is no proof that this is the case. It has also been assumed that both Smith and Johnson were pen names for individual people, but there is no proof of that either and there remains every possibility that both were names that could have disguised two or more writers working together in a team. There is also the assumption that the Captain Johnson who wrote the book on pirates in 1724 was *the same person* who wrote the book in 1734, again, with no proof. Indeed, when considering the authorship of the first edition and its related volumes, one does well to consider that any explanation is still possible.

Smith, it has been argued from hints in the introduction to the second volume of his 1714 edition, may have been the satirist Ned Ward (1667–1731), the author of the well-known periodical about London life *The London Spy*. Johnson, it was once believed, was none other than the author Daniel Defoe (1660–1731) but the argument has now lost weight. A more recent suggestion is that Johnson was the newspaper owner, printer and journalist Nathaniel Mist (d. 1737) (for whom Defoe worked), a proposal that is supported by some – albeit indefinite – written evidence. Part of the attraction of both Defoe and

3

Jos. Nicholls Delin. *I. Basire s.*

Captain Teach commonly call'd Black Beard.

Mist as possible authors is that these men, at different times of their lives, were imprisoned. Defoe was accused of Seditious Libel which led to the pillory and a sentence in Newgate. Mist, a known Jacobite, was in trouble with the authorities on no fewer than fourteen occasions with several prison sentences and also a visit to the pillory. And so, yes, they were authors, but they were also criminals: if they did write the book, to some extent they had a vested, and insider, knowledge of their subject matter as well as access to criminals for material.

Part of the charm of the 1734 volume, therefore, is that the identity of its author/s remains a mystery. Perhaps the only secure facts we have are that Johnson was a man of the sea – his accounts of the pirates are littered with convincing and accurate descriptions of the realities of life at sea; that he had intimate and accurate knowledge of the West Indies; and that he had access to incoming reports about pirates in the same way that a good fishmonger has access to fresh fish: he had his ear to the sea, perhaps a network of informers from whom he could accurately take the pulse of the maritime news. We also know that whoever wrote the 1734 book was more than happy to freely take material from Smith's book to make a few sovereigns of his own – this book itself is a brazen act of literary robbery – an activity we might describe now, particularly in relation to music, as piracy.

This question of authorship hobbles us as historians, but so too does the material in the 1734 book itself. It is an unpredictable mixture of fact and fiction – but presented as fact. Some of the characters – not least the first, which is a life of Shakespeare's John Falstaff – are entirely fictional, plucked from myth or literary works. But others are real, even though their crimes, appearance or behaviour *seem* unreal. What is the attraction of the pirate Blackbeard – who ignites fireworks in his beard and hair to scare off his enemies and impress his victims as the incarnation of Lucifer himself – if not that he is something so fantastical that you *couldn't* make it up? Some of the actions of those who are real, however, we also know to have been fabricated.

The result of all of this is that the book is a challenge as much as it is a source of entertainment; to read it is to be entertained and informed but it is also to play a game with – and perhaps even to *spar* with – an author who lived 285 years ago but who is now joined directly to you through the words of this new edition. As you read this, know that you are in the hands of a master storyteller as well as a consummate historian, who deliberately weaves truth and lies together, at once telling us that we can 'depend' on the 'authenticity' of his tale and then suddenly pulling away the rug by including the implausible. In our modern world beset with fake news, such a challenge as is posed by this text is one that we must all be able to meet, and to learn these skills of the historian our only recourse.

But with this challenge in mind, the 1734 book opens up a world of entertainment and historical enquiry. As a contemporary document it is a political satire and a commentary on crime; as a popular literary work it is a precursor to the novel as much as it is to popular biography and more general popular history; as an *object*, the British Library's First Edition – from which this particular edition on the Rogues comes – is evidence of publishing and printing techniques and its healthy size and impressive engravings suggestive of a target audience with a disposable income and the desire to be seen as well-read – it is an early coffee-table book made for display as much as for reading; as a source of artwork it is an important contribution to what we know about the development of illustration; as an historical source it is unparalleled in what it tells us about certain types of crime; as an anonymous work it is a contribution to our understanding of the use of pen names, a fascinating history of its own which includes Charlotte Brontë, Agatha Christie, Stephen King and J.K. Rowling. The list of themes in the book ripe for exploration goes on and on. The more you look, the more you discover; the more you discover, the more questions you raise.

To read it is to be entertained and intrigued, shocked and bewildered. As you read it and experience those emotions, consider the bridge across time that this book has created, and know that thousands of people have similarly been lured by its title to pick it up, lured by its introduction to look inside, and lured by these lives into a world where innocence and evil, truth and lies, and past and present, all lie side by side. So read this new edition, but as you do so give half a thought to your historical shadow, that person who has picked it up, thumbed through the pages, and is now reading it in 1734.

Publishing this extraordinary volume now will, hopefully, bring it to the large audience it deserves, lead to further research to help us understand it, and engage people with the very stuff of history and with the skills of *being* a historian: read it and let me know which bits *you* believe.

@DrSamWillis

A GENERAL HISTORY OF ROGUES

As ever with Captain Johnson there is plenty of fiction in this volume to go with fact, cartoons to go with flesh and blood. Never forget that *A General History of the Lives and Adventures of the Most Famous Highwaymen, Murderers, Street-Robbers, &c.* (1734) was meant for entertainment as much as (and sometimes far more than) it was for education and reliable information; to enjoy it, you must allow the lines that mark your own perception of what a history book 'should' be to blur and perhaps also your understanding of what is – or is not – a crime.

Some crimes are obvious – such as cannibalism, gruesomely depicted in the chapter on Sawney Beane. But even in that particular story, when Johnson explores the very extremes of credulity in his audience, there is important and accurate history to be found. Are you after something racy and of pure invention? Look no further than this wonderful tale, presented here, as all of Johnson's stories are, as cast-iron fact: 'The following account, though as well attested as any historical fact can be', says Johnson. Hmm, let us see. This Mr Beane lived in a cave in Scotland (more specifically on a headland in the Firth of Clyde) with his wife, their many children and numerous grandchildren conceived through incest between the children. Some accounts give the number at almost 50. This mighty clan survived by ambushing people near their cave and then eating them, pickling the leftovers in barrels. Let's allow Johnson to tell it, for he tells it best.

> As soon as they had robb'd and murder'd any man, woman, or child, they used to carry off the carcass to the den, where cutting it into quarters, they would pickle the mangled limbs, and afterwards eat it; this being their only sustenance: and, notwithstanding, they were at last so numerous, they commonly had superfluity of this their abominable food; so that in the night-time they frequently threw legs, and arms of the unhappy wretches they had murdered, into the sea, at a great distance from their bloody habitation. The limbs were often cast up by the tide in several parts of the country, to the astonishment and terror of all the beholders

Unsurprisingly this story was so potent that it has survived for many centuries and is still known and retold in Scotland today. In fact, it became so popular in the eighteenth century that Scots actually became known by the English as 'Sawneys', and therein perhaps lies some truth in the tale. Some (most) historians believe that the story was created in the intense fire of anti-Scottish sentiment that burned in England for many generations, and especially fiercely in the first half of the eighteenth century. The English and Scottish parliaments were unified by the Act of Union of 1707 but this 'union' led to intense transnational comparisons and loathing as both sides sought to identify themselves independently in spite of this new political union which stated that all Scots and English were now, in fact, one. There were Jacobite rebellions in 1715 and 1719, and in 1745, just 12 years after *A General History of the Lives and Adventures of the Most Famous Highwaymen, Murderers, Street-Robbers, &c.* was published, the Jacobites rose up again with more success than ever before. What better way to celebrate English identity by denigrating the Scots in 1734 than to share this story of uncontrollable incestuous breeding, inconceivable savagery and bestial behaviour, and to do so on the widest possible of platforms? The story might be nonsense but in its telling Charles Johnson has revealed something about himself: whoever he (or she) was,★ they were either anti-Scottish or keenly alert to the commercial value of anti-Scottish sentiment at the time.

★ See pp.3–5 and note that the inclusion of this anti-Scottish story may well be a powerful argument against the author being Nathaniel Mist, with his known Jacobite sympathies.

Sheppard, after escaping from Newgate, persuades a Shoemaker to knock his Irons off.

9

At the other end of this scale running between fact and fantasy is Jonathan Wild, a man so much of flesh and blood that his skeleton still exists; it is on display at the Royal College's Hunterian Museum in London. In this period, autopsies were carried out on the most notorious of criminals and Wild was certainly one of them. As gang-leader, Wild stole with one hand but in his official role as Thief-Taker General, he received rewards for returning those goods with the other. He even helped catch the criminals 'responsible' – by fingering innocents. Wild was loved by the press in the same way that the pirate Captain Kidd was. Kidd once held an official position with a Royal warrant but 'turned pirate', and so, too, did Wild embrace the dark side. His crime, therefore, was not just theft but *betrayal*: he betrayed the trust placed in him by upright society, the trust that held – just – society together. His was exactly the type of crime that terrified the establishment.

Alongside Wild and Beane there is a kaleidoscope of criminality, a fascinating history in its own right, for there are crimes and criminals that we might recognise here – swindlers, pickpockets, murderers and thieves, and even a bril-liant tale of an imposter, the enthralling German Princess, who claimed to be the daughter of the Lord of Holmsteim but was, in fact, the daughter of a chorister at Canterbury cathedral. There are also, however, crimes that will be new to most. Who has heard, for example, of the wool-drawers, 'whose trade is to snatch away cloaks, hats, or perukes, from towners'? Johnson adds just a splash of colour, noting that this was 'a very sly sort of theft, practis'd only in the night'. Other crimes no longer exist – at least not in name. Take housebreaking. During the eighteenth century, breaking into a dwelling at night was seen as burglary in English common law but breaking into a dwelling during the day was a comple-tely separate offence, known as housebreaking.

For all of the variety of crimes represented in the original 1734 book, it is interesting and important that they are not disclosed in the chapter titles which are nothing more than a beguilingly ordinary name: the stories were carefully created with the pleasure of the readers' discovery in mind. The 1734 book itself was a cunning plot, a carefully laid trap. A large part of the pleasure that one derives from reading these biographies, therefore, lies in the *finding-out*. What ghastly crime has this, once innocent, person stooped to? What, for example, could that nice-sounding, next-door-neighbourly parson's son Tom Taylor have done? Pickpocket, I'm afraid; and caught by a gentleman in a theatre who had deliberately sewn fishhooks into his pockets so as to catch the likes of Taylor. And what of the charming Deborah Churchill, given an excellent education and brought up well by honest parents? Thief and prostitute and accessory to murder, I'm afraid. 'Abandoned . . . to all manner of filthiness and uncleanness.' Regularly abused. In one nasty incident 'kicked . . . about the room like a foot ball.' Or the man with the trustworthy name of Jack Goodwin? Conman and swindler, I'm afraid. In one instance he convinced a homeless man to let him seal his eyes shut with candlewax – all so that Jack could play the role of blind-man's guide, luring unsuspecting passers-by with fat wallets into his path.

These criminal lives therefore stand testament to the original publisher's awareness and clever manipulation of the commercial value of the fall of man as experienced in the first half of the eighteenth century, and it is lurid not only in the description of the heinous crimes but also in what might await you should you be caught. There are hangings, whippings, burnings and brandings, hard labour and transportation (your punishment could be measured in miles as easily as in years), but so too the brutality of simple incarceration. In the life of the nice-sounding Thomas Sharp (fraudster and thief, I'm afraid) we have a particularly spectacular description of Newgate, at the time London's oldest and most notorious gaol.

> 'Tis a dwelling in more than Cimmerian darkness, an habitation of misery, a confus'd chaos, without any distinction, a bottomless pit of violence, and a Tower of Babel, where are all speakers, and no hearers. There is mingling the noble with the ignoble, the rich with the poor, the wise with the ignorant, and the debtors with the worst of malefactors. It is the grave of gentility, the banishment of courtesy, the poison of honour, the centre of infamy, the paradise of cousenage, the hell of tribulation, the treasure of despair, the refuge of vengeance, and den of foxes. There he that yesterday was great, to-day is mean; he that was well fed abroad, there starves; he that was richly clad, is stark naked; he that commanded, obeys; and he that lay in a good bed, is forc'd to rest himself on the hard boards, or cold stones ... There hunger is their appetite; their times of meals, always when they get any thing to eat; their table, the floor; their sauce, the filthy stinks of their wards; and their musick, nothing but snoring, sneezing, and belching.

To read these biographies was (and still is), therefore, to wallow in human guilt and sin; to feverishly scratch a terrible itch. The reading – or perhaps we should say consumption – of this book would have given the reader a distinct and illicit pleasure. No doubt the book was sometimes even *read* illicitly. In some god-fearing morally upright households even to have the book in your possession would have been a crime, and actually to read it an unforgivable one. Perhaps for a truly authentic contemporary experience as a reader, you should take this new edition into the downstairs closet and lock the door to read in secret; or slip it into a backpack and ride to a nice spot under an isolated tree. And between bouts of rushed and hushed forbidden reading, you must hide it – perhaps under a pillow, perhaps even in plain sight, where this despicable, corrupting bible of crime can lurk, disguised in a tower of acceptable literature. Ah yes, I see a spot ... just there on your shelves ... between *Nigella Christmas* and the Ordnance Survey's *Circular Walks on Dartmoor* ... perfect. No one will ever know what you *really* want to read. Let's keep it a secret between you and me.

Fett. delin.   I.Bagre. sculp.

Colonel Jack Robbing Mrs Smith going to Kentish Town

THE LIFE OF
COLONEL JACK

I n this account of the life of Colonel Jack, as written by himself, there is room for just and copious observations on the blessings and advantages of a sober and a well-govern'd education, and the ruins of many thousands of youths of all kinds for want of it: also how much publick-schools and charities might be improv'd to prevent the destruction of so many unhappy children, as in this city are every year bred up for the gallows. The miserable condition of unfortunate children, many of whose natural tempers are docible, and would lead them to learn the best things rather than the worst, are truly deplorable, and is abundantly seen in the history of this man's childhood, where though circumstances form'd him by necessity to be a thief, a strange rectitude of principles remain'd with him, and made him early abhor the worst part of his trade, and at last wholly leave it off. If he had come into the world with the advantages of education, and been well-instructed how to improve the generous principles he had in him, what a man might he not have been?

The various turns of his fortune in the world, make a delightful field for the reader to wander in. Every wicked reader will be here encouraged to a change, and it will appear, that the best and only good end of a wicked misspent life is repentance. While these things, and such as these are the end and designs of the undertakers of this present book, I think no apology need be made for any single life, no, nor for the whole, if discouraging every thing that is evil, and encouraging every thing which is virtuous and good: I say, if these appear to be the scope and design of publishing such stories, no objection can be against it, neither is it of the least moment to inquire whether the Colonel hath told his own story true or not. If he has made it a history, or a parable, it will be equally useful and capable of doing good, and in that it recommends itself without any further introduction.

Seeing my life has been such a chequer-work of nature, and that I am able now to look back upon it, from a safer distance, than is ordinary to the fate of the clan, to which I once belong'd, I think my history may find a place in the world, as well as some, who I see are every day read with pleasure, though they have in them nothing so diverting or instructing, as I believe mine will appear to be.

My original may be as high as any bodies, for ought I know; for my mother kept very good company; but that part belongs to her story more than to mine: all I know of it is by oral tradition thus: my nurse told me my mother was a gentlewoman; that my father was a man of quality, and she (my nurse) had a good piece of money given her to take me off his hands, and deliver him and my mother from the importunities that usually attend the misfortune of having a child to keep that should not be seen or heard of.

My father, it seems, gave my nurse something more than was agreed for, at my mother's request, upon her solemn promise, that she would use me well, and let me be put to school; and charged her, that if I lived to come to any bigness, capable to understand the meaning of it, she should always take care to bid me remember, that I was a gentleman; and this, he said, was all the education he would desire of her for me; for he did not doubt, but that some time or other, the very hint would inspire me with thoughts suitable to my birth; and that I would certainly act like a gentleman, if I believ'd myself to be so.

But my disasters were not directed to end as soon as they began; 'tis very seldom that the unfortunate are so but for a day, as the great rise by degrees of greatness to the pitch of glory in which they shine; so the miserable sink to the depth of their misery by a continued series of disasters, and are long in the tortures and agonies of their distressed circumstances before a turn of fortune, if ever such a thing happens to them, gives them a prospect of deliverance.

My nurse was as honest to the engagement she had enter'd into, as could be expected from one of her employment; and particularly as honest as her circumstances would give her leave to be; for she bred me up very carefully with her own son, and with another son of shame, like me, who she had taken upon the same terms.

My name was John, as she told me; but neither she nor I knew any thing of a sirname that belonged to me; so that I was left to call myself Mr Any Thing what I pleased, as fortune and better circumstances should give occasion. It happen'd, that her own son (for she had a litle boy about one year older than I) was called John too, and about two years after, she took another son of shame, as I call'd it above, to keep, as she did me, and his name was John too. But my nurse, who may be allow'd to distinguish her own son a little from the rest, would have him call'd Captain, because forsooth he was the eldest.

I was provok'd at having this boy called Captain, and cried and told my nurse **15** I would be called Captain; for she told me I was a gentleman, and I would be a captain, that I would. The good woman, to keep the peace, told me, 'Ay, ay, I was a gentleman, and therefore I should be above a captain, for I should be a colonel, and that was a great deal better than a captain: for, my dear,' says she, 'every tarpawlin, if he gets but to be lieutenant of a press-smack, is called captain; but colonels are soldiers, and none but gentlemen are ever made colonels: besides,' says she, 'I have known colonels come to be lords, and generals though they were bastards at first; and therefore you shall be called Colonel.' Well I was hush'd indeed, with this for the present, but not thoroughly pleased, till a little while after, I heard her tell her own boy, that I was a gentleman; and therefore he must call me Colonel; at which her boy fell a crying, and he would be called Colonel too; so then I was satisy'd that it was above a captain. So universally is ambition seated in the minds of men, that not a beggar boy, but has his share of it. Before I tell you much more of our story, it would be very proper to give something of our several characters, as I have gather'd them up in my memory, as far back as I can recover things either of myself, or my brother Jacks, and they shall be brief and impartial.

Capt. Jack, the eldest of us all by a whole year, was a squat, big, strong made boy, and promised to be stout when grown up to be a man, but not tall. He was an original rogue; for he would do the foulest and most villainous things even by his own inclination; he had no taste or sense of being honest, no not even to his brother rogues, which is what other thieves make a point of honour of; I mean that of being honest to one another.

Major Jack was a merry, facetious, pleasant boy, and had something of a gentleman in him: he had a true manly courage, fear'd nothing, and yet, if he had the advantage, was the most compassionate creature alive, and wanted nothing but honesty to have made him an excellent man. He had learnt to write and read very well, as you will find in the process of this story.

As to myself, I pass'd among my comrades for a bold resolute boy; but I had a different opinion of myself; and therefore shun'd fighting as much as I could. I was wary and dexterous at my trade, and was not so often catched as my fellow-rogues. I mean while I was a boy, and never after I came to be a man, no not once for twenty six years, being so old in the trade, and still unhang'd.

I was almost ten years old, the Captain eleven, and the Major eight, when our good old nurse died, her husband was drown'd a little before in the *Gloucester* frigate, which was cast away going to Scotland with the Duke of York, in the reign of King Charles II and the honest woman dying very poor, the parish was obliged to bury her. The good woman being dead, we were turned loose to the world, rambling about all three together, and the people in Rosemary Lane and Ratcliffe, knowing us pretty well, we got victuals easy enough; as for lodging, we lay in the summer-time on bulk-heads, and at shop-doors, as for a bed, we knew nothing what belong'd to it for many years after my nurse died; but in winter got into the ash-holes, and nealing-arches in the glass-houses, where we were accompanied by several youngsters like ourselves; some of whom persuaded the Captain to go a kid-napping with them, a trade at that time much followed: the gang used to catch children in the evening, stop their mouths, and carry them to such houses, where they had rogues ready to receive them, who put them on board ships bound to Virginia, and when they arrived there, they were sold. This wicked gang were at last taken, and sent to Newgate; and Capt. Jack, among the rest, though he was not then much above thirteen years old, and being but a lad, was ordered to be three times whipped at Bridewell, the recorder telling him, it was done in order to keep him from the gallows: we did what we could to comfort him; but he was scourged so severely, that he lay sick for a good while; but as soon as he regain'd his liberty, he went to his old gang, and kept among them as long as that trade lasted; for it ceased a few years afterwards.

The Major and I, though very young, had sensible impressions made on us for some time by the severe usage of the Captain; but it was within the year, that the Major, a good-condition'd easy body was wheedled away by a couple of young rogues to take a walk with them. The gentlemen were very well matched for the oldest of them was not above fourteen, the business was to go to Bartholomew-Fair, and the end of going there was to pick pockets.

The Major knew nothing of the trade, and therefor was to do nothing, but they promised him a share with them, for all that, as if he had been as expert as themselves; so away they went. The two dexterous rogues managed it so well, that by about eight o'clock at night, they came back to our dusty quarters at the glass-house, and sitting them down in a corner, they began to share their spoil by the light of the glass-house fire: the Major lugg'd out the goods, for as fast as they made any purchase, they unloaded themselves, and gave all to him, that if they had been taken, nothing might be found about them. It was a devilish lucky day to them; the Devil certainly assisting them to find their prey, that he might draw in a young gamester, and encourage him to the undertaking, who had been made backward before by the misfortune of the Captain. The list of their purchase the first night was as follows:

1. A white handkerchief from a country wench, as she was staring up at a jack-pudding: there was three shillings and six-pence, and a row of pins tied up in one end of it.
2. A coloured handkerchief out of a young country fellow's pocket, as he was buying a China orange.
3. A ribband-purse with eleven shillings and three pence, and a silver thimble in it, out of a young woman's pocket, just as a fellow offered to pick her up.— N. B. She miss'd her purse presently; but not seeing the thief, charged the man with it that would have picked her up, and cried out, 'A pickpocket!' and he fell into the hands of the mob, but being known in the street, he got off with great difficulty.

4. A knife and fork that a couple of boys had just bought, and were going home with; the young rogue that took it, got it within the minute after the boy had put into his pocket.
5. A little silver-box with seven shillings in it, all in small silver, 1 *d.* 2 *d.* 3 *d.* 4 *d.* pieces.
6. Two silk handkerchiefs.
7. A jointed-baby, and a little looking-glass, stoln off a toy-seller's stall in the fair.

All this cargo to be brought home clear in one afternoon, or evening rather, and by only two little rogues, so young, was, it must be confessed, extraordinary; and the Major was elevated the next day to a strange degree; for he came to me very early, and called me out into a narrow lane, and shewed me almost his little hand full of money. I was surpriz'd at the sight, when he puts it up again, and bringing his hand out, 'Here,' says he, 'you shall have some of it,' and gives me a six-pence and a shilling's worth of the small silver pieces. This was very welcome to me, who never had a shilling of money together before in all my life, that I could call my own. I was very earnest to know how he came by this wealth; he quickly told me the story; and that he had for his share seven shillings and six-pence in money, the silver-thimble, and a silk-handkerchief.

We went to Rag-Fair, and bought each of us, a pair of shoes and stockings, and afterwards went to a boiling cooks in Rosemary-Lane, where we treated ourselves nobly; for we had boil'd beef, pudding, a penny-brick, and a pint of strong-beer, which cost us seven-pence in all. That night the Major triumph'd in our new enjoyment, and slept in the usual place, with an undisturb'd repose: the next day the Major and his comrades went abroad again, and were still successful, nor did any disaster attend them for many months; and by frequent imitation and direction, Major Jack became as dexterous a pick-pocket as any of them, and went through a long variety of fortune, too long to enter upon now, because I am hast'ning to my own story, which at present is the main thing I have to set down.

Overcome by the persuasions of the Major, I enter'd myself into his society, and went down to Billinsgate with one of them, which was crouded with masters of coal-ships, fish-mongers, and oyster-women. It was the first of these people my comrade had his eye upon: so he gives me my orders, which was thus:

'Go you,' says he, 'into all the ale-houses as we go along, and observe where any people are telling of money, and when you find any, come and tell me.' So he stood at the door, and I went into the houses. As the collier masters generally sell their coals at the gate, as they call it; so they generally receive their money in those ale-houses, and it was not long before I brought him word of several. Upon this, he went in and made his observations; but found nothing to his purpose. At length I brought him word, that there was a man in such a house, who had received a great deal of money of somebody, I believed, of several people; and that it lay all upon the table in heaps, and he was very busy writing down the sums, and putting it up in several bags: 'Is he,' says he, 'I'll warrant him, I will have some of it;' and in he goes, walks up and down the house, which had several open tables and boxes in it, and listen'd to hear, if he could learn what the man's name was, and he heard somebody call him Cullam, or some such name, then he watches his opportunity, and steps up to him, and tells him a long story, 'That there was two gentlemen at the gun-tavern sent him to enquire for him, and to tell him, they desired to speak with him.'

The collier master had got his money before him just as I had told him, and had two or three small payments of money, which he had put up in little black dirty bags, and laid by themselves; and as it was hardly broad day, he found means in delivering his message, to lay his hand upon one of those bags, and carry it off perfectly undiscover'd. When he had got it, he came out to me, who stood but at the door, and pulling me by the sleeve, 'Run, Jack,' says he, 'for our lives;' and away he scours, and I after him, never resting, or scarce looking about me, till we got quite into Moorfields. But not thinking ourselves safe there, we run on till we got into the fields, and finding a by-place, we sat down, and he pulls out the bag, 'Thou art a lucky boy, Jack,' says he, 'thou deservest a good share of this job, truly; for 'tis all along of thy lucky news'; so he pours it all out into my hat; for, as I told you, I now wore a hat.

How he did to whip away such a bag from any man who was awake and in his senses, I can't tell: there was about seventeen or eighteen pound in the bag, and he parted the money, giving me one third, with which I was very well contented. As we were now so rich, he would not let me lie any longer about the glass-house, or go naked and ragged, as I had done; but obliged me to buy two shirts, a waistcoat, and a great-coat; for a great-coat was more proper for our

19

business than any other. So I cloathed myself, as he directed, and we lodged together in a little garret.

Soon after this, we walk'd out again, and then we tried our fortune in the places by the Exchange a second time. Here we began to act separately, and I undertook to walk by himself, and the first thing I did accurately, was a trick I play'd that argued some skill for a new beginner; for I had never seen any business of that kind done before, I saw two gentlemen mighty eager in talk, and one pulled out a pocket-book two or thre times, and then slipt it into his coat-pocket again, and then out it came again, and papers were taken out, and others put in, and then in it went again; and so several times, the man being still warmly engaged with another man, and two or three others standing hard by them the last time he put his pocket-book into his pocket with his hand, and the book lay end-way, resting upon some other book, or something else in his pocket; so that it did not go quite down, but one corner of it was seen above his pocket. When seeing the book pass and repass, I brushed smoothly, but closely by the man, and took it clean away, and went directly into Moorfields, where my fellow rogue was to meet me. It was not long before he came: I had no occasion to tell him my success; for he had heard of the action among the crowd. We searched the book, and found several goldsmith's and other notes: but the best of the booty was in one of the folds of the cover of the book. There was a paper full of loose diamonds. The man, as we understood afterwards, was a Jew, and dealt in those glittering commodities.

We agreed that Will (which was my comrade's name) should return to the Change to hear what news was stirring, and there he heard of a reward of one hundred pound for returning the things. The next day he went to the gentleman, and told him he had got some scent of his book, and the person who took it, and who, he believed, would restore it, for the sake of the reward, provided he was assured that he should not be punish'd for the fact. After many preliminaries, it was concluded, that Will should bring the book, and the things lost in it, and receive the reward, which on the third day, he did, and faithfully paid me my share of it.

Not long after this, it fell out, we were strolling about in Smithfield on a Friday: there happened to be an old country gentleman in the market, selling some very large bullocks; it seems they came out of Sussex, for we heard him say, there were no such bullocks in the whole county of Sussex. His Worship, for so they call'd him, had received the money for these bullocks at a tavern, whose sign I have forgot now, and having some of it in a bag, and the bag in his hand, he was taken with a sudden fit of coughing, and stands to cough, resting his hand with the bag of money in it, upon a bulk-head of a shop, just by the Cloyster-Gate in Smithfield, that is to say, within three or four doors of it: we were both just behind him, says Will to me, 'Stand ready': upon this, he makes an artificial stumble, and falls with his head just against the old gentleman in the very moment when he was coughing ready to be strangl'd and quite spent for want of breath.

The violence of the blow, beat the old gentleman quite down; the bag of money did not immediately fly out of his hand, but I ran to get hold of it, and gave it a quick snatch, pulled it clean away, and run like the wind down the Cloyster with it, till I got to our old rendezvous. Will in the mean time, fell down with the old gentleman, but soon got up. The old knight, for such, it seems he was, was frighted with the fall, and his breath so stopp'd with his cough, that he could not recover himself to speak 'till some time, during which, nimble Will, was got up again, and walk'd off; nor could he call out stop thief, or tell any body he had lost any thing for a good while; but coughing vehemently till he was almost black in the face, he at last brought it out, 'The rogues have got away my bag of money.'

All this while the people understood nothing of the matter; and as for the rogues indeed, they had time enough to get clear away, and in about an hour, Will came to the rendezvous; there we sat down on the grass again, and turned out the money, which proved to be eight guineas, and five pounds eight shillings in silver: this we shar'd upon the spot, and went to work the same day for more; but whether it was, that being flush'd with our success, we were not so vigilant, or that no other opportunity offer'd, I know not, but we got nothing more that night, nor so much as any thing offer'd itself for an attempt.

The next adventure was in the dusk of the evening, in a court which goes out of Grace-Church Street into Lombard-Street, where the Quaker's Meeting-House is, there was a young fellow, who, as we learn'd afterwards, was a woollen-draper's apprentice in Grace-Church Street, it seems he had been receiving, a sum of money, which was very considerable, and he comes to a goldsmiths in Lombard Street with it, paid in the most of it there, insomuch that it grew dark; and the goldsmith began to be shutting in shop, and candles to be lighted, we watched him in there, and stood on the other side of the way, to see what he did, when he paid in all the money he intended, he stayed a little longer to take notes for what he had paid. At last he comes out of the shop with still a pretty large bag under his arm, and walks over into the court, which was then very dark, in the middle of the court is a boarded entry, and at the end of it a threshold, and as soon as he had set his foot over the threshold, he was to turn on his left hand into Grace-Church Street.

'Keep up,' says Will to me, 'be nimble,' and as soon as he had said so, he flies at the young man, and gives him such a violent thrust, that pushed him forward with too great a force for him to stand; and as he strove to recover the threshold, took hold of his feet, and he fell forward. I stood ready, and presently fell out the bag of money, which I heard fall, for it flew out of his hand. I went forward with the money, and Will finding I had it, run backward. And as I made along Fenchurch-Street overtook me, and we scoured home together. The poor young man was hurt a little with the fall, and reported to his master as we heard afterwards, that he was knocked down: his master was glad the rest of the money was paid in to the banker, and made no great noise at the loss, only cautioned his apprentice to avoid such dark places for the future,

This booty amounted to 14 *l.* 18 *s.* apiece, and added extremely to my store; which began to grow too big for my management; but still I was at a loss with whom to trust it. A little after this, Will brought me into the company of two more young fellows; we met at the lower part of Gray's-Inn Lane, about an hour before sun set, and went out into the fields, towards a place called the Pindar of Wakefield, where are abundance of brick-hills; here it was agreed to spread from the field path, to the road-way, all the way towards Pancrass church, to observe any chance game; which, as they called it, they might shoot flying. Upon the path within the bank on the side of the road going towards Kentish Town, two of our gang, Will, and one of the other met a single gentleman, walking apace towards the town, being almost dark, Will cryed, 'Mark, ho,' which, it seems was the word at which we were all to stand still at a distance, come in if he wanted help, and give a signal if any thing appeared that was dangerous.

Will steps up to the gentleman, stops him, and put the question, that is, 'Sir, your money'; the gentleman seeing he was alone, struck at him with his cane, but Will a nimble strong fellow, flew in upon him, and with strugling got him down, then he begged for his life. Will having told him with an oath, that he would cut his throat in that moment. While this was doing, comes a hackney coach along the road, and the fourth man who was that way cries 'Mark, ho,' he which was to intimate that it was a prize, not a surprize, and accordingly the next man went up to assist him, where they stop'd the coach, which had a doctor of physick, and a surgeon in it, who had been to visit some considerable patient, and I suppose had considerable fees; for here they got two gold purses, one with 11 or 12 guineas, the other six, with some pocket money, two watches, one diamond ring, and the surgeon's plaister box, which was most of it full of silver instruments.

While they were at this work Will kept the man down, who was under him, and tho' he promis'd not to kill him, unless he offered to make a noise, yet he would not let him stir, till he heard the noise, of the coach going on again, by which he knew the job was over on that side. Then he carried him a little out of the way, ty'd his hands behind him, and bid him lie still and make no noise, and he would come back in half an hour, and untie him upon his word, but if he cry'd out he would come back and kill him. The poor man promis'd to lie still and make no noise, and did so, and had not above 11 s. 6 d. in his pocket, which Will took, and came back to the rest; but while they were together, I who was on the side of the Pindar of Wakefield, cry'd 'Mark, ho,' too.

What I saw was a couple of poor women, one a kind of a nurse, and the other a maid-servant, going for Kentish Town. As Will knew I was but young at the work, he came flying to me, and seeing how easy a bargain it was, he said 'Go Col. fall to work'. I went up to them, and speaking to the elderly woman, 'Nurse' said I, 'don't be in such haste, I want to speak with you,' at which they both stopp'd, and looked a litle frighted, 'don't be frighted sweet-heart' said I to the maid, 'a little of that money in the bottom of your pocket, will make all easy, and I'll do you no harm'; by this time Will came up to us, for they did not see him before, then they began to scream out, 'hold' says I, 'make no noise, unless you have a mind to force us to murther you whether we will or no, give me your money presently, and make no words, and we shan't hurt you.' Upon this the poor maid pull'd out 5 s. 6 d. and the old woman a guinea and a shilling, crying heartily for her money, and said it was all she had in the world; well we took it for all that, tho' it made my heart bleed to see what agony the poor woman was in at parting with it; and I ask'd her where she lived, she said her name was Smith, and she lived at Kentish Town, I said nothing to her, but bid them go on about their business; and I gave Will the money; so in a few minutes we were all together again; says one of the other rogues 'come this is well enough for one road, it's time to be gone'. So we jog'd away, crossing the fields out of the path towards Tottenham-Court; but 'hold' says Will, 'I must go and untie the Man.' 'D—m him,' says one of them, 'let him lye,' 'no' says Will, 'I won't be worse than my word, I will untye him.' So he went to the place, but the man was gone; either he had untied himself, or some-body had passed by, and he had called for help, and so was untied, for he could not find him, nor make him hear, tho' he ventured to call twice for him aloud.

This made us hasten away the faster, and getting into Tottenham Court Road, they thought it was a little too near, so they made into the town at St Giles's, and crossing to Piccadilly went to Hyde Park Gate; here they ventured to rob another coach, that is to say, one of the two other rogues and Will, did it between the Park Gate and Knights-bridge; there was in it only a gentleman and a whore that he had pick'd up it seems at the Spring-Garden a little farther, they took the gentleman's money, and his watch, and his silver hilted sword; but when they came to the slut, she damn'd them and cursed them for robbing the gentleman of his money, and leaving him none for her; as for herself she had not one sixpenny-piece about her, tho' she was indeed well enough dressed too. Having made this adventure, we parted, and went each man to his lodging.

Two days after this, Will came to my lodging, for I had now got a room by myself, and appointed me to meet him the next evening at such a place. I went, but to my great satisfaction miss'd him; but met with the gang at another place, who had committed a notorious robbery near Hounslow; where they wounded a gentleman's gardner, so that I think he died, and robbed the house of a very considerable sum of money and plate. This, however, was not so clean'd carried, but the neighbours were alarm'd, the rogues pursued, and being at London with the booty, one of them was taken; but Will being a dextrous fellow made his escape with the money and plate. He knew nothing that one of his comrades were taken, and that they were all so closely pursued that every one was obliged to shift for himself. He happened to come home in the evening, as good luck then directed him. Just after search had been made for him by the constables, his companion who was taken, having upon promise of favour, and to save himself from the gallows, discovered his confederates; and Will among the rest, as the principal party in the whole undertaking, he got notice of it, and left all his booty at my lodging, hiding it in an old coat that lay under my bed, leaving word he had been there, and had left the coat that he borrowed of me, under my bed. I knew not what to make of it, but went up stairs, and finding the parcel, was surprized to see wrapped up in it, above a hundred pounds in plate and money, and heard nothing of Brother Will, as he called himself, for three or four days, when we sold the plate after the rate of two shillings per ounce, to a pawn-broker near Cloth-Fair.

About two days afterwards, going upon the strole, who should I meet but my former brother Captain Jack? When he saw me, he came close to me in his blunt way, and says, 'Do you hear the news?' I asked him, 'What news?' He told me, 'My old comrade and teacher was taken, and that morning carried to Newgate; that he was charged with a robbery and murder, committed somewhere beyond Brentford; and that the worst was, he was impeached.' I thanked him for his information, and for that time parted; but was the very next morning surpriz'd, when going cross Rag-Fair, I heard one call 'Jack?' I look'd behind me, and immediately saw three men, and after them a constable, coming towards me with great fury, I was in a great surprize, and started to run; but one of them clapped in upon me, got hold of me, and in a moment the rest surrounded me, and told me they were to apprehend a known thief, who went by the name of one of the Three Jacks of Rag-Fair; for that he was charged upon oath, with having been a party in a notorious robbery, burglary, and murther, committed in such a place, and on such a day.

Not to trouble the reader with an account of the discourse that past between the Justice, before whom I was carried, and myself. I shall, in brief, inform him, that my brother Capt. Jack. who had the forwardness to put it to me, whether I was among them or no; when in truth he was there himself, had the only reason to fly, at the same time that he advised me to shift for myself; so that I was discharged, and in about three weeks after, my master and tutor in wickedness, poor Will, was executed for the fact.

I had nothing to do now but to find out the Captain, who, though not without some trouble, I at last got news of, and told him the whole story: he presently discover'd by his surprize, that he was guilty, and after a few words more, told me, 'It was all true, that he was in the robbery, and had the greatest part of the booty in keeping; but what to do with it, or himself he did not know; but thought of flying into Scotland,' asking me, 'if I would go with him?' I consented, and the next day he shewed me twenty two pound he had in money. I honestly produced all the money I had left, which was upwards of sixteen pounds. We set out from London on foot, and travelled the first day to Ware; for we had learn'd so much of the road, that our way lay thro' that town; from Ware we travelled to Cambridge, though that was not our direct road: the occasion was this: in our way through Puckridge, we baited at an inn, and while we were there, a countryman came and hung his horse at the gate, while he went in to drink: we sat in the gate-way, having called for a mug of beer, we drank it up; we had been talking to the hostler about the way to Scotland, and he bid us ask the road to Royston: 'But,' says he, 'there is a turning just here a little farther, you must not go that way; for that goes to Cambridge.'

We had paid for our beer, and sat at the door only to rest us, when on the sudden comes a gentleman's coach to the door, and three or four horsemen rode into the yard, and the hostler was obliged to go in with them; says he to the Captain, 'Young man, pray take hold of the horse,' meaning the countryman's horse I mention'd above, 'and take him out of the way that the coach may come up': he did so, and beckoned to me to follow him: we walk'd together to the turning; says he to me, 'Do you step before, and turn up the lane, I'll overtake you'; so I went on up the lane, and in a few minutes, he was got upon the horse, and at my heels, and bidding me get up, and take a lift.

I made no difficulty of doing so, and away we went at a good round rate, having a strong horse under us. We suspected the countryman would follow us to Royston, because of our directions from the hostler; so that we went towards Cambridge, and went easier after the first hour's riding, and coming thro' a town or two, we alighted by turns, and did not then ride double; but by the way picked a couple of good shirts of a hedge; and that evening got safe to Cambridge, where the next day I bought a horse for myself, and thus equipped, we jogged on, through several places, till we got to Stamford in Lincolnshire, where it was impossible to restrain my Captain from playing his pranks, even at church, where he went, and placed himself so near an old lady, that he got her gold watch from her side unperceived; and the same night we went away by moon-light, after having the satisfaction to hear the watch cried, and ten guineas offered for it again, he would have been glad of the ten guineas instead of the watch, but durst not venture to carry it home. We went through several other places, such as Grantham, Newark, and Nottingham, where we play'd our tricks; but at last we got safe to Edinborough, without any accident but one, which was crossing a ford, the Captain was really in danger of drowning, his horse being driven down by the stream, and fell under him; but the rider had a proverb on his side, and got out of the water.

At Edinborough we remain'd about a month, when on a sudden my Captain was gone, horse and all, and I knew nothing what was become of him, nor did I ever see or hear of him for eighteen months after, nor did he so much as leave the least notice for me, either where he was gone, or whether he would re-return to Edinborough again or no. I took his leaving me very heinously, not knowing what to do with myself, being a stranger in the place, and on the other hand my money abated a-pace too. I had for the most part of this time my horse upon my hands to keep; and as horses yield but a sorry price in Scotland, I found no opportunity to sell him to any advantage: however, at last I was forced to dispose of him.

Being thus eased of my horse, and having nothing at all to do, I began to consider with myself what would become of me, and what I could turn my hand to. I had not much diminished my stock of money; for though I was all the way so wary, that I would not join with my Captain in his desperate attempts, yet I made no scruple to live at his expence. In the next place, I was not so anxious about my money running low, because I had made a reserve, by leaving upwards of ninety pounds in a friend's hands at London; but still I was willing to get into some employment for a livelihood. I was sick of the wandering life I had led, and resolved to be a thief no more, but stuck close to writing and reading for about six months, till I got into the service of an officer of the customs, who imploy'd me for a time; but as he set me to do little but pass and repass between Leith and Edinborough, leaving me to live at my own expence till my wages should be due, I run out the little money I had left in cloaths and subsistance, and a little before the year's end, when I was to have twelve pounds English money, my master was turned out of his place, and which was worse, having been charged with some misapplications, was obliged to take shelter in England; so we that were servants, for there were three of us, were left to shift for ourselves. This was a hard case for me in a strange place, and I was reduced by it to the last extremity. I might have gone for England, an English ship being there; the master proffered to take my word for ten shillings, till I got there: but just as I was upon going, Captain Jack appeared again.

I have mentioned how he left me, and that I saw him no more for eighteen months. His ramble and adventures were many in that time he went to Glasgow, played some very remarkable pranks there, escaped, almost miraculously, the gallows, got over to Ireland, wandered about there, turn'd rapparee, did some villainous things there, escaped from Londonderry over to the Highlands, and about a month before, I was left destitute at Leith, by my master, noble Captain Jack came in there, on board the ferry-boat from Fife, being, after all his adventures and successes, advanc'd to the dignity of a foot-soldier in a body of recruits rais'd in the north for the regiment of Douglas.

After my disaster, being reduc'd almost as low as Jack, I found no better shift before me, at least not for the present, than to enter my self a soldier too; and thus we were rak'd together, with each of us a musket upon our shoulders. I was extremely delighted with the life of a soldier; for I took the exercises naturally, that the serjeant, who taught us to handle our arms, seeing me so ready at it, ask'd me if I had never carried arms before. I told him no. At which he swore, though jesting, 'they call you Colonel,' says he, 'and I believe you will be a colonel, or you must be some colonel's bastard, or you would never handle your arms as you do at once or twice showing.' Whatever was my satisfaction in that part, yet other circumstances did not equally concur to make this life suit me; for after we had been about six months in this figure, we were inform'd that we were to march for England, and be shipp'd off at Newcastle, or Hull, to join the regiment in Flanders. Poor Captain Jack's case was particular; he durst not appear publickly at Newcastle, as he must have done had he march'd with the recruits. In the next place, I remember'd my money in London, which was almost 100 *l.* and if it had been ask'd all the soldiers in the regiment which of them would go to Flanders a private centinel, if they had 100 *l.* in their pockets, I believ'd none of them would have answer'd in the affirmative.

These two circumstances concurring, I began to be very uneasy and very unwilling in my thoughts to go over into Flanders a poor musketeer, to be knock'd on the head for 3 *s.* 6 *d.* a week. While I was daily musing on the hardship of being sent away, as above, Captain Jack comes to me one evening, and ask'd me to take a walk with him into the fields, for he wanted to speak with me. We walk'd together here, and talk'd seriously of the matter, and at last concluded to desert that very night. The moon affording a good light, and Jack had got a comrade with him thoroughly acquainted with the way cross the Tweed, and when he arrived there we were on English ground, and safe enough, from thence we propos'd to get to Newcastle, and get some collier ship to take us in, and carry us to London.

About half an hour past eight in the morning we reach'd the Tweed, and here we overtook two more of the same regiment, who had deserted from Haddingtown, where another part of the recruits were quarter'd. Those were Scotsmen, and very poor, having not one penny in their pockets; and when they saw us, who they knew to be of the same regiment, they took us to be pursuers; upon which, they stood upon the defence, having the regiment swords on, as we had, also, but none of the mounting or cloathing, for we were not to receive the clothes till we came to the regiment in Flanders. It was not long before we made them understand that we were in the same condition with themselves, and so we became one company. Our money was ebb'd very low, and we contriv'd to get into Newcastle in the dusk of the evening, and even then we durst not venture into the publick parts of the town, but made down towards the river below the town: here we knew not what to do with ourselves, but, guided by our fate, we put a good face upon the matter, went into an alehouse, sat down, and called for a pint of beer.

The woman of the house appear'd very frank, and entertain'd us chearfully; so we, at last, told her our condition, and ask'd her if she would not help us to some kind master of a collier, who would give us a passage to London by sea. The subtil Devil, who immediately found us proper fish for her hook, gave us the kindest words in the world, and told us she was heartily sorry she had not seen

29

us one day sooner; that there was a collier-master of her particular acquaintance who went away but with the morning tide; that the ship was fallen down to Sheilds, but she believ'd was hardly over the bar yet, and she would send to his house and see if he was gone on board (for sometimes the masters do not go away till a tide after the ship); and she was sure, if he was not gone, she could prevail with him to take us all in; but then she was afraid we must go on board immediately, the same night.

We begg'd of her to send to his house, for we knew not what to do; for as we had no money, we had no lodging, and wanted nothing but to be on board. We look'd upon this as a mighty favour, that she sent to the master's house; and, to our greater joy, she brought us word, about an hour after, that he was not gone, and was at a tavern in the town, whither his boy had been to fetch him; and that he had sent word he would call there in his way home. This was all in our favour, and we were extremely pleas'd with it. In about an hour he comes into the room to us; 'Where are these honest gentlemen soldiers,' says he, 'that are in such distress?' We stood all up, and paid our respects to him. 'Well, gentlemen,' said he, 'and is all your money spent?'

'Indeed it is,' said one of our company, 'and we will be infinitely obliged to you, Sir, if you will give us a passage. We will be very willing to do any thing we can, in the ship, though we are not seamen.'

'Why,' says he, 'were none of you ever at sea in your lives?'

'No,' says we, 'not one of us.'

'You will be able to do me no service, then; for you will all be sick. However, for my good landlady's sake here, I'll do it. But are you all ready to go on board? for I go on board, my self, this very night.'

'Yes, Sir,' says we, again, 'we are ready to go, this very minute.'

'No, no,' said he, very kindly, 'We'll drink together. Come, landlady,' says he, 'make these honest gentlemen a sneaker of punch.'

We look'd at one another, for we knew we had no money, and he perceiv'd it. 'Come, come,' said he, 'don't be concern'd at your having no money; my landlady, here, and I, never part with dry lips. Come, good wife, make the punch, as I bid you.'

We thanked him, and said, 'God bless you, noble captain,' a hundred times over, being over-joy'd at our good luck. While we were drinking the punch, he told the landlady he would step home, and order the boat to come at high-water, bad her get something for supper, which she did.

In less than an hour, our captain came again, and came up to us, and blam'd us that we had not drank the punch out. 'Come,' said he, 'don't be bashful; when that's out, we can have another: when I am obliging poor men, I love to do it handsomely.'

We drank on, and drank the punch out; more was brought up, and he push'd it about a-pace: then came up a leg of mutton. I need not say we fed heartily, being several times told we should pay nothing. After supper was done, he bids my landlady ask if the boat was come; and she brought word no, it was not high-water by a great deal. Then more punch was call'd for, and, as was afterwards confess'd, something more than ordinary was put into it, that, by the time the punch was drank out, we were all intoxicated, and, as for me, I fell a-sleep.

At last, I was rouz'd, and told that the boat was come: so I, and my drunken comrades, tumbled out, almost one over another, into the boat, and away we went with our captain. Most of us, if not all, fell a-sleep till after some time, though how much, or how far going, we knew not. The boat stopp'd, and we were wak'd, and told we were at the ship's side, which was true, and, with much help, and holding us, for fear we should fall over board, our captain, as we call'd him, call'd us thus: 'Here. Boatswain, take care of these gentlemen, give them good cabins, and let them turn into sleep, for they are very weary.' And so, indeed, we were, and very drunk too.

Care was taken of us, according to order, and we were put into very good cabins, where we were sure to go immediately to sleep; in the mean time, the ship, which was indeed just ready to go, and only on notice given, had come to an anchor for us at Sheilds weigh'd, stood over the bar, and went off to sea, and when we wak'd, and began to peep abroad, which was not till near noon the next day, we found our selves a great way at sea, the land in sight, indeed, but at a great distance, and all going merrily on for London, as I thought. We were very well us'd, and very well satisfy'd with our condition, for about three days; when we began to enquire whether we were not almost come, and how much longer it would be before we should come into the river. 'What river?' says one of the men. 'Why the Thames,' says my Captain Jack. 'The Thames,' says the sailor, 'what d'ye mean by that? What ha'n't you had time enough to be sober, yet?' So Captain Jack said no more, but look'd very silly, when, a while after, some other of us ask'd the same question, and the seaman, who knew nothing of the cheat, began to smell a rat, and, turning to the other Englishman, who came with us, 'Pray,' says he, 'where do you fancy you are going, that you ask so often about it?' 'Why to London,' says he, 'where should we be going? We agreed with the captain to carry us to London.'

'Not with the captain' says he, 'I dare say, poor men you are all cheated, and I thought so, when I saw you come aboard with that kidnapping rogue Gilliman, poor Men' adds he, 'you are all betray'd for the ship is bound to Virginia.' As soon as we heard this news, we were raving mad, drew our swords and swore revenge; but we were soon over-powered and carried before the captain, who told us, he was sorry for what had happened, but that he had no hand in it, and it was out of his power to help us, and let us know very plainly what our condition was, namely, that we were put on board his ship as servants to Maryland, to be delivered to a person there, but that however, if we would be quiet and orderly in his ship, he would use us well in the passage; but if we were unruly, we must be handcuffed and kept between deck, for it was his business to take care no disturbance happened in the ship.

'No hand in it! Damn him' says my Captain Jack, aloud, 'do you think he is not a confederate in this villainy? would any honest man receive innocent people on board his ship, and not enquire of their circumstances, but carry him away, and not speak to them? Why does he not set us on shore again, I tell you he is a villain, and none but him; why does he not compleat his villainy, and murder us, and then he'll be free from our revenge? But nothing else shall deliver him from my hands, but sending us to the D——l, or going thither himself; and I am honester in telling him so fairly, than he has been to me.'

All this discourse availed nothing, we were forced to be quiet, and had a very good voyage, no storms all the way; but just before we arrived, one of the Scotsmen asked the captain of the ship, whether he would sell us, 'Yes' said he; 'Why then Sir,' says the Scotsman, 'the Devil will have you at the hinder end of the bargain.' 'Say you so,' says the captain, smiling, 'well, well, let the Devil and I alone to agree about that, do you be quiet, and behave civily as you should do.'

When we come ashore, which was on the banks of a river they call Potomack, Jack says, 'I have something to say to you Captain; that is, I have promised to cut your throat, and depend upon it I will be as good as my word.' Our captain or kidnapper, call him as you will, made no answer, but delivered us to the merchant to whom we were consigned, who again disposed off as he thought fit; and in a few days we were separated.

As for my Captain Jack, to make short of the story, that desperate rogue had the good luck to have an easy good master, whom he abused very much; for he took an opportunity to run away with a boat, which his master entrusted him, and another with, to carry provisions to a plantation down the river. This boat and provisions they run away with, and sailed north to the bottom of the bay, as they call it, and there quitting the boat, they wandered through the woods, till they got into Pensylvania; from whence they made shift to get a passage to New England, and from thence home; where falling in among his old companions, and to his old trade, he was at length taken and hanged about a month before I came to London, which was near twenty years afterwards.

My part was harder at the beginning, tho' better at the latter end; I was sold to a rich planter, whose name was Smith. During this scene of life I had time to reflect on my past hours; and tho' I had no great capacity of making a clear judgment and very little reflections from conscience, yet it made some impressions upon me. I behaved my self so well, that my master took notice of me, and made me one of his overseers; and was so kind as to send my note of my friends hand for the 93 *l*, before-mentioned, to his correspondent; who received and returned me the money. My good master a little time after, says to me, 'Colonel don't flatter me, I love plain dealing; liberty is precious to every body, I give you yours, and will take care you shall be well used by the country, and will get you a good plantation.'

I insisted I would not quit his service, for the best plantation in Maryland, that he had been so good to me, and I believed I was so usefull to him, that I could not think of it; and at last I added I hoped he could not believe but I had as much gratitude as a black man.

He smiled and said he would not be served upon these terms, that he did not forget what he had promised, nor what I had done in his plantation; and that he was resolved in the first place to give me my liberty, so he pulls out a piece of paper, and throws it to me; 'There,' says he, 'is a certificate of your coming on shore, and being sold to me for five years, of which you have lived three with me, and now you are your own master.'

I bowed and told him, that I was sure if I was my own master, I would be his servant, as long as he would accept of my service. He told me he would accept of my service, on these two conditions. First, that he would give me 30 *l.* pr. ann. and my board, for my managing the plantation I was then imploy'd in. And secondly, that at the same time he would procure me a new plantation to begin with upon my own account; 'for Jack,' says he, smiling, 'tho' you are but a young man, 'tis time you was doing something for your self.'

Not long after, he purchased in my name about 30 acres of land, near his own plantation, as he said, that I might the better take care of his. My master, for such I must still call him, generously gave it me; 'but Colonel' says he, 'giving you this plantation is nothing at all, if I do not assist you to support it, and to carry it on, and therefore I will give you credit, for whatever is needful. Such as tools, provisions, and some servants to begin. Materials for out-houses, and hogs, cows, horses, for stock, and the like; and I'll take it out of your returns from abroad, as you can pay it.'

Thus got to be a planter, and encouraged by a kind benefactor, that I might not be wholly taken up with my new plantation; he gave me freely without any consideration, one of his slaves named Mouchat, whom I always esteemed. Besides this, he sent to me two servants more, a man and a woman; but these he put to my account as above. Mouchat and these two fell immediately to work for me, they began with about two acres of land, which had but little timber on it at first, and most of that was cut down by the two carpenters who built my house. It was a great advantage to me, that I had so bountiful a master who help'd me out in every case; for in this very first year, I received a terrible blow; having sent a large quantity of tobacco, to a merchant at London, by my master's direction, which arrived safe there. The merchant was ordered to make the return in a sorted cargo of goods for me, such as would have made a man of me all at once; but to my inexpressible terror and surprize, the ship was lost, and that just at the entrance into the Capes, that is to say, the mouth of the bay; some of the goods were recovered, but spoiled. In short, nothing but the nails, tools, and iron-work were good for any thing; and tho' the value of them was very considerable in porportion to the rest; yet my loss was irreparably great, and indeed, the greatness of the loss consisted in its being irreparable.

I was perfectly astonished at the first news of the loss, knowing that I was in debt to my patron or master, so much, that it must be several years before I should recover it; and as he brought me the bad news himself he perceived my disorder; that is to say, he saw I was in the utmost confusion, and a kind of amazement; and so indeed I was, because I was so much in debt. But he spoke chearfully to me, 'Come' says he, 'do not be so discouraged, you may make up this loss,' 'No Sir,' says I, 'that never can be, for it is my all, and I shall never be out of debt'; 'Well,' says he, 'you have no creditor, however, but me, and now remember I once told you, I would make a man of you, and I will not disappoint you'; for this disaster I thank'd him, and did it with more ceremony and respect than ever, because I thought myself more under the hatches than I was before: but he was as good as his word, for he did not baulk me in the least, of any thing I wanted, and as I had more iron-work saved out of the ship in proportion, than I wanted, I supplied him with some part of it, and took up some linnen and cloaths, and other necessaries from him in exchange, and now I began to encrease visibly; I had a large quantity of land cured, that is freed from timber, and a very good crop of tobacco in view, and I got three servants more, and one black man; so that I had five white servants, and two black; and with this my affairs went very well on; the first year indeed I took my wages or sallary, of 30 *l.* a year, because I wanted it very much; but the second and third year, I resolved not to take it, but to leave it in my benefactor's hands, to clear off the debt I had contracted.

At the same time my thoughts dictated to me, that tho' this was the foundation of my new life, yet that this was not the superstructure, and that I might still be born for greater things than these, that it is honesty and virtue alone, that made men rich and great, and gave them fame, as well as figure in the world, and that therefore I was to lay my foundation in these, and expect what might follow in time. To help these thoughts as I had learned to read and write when I was in Scotland; so I began now to love books, and particularly, I had an opportunity of reading some very considerable ones, some of which I bought at a planter's house, who was lately dead, and his goods sold, and others I borrowed. I considered my present state of life, to be my meer youth, tho' I was now above

35

30 years old, because in my youth I had learned nothing; and if my daily business, which was now great, would have permitted, I would have been content to have gone to school; however, fate which had something else in store for me, threw an opportunity into my hand, namely, a clever fellow that came over a transported felon from Bristol, and fell into my hands for a servant. He had led a loose life that he acknowledged, and being driven to extremities, took to the high-way, for which had he been taken, he would have been hanged; but falling into some low priz'd rogueries afterwards, for want of opportunity for worse, was catched, condemn'd, and transported, and, as he said, was glad he came off so.

He was an excellent scholar, and I perceiving it, asked him one time, if he could give a method how I might learn the Latin tongue; he said, smiling, yes, he could teach it me in three months, if I would let him have books, or even without books if he had time. I told him a book would become his hand better than a hoe, and if he could promise to make me but understand Latin enough to read it, and understand other languages by it, I would ease him of the labour which I was now obliged to put him to; especially if I was assured that he was fit to receive that favour of a kind master. In short, I made him to me, what my kind benefactor made me to him; and from him I gained a fund of knowledge, infinitely more valuable than the rate of a slave, which was what I paid for it; but of this hereafter.

In this posture I went on for 12 years, and was very successful in my plantation, and had gotten by means of my master's favour, who now I called my friend, a correspondent in London, with whom I traded; shipped over my tobacco to him, and received Europian goods in returns, such as I wanted to carry on my plantation, and sufficient to sell to others also. In this interval, my good friend and benefactor died; and I was left very disconsolate, on account of my loss, for it was indeed a great loss to me; he had been a father to me, and I was like a forsaken stranger without him; tho' I knew the country and the trade too well enough, and had for some time chiefly carried on his whole business for him, yet I seem'd now at a loss, my councellor and my chief supporter was gone; and I had no confidant to communicate myself to, on all occasions as formerly, but there was no remedy. I was however, in a better condition to stand alone than ever: I had a very large plantation, and had near 70 black and other servants.

Now I looked upon myself as one buried alive in a remote part of the world, where I could see nothing at all, and hear but a little of what was seen, and that little not till at least half a year after it was done, and sometimes a year or more, and in a word, the old reproach often came in my way, namely, that even this was not yet the life of a gentleman. However, I now began to frame my thoughts for a voyage to England, resolving then to act as I should see cause, but with a secret resolution to see more of the world if possible, and realize those things to my mind, which I had hitherto only entertained remote ideas of, by the help of books.

It was three years after this, before I could get things in order, fit for my leaving the country: in this time I delivered my tutor from his bondage, and would have given him his liberty, but to my great disappointment I found that I could not empower him to go for England till his time was expired, according to the certificate of his transportation, which was register'd; so I made him one of my overseers, and thereby raised him gradually to a prospect of living in the same manner, and by the like steps, that my good benefactor raised me, only that I did not assist him to enter upon planting for himself as I was assisted, neither was I upon the spot to do it, but this man by his diligence and honest application delivered himself, even unassisted, any farther than by making him an overseer, which was only a present ease and deliverance from the hard labour and fare, which he endured as a servant. However, in this trust he behaved so faithfully, and so diligently, that it recommended him in the country, and, when I came back. I found him in circumstances very differing from what I left him in; besides, his being my principal manager for near 20 years, as you shall hear in its place.

I was now making provision for my going to England, after having settled my plantation in such hands as was fully to my satisfaction. My first work was, to furnish myself with such a stock of goods and money as might be sufficient for my occasions abroad, and, particularly, might allow to make large returns to Maryland, for the use and supply of all my plantations; but when I came to look nearer into the voyage, it occurr'd to me that it would not be prudent to put my cargo all on board the same ship that I went in: so I shipp'd, at several times, five hundred hogsheads of tobacco, in several ships, for England, giving notice to my correspondent, in London, that I would embark about such a time to come over

37

myself, and ordering him to insure for a considerable sum proportion'd to the value of my cargo.

About two months after this, I left the place, and embark'd for England in a stout ship, carrying 24 guns, and about 600 hogsheads of tobacco; and we left the capes of Virginia on the first of August —. We had a very sour and rough voyage for the first fortnight, though it was in a season so generally noted for good weather. We met with a storm, and our ship was greatly damag'd, and some leaks we had, but not so bad, but, by the diligence of the seamen, they were stopp'd; after which, we had tolerable weather, and a good sea, till we came into the soundings, for so they call the mouth of the British Channel. In the grey of the morning a French privateer, of 26 guns, appear'd, and crowded after us with all the sail they could make. Our captain exchang'd a broad-side or two with them, which was terrible work to me; for I had never seen such before; the Frenchman's guns having rak'd us, and kill'd and wounded six of our men. In short, after a fight long enough to shew us that if we would not be taken, we must resolve to sink by her side, for there was no room to expect deliverance, and a fight long enough to save the master's credit, we were taken, and the ship carried away for St Malo's. I had, however, besides my being taken, the mortification to be detain'd on board the cruiser, and seeing the ship I was in, mann'd with Frenchmen, set sail from us. I afterwards heard that she was re-taken by an English man of war, and carried into Portsmouth.

The rover cruis'd abroad again, in the mouth of the Channel, for some time, and took a ship richly laden, bound homeward from Jamaica. This was a noble prize for the rogues, and they hastened away with her to St Malo's, and from thence I went to Bourdeaux, where the captain ask'd me if I would be deliver'd up a state prisoner, get myself exchanged, or pay 300 crowns. I desir'd time to write to my correspondent in England, who sent me a letter of credit, and in about six weeks I was exchang'd for a merchant prisoner in Plymouth. I got passage from hence to Dunkirk, on board a French vessel; and having a certificate of an exchang'd prisoner from the intendant of Bourdeaux, I had a passport given me to go into the Spanish Netherlands, and so whither I pleas'd. I went to Ghent, afterwards to Newport, where I took the packet boat, and came over to England, landing at Deal instead of Dover, the weather forcing us into the Downs.—When I came to London, I was very well receiv'd by my friend to whom I had consign'd my effects; for all my goods came safe to hand, and my overseers I had left behind, had shipp'd, at several times, 400 hogsheads of tobacco, to my correspondent, in my absence. So that I had above 1000 *l*. in my factor's hands, and 200 hogsheads besides, left in hand, unsold.

I had nothing to do now but entirely to conceal myself from all that had any knowledge of me before; and this was the easiest thing in the world to do, for I was grown out of every body's knowledge, and most of those I had known, were grown out of mine: my Captain who went with me, or rather who carried me away, I found by enquiring at the proper place, had been rambling about the world, came to London, fell into his old trade, which he could not forbear, and growing an eminent highwayman, had made his exit at the gallows, after a life of 14 years most exquisite and successful rogueries; the particulars of which, would make, as I observed, an admirable history. My other brother Jack, who I called Major, followed the like wicked trade; but was a man of more gallantry and generosity, and having committed innumerable depredations upon mankind, yet had always so much dexterity, as to bring himself off, till at length he was laid fast in Newgate, and loaded with irons, and would certainly have gone the same way as the Captain, but he was so dextrous a rogue, that no gaol, no fetters would hold him; and he with two more, found means to knock off their irons, work'd their way thro' the wall of the prison, and let themselves down on the outside, in the night: so escaping, they found means to get into France, where he followed the same trade, and that with so much success, that he grew famous by the name of Anthony, and had the honour with three of his comrades, who he had taught the English way of robbing generously, as they called it, without murthering, or wounding, or ill-using those they robb'd, to be broke upon the wheel, at the Greve in Paris.

All these things I found means to be fully informed of, and to have a long account of the particulars of their conduct from some of their comrades, who had the good fortune to escape, and who I got the knowledge of, without letting them so much as guess at who I was, or upon what account I enquir'd.

I was now at the height of my good fortune, and got the name of a great merchant. I lived single, and in lodgings, and kept a French servant, being very desirous of improving myself in that language, and received 5 or 600 hogsheads a-year from my own plantations, and spent my time in that, and in supplying my people with necessaries at Maryland, as they wanted them.

In this private condition I continu'd about two years more, when the Devil owing me a spleen ever since I refus'd being a thief, paid me home, with interest, by laying a snare in my way, which had almost ruin'd me.

There dwelt a lady in the house opposite to the house I lodg'd in, who made an extraordinary figure, and was a most beautiful person. She was well bred, sung admirably fine, and sometimes I could hear distinctly, the houses being over-against one another in a narrow court. This lady put her self so often in my way, that I could not in good manners forbear taking notice of her, and giving the ceremony of my hat, when I saw her at her window, or at the door, or when I pass'd her in the court: so that we became almost acquainted at a distance. Sometimes she also visited at the house I lodg'd at, and it was generally contriv'd that I shou'd be introduc'd when she came. And thus, by degrees, we became more intimately acquainted, and often convers'd together in the family, but always in publick, at least for a great while. I was a meer boy in the affair of love, and knew the least of what belong'd to a woman, of any man in Europe of my age; the thoughts of a wife, much less a mistress, had never so much as taken the least hold of my head, and I had been, till now, as perfectly unacquainted with the sex, and as unconcern'd about them, as I was when I was ten years old, and lay in a heap of ashes at the glass-house.

She attack'd me without ceasing, with the fineness of her conduct, and with arts which were impossible to be ineffectual. She was ever, as it were, in my view, often in my company, and yet kept her self so on the reserve, so surrounded continually with obstructions, that for several months after she could perceive I sought an opportunity to speak to her. She render'd it impossible, nor could I ever break in upon her, she kept her guard so well.

This rigid behaviour was the greatest mystery that could be, considering, at the same time, that she never declin'd my seeing her, or conversing with me in publick, but she held it on. She took care never to sit next me, that I might slip no paper into her hand, or speak softly to her. She kept some body or other always between, that I could never come up to her. And thus, as if she was resolv'd really to have nothing to do with me, she held me at the bay several months. In short, we came nearer and nearer every time we met, and at last gave the world the slip, and were privately married, to avoid ceremony, and the publick inconveniency of a wedding.

No sooner were we married, but she threw off the mask of her gravity and good conduct, and carried it to such an excess, that I could not but be dissatisfied at the expence of it. In about a twelve-month she was brought to bed of a fine boy; and her lying in cost me, as near as I can now remember, 136 *l.* which, she told me, she thought was a trifle. Such jarring continually between us, produced a separation; and she demanded 300 *l.* per annum for her maintenance. In the interim of this, by means of two trusty agents, I got proof of my spouse's being caught several times in bed with another person, and by whom she had a daughter. I sued her in the ecclesiastical court, in order to obtain a divorce; and, as she found it impossible to avoid it, she declin'd a defence, and I gain'd a legal decree of divorce.

Things being at this pass, I resolv'd to go over to France, where I fell into company with some Irish officers of the regiment of Dillon, where I bought a company, and so went into the army directly. Our regiment, after I had been some time in it, was commanded into Italy, and one of the most considerable actions I was in, was the famous attack upon Cremona in the Milaneze, where the Germans being treacherously let into the town by night, through a kind of common-shore, surpriz'd the town, and took the Duke de Villeroy prisoner, beating the French troops into the citadel, but were in the middle of their victory so boldly attack'd by two Irish regiments, that, after a most desperate fight, and not being able to break through us to let in their friends, were obliged to quit the town, to the eternal honour of those Irish regiments. Having been in several campaigns, I was permitted to sell my company, and got the Chevalier's Brevet for a colonel, in case of raising troops for him in Great-Britain. I, accordingly, embark'd on board the French fleet, for the Firth of Edinburgh; but they over-shot their landing-place: and this delay gave time to the English fleet, under Sir George Byng, to come to an anchor just as we did.

Upon this surprize, the French admiral set sail, and, crouding away to the north, got the start of the English fleet, and escap'd, with the loss of one ship only, to Dunkirk; and glad I was to set my foot on shore again, for all the while we were thus flying for our lives, I was under the greatest terror imaginable, and nothing but halters and gibbets run in my head, concluding, that if I had been taken, I should certainly have been hang'd.

I took my leave of the chevalier and the army, and made haste to Paris, a place full of gallantry, and where I again foolishly tried my fate in matrimony; for in less than three months I caught my good natur'd wife in bed with a French marquiss, whom I the next day fought, and left for dead. I took post horses for Flanders, and, at last, got safe once more to London, from which place I embark'd for Virginia, and had a tolerable voyage thither, only that we met with a pyrate ship, who plunder'd us of every thing they could come at that was for their turn: but, to give the rogues their due, though they were the most abandon'd wretches that ever were seen, they did not use us ill; and, as to my loss, it was not considerable.

I found all my affairs in very good order at Virginia, my plantations prodigiously increas'd, and my manager, who first inspir'd me with travelling thoughts, and made me master of any knowledge worth naming, receiv'd me with a transport of joy, after a ramble of four and twenty years. I was exceedingly satisfied with his management, for he had improv'd a very large plantation of his own, at the same time; however, I had the mortification to see two or three of the Preston gentlemen there, who being prisoners of war, were spar'd from the publick execution, and sent over to that slavery, which, to gentlemen, must be worse than death.

During my stay here, I married a maid I brought over from England, who behav'd her self, for some time, extraordinary well, but at last turn'd whore, like the rest, got the foul disease, and died; and I, not liking to stay long in a place I was so much talk'd of, sent to one of my correspondents for a copy of the general free pardon then granted, and wherein it was manifest I was fully included.

After I had settled my affairs, and left the same faithful steward, I again embark'd for England, and, after a trading voyage (for we touch'd at several places in our way), I arriv'd safe, determining to spend the remainder of my life in my native country; for here I enjoy the moments which I had never before known how to employ, I mean that of looking back upon an ill-spent Life.

Perhaps, when I wrote these things down, I did not foresee that the writings of our own stories would be so much the fashion in England, or so agreeable to others to read, as I find custom, and the humour of the times, has caus'd it to be. If any one that reads my story pleases to make the same just reflections, which I acknowledge I ought to have made, he will reap the benefit of my misfortunes, perhaps, more than I have done my self, 'tis evident, by the long series of changes and turns which have appear'd in the narrow compass of one private mean person's life, that the history of men's lives may be many ways made useful and instructing to those who read them, if moral and religious improvement, and reflections, are made by those that write them.

43

SAWNEY BEANE at the Entrance of his Cave.

THE LIFE OF

SAWNEY BEANE

T he following account, though as well attested as any historical fact can be, is almost incredible, for the monstrous and unparallel'd barbarities that it relates; there being nothing that we have ever heard of, with the same degree of certainty, that may be compar'd with it, or that shews how far a brutal temper, untam'd by education and knowledge of the world, may carry a man in such glaring and horrible colours.

Sawney Beane was born in the county of East Lothian, about eight or nine miles eastward of the city of Edinburgh, some time in the reign of Queen Elizabeth, whilst King James I govern'd only in Scotland. His parents work'd at hedging and ditching for their livelihood, and brought up their son, to the same occupation. He got his daily bread in his youth by these means; but being very much prone to idleness, and not caring for being confined to any honest employment, he left his father and mother, and ran away into the desart part of the country, taking with him a woman as viciously inclin'd as himself. These two took up their habitation in a rock by the sea-side, on the shore of the county of Galloway, where they lived upwards of 25 years without going into any city, town, or village.

In this time they had a great number of children and grand-children, whom they brought up after their own manner, without any notions of humanity or civil society. They never kept any company, but among themselves, and supported themselves wholly by robbing; being, moreover, so very cruel, that they never robb'd any one, whom they did not murder.

By this bloody method, and their living so retiredly from the world, they continued such a long time undiscovered, there being no body able to guess how the people were lost that went by the place where they lived. As soon as they had robb'd and murder'd any man, woman, or child, they used to carry off the carcass to the den, where cutting it into quarters, they would pickle the mangled limbs, and afterwards eat it; this being their only sustenance: and, notwithstanding, they were at last so numerous, they commonly had superfluity of this their abominable food; so that in the night-time they frequently threw legs, and arms of the unhappy wretches they had murdered, into the sea, at a great distance from their bloody habitation. The limbs were often cast up by the tide in several parts of the country, to the astonishment and terror of all the beholders, and others who heard of it. Persons who have gone about their lawful occasions fell so often into their hands, that it caused a general outcry in the country round about, no man knowing what was become of his friend or relation, if they were once seen by these merciless cannibals.

All the people in the adjacent parts were at last alarm'd, at such a common loss of their neighbours, and acquaintance; for there was no travelling in safety near the den of these wretches. This occasioned the sending frequent spies into these parts, many of whom never return'd again, and those who did, after the strictest search and enquiry, could not find how these melancholy matters happen'd. Several honest travellers were taken up on suspicion, and wrongfully hang'd upon bare circumstances; several innocent inn-keepers were executed for no other reason than that persons who had been thus lost, were known to have lain at their houses, which occasion'd a suspicion of their being murdered by them, and their bodies privately buried in obscure places, to prevent a discovery. Thus an ill-plac'd justice was executed with the greatest severity imaginable, in order to prevent these frequent atrocious deeds; so that not a few inn-keepers, who lived on the western road of Scotland, left off their business, for fear of being made examples, and followed other employments. This on the other hand occasion'd many great inconveniencies to travellers, who were now in great distress for accommodation for themselves and their horses, when they were disposed to bait, or put up for lodging at night. In a word, the whole country was almost depopulated.

Still the King's subjects were missing as much as before; so that it was the admiration of the whole kingdom how such villainies could be carried on, and not the villains to be found out. A great many had been executed, and not one of them all made any confession at the gallows; but stood to it at the last, that they were perfectly innocent of the crimes for which they suffer'd. When the magistrates found all was in vain, they left off these rigorous proceedings, and trusted wholly to Providence, for the bringing to light the authors of these unparallel'd barbarities, when it should seem proper to the Divine Wisdom.

Sawney's family was at last grown very large, and every branch of it, as soon as able, assisted in perpetrating their wicked deeds, which they still follow'd with impunity. Sometimes they would attack four, five, or six footmen together, but never more than two if they were on horse-back. They were, moreover so careful, that not one whom they set upon should escape, that an ambuscade was placed on every side to secure them, let them fly which way they would, provided it should ever so happen that one or more got away from the first assai- **47** lants. How was it possible they should be detected, when not one that saw them ever saw any body else afterwards? The place where they inhabited was quite solitary and lonesome; and when the tide came up, the water went for near two hundred yards into their subterraneous habitation, which reached almost a mile under ground; so that when some who had been sent arm'd to search all the by-places about, have past by the mouth of their cave; they have never taken any notice of it, not supposing that any thing human would reside in such a place of perpetual horror and darkness.

The number of the people these savages destroyed was never exactly known; but it was generally computed that in the twenty-five years they continued their butcheries, they had washed their hands in the blood of a thousand at least, men, women, and children. The manner how they were at last discover'd was as follows:

A man and his wife behind him on the same horse, coming one evening home from a fair, and falling into the ambuscade of these merciless wretches, they fell upon them in a most furious manner. The man, to save himself as well as he could, fought very bravely against them with sword and pistol, riding some of them down, by main force of his horse. In the conflict the poor woman fell from behind him, and was instantly murdered before her husband's face; for the female cannibals cut her throat, and fell to sucking her blood with as great a gust, as if it had been wine. This done, they ript up her belly, and pulled out all her entrails. Such a dreadful spectacle made the man make the more obstinate resistance, as expecting the same fate, if he fell into their hands. It pleased Providence, while he was engaged, that twenty or thirty from the same fair came together in a body; upon which, Sawney Beane and his blood-thirsty clan withdrew, and made the best of their way through a thick wood to their den.

This man, who was the first that had ever fell in their way, and came off alive, told the whole company what had happened, and shewed them the horrid spectacle of his wife, whom the murderers had dragg'd to some distance, but had not time to carry her entirely off. They were all struck with stupefaction and amazement at what he related, took him with them to Glasgow, and told the affair to the provost of that city, who immediately sent to the King concerning it.

In about three or four days after, his Majesty himself in person, with a body of about four hundred men, set out for the place where this dismal tragedy was acted, in order to search all the rocks and thickets, that, if possible, they might apprehend this hellish cure, which had been so long pernicious to all the western parts of the kingdom.

The man who had been attacked was the guide, and care was taken to have a large number of blood-hounds with them, that no human means might be wanting towards their putting an entire end to these cruelties.

No sign of any habitation was to be found for a long time, and even when they came to the wretches cave, they took no notice of it, but were going to pursue their search along the sea shore, the tide being then out. But some of the blood-hounds luckily enter'd this Cimmerian den, and instantly set up a most hideous barking, howling, and yelping; so that the King, with his attendants, came back, and looked into it. They could not yet tell how to conceive that any thing human could be concealed in a place where they saw nothing but darkness. Nevertheless, as the blood-hounds encreased their noise, they went farther in, and refused to come back again, they began to imagine there was some reason more than ordinary. Torches were now immediately sent for, and a great many men ventur'd in through the most intricate turnings and windings, till at last they arrived at that private recess from all the world, which was the habitation of these monsters.

Now the whole body, or as many of them as could, went in, and were all so shocked at what they beheld, that they were almost ready to sink into the earth. Legs, arms, thighs, hands, and feet of men, women, and children, were hung up in rows, like dried beef. A great many limbs lay in pickle, and a great mass of money, both gold and silver, with watches, rings, swords, pistols, and a large quantity of cloaths, both linnen and woollen, and an infinite number of other things, which they had taken from those whom they had murder'd, were thrown together in heaps, or hung up against the sides of the den.

Sawney's family at this time, besides him, consisted of his wife, eight sons, six daughters, eighteen grandsons, and fourteen grand-daughters, who were all begotten in incest.

These were all seiz'd and pinion'd, by his Majesty's order in the first place; then they took what human flesh they found, and buried it in the sands, afterwards loading themselves with the spoils which they found, they return'd to Edinburgh with their prisoners, all the country, as they passed along flocking to see this cursed tribe. When they were come to their journey's end, the wretches were all committed to the talbooth, from whence they were the next day conducted under a strong guard to Leith, where they were all executed without any process, it being thought needless to try creatures who were even professed enemies to mankind.

The men had first their privy-members cut off, and thrown into the fire before their faces, then their hands and legs were severed from their bodies; by which amputations they bled to death in some hours. The wife, daughters, and grand-children, having been made spectators of this just punishment inflicted on the men, were afterwards burnt to death in three several fires. They all in general died without the least signs of repentance; but continued cursing and venting the most dreadful imprecations to the very last gasp of life.

Hannah Blay

THO: SAVAGE *Returning to* HANNAH BLAY's *Lodging*

J. Nicholls *Delin.*

J. Basire *sculp.*

THE LIFE OF
THOMAS
SAVAGE

This unhappy wretch was born of very honest parents in the parish of St Giles's in the Fields, and between fourteen and fifteen years of age, bound apprentice to one Mr Collins a vintner, at the Ship-Tavern at Ratcliff-Cross, with whom he led but a very loose and profligate sort of life for about two years.

Breaking the Sabbath (by his own confession, he having never once heard a whole sermon during that time) was the first inlet to all his other vices, especially whoredom, drunkenness, and theft: for he used commonly to pass away the Sabbaths at a bawdy-house in Ratcliff-Highway, with one Hannah Blay, a vile common strumpet, who was the cause of his ruin, and brought him to his shameful end.

He was carried at first to drink there by an acquaintance, who afterwards went to sea; but having once found the way, he went after that alone, without his companion, and would often carry a bottle or two of wine to junket with her. This however, not satisfying her wicked desires, she told him frequently, 'That if he would enjoy her company, he must bring good store of money with him': to this he always replied, 'That he could bring none but his master's; and that he had never wronged him of two-pence in his life.' Nevertheless she still continued urging him to rob him privately, but he answer'd, 'he could not because the maid was always at home with him.' 'Hang her, a jade,' (said this limb of the Devil) 'knock her brains out, and I'll receive the money, and go any where with you beyond sea, to avoid the stroke of justice.'

She was often giving him this bad advice, and preaching this infernal doctrine; and she repeated it in particular on the very day when he unhappily took her counsel, and perpetrated the murder. For being at her house in the morning, she made him drunk with burnt brandy, and he wanting a groat to pay his reckoning, she again perswaded him to knock the maid's brains out, and bring her what money he could find.

Hereupon he went home between twelve and one o'clock, and seeing his master standing at the street door, did not dare to go in that way, but climbed over a wall, and getting in at the back-door, went into the room, where his fellow-servants were at dinner: 'O Sirrah,' said the maid to him, 'you have been now at the bawdy-house, you will never leave it till you are utterly ruin'd thereby.'

These words provok'd him highly, and he was so much enraged at her, that from that moment the Devil took firm possession of him, and he fully resolved, even while he was at dinner, to be her butcher. Accordingly, when his master, with the rest of the family were gone to church, leaving only the maid and Tom Savage at home, he goes into the bar, and fetches a hammer, with which he began to make a great noise, as he sat by the fire, by knocking on the bellows. Hereupon, says the maid to him, 'Sure the boy is mad! Sirrah, what do you make this noise for?'

To this he made no answer, but going to the kitchen window began to knock, and make the same noise there, of which the maid then taking no notice, he, to provoke her, got on the clean dresser, and walk'd up and down thereon several times with his dirty shoes. This piece of malice exasperating the maid, so that she scolded at him pretty heartily, he threw the hammer at her suddenly with such violence, that hitting her on the head, it fell'd her to the ground, and she shriek'd out. He then went and took up the hammer, intending to repeat the blow, but laid it down again thrice, not being yet harden'd enough in cruelty, to strike her any more; but at last taking it up the fourth time, the Devil had then gain'd such an absolute mastery over him, that he gave her several strokes with all the force he could, and quickly dispatch'd her out of the world.

The inhuman wretch having perpetrated this hellish piece of barbarity, immediately broke open a cupboard in his master's chamber, and taking out a bag, wherein was about sixty pounds, hid it under his coat, and went out at a back-door directly away to Hannah Blay again. When he came there, and had informed her what he had done, the cunning slut, who was harden'd in wickedness, would fain have had the money from him; but he would part with no more than half-a-crown, which having given her, he went away without the least remorse for what he had done.

But he had not gone very far, when meeting with a stile, he sat him down thereon to rest himself, and then began to reflect on the horrid deed he had perpetrated, and to cry out to himself, 'Lord, what have I done!' wishing that he could have recalled the fatal blows, even at the price of ten thousand worlds, if so many had been in his power. After this, he was in so much horror and dread of mind, that he stirred not a step, but he thought every one he met, came to apprehend him.

That night he reach'd Greenwich, where he took up his lodging, telling the people of the house he was going to Gravesend; but being got to bed, he could not sleep, through the terror of a guilty conscience, but got up again, and walked about the room for several hours. Next morning the mistress of the house, perceiving he had a large quantity of money in a bag not sealed up, began to examine him about it, doubting he came not by it honestly. Hereupon, to avoid her just suspicion, he told her, 'He was carrying it down to Gravesend to his master, who was a wine-cooper, and lived on London-Bridge; and that if she would not believe him, she might send to his mistress, and in the mean time he would leave the money in her hands.'

This was agreed upon, and accordingly he wrote a note himself to his pretended mistress, which was to be carried by some people, who were then going to London, whilst he went his way, wandering towards Woolwich, where he was in the ship-yard, much about the time the hue-and-cry came to Greenwich of a murder committed at Ratcliff-Cross by a youth, upon a maid, who was his fellow-servant; and that he had also robb'd his master of a bag of money.

Upon this news the mistress of the house, where he lay, presently concluded, that it was the same youth who had lodg'd there, and that the bag he had left with her was that whereof he had robb'd his master. Hereupon, she immediately dispatch'd several men in search of him, who found him a-sleep in an alehouse, with his head upon a table, and a pot of beer by him. Upon this, one of the men calling him by his name, said, 'Tom, did not you live at Ratcliff?' He answer'd, 'Yes.' 'And did not you murder your fellow-servant.' He answer'd likewise in the affirmative. 'And you took so much money from your master?' He acknowledg'd all. 'Then,' continued he, 'you must go along with us.' To which he replied, 'Yes, with all my heart.' Accordingly they went forthwith to Greenwich, to the house where he had lain the night before.

By that time he got thither, his master and some friends were arriv'd there likewise, who exaggerated to him the barbarity of the fact, wherewith he was not much affected at first, though a little after he burst out into tears: from thence he was carried back to Ratcliff, and had before a Justice of Peace, who committed him to Newgate.

Being now in safe custody, he was visited by one Mr Baker, to whom, after some little acquaintance, he gave the foregoing account; and he found him at first but little sensible of the heinousness of the crime he had committed. But the next time, asking him whether he was sorry for the fact, he answer'd with tears in his eyes, wringing his hands, and striking his breast, 'Yes, Sir; for it cuts me to the heart to think that I should take away the life of an innocent creature; and that is not all, but for any thing I know, I have sent her soul to Hell. Oh! how can I think of appearing before God's tribunal, when she shall stand before me, and say, "Lord, this wretch took away my life, and gave me not the least time to consider of the state of my soul, that so I might have repented of my sins, and have turned to thee; he gave me no warning at all, Lord." Oh: then, what will become of me?'

He was then visited by Mr Robert Franklyn, Mr Thomas Vincent, Mr Thomas Doolittle, and Mr James Janeway, who ask'd him, 'if he was the person that murder'd the maid at Ratcliff?' To which he answer'd, 'Yes.' Hereupon they endeavoured to set the sin home upon his conscience, telling him the danger he was in not only of a temporal but of an eternal death, without true repentance, and a sincere and strong faith.

The day that he went down to the sessions, his fellow-prisoners gave him something to drink, which very much disorder'd him; and Hannah Blay, whom he had accused, and who was taken into custody thereupon, was heard to say to him: 'Others have made you drunk to-day, but I will make thee drunk to-morrow.' He lamented this back-sliding grievously, but said, 'that it was not the quantity he had drank, which was much less than he was able to drink at other times, without being in the least disorder'd; but it was something they had infused into his liquor to intoxicate his senses'; which made him ever afterwards very cautious and fearful of drinking in their company.

After he had received sentence of death, he was again visited by Mr Baker; and the Saturday before his execution was again with him, when Savage said to him, taking him by the hand, 'Oh! my dear friend, come hither': then opening his coffin, 'look here,' continued he, 'this is the ship wherein I must launch out into the ocean of eternity: is it not a terrible thing to see one's own coffin and burial cloaths, when at the same time (as to my bodily health) I am every whit as well as you?'

On the Sunday, expecting to be executed next day, he desir'd to be alone, and spent it in prayer, and other religious duties. Next morning the sheriff's men and cart came for him, but the Sheriff of Middlesex not having notice, it was deferred till Wednesday, when looking upon his cloaths that he had put on to die in, he said, 'What, have I got on my dying cloaths? Dying cloaths, did I say? They are my living cloaths, the cloaths out of which I shall go into eternal glory: they are the best cloaths that ever I put on.'

Being brought to the place of execution at Ratcliff-Cross, he made a short speech, wherein he exhorted people, both old and young, 'to take warning by his untimely end, how they offended against the laws of God and man.' After which, having said a very pathetick prayer, and breath'd forth such pious ejaculations, as drew tears from the eyes of the beholders, he was turn'd off the cart, and struggl'd for a while, heaving up his body: which a young man, his friend, perceiving, he struck him several blows upon his breast with all his strength, to put him out of his pain, till no motion could be perceived in him; wherefore after he had hung a considerable time, and was to all appearance dead, the people moving a way, the sheriff ordered him to be cut down: when being received into the arms of some of his friends, he was convey'd into a house not far from the place of execution. There being laid upon a table, he began, to the astonishment of the beholders, to breath, and rattle in the throat, so that it was evident life was whole in him. Hereupon he was carry'd from thence to a bed in the same house, where he breath'd more strongly, and opened his eyes and mouth, though his teeth were set before, and he offer'd to speak but could not recover the use of his tongue.

However, his reviving being blaz'd abroad within an hour, the sheriffs officers came to the house where he was, and carrying him back to the place of execution, hung him up again till he was really dead: after which his body was carried by his mourning friends to Islington, and buried October 28. 1668, being seventeen years of age.

AN ACCOUNT OF
THE MURDER OF
JOAN NORCOTT

T he following relation was found among the papers of Sir John Maynard, an eminent lawyer, and formerly one of the commissioners of the Great Seal of England. We think proper to give it in his own words.

The Case, or rather History of a Case, that happen'd in the country of Hertford, I thought good to report here, though it happened in the fourth year of King Charles I that the memory of it may not be lost, by miscarriage of my papers, or otherwise. I wrote the evidence that was given, which I and many others did hear; and I wrote it exactly according to what was deposed at the tryal, at the Bar of the King's Bench, *viz*.

Joan Norcott, wife of Arthur Norcott, being murder'd, the question was, 'How she came by her death?' The coroner's inquest, on view of the body, and depositions of Mary Norcott, John Okeman, and Agnes his wife, inclin'd to find Joan Norcott, *felon de se*. For they inform'd the coroner and jury, that she was found dead in her bed, the knife sticking in the floor, and her throat cut. That the night before, she went to bed with her child, her husband being absent; and that no other person, after such time as she was gone to bed, came into the house: that the examinants, lying in the outer room, must needs have seen or known if any stranger had come in.

The jury, upon these evidences, give up their verdict to the coroner, that she was *felon de se*. But afterwards, upon rumour among the neighbourhood, and their observation, divers circumstances, which manifested that she did not, nor, according to those circumstances, could not possibly murder herself, the jury, whose verdict was not yet drawn up in form by the coroner, desired the coroner, that the body which was buried, might be taken out of the grave, which the coroner assented to; so that thirty days after her death, she was taken up in the presence of the jury, and a great number of people; whereupon the jury changed their verdict. The persons being tried at Hertford Assizes, were acquitted; but so much against the evidence, that Judge Harvey let fall his opinion, that it were better an appeal were brought, than so foul a murder escape unpunished. Whereupon Pascha 4 Car. they were tried on the appeal which was brought by the young child against his father, grandmother, aunt, and her husband Okeman; and because the evidence was so strange, I took exact and particular notice, and it was as follows:

After the matters above-mention'd were related, an antient and grave person, minister of the parish where the fact was committed, (being sworn to give evidence according to custom) deposed, 'that the body being taken out of the grave, thirty days after the party's death, and lying on the grass, and the four defendants press'd, they were required each to touch the dead body, Okeman's wife fell on her knees, and pray'd God to shew some token of her innocency, or to that purpose, her very words I have forgot. The appellees did touch the dead body, which was before of a livid and carrion colour' (that was the verbal expression *in terminis* of the witness) 'whereupon the brow of the dead began to have a dew, or gentle sweat arise on it, which increased by degrees, till the sweat ran down by drops on her face. The brow changed to a lively colour, and the dead open'd one of her eyes, and shut it again; and this opening of the eye was done three several times: she likewise thrust out the ring or wedding-finger, three times, and pulled it in again, and the finger dropped blood from it on the grass.'

Sir Nicholas Hyde, Lord Chief Justice, seeming to doubt the evidence, asked the evidence, 'Who saw this besides you?'

Witness. 'I cannot swear what others saw; but, my Lord, I do believe the whole company saw it; and, if it had been thought a doubt, proof would have been made of it, and many would have attested with me.'

Then the witness, observing some admiration in the auditors, spake farther.

'My Lord, I am minister of the parish, and have long known all the parties; but never had any occasion of displeasure against any of them, nor any thing to do with them, or they with me, but as I was their minister. The thing was wonderful to me; but I have no interest in the matter, only as I am called upon to testify the truth, I have done it.'

This witness was a very reverend person, as I guess'd, about seventy years of age; his testimony was deliver'd gravely, and temperately, but to the great admiration of all the auditory; whereupon applying himself to the Lord Chief Justice, he said farther.

'My Lord, my brother here present is minister of the next parish, adjacent, and I am assured he saw all done that I have affirm'd.'

Here that person was also sworn to give evidence, and deposed the same in every point, *viz.* the sweating of the brow, the change of the colour, the opening of the eye, the thrice moving of the finger, and drawing it in again. Only the first witness added, 'that he himself dipped his finger in the blood, which came from the dead body, to examine it', and he swore, 'that he believed it was blood.'

I conferred afterwards with Sir Edward Powel, Barrister at Law, and others, who all concurred in the observation; and for myself, if I were upon my oath, I can testify, that these depositions, especially the first witness, are truly reported in substance.

The other evidence was given against the prisoners, *viz.* the grandmother of the plaintiff, and against Okeman and his wife. That they confessed that they lay in the next room to the dead person that night; and that none came into the house till they found her dead in the morning. Therefore, if she did not murder herself, they must be the murderers.

To prove that she did not murder herself it was farther deposed.

First, 'That she lay in a composed manner in her bed, the bed-cloaths nothing at all disturbed, and her child by her in bed.'

Secondly, 'That her neck was broke, and she could not possibly break her neck in the bed, if she first cut her throat, nor *contra.*'

Thirdly, 'That there was no blood in the bed, saving a tincture of blood on the bolster; whereon her head lay; but no substance of blood at all.'

Fourthly, 'That from the bed's head, there was a stream of blood on the floor, which ran along till it ponded in the bending of the floor, in a very great quantity; and that there was also another stream of blood on the floor, at the bed's feet, which ponded also on the floor, to another great quantity, but no continuance or communication of blood, at either of these two places, from one to the other, neither upon the bed; so that she bled in two places severally.' And it was deposed, 'That upon turning up the mat of the bed, there were found clots of congeal'd blood in the straw of the mat underneath.'

Fifthly, 'That the bloody knife was found in the morning, sticking in the floor, at a good distance from the bed; and that the point of the knife, as it stuck, was towards the bed, and the haft from the bed.'

Lastly, 'That there was the print of a thumb and four fingers of a left hand.'

Sir Nicholas Hide, Lord Chief Justice, said to the witness, 'How can you know the print of a left-hand, from the print of a right in such a case?'

Witness. 'My Lord, it is hard to describe; but if it please that honourable Judge to put his left-hand upon your left-hand, you cannot possibly place your own right-hand in the same posture.' This was tried, and approved.

The prisoners had now time to make their defence; but gave no evidence to any purpose; whereupon the jury departed out of the court; and returning, acquitted Okeman, and found the other three guilty; who being severally demanded what they could say, why judgment should not be pronounced, they only cried out after one another, 'I did not do it, I did not do it.'

Judgment was given, and the grandmother and the husband executed; but the aunt, being with child, had the priviledge to be spared execution.

I enquired, if they confessed any thing at the gallows, but could not hear that they did.

Thus far the learned knight has continued his account of this surprizing occurrence, and we have all the reason in the world to believe, he really heard and saw what he has related, he being a man of too much candour and good-sense to be either imposed upon himself, or to impose upon others in an affair of this nature. 'Twas the extraordinary effect that the observing of this tryal had upon his own mind, which made him so careful to transmit it to posterity; doubtless, that the nature of the facts might be examined.

A question may here naturally arise, 'Whether or no the evidence of the two ministers would have been sufficient to have convicted these persons of murder, if there had been no circumstantial proofs of their guilt produced by other witnesses?'

Without pretending to decide in such a nice point, we shall only make two or three general observations on what Sir John Maynard has reported, and then leave the judicious reader to determine for himself.

In the first place, if the effects that appeared upon the relations touching the dead body, were caused by that natural sympathy, which some stickle so much for, how does it yet appear, that these effects were signs of guilt in the persons who touched; since those who give us instances of this power in nature, generally produce stronger proofs of its operation in cases of extraordinary love and esteem, than on any other account whatsoever?

Secondly, we have no rules from revelation, whereby to judge of supernatural appearances; so that if this sweating and moving was the immediate work of Providence, how can we tell for what end it was design'd; or how were they who saw it able to determine, whether or no it was done to discover the murderers, unless the proofs had been yet plainer? For if God realy had an hand in these things, he might as well have made the dead body speak, or any thing else, as have caused it to sweat, or move a lip, a hand, or an eye; and it is reasonable to suppose that the Divine Being will always make that familiar to our senses, which he designs for our sudden conviction in any particular. The miracles of Moses and our Saviour were of this nature.

Thirdly, we have no reason to expect any thing out of the common course of nature; and therefore there is no provision made by our laws, for what may happen out of this ordinary way. Now whether or no a person can be convicted upon what has never before been admitted, or even thought of, as the proof of any fact, is a point to be decided before we can determine the validity of our clergymens evidence; because we can't account for any appearance is not a sufficient proof that the said appearance is sent for our information. With any reasonable man, I think it should be the direct contrary.

But perhaps these reflections may be thought foreign to my purpose; or otherwise, some may imagine, that I am endeavouring to exclude Providence from having any share in the discovery I have been relating. In answer to the first objection, I shall only say, that the best histories now extant receive their value from the judicious observations of their authors; and that I only endeavour to imitate. As to the excluding Providence from having the direction of second causes, I am so far from it, that I think it every one's duty to trace the marks of the Divine Power in all occurrances. Nevertheless, we dishonour, rather than honour the disposer of all things, when we attribute to him what on a like occasion would seem unworthy a wise man, and which, perhaps, has no fitness for the end we apply it, but only in our own fancies.

What has been here said, does not at all suppose that the relations of Joan Norcott were not guilty of the murder, there being other proofs enough to convict them. Nor does it call in question the veracity either of Sir John Maynard, or the clergymen, who deposed these strange things, but only the validity of the facts themselves in the case for which they were produced.

THE LIFE OF
MAJOR GEORGE
STRANGWAYES

Mr George Strangwayes, was the second son of Mr James Strangwayes, of Mussen in Dorsetshire, a gentleman of an antient and unblemished family. He was a person that had a brave and generous soul, in a stout and active body; being tall of stature, and framed to the most masculine proportion of man. The virtues of his father he rather seem'd to improve than degenerate from, till he was hurried on by an ungovernable passion to commit the horrid fact which we are going to relate.

As his constitution in his youth made him fitter to follow Mars than the Muses, he attained to the degree of a Major in the service of King Charles I which military office he executed with a great deal of bravery and gallantry, during the whole course of the Civil War: yet was he not a stranger to those arts that finish a gentleman; for (as Mr Dryden says of my Lord Roscommon) 'He had made both Minerva's his own'. In the most important consultations he had always a head as dexterous to advise, as a heart daring to act. Only in love he appeared either unskilful, or unsuccessful; for he was never married.

The father of Mr Strangwayes died about ten years before the unhappy accident happened, which brought destruction upon his son: at his death the Major was left in possession of Mussen farm, and his eldest sister, Mrs Mabellah Strangwayes, was constituted executrix by will.

This sister, being then an antient maid, rented her brother's farm, and stock'd it at her own cost; engaging herself to him in a bond of 350 *l.* which she borrow'd towards the procuring of the said stock. The Major, presuming upon her continuance of a single life, and expecting that the greatest part, if not all of her personal estate, would in time revert to him as her heir, entrusted her, not only with the bond, but also with that part of the stock, and such utensils of the house, as, by his father's will, properly belonged to him. His reason for doing this was, that they would be more secure by passing for hers, forasmuch as his whole estate was liable to sequestration; by which, at that time of day, a great many thousand loyal gentlemen were ruined. Sad times, indeed, when honesty, which, by those who have just notions of Providence, is esteemed a common preservative against calamity, was the principal means that made people obnoxious to it! But this was not the only age, in which that noble principle had been out of fashion.

His estate being thus in a fair probability of being preserved from those vultures of the Commonwealth, who had then the administration of publick affairs, he lived for some time very happily with his sister, of whose prudence and discretion he had a very high opinion, at his farm of Mussen.

But all on a sudden the scene altered, and she whom he thought sufficiently proof against all inclinations to matrimony, began to express some affection for Mr Fussel, a gentleman well esteemed at Blandford, the place of his residence, and of much repute for his eminent abilities in matters of law.

Mrs Mabellah Strangwayes had now contracted an intimacy with Mr Fussel, and she made it the least part of her care to disguise her sentiments concerning him; so that it was not long before her brother came to a perfect knowledge of their mutual resolutions. Whether it was that he had any former dislike to the man, or that he imagined one of that profession might injure him in his property; or whether it was only the being disappointed in the hopes he had conceiv'd of enjoying after his sister the whole substance of the family, is not easy to determine; but certain it is, that he no sooner heard of a proposal of marriage between this gentleman and his sister, than he shewed himself absolutely against it, and took an opportunity of telling his sister privately, how much he disapproved her design. Mrs Mabellah, as freely told him how stedfast she was in her purpose; upon which he broke out into the most violent expressions of passion, affirming with bitter imprecations, that if ever she married Mr Fussel, he would certainly be the death of him soon afterwards.

These family quarrels soon occasion'd a separation between our unhappy brother and sister; and the rupture was still encreased by mutual complaints between them. She pretends, that he unjustly detains from her much of the stock of the farm, which, either by her father's will, or her own purchase, was lawfully hers; at the same time he denies that ever he sealed the afore-mentioned bond, insinuating, that it was only a forgery of her brother's. The Major, on the other hand, cried out as loudly against his sister, accusing her with nothing less than a design to defraud him of part of his estate, besides the money due by the bond. These were the differences, which first fomented a rage that was not to be quenched but by blood.

Soon after their parting Mrs Mabellah, and Mr Fussel were married, and the grievances between the brother and sister commenced a law-suit; for the prose-cuting of which, as well as for the carrying on of several other causes which he was employ'd in, he being a man of great business, Mr Fussel was come up to London, it being Hilary-term, at the unhappy time when he lost his life, in the following manner:

Mr Fussel lodged up one pair of stairs, at the sign of the George and Half-Moon, three doors from the Palsgrave's-Head Tavern, without Temple-Bar, opposite to a pewterer's shop. He came in one evening between nine and ten, and retired to his study, which fronted the street, sitting behind a desk, with his face towards the window, the curtains being so near drawn, that there was but just room enough left to discern him. In this manner he had not sat above a quarter of an hour, before two bullets shot from a carbine, struck him, the one through the forehead, and the other in about his mouth, a third bullet, or slug, stuck in the lower part of the timber of the window, and the passage, by which the two former entered, was so narrow, that little less than an inch over or under had obstructed their passage.

He drop'd down upon his desk without so much as a groan; so that his clerk, who was in the room at the same time, did not at first apprehend any thing of what was done; till at last perceiving him lean his head, and knowing him not apt to fall asleep as he wrote, he imagined something more than ordinary was the matter. Upon this he drew near, to be satisfy'd, when he was suddenly struck with such horror and amazement at the unexpected sight of blood, that, for the present he was utterly incapable of action. As soon as he had recollected himself, he called up some of the family, by whose assistance he discovered what an unhappy accident had bereaved him of his master. Instantly they all ran down into the street, but could see nothing that might give them the least information, every thing appearing, as they conceived, more silent and still than is usual at that time of night, in the publick parts of the city. Officers were sent for, and Mr Fussel's son (for he had been married before) was acquainted with the melancholy news; who immediately made use of all the means he could think of to discover the authors of this horrid fact.

Several places were searched in vain; and a barber, who lodged in the same house with Mr Fussel, was apprehended on suspicion, he having been absent at the time when the deed was perpetrated.

While they were considering what could induce any body to such an action, young Fussel called to mind those irreconcileable quarrels which had for some time subsisted between his father, and his Uncle Strangwayes; and thereupon proposes the apprehending him to the officers, which motion, they, in general, approved of.

They now proceed to put it in execution, and between two and three in the morning, the Major is apprehended in his bed, at his lodging, over-against Ivy-Bridge in the Strand, at the house of one Mr Pym, a taylor, next door to the Black-Bull-Inn, which is now Bull-Inn Court.

Being in the custody of the officers, he was had before Justice Blake, before whom he denied the fact, with an undaunted confidence. However, as there was so much room for suspicion, the Justice committed him to Newgate, where remaining till next morning, he was then convey'd to the place where Mr Fussel's body was. When he came there, he was commanded to take his dead brother-in-law by the hand, and touch his wounds before the coroner's inquest, a method mightily relied on by the defenders of sympathy.

But there having been nothing discovered by this experiment, he was remanded back to prison, and the jury proceed in their inquiry, though with little hopes of satisfaction. Several ways were propounded by the foreman, for the detection of the murderer; one of which was, 'that all the gunsmith's in London, and the adjacent places, should be examined what guns they had either lent or sold that day'. This, in the opinion of most of the jurymen, was an unpracticable task; and one Mr Holloway, a gunsmith in the Strand, who was one of the number, told them all, 'that the men of his profession were so numerous, that he thought it next to impossible for them to make such an enquiry without missing many; that, for his own part, he had that day lent a carbine, and did not question but several of the trade did the same every day that passed'. This saying of Mr Holloway's, was presently taken hold of by the foreman, who desired him, for the satisfaction of them all, to declare whom he had lent the said piece to: Mr Holloway, after some small recollection, answered, 'to one Mr Thompson in Long-Acre, who had formerly been a Major in the King's Army, and was now married to a daughter of Sir James Aston'. Upon this, a speedy search was made after Major Thompson, who being abroad, his wife was taken into custody, and detained a prisoner, till her husband should be produced, though she cleared herself very handsomely from having any knowledge of borrowing, or even seeing any such thing as a gun.

Mr Thompson was that morning gone into the country on some urgent occasions; but on the first news of his wife's confinement, he returned hastily to London, where being examined before a Justice of the Peace, he confessed, 'that he had borrowed a carbine of Mr Holloway, at the time mentioned, for the use of Major Strangwayes, who told him, that all he intended to do with it, was to kill a deer; and that having loaded it with a brace of bullets and a slug, he delivered it to the said Major Strangwayes, in St Clements's church-yard, between the hours of seven and eight at night'.

This was all the certain intelligence they could get of what passed before the firing of the gun. Who did the desperate deed was never known; for Mr Strangwayes carried that great secret with him to the grave, refusing to confess any thing before man, and reserving this discovery for the general assize hereafter, when the inmost recesses of mens hearts shall be laid open. Thus much farther they learned of Major Thompson, 'that between the hours of ten and eleven, Major Strangwayes brought back the gun to his house, left it, and retired to his lodging'.

These circumstances were enough to increase the suspicion of the inquisitive jury, and when they were told to Mr Strangwayes, he seemed to be struck with terror, so that he continued some moments in a profound silence; afterwards he acknowledged in a very pathetick manner, that the immediate hand of God was in the affair, for nothing less could have brought about such a wonderful detection. He farther owned, that the night the murder was committed, he left one at his quarters to personate him, whom he took care to introduce about seven in the evening, while the people of the house were employ'd in their necessary affairs, and not at leisure to take any notice of his actions. This friend, he said, walked about the chamber, so as to be heard of all the family, which occasioned them to give a wrong deposition, concerning his being at home, when he was examined before the magistrate. He added, that when the fact was committed (by whom, as we have observed already, he would never confess) he returned to his lodging, found means to discharge his friend, then hastened to bed, and lay there till he was apprehended, at three in the morning.

On the 24th of February, 1657–8 Major George Strangwayes was brought to his tryal, at the Sessions-House in the Old Bailey; where his indictment being read, and he commanded to plead, he absolutely refused to comply with the method of the court, 'unless,' he said, 'he might be permitted, when he was condemned, to die in the same manner as his brother-in-law had done. If they refused this,' he told them, 'he would continue in his contempt of the court, that he might preserve his estate, which would be forfeited on his conviction, in order to bestow it on such friends as he had most affection for, as well as to free himself from the ignominious death of a publick gibbet.'

Many arguments were urged by the Lord Chief Justice Glyn, and the rest of the bench, to induce him to plead; particularly, the great sin he committed, in refusing to submit to the ordinary course of the law, and the terror of the death, which his obstinate silence would oblige them to inflict upon him. But these, and all the other motives they made use of, were ineffectual; he still remained immoveable, refusing either to plead, or to discover who it was that fir'd the gun; only affirming, both then, and always afterwards till his death, 'that whoever did it, it was done by his direction'.

When the court perceiv'd they could work nothing on him, the Lord Chief Justice read the following dreadful sentence:

> That the Prisoner be sent back to the Place from whence he came, and there put into a mean Room, where no Light can enter; that he be laid upon his Back, with his Body bare, save something to cover his Privy

Parts; that his Arms be stretched forth with a Cord, one to one Side of the Prison, and the other to the other Side of the Prison, and in like Manner his Legs shall be used; that upon his Body be laid as much Iron and Stone as he can bear, and more; that the first Day he shall have three Morsels of Barley-Bread, and the next Day he shall drink thrice of the Water in the next Channel to the Prison Door, but no Spring or Fountain Water; and this shall be his Punishment till he dies.

Sentence being past upon him, he was remanded back to Newgate, where he was attended by several eminent and pious divines till the day of his death namely, Dr Wild, Dr Warmstrey, Mr Jenkins, Mr Watson, and Mr Norton.

Monday, the last day of February, was the fatal day appointed for executing the judgment past on him, when about eleven o'clock in the forenoon, the sheriffs of London and Middlesex, accompanied with several of their officers, came to the press-yard in Newgate. After a short stay, Major Strangwayes was guarded down, cloathed all in white, waistcoat, stockings, drawers, and cap, over which was cast a long mourning cloak. From whence he was conducted to the dungeon, the dismal place of execution, being still attended with a few of his friends, among whom was the Reverend Dr Warmstrey, to whom turning, he said, 'Sir, will you be pleased to assist me with your prayers?' The Doctor answer'd, 'Yes, Major, I come on purpose to officiate in that Christian work: the Lord strengthen your faith, and give you confidence and assurance in Jesus Christ.'

After they had spent some time in prayers, the Major addressed himself to the company in general, and with a voice something more elevated than ordinary, spoke as follows:

'I thank my God, I never had a thought in my heart to doubt the truth of the religion I profess: I die a Christian, and am assured of my interest in Christ Jesus, through whose merits I question not but e'er long, my soul shall triumph over her present afflictions in an eternity of glory, being reconciled to God by the blood of my Saviour. The Lord bless you all in this world, and bring you at last to a world of blessedness, which is the reward of the elect. The Lord bless me in this last and dreadful tryal: so let us all pray, Jesus, Jesus, have mercy on me!'

Having said this, he took his solemn last leave of all his lamenting friends, and prepared himself for the dreadful assault of death, with whom he was speedily to encounter. He desired his friends, when he gave the signal, to lay on the weights, and they placed themselves at the corners of the press for that purpose.

His arms and legs were extended, according to the sentence, in which action he cried out, 'Thus were the sacred limbs of my ever-blessed Saviour stretched forth on the cross, when he suffered to free the sin-polluted world from an eternal curse.' Then crying with a sprightly voice, 'Lord Jesus receive my soul', which were the words he had told them, his mournful attendants performed their dreadful task. They soon perceived, that the weight they laid on was not sufficient to put him suddenly out of pain, so several of them added their own weight, that they might the sooner release his soul. While he was dying, it was horrible to all that stood by, as well as dreadful to himself, to see the agonies he was put into, and hear his loud and doleful groans. But this dismal scene was over in about eight or ten minutes, when his spirit departed, and left her tortured mansion, till the great day that shall unite them again.

His body having lain some time in the press, was brought forth, and exposed to publick view, so that a great many beheld the bruises made by the press, one angle of which being purposely placed over his heart, he was the sooner deprived of life, though he was deny'd what is usual in these cases, to have a sharp piece of timber under his back to hasten the execution. The body appeared void of scars, and not deform'd with blood, save where the extremities of the press came, on the breast, and upper part of the belly. The face was bloody, but not from any external injury, but the violent forcing of the blood from the larger vessels into the veins of the face and eyes. After the dead corps had been thus examined, it was put into a coffin, and in a cart that attended at the prison door, convey'd to Christ-Church, where it was interr'd.

While he was under sentence, he wrote the following letter to Major Dewey, a Member of Parliament, who had married one of his sisters:

> Dear Brother,
>
> I hope for forgiveness from you and the rest of my friends; for my conscience bears me witness that I was grievously provoked by my brother-in-law's wrongs. It was after he had abused me by prosecutions,

and refused to fight me in single combat, that I suffer'd myself to be tempted to do what I did, though I intended only to have terrified, and not kill'd him. In a word, each hath his desert; he fell to my revenge, and I to the law: I suffer willingly, being satisfy'd, that my crime is cancel'd before the Almighty. From

Your dying brother,

G. STRANGWAYES.

'Tis said the Major had often fallen into most impetuous storms of rage at the sight of Mr Fussel, and had offered him odds in length of weapon, to fight with him: once in particular, he met him in Westminster-Hall, when they had a cause there depending, and told him, 'that Calice-Sands was a much fitter place for them, who were both Cavaliers, to dispute in, than that court, where most of the judges were their enemies'. But Mr Fussel not only refused that way of deciding their quarrel, but indicted him as a challenger, which added fuel to his former rage, and put him upon the dreadful manner of satisfying his passion, for which he suffered.

AN ACCOUNT OF
THE MURDER OF
THE REV. MR
JOHN TALBOT

T his gentleman had been chaplain to a regiment in Portugal, in the reign of King Charles II where he continued in the discharge of his office, till the recalling of the said regiment: when arriving in London, he preached three months at St Alphage in the Wall. Afterwards he was curate at a town called Laindon in Essex, where a law suit commenced between him and some persons of the said parish, upon the account of which, he came up to London at the unhappy time when a period was put to his life in the following manner.

Several profligate abandon'd wretches, to the number of six men, and one woman, took into their heads one day to way-lay, rob, and murder this poor man. Whether hearing his business, they might think he had a pretty deal of money about him: or whether they acted at the instigations of some of Mr Talbot's enemies, is not certain; however it was, they dogged him from four a-clock in the afternoon, whethersoever he went. The names of some of these miscreants were, Stephen Eaton, a confectioner; George Roades, a broker; Henry Prichard, a taylor; and Sarah Swift.

Mr Talbot had received information, that his adversaries design'd to arrest him, which made him a little circumspect while he was abroad; for every one who took any notice of him, he imagined to be an officer. This occasioned him the sooner to be alarm'd when he saw himself followed by five or six people, from place to place; so that turn which way soever he would, he was certain of meeting one or more of them.

After he had shifted about a long time to no purpose, in order to avoid, as he thought, their claping a writ on his back, he betook himself to Gray's-Inn, whither being still pursued, he had there a good opportunity to take particular and accurate notice of some or all of these evil-disposed persons. Here he took shelter a little while, and writ letters to some of his acquaintance and friends, requesting them to come and lend him their assistance in order to secure his person.

The persons whom he sent to failing him, he got admittance into the chambers of one of the gentlemen of the place, where he stay'd till he supposed all the danger was over; then taking a little refreshment, he took the back way, through Old-Street, and so over the fields to Shoreditch.

Not long after he had got into the fields, he perceived the same persons at his heels, who had dogged him before. He was now more surpriz'd than ever, it being eleven a-clock at night. The most probable method of escaping that he could see, was by breaking through a reed-hedge, to a garden-house; but before he could reach the place, one or more of the villains seiz'd him, and began to pick his pockets. They found about twenty shillings, and his knife, with which they attempted to kill him, by cutting his throat.

Whether it was by chance, or these wretches pretended to an extraordinary skill in butchering men, is uncertain; but they first cut out a piece of his throat, about the breadth of a crown-piece, without touching the wind-pipe; and then, in the dependant part of the orifice, they stabbed him with the knife so deep, that the point almost reached his lungs. However, Providence so far over-ruled their cruelty, that they did not cut the reccurent nerves, which would have stopped his speech, not the jugular veins and arteris, which if they had done, he had instantly bled to death without remedy, and then possibly no discovery had been made.

There was a cut in the collar of his doublet, which seemed to shew that they attempted this piece of butchery before they stripped him; but then the nature of the wound intimated, on the contrary, that they pulled off his coat and doublet before they accomplished their design.

This bloody deed was perpetrated at Anniseed-Clear, on Friday night, the second of July, 1669. While the wretches were committing their butchery, the dogs bark'd, and the beasts bellow'd in an uncommon manner; so that several gardeners rose out of their beds to prepare for the market, supposing it had been day-light, soon after it thunder'd and rain'd in a terrible manner, which drew several brick-makers out of their lodgings to secure their bricks from the weather, and was also the occasion that the murderers did not get far from the place where their barbarity was acted before they were apprehended, so that heaven and earth seem'd to unite in crying out against the inhuman deed, and detecting the wicked authors of it.

Some of the brick-makers, who had been alarm'd by the thunder and rain, discover'd Mr Talbot lying in his shirt and drawers all bloody: these gave notice to their companions, who also came up. They then raised him, and cherished him with a dram which one of them had at hand; whereupon he immediately pointed which way the murderers went. The watch near Shoreditch were soon inform'd what had happen'd, and some of them came as well to take care of the wounded gentleman, as to apprehend the authors of his misfortune. One of the number quickly discover'd a man lying among the nettles, and called up his companions, supposing he also had been murder'd; but when they came to a nearer examination, they saw a bloody knife on one side of him, and the Minister's doublet on the other. Upon these circumstances, presuming he was guilty of the murder, they apprehended him. At first he feign'd himself a-sleep, and then suddenly starting up, he attempted to make his escape, but in vain. A pewter pot, with the mark was newly scraped out, was found near him, and one of the watchmen broke his head with it, which made him a little more tractable. In the mean time, Mr Talbot, by the great care of the officers of the night, was carried to the Star Inn at Shoreditch church, where he was put to bed, and whither a surgeon was sent for to dress, and take care of his wounds.

This man, who was apprehended, was Eaton, the confectioner, he was carried before Mr Talbot, who instantly knew him, and by writing, declared that he was the man who cut his throat; and that five more men, and a woman, were his associates. A second time, upon Mr Talbot's own request, Eaton was brought before him, when he continued his former accusation against him; whereupon he was carried before Justice Pitfield, and by him committed to Newgate. It was not long after Eaton, before the woman was found, who also pretended to be a-sleep. Mr Talbot swore as positively to her, as he had done to the other, and enquired of the constable whether her name was not Sarah? For he had heard one of her comrades say to her, when in Holborn, 'Shall we have a coach Sarah?' The constable demanded her name, and she not suspecting the reason, told him right, which confirmed the evidence of the dying gentleman. Shortly after a third, and then a fourth was taken, who were also committed to Newgate, Mr Talbot knowing one of these also.

The care of Mr Talbot's wounds was committed to one Mr Litchfield, an able surgeon, who diligently attended him; and that nothing might be omitted which might conduce to his recovery, Dr Hodges one of the physicians employ'd by the city, during the dreadful visitation in 1665 was likewise called. To these, at the request of the minister of the Charter-house, Dr Ridgely was added. By their joint direction, he was in a fare way to be cured, no ill symptoms appearing from Monday morning to the Sabbath day following, either upon account of his wounds, or otherwise; for though he lay some time in the wet, yet thro' the experience of these gentlemen, he was kept from a fever. Several other surgeons also freely offered their assistance.

About noon on Sunday he was dressed, the wound look'd well, and he seem'd more chearful than ordinary; but within two or three hours after, a violent fit of coughing seiz'd him, which broke the jugular vein, and caused such an effusion of blood, that he fainted, and his extreme parts were cold, before any one could come to his assistance. The flux was once stop'd, but upon coughing he bled again, so that his case was almost past hopes.

About one or two next morning, he sent for Dr Atfield, minister of Shoreditch church; and though he had before said little more than ay or no, and his physicians desired him not to strain those parts where his danger lay, but rather write his mind; notwithstanding all this, he talk'd very familiarly to the doctor, telling him, 'that he hoped to be saved by the merits of Jesus Christ only'. Then the doctor pressed him to declare, whether he were still fully satisfy'd as to the persons he swore against: to which he readily answered, 'that he was certain he was not mistaken in what he had done'. Being asked whether or no he could freely forgive them, he replied, 'that he pray'd for the welfare of their souls, but desired the law might be executed on their bodies'. In a word, this reverend gentleman seemed very submissive under this severe dispensation, believing a Providence in every thing that happens. The doctor pray'd by him, and departed, and within two hours after, he expired, having been very devout and composed to the last moment.

Several attestations were made before the Justice, and at the tryal of the prisoners, concerning Mr Talbot's having been dogg'd and murdered, by those who had either seen him the day before, or came up to him first, when he was left in the lamentable condition we have beens describing. Mr Went, in particular, who was constable of the night, when this murder was committed, gave a particular relation of taking the prisoners, and of what Mr Talbot said and wrote, when he saw any one of them. The papers which the deceased wrote were likewise produced in court, and it was observable that he particularly exclaim'd against the woman, whom he called bloody every time he mentioned her, affirming, that she said to her companions several times, 'Kill the Dog, kill him.'

The facts and circumstances were so plain, that the jury found all the four that had been taken, guilty of the murder, not one of them being able to give a satisfactory account of themselves, or to prove where they were after six o'clock, the night the bloody deed was done. The names of these four was given at the beginning of this relation.

Mr Cowper, the coroner, and Mr Litchfield the surgeon, gave in their informations, an exact account of Mr Talbot's wound, and both of them deposed, 'that they verily thought it to be the occasion of his death'. Mr Litchfield said, 'The knife, realy penetrated his lungs.'

The night before Mr Talbot died, he wrote to Mr Went the constable, desiring him to go to the ordinary, and enquire with him of Eaton, whether any of Laindon's people, employ'd or abetted him in the fact he had committed, if they did, to get their names of him. But Eaton persisted in denying, not only that, but even the fact itself, telling them in the most solemn manner, 'that, to his knowledge, he never in his life saw Mr Talbot, till he was brought before him, after he was taken'. Sarah Swift likewise being questioned concerning her guilt, and urged to confess what she knew, she answered, 'that she would burn in Hell before she would own any thing of the matter'. To such an uncommon degree had these wretches hardened themselves in their crimes.

Mr Talbot wrote also several letters to his friends, with an exact account of the manner how he had been followed for seven hours together, and how he was at last set upon, and used in the barbarous manner herein related; but the substance of these letters being interspersed in the story itself, it is needless to give them at large.

On Wednesday the 14th of July, 1669 Stephen Eaton, George Roades, and Sarah Swift were convey'd in a cart to Tyburn, where the two men confessed the murder; but the woman continued obstinate to the last. Henry Prichard was reprieved upon some favourable circumstances that were produced.

'Tis wonderful what could excite these poor creatures to pursue the blood of an innocent man at this unaccountable rate, and indeed 'tis scarce to be imagin'd, that they should pitch upon one from whom they could have no very great expectations, unless they had been hired to do it, or had some personal quarrel with him, which latter could not be true. However as none of them own'd who were their abettors, or whether they were employ'd at all or no, we must not take upon us to judge in this case; but leave the decision of this point to that great and awful day, when the secrets of men's hearts shall be revealed, and every thing that has been hid shall be made manifest.

THE LIFE OF
MARY CHANNEL

The following life was sent us by a gentleman unknown, who has assured us the facts were all within his own knowledge, and desired it might be immediately inserted. We take this opportunity to thank our ingenious correspondent, whosoever he may be, and to assure him, or any other gentleman who can furnish us with the lives of any extraordinary malefactors, that the same care and expedition shall always be made use of in publishing what they may communicate.

Mary Channel was the daughter of one Mr Woods, a person of good repute, who resided in a little village near Dorchester in the county of Dorset. He was a person of known wealth, and good credit, who by his industry and diligence, daily encreased his riches: and perceiving his daughter to be of a promising disposition, and amiable both in body and mind, he gave her a liberal education, to improve and refine those good qualifications by art and study, wherewith she was liberally endow'd by the bounty of nature. She made so speedy a progress in her learning, that she soon outvied her schoolfellows; and the strong imaginations, polite behaviour, and majestick graces in her carriage, so lively display'd themselves, that she became the mirrour and discourse of all who knew her. Though her birth gave place to those of the highest rank and quality, yet her education was not inferior to them; and her incomparable wit, united with her beautiful presence, rendered her so agreeable, that she was to be preferr'd even to many of a superior rank.

But it's doing justice to give her a more ample description: her eyes then were said to be large, and full of vivacity; her inimitable complexion was like a mixture of lillies and roses; her shape small and delicate: to all this she had an air of majesty, worthy of her character, and knew how to explain herself with an admirable grace. Her charms were capable of triumphing over the heart of a prince: for wit, beauty, and an affluence of fortune, perfections seldom found together, were all united in her person, whereby the young men invented a thousand stratagems to rival each other's views; but she became envied by her neighbouring virgins.

Her charms did not consist in adorning and dressing herself in magnificent and gay attire, decked with pearls and diamonds, which gives a false gloss of beauty to persons, whose natures are opposite, and only serve to brighten the lustre of their pretended fine qualities. In a word, she was generally esteemed the most celebrated wit, and accomplished beauty of her age.

> Not she for whom the Lapithides took Arms,
> Nor Sparta's Queen could boast such heavenly Charms.
>
> GARTH.

Being now in the flower of her youth, and bloom of her beauty, she had several suitors of good repute, who all became captives to her beauty, and hardly did they find themselves ensnared, but they had the boldness to flatter themselves with the hopes of one day possessing such a charming object. Amongst the rest, one Mr Channel, a wealthy grocer of Dorchester, came to pay his respects to her, who for the great riches he enjoy'd, was gratefully accepted by her parents, though by her altogether contemn'd and slighted: he had nothing to recommend him but his wealth, which was so much superior to the rest of her suitors, as his person was inferior to them; his limbs and body were in some measure ill-proportion'd, and his features in no wise agreeable; but what render'd him the more detestable and ridiculous in her sight, was his splay-foot, which did not in the least concur with her sublime and lofty temper, which was capable of encouraging none but amiable young gallants, whom she was free in entertaining with her company, though not any ways inconsistent with her honour; for (to give her her due) she generally bore the character of modest. But the proverb (*Pecuniæ obedient omnia*) is too often fulfilled. Her father, therefore, evidently perceiving the addresses of Mr Channel were gratify'd, and accepted by her with scorn and reproofs, entreated her to receive him with less disdain, and listen to his respectful addresses. These admonitions and sollicitations wrought no influence on her, and all her father's advice and instructions (on this account) were fruitless, and to no effect; for she still persisted, saying, 'she could by no means love him'. He then took a new method to ripen her love towards Mr Channel, by menacing her with his utmost displeasure, in case of her resistance, and by even compelling her to express a kindness for him whom she utterly abhorred. Her slight and slow advances also greatly grieved and disquieted her lover; yet whenever he studied what measures to take in his own justification, love had always the upper hand, and he was thus perswaded to accomodate the slights and injuries his charmer had shewn him. Yet, however, contrary to her inclinations, his addresses might be sometimes out of gratitude, and to soften her parents threats, she affected a beseeching air of tenderness, which her father at first took for a mark of obedience, and her suitor for the greatest proofs of love; but they were both ignorant of the motive that induced her to behave after such a manner, which only served to appease and mitigate the irreconcilable wrath of her parents; for the compliments she made were with a dissembled and ironical pleasure. Yet, this outward courtesy soon vanished; for animating and aspiring her lover with fresh hopes of attaining his desired success, and being thus encouraged, he pursued his inclinations with greater force than before. Hereupon being weary of his fond familiarities, she determined to abandon herself from him, and never more admit him into her presence or society. She had no sooner put her design in execution, but it reached her father's ears, who upon this revelation, discovering her false pretexts, and counterfeiting air, kept a more strict guard, and watchful eye over her behaviour and conduct; and forthwith continued his absurd and unreasonable expostulations, and imprudent menaces to enforce and augment her love. She in vain endeavoured to excuse herself, by disputing the most solid and rational arguments; but how much the more she persisted, by so much the more her parents resolution was incensed and irritated, pressing her to consent to a speedy marriage, and telling her she would discharge the duty, under which she was obligated to them, by assenting to, and complying with their commands. 'Alas,' said she, 'how easy is it to be dutiful, when it's agreeable to the inclination? But how difficult a thing is it to retain and discharge one's duty when it's contrary to and exclusive of the limits of nature? If this be a duty, and I, unhappy I, compelled to obey and embrace it; then — hard is my fate! His possessions indeed, are larger than others: he has made a purchase then, of my mercenary heart!' She often uttered these and such like expressions, to endeavour, (if possible) to recall her father's resolution, though to no purpose. Permit me here to recite the opinion of a celebrated author, treating on the like subject; which intimates much in the favour and behalf of Mrs Channel, as touching her marriage, and which every impartial person cannot but allow to be equity. 'I confess' (says he) 'it is just and proper, that children should pay obedience to their parents commands; but it is also very convenient, and much better, that parents should allow their children to embrace what condition of life they like best; and since marriage is a knot which is untied only by death, both parties should be entirely satisfy'd in the tying it.' At length, being continually fatigued and importuned by her parents to have the marriage solemniz'd, she consented, tho' with the greatest reluctance: and on the day appointed, the ceremony was ordained.

> Thus far obliging Love employ'd her Art,
> But now Revenge must act a Tragick Part.
>
> TATE.

Having now gratify'd her parents desire, and yielded to their compulsions, by putting the finishing stroke to her marriage, she still continued her slights and contempts towards her husband, and he became the intire object of her scorn. Soon after the solemnization of the marriage, she began to plot and contrive new scenes of tragedies, and her thoughts were chiefly employ'd, and taken up in studying what measures to take to get rid of her husband, and set herself at liberty. Nothing would satisfy her enormous desires but his death, which she determined to expiate by poison: and in order thereto, she sent her maid to the apothecary's for some white mercury, telling her, 'twas to kill rats and mice; tho' 'tis certain her design was reverse, which she intended to fulfil as soon as opportunity would give reins to her vicious inclinations. A little after she gave orders for rice milk to be made for breakfast: that morning particularly, she was observed to demonstrate a seeming diligence in procuring every one their proper messes; and no one was permitted to serve her husband but herself. Accordingly she prepar'd and gave him the poisonous draught, mix'd, and infused with the mercury, which she had reserved for this desperate use, and which proved his fatal dish. After he had eaten somewhat liberally, he discovered an ill savour in his milk, and said it tasted amiss. Hereupon he offered his wife's brother (a youth who boarded with him) to taste it; but she would by no means permit her brother to comply with this reasonable request, which caused a strong suspicion throughout the family. Then Mr Channel required the maid to taste it; but she had no sooner taken it into her hands, than her mistress in a violent passion caught it from her, and forthwith convey'd it away, and cast it into the house of office. It was now too late to recal what had past, or to seek for refuge, for his body presently began to swell vehemently, which the domesticks perceiving, immediately sent for a doctor; but the infused mercury had so great an effect upon him, that no remedy could expel it; and he expired before the physicians came to his assistance. Having thus resign'd his breath, and there being visible proofs of his being poison'd, 'twas not without reason she was suspected to be the principal and only actress and procurer thereof. Hereupon, she was immediately seiz'd, and convey'd before a Justice, before whom she entirely denied the fact; nevertheless, on her servants information, he committed her to Dorchester gaol.

At the assizes ensuing at Dorchester, she was brought to receive her trial, but she pleaded her belly; upon which she was conducted back to gaol to be kept in custody 'till after her delivery; but a jury of matrons being empannelled, they brought her in, 'Not quick with child': upon which she was a second time carried to receive her trial, and the indictment being read, she pleaded, Not Guilty. Her maid deposed, she fetched the mercury for her, and the apothecary to the same effect. She made an excellent defence, wherein she endeavoured to extenuate her guilt, and prove her innocence: she said her parents compulsions had brought this her shame and disgrace on her, by forcing her, contrary to her inclinations, to wed one whom she so utterly despised; and desired the judge to consider her youth, and that as for the mercury, she solemnly protested she intended it for no other purpose than for killing rats and mice, (which she had also told the Justice before her commitment) which if it was her real intention, happy it would have been for her had she continued her resolution; but this was looked upon as a fallacious and counterfeit pretext or excuse. In fine, the defence she made (whether it was real or pretended) was so full of wit and ingenuity, and uttered with such an extraordinary courage and humility, that it caused admiration in the judges, and pity and compassion in all who heard her trial. But this availed nothing; for the evidences appearing plain against her, and the friends of her deceased husband, being very substantial people, she received sentence to be burnt at the stake till she was dead.

The day, whereon she was to suffer being come, she was guarded by proper officers to the place of execution, with her hood veil'd over her face; being at the stake, she was exhorted to make a free confession, but would not, and further declared, 'that she had no more to add to her former confession'; whether she confessed the fact to her maid in private (as was supposed) is uncertain. After she had uttered some private ejaculations, she pulled off her gown and white silk hood, and delivered them to her maid, who accompanied her to the stake. And then — suffered death, according to the sentence before pronounced against her, declaring her faith in Christ; and to the last continued to exclaim against her parents constraints, which had been the sole cause of her torturing death. Thus at a small distance from the town of Dorchester, she yielded her breath, in or about the month of April, Anno Domini 1703, in the 18th year of her age; being greatly bewailed and lamented, though the sentence was acknowledged to be just and lawful.

Her parents being troubled at their daughter's miserable end, and not being able to sustain the injurious reflections and reproaches of the country, took coach the same day, and came for London.

> Parents by these Examples strictly prove,
> Ne'er to enforce, or cross your Children's Love;
> But that submit, to Providence above.

83

J. Nicholls delin.   J. Basire sculp.

The German Princess *with her Suppos'd* Husband *and* Lawyer.

THE LIFE OF

THE GERMAN
PRINCESS

This woman was so called from her pretending to be born at Collogn in Germany, and that her father was Henry Van Wolway a doctor of the civil law, and Lord of Holmsteim. But this story was of a piece with her actions, for she was really the daughter of one Meders a chorister at the Cathedral of Canterbury, as, some say, only an indifferent trader of that city, in which she was born the 11th of January, 1642. We can say little of her education, only from her inclinations afterwards we may suppose she had as much learning as is commonly given to her sex. She took great delight in reading, especially of romances, and books of knight errantry; *Parismus and Parismenus, Don Bellianis of Greece,* and *Amadis de Gaul,* were some of her favourite authors; and she was so touched with the character of Oriana in the latter, that she frequently conceited herself a princess, or a lady of high quality. Casandra and Cleopatra were also read in their turns, and her memory was so tenacious, that she could repeat a great part of their amours and adventures very readily.

Her marriage was not agreeable to the high opinion she had entertained of her own merit, instead of a knight, or a squire at least, which she had promised herself; she took up with a journeyman shoemaker whose name was Stedman, by whom she had two children, who both died in their infancy. This man being unable to maintain her extravagances, and support her in the splendour she always aim'd at, she was continually discontented, till at last she resolv'd to leave him, and seek her fortune. A woman of her spirit is never long in executing things of this nature, she made an elopement, she went to Dover, she married another husband who was a surgeon of that town.

Information of this affair was soon taken, and she was apprehended and indicted at Maidstone, for having two husbands, but by some masterly stroke, which she never wanted on a pressing occasion, she was quickly acquitted. This emboldened her to a third marriage, with one John Carleton, a Londoner, which was the occasion of her being first publickly known in town; for some of her old acquaintance giving Carleton's brother an account of her former weddings, she was again taken, committed to Newgate, and try'd at the Old-Bailey for polygamy. Here again the evidence against her was insufficient, so that she was a second time acquitted.

'Tis requisite, before we proceed any further in our relation, to observe, that between the two last marriages, she embark'd on board a merchant ship which carried her to Holland from whence she travelled by land to the place she had so often talk'd of, the city of Collogn, where being now mistress of a considerable sum of money; she took a fine lodging at a house of entertainment, and lived in greater splendour than she had ever before done. As it is customary in England, to go to Epsom or Tunbridge Wells in the summer season, so in Germany, the quallity usually frequent the spaw: here our adventuress had the picking of a few feathers from an old gentleman who fell in love with her, and who had a good estate not many miles distant from Collogn, at Liege or Luget: by the assistance of the landlady she managed this affair with so much artifice, that he presented her with several fine and valuable jewels, besides a gold chain, with a very costly medal, which had been formerly given him for some remarkable good service, under Count Tilley against the valiant King of Sweden, Gustavus Adolphus. The foolish old dotard, urged his passion with all the vehemence of a young vigorous lover, pressing her to matrimony, and making her very large promises, till at last she gave her consent to espouse him in three days, and he left the preparation of things necessary to her care, giving her large sums of money for that purpose. Madam now perceived it was high time to be gone, and, in order to her getting off with the greater security, she acquainted her landlady with the design, who had before shared pretty largely in the spoils of the old captain. The hostess to be sure, was willing to hearken to any proposal that would help her a little more to fleece the doting inamorate.

The Princess, however, was resolved this time to have all the booty to herself; and to accomplish this, she perswaded her landlady to go into the town, and get a place for her in some carriage that did not go to Collogn; because, she said her lover should not know whether to follow her. The old trot saw that this precaution was very necessary, and therefore a way goes she, to provide for the safety of her guest, who was now sufficiently to reward her out of her dotard's favours. This was all our adventuress wanted, for as soon as she found herself left alone, she broke open a chest, where she had observed her landlady to put all her treasure, and there she found not only what she had shared with her out of the old man's benevolence, but also an additional sum of money not inconsiderable. There is little reason to tell the reader that she took all that was worth taking, there being none of her character apt to spare what it is in their power to seize, tho' it be from a brother or sister of their own profession. Madam soon pack'd up her parcel, and having before privately made sure of a passage to Utrecht. She fled thither, from thence she went to Amsterdam where she sold her gold chain, medal, and some of the jewels, then proceeded to Rotterdam, and then, to the Brill, where she took shipping for England.

She landed at Billingsgate one morning very early, about the latter end of March, in the year, 1663 but found no house open till she came to the Exchange Tavern, where she first obtained the title of the German Princess, in the following manner.

She was got into the aforesaid tavern, in company with some gentlemen, who she perceived, were pretty full of money. These gentlemen addressing her in the manner usual on such occasions, she immediately feigned a cry which she had always at command. The tears trickled down her cheeks, she sigh'd, she sobb'd, and, the cause being demanded, told them, that she little thought once of being reduced to such a wretched necessity as she was now in, of exposing her body to the pleasure of every bidder. Here she repeated the history of her extractions and education, telling them a great deal about her pretended father, the Lord Henry Van Wolway; who, she said, was a sovereign Prince of the Empire, independent of any man but his sacred Imperial Majesty. 'Certainly,' continued she, 'any gentleman may suppose what a mortification it must be to a woman born of such noble parents, and bred up in all the pomp of a court, under the care of an indulgent father, to suffer as I now do; yet why did I say indulgent father? Alas! was it not his cruelty that banished me his only daughter, from his dominions, only for marrying a nobleman of the court, whom I loved to excess, without his knowledge? Was it not my father that occasioned my dear lord and husband to be cut off in the bloom of his age, by falsly accusing him of a design against his person, a deed which his virtuous soul abhorred.' Here she pretended her sorrow would permit her to rehearse no more of her misfortunes, and the whole company was touched with compassion at the melancholly relation, which she so well humoured, that they all looked upon it as true, giving her out of mere pity, all the money they had about them, promising to meet her again with more. This they also accomplished, and ever afterwards called her, the poor unfortunate German Princess; which name she laid claim to in all companies.

The Exchange Tavern was kept by one Mr King, who was the same as kept it when our Princess received her honourary title. As she was now come from foreign parts, with a great deal of riches, he believed more than ever the truth of what she had before affirmed: nor was madam backwards in telling him that she had raised all her wealth by private contribution from some Princes of the Empire, who were acquainted with her circumstances, and to whom she had made herself known. Adding, that not one of those who had given her any thing, dared to acquaint her father that they knew where she was, because they were all his neighbours, and vastly inferior to him in the number and strength of their forces, 'For,' said she, 'my father is so inexorable, that he would make war upon any prince, who he knew extended his pity to me.'

John Carleton, whom we mentioned before as her third husband, was brother-in-law to Mr King. He made his addresses to the Princess Van Wolway, in the most dutiful and submissive manner that could be imagined, making use of his brother's interest, to negotiate the affair between them, till with a great deal of seeming reluctance at marrying one of common blood, her Highness consented to take him to her embraces. Now was Mr Carleton as great as his Majesty, in the arms of an imaginary princess; he formed to himself a thousand pleasures, which the vulgar herd could have no notion of; he threw himself at her feet in transport, and made use of all the rhetoric he could collect, to thank her for the prodigious honour she had done him. But alas! how was he surprized, when Mr King presented him with the following letter.

> SIR,
>
> I am an entire Stranger to your Person, yet common Justice and Humanity obliges me to give you Notice, that the pretended Princess, who has passed herself upon your Brother, Mr John Carleton, is a Cheat and an Impostor.
>
> If I tell you, Sir, that she has already married several Men in our County of Kent, and afterwards made off with all the Money she could get into her Hands, I say no more than could be proved, were she brought in the Face of Justice.
>
> That you may be certain I am not mistaken in the Woman, please to observe that she has high Breasts, a very graceful Appearance, and speaks several Languages fluently.
>
> Yours unknown,
>
> T. B.

After Mrs Carleton (for so we may at present call her) had got rid of her husband, and of the prosecution for marrying him, she was entertained by the players, who were in hopes of gaining by a woman, who had made such a considerable figure on the real theatre of the world. The house was very much resorted to upon her acccount, and she got a great deal of applause in her dramatical capacity, by the several characters she performed, which were generally either Jilt, Coquette, or Chamber-Maid, either of which was agreeable to her artful intrigueing genius; but what contributed most to her fame, was a play, written purely upon her account, called the *German Princess*, from her name, and in which she performed a principal part, besides speaking the following epilogue.

> I've past one Trial, but it is my Fear
> I shall receive a rigid Sentence here:
> You think me a bold Cheat, put Case 'twere so,
> Which of you are not? Now you'd swear I know.
> But do not, lest that you deserve to be

Censur'd worse than you can Censure me:
The World's a Cheat, and we that move in it,
In our Degrees, do exercise our Wit;
And better 'tis to get a glorious Name,
However got, than live by common Fame.

The Princess had too much mercury in her constitution to be long settled in any way of life whatsoever: the whole City of London was too little for her to act in, how was it possible then that she should be confined in the narrow limits of a theatre? She did not, however, leave the stage so soon but she had procured a considerable number of adorers, who having either seen her person, or heard of her fame, were desirous of a nearer acquaintance with her. As she was naturally given to company and gallantry, she was not very difficult of access; yet when you were in her presence, you were certain to meet with an air of indifferency.

There were two of her bullies who doted on her beyond all the rest, a couple of smart young fellows, who had abundance more in their pockets, than they had in their heads. These from a difficiency of wit in themselves, were very fond in the large quantity of that commodity which they discovered in our Princess, and for that reason were frequently in her company. There is no doubt but they had other designs than just to converse with her, for they several times discovered an inclination to come a little nearer to her body: and madam was not so ignorant, but she knew their meaning by their whining; she therefore gave them encouragement, till she had drained about 300 *l.* apiece out of them, and then, finding their stock pretty well exhausted, she turn'd them both off, telling them she wondered how they could have the impudence to pretend love to a princess.

After this, an elderly gentleman fell into the same condition, at seeing her, as several had done before, tho' he was fifty years of age, and not ignorant of her former tricks. He was worth about 400 *l.* per annum, and immediately resolv'd to be at the charge of a constant maintenance, provided she would consent to live with him. To bring about which he made her several valuable presents of rings, jewels, &c. At last, after a long siege, he became master of the fort; yet in such a manner, that it seemed rather to be surrender'd out of pure love and generosity, than from any mercenary views, for she always protested against being corrupted, so far as to part with her honour, for the sake of filthy lucre, which is a common artifice of the sex. Our gentleman, tho', as has been remark'd, he was sensible what she was; yet by degrees he became so enamour'd, as to believe every thing she said, and to look upon her as the most virtuous woman alive.

Living now as man and wife, she seem'd to redouble her endearments, and to give them all a greater air of sincerity, so that he was continually gratifying her with some costly present or another, which she always took care to receive with an appearance of being ashamed he should bear so many obligations on her, telling him continually that she was not worthy of so many favours. Thus did she vary her behaviour, according to the circumstances and temper of the person she had to deal with. At last, our old lover came home one night very much in liquor, and gave her a jewel of 5 *l.* value, and our Princess thought this as proper a time as any she was like to meet with, for her to make the most of his Worship's passion. Accordingly having got him to bed, and seen him fast asleep, which he soon was at this time, she proceeded to rifle him, finding his pocket-book, with a bill for 100 *l.* upon a goldsmith in the City, and the keys of his trunks, and escritoires.

She now proceeded to secure all that was worth her while; among other things, she made herself mistress of 20 pieces of old gold, a gold watch, a gold seal, an old silver watch, and several pieces of plate, with other valuable move-ables, to the value in all of 150 *l.* Now she thought it best for her to make off as fast as she could with her prize. So as soon as it was day she took coach, and drove to the goldsmith, who mistrusted nothing, having seen her before with the gentleman, and instantly paid the 10 *l.* upon which she delivered up the bill.

Having thus over-reached her old lover, madam took a convenient lodging, at which she past for a virgin, with a fortune of a 1000 *l.* left her by an uncle; to this she added, that her father was very rich, and able to give her as much more, but that disliking a man whom he had provided for her husband, she had left the country, and retired to London; where she was in hopes none of her relations would find her. That this story might appear the more probable, she contrived letters from a friend which were brought her continually; and in which, she pretended, she received an account of all that past, with respect to her father and lover. These letters being loosely laid about the chamber, were pick'd up by her landlady, who out of curiosity perused the contents, and by that means became

more and more satisfied in her tennant. This landlady had a nephew of considerable substance, and it was now all her endeavour to make a match between him
and her young gentlewoman, whom she soon brought to be pretty intimately
acquainted together.

The new lover presents her with a watch, as a token of his esteem for her
person, but the poor innocent creature refused it with abundance of modesty.
However, she was at last prevailed upon to accept this little favour, and the young
man thought himself with one foot in paradise already, that she was so conde-
scending. Their amour after this, went on to both their satisfactions; madam
seeing a fair prospect of making a penny of her inamorato, and he not in the
least doubting but he should obtain his wish, and one day or another enjoy that
heaven of bliss, which, as he frequently expressed it, was treasured in her arms.

One day as they were conversing together, and entertaining each other with all
the soft and tender endearments of young lovers, a porter knocks at the door, and
upon being admitted, delivers a letter to our lady, being introduced by the maid,
who had received her instructions before-hand. Madam immediately opens and
reads the letter, but scarce had she made an end, before altering her countenance,
she shrieked out, 'Oh! I am undone, I am undone.' All the company could scarce
prevent her falling into a swoon, tho' the smelling bottle was at hand, and her young
lover sitting by her; who, to be sure, did not fail to use all the rhetoric he was master
of, in order to comfort her, and learn the cause of her surprise. 'Sir,' quoth she at last,
'since you are already acquainted with most of my concerns, I shall not make a
secret of this: therefore, if you please, read this letter, and know the occasion of my
affliction.' The young gentleman received it at her hands, and read as follows.

Dear Madam,

I have several Times taken my Pen in Hand, on purpose to write to you,
and as often laid it aside again, for fear of giving you more Trouble than
you already labour under. However, as the Affair so immediately concerns
you, I cannot in Justice hide what I tremble to disclose, but must in Duty
tell you the worst of News, whatever may be the Consequence of my so
doing.

Know then, that your affectionate and tender Brother is Dead. I am
sensible how dear he was to you, and you to him; yet let me intreat you

for your own sake to aquiesce in the Will of Providence as much as possible, since our Lives are all at his disposal who gave us Being.

I could use another Argument to comfort you, that with a Sister less loving than you would be of more Weight than that I have urged, but I know your Soul is above all mercenary Views. I cannot, however, forbear just to inform you that he has left you all he had; and you know further, that your Father's Estate of 200 *l.* per Annum, can now devolve upon No-Body after his Decease, but yourself, who are now his only Child.

What I am next to acquaint you with, may perhaps be almost as bad as the former Particular. Your hated Lover has been so importunate with your Father, especially since your Brother's Decease, that the old Gentleman resolves, if ever he should hear of you any more, to marry you to him, and he makes this the Condition of your being received again into his Favour, and having your former Disobedience, as he calls it, forgiven: While your Brother lived, he was every Day endeavouring to soften the Heart of your Father, and we were but last Week in Hopes he would have consented to let you follow your Inclinations, if you would come Home to him again; but now there is never an Advocate in your Cause, who can Work upon the old Man's peevish Temper; for he says, as you are now his sole Heir, he ought to be more Resolute in the Disposal of you in Marriage.

While I am Writing, I am surprised with an Account that your Father and Lover are both preparing to come to London, where they say they can find you out. Whether or no this be only a Device, I cannot tell, nor can I imagine where they could receive their Information if it be true: However, to prevent the Worst, consider, whether or no you can cast off your old Aversion, and submit to your Father's Commands; for if you cannot, it will be most adviseable, in my Opinion, to change your Habitation. I have no more to say in the Affair, being unwilling to direct you in such a very nice Circumstance, the Temper of your own Mind will be the best Instructor you can apply to, for your future Happiness or Misery, during Life, depends on your Choice. God grant that every Thing may turn for the Better.

From your Friend,

S. E.

Our young lover having read the letter, found that she had real cause to be afflicted. Pity for her, and above all, a concern for his own interest, and the fear of losing his mistress to the country lover, thro' the authority of her father, put him upon perswading her to remove from her habitation, and come to reside with him, having very handsome rooms, fit for the reception of a person of such high quality. Thither she went the next day, with her maid, who knew her design, and had engaged to assist her therein to the utmost of her ability. When they were come into madam's bed-chamber, they resolved not to go to rest, that they might be ready to move off in the morning at the first opportunity. By turns they slept in their cloths on the bed, and towards morning when all were fast, but themselves, they went to work, broke open a trunk, took a bag with 100 *l.* in it, and several suits of apparel, and then slipt out, leaving our poor lover to look for his money and mistress together when he was stirring, who were both by that time far enough out of his way.

In a word, it would be impossible to relate half the tricks which she play'd, and mention half the lodgings in which she at times resided. Seldom did she miss carrying off a considerable booty wheresoever she came; at best she never fail'd of something, for all was fish that came to her net, where there was no plate, a pair of sheets, half a dozen napkins, or a pillowbier; nay, even things of a less value than these would serve her turn, rather than she would suffer her hands to be out of practice. Captain Smith, for the sake of swelling her life, has made her the actress of several things which he has in other places apply'd to other people. We can see no cause he had to do thus, since there are many more genuine facts that have come to our knowledge than we shall insert.

One time she went to a mercer's in Cheapside, with her pretended maid, where she agreed for as much silk as came to 6 *l.* and pulled out her purse to pay for it, but there was nothing therein but several particular pieces of gold, which she pretended to have a great value for: the mercer to be sure, would not be so rude as to let a gentlewoman of figure part with what she had so much esteem for; so he ordered one of his men to go along with her to her lodgings, and receive the money there. A coach was ready which she had brought along with her, and they all three went up into it. When they came to the Royal-Exchange, madam ordered the coachman to set her down, pretending to the mercer that she wanted to buy some ribbons suitable to the silk; upon which he suffered the maid, without any scruple, to take the goods along with her, staying in the coach for their return. But he might have staied long enough, if he had attended till they came again, for they found means to get off into Threadneadle-Street, and the young man having waited till he was quite weary, made the best of his way home to rehearse his misfortune to his master.

Something of a piece with this, was a cheat she put upon a French master weaver in Spittlefields, of whom she bought to the value 40 *l.* taking him home with her to her lodging, and bidding him make a bill of parcels, for half the silk was for a kinswoman of hers in the next room. The Frenchman sate down very orderly to do as she bid him, whilst she took the silk into the next room for her niece to see it: half an hour he waited pretty contentedly, drinking some wine, which madam had left him. At last beginning to be a little uneasy, he made bold to knock, when the people of the house came up, and upon his asking for the gentlewoman, told him she had been gone out some time, and was to come there no more. The poor man seeming surprised, they took him into the next room, and shewed him a pair of back stairs which was the proper way to her appartment. Monsieur was at first in a passion with the people, till they convinced him that they knew nothing of his gentlewoman, any more than that she had taken their room for a month, which being expired, she was removed they could not tell whether.

The next landlord she had was a taylor, whom she employed to make up what she bilked the mercer and weaver of. The taylor imagines he has got an excellent job, as well as a topping woman for his lodger, so he fell to work immediately, and by the assistance of some journeymen which he hired on this occasion, he got the cloths finished against a day which she appointed, when she pretended she was to receive a great number of visiters. Against the same time she gave her landlady 20 *s.* to provide a supper, desiring her to send for what was needful, and she would pay the overplus next day. Accordingly an elegant enter-tainment was prepared. Abundance of wine was drank, and the poor taylor was as drunk as a beast. This was what our Princess wanted, for the landlady going up to put her husband to bed, she and all her guests slip'd out, one with a silver tankard, another with a salt, her maid with their cloths which was not on their backs; and, in a word, not one of them all went off empty-handed. Being got into the street, they put the maid and the booty into the coach, getting themselves into others, and driving by different ways to the place of their next residence, not one of them being discovered.

Another time, she had a mighty mind, it seems, to put herself into mourning, to which purpose, she sent her woman to a shop in the New-Exchange in the Strand, where she had bought some things the day before, to desire that the people would bring choice of hoods, knots, scarves, aprons, cuffs, and other mourning accoutrements, to her lodging instantly, for her father was dead, and she must be ready in so many days to appear at his funeral. The woman of the shop presently look'd out the best she had of each of these commodities, and made the best of her way to madam's quarters. When she came there, the poor lady was sadly indispos'd, so that she was not able to look over the things till after dinner; when, if Madam Millener wou'd please to come again, she did not doubt but they shou'd deal. The good woman was very well satisfy'd, and refus'd to take her goods back again, but desir'd she might trouble her Ladyship so far as to leave them there till she came again; which was very readily granted. At the time appointed comes our tradeswoman, and asks if the gentlewoman above stairs was at home, but was told, to her great mortification, that she was gone out they could not tell whither, and that they believ'd she would never return again; for she had found means, before her departure, to convey away several of the most valuable parts of furniture in the room which she had hir'd. The next day confirm'd their suspicion, and made both the landlord and millener give her up for an impostor, and their goods for lost.

Being habited, *à la mode*, all in sable, she took rooms in Fuller's-Rents in Holborn, and sent for a young barrister of Gray's-Inn. When Mr Justinian came, she told him she was heir to her deceas'd father, but that having an extravagant husband, with whom she did not live, she was willing to secure her estate in such a manner as that he might not enjoy the benefit of it, or have any command over it, for, if he had, she was certain of coming to want bread in a little time. Here she wept plentifully, to make her case have the greater effect, and engage the lawyer to stay with her till the plot she had laid could be executed. While the grave young man was putting his face into a proper position, and speaking to the affair in hand with all the learning of Coke, a woman came up stairs on a sudden, crying out, 'O Lord, Madam, we are all undone! for my master is below. He has been asking after you, and swears he will come up to your chamber. I am afraid the people of the house will not be able to hinder him, he appears so resolute.' 'O heavens!' says our counterfeit, 'what shall I do?' 'Why?' says the lawyer. 'Why?' quoth she, 'I mean for you, dear me, what excuse shall I make for your being here? I dare not tell him your quality and business; for that would endanger all: and, on the other side, he is extremely jealous. Therefore, good Sir, step into that closet till I can send him away.' The lawyer being surpriz'd, and not knowing what to do so on a sudden, complied with her request, and she lock'd him into the closet, drawing the curtains of the bed, and going to the door to receive her counterfeit husband, who, by this time, had demanded entrance.

No sooner was our gentleman enter'd, but he began to give his spouse the most opprobrious language he could invent. 'O Mrs Devil,' says he, 'I understand you have a man in the room! a pretty companion for a poor innocent woman, truly! one who is always complaining how hardly I use her. Where is the son of a whore? I shall sacrifice him this moment. Is this your modesty, Madam? This your virtue? Let me see your gallant immediately, or, by the light, you shall be the first victim yourself.' Upon this, he made to the closet-door, and forc'd it open in a great fury, as he had before been directed. Here he discovers our young lawyer, all pale, and trembling, ready to sink through the floor at the sight of one from whom he could expect no mercy. Out flies the sword, and poor Littleton was upon his marrow-bones in a moment. Just in this instant madam interpos'd, being resolv'd rather to die herself than see the blood of an innocent man spilt in her apartment, and upon her account. A companion, also, of our bully husband, stepp'd up, and wrested the sword out of his hand by main strength, endeavouring to pacify him with all the reason and art he was master of. But still, that there might be no appearance of imposture, the more they strove, the more enrag'd our injur'd poor cornuto appear'd, for such he thought to make the lawyer believe he imagin'd himself.

They cou'd not, however, so effectually impose on our limb of the law, as that he discern'd nothing of the artifice: he began to see himself trapann'd, and ventur'd to speak in his own behalf, and tell the whole truth of the story. But he might as well have said nothing; for the other insisted upon it that this was only pretence, and that he came there for other purposes. His honour was injur'd, and nothing would serve but blood, or other surficient reparation. It was at last

97

referr'd to the arbitration of the other man, who came with the sham husband; and he propos'd the sum of 500 *l.* to make up the matter. This was a large sum, and, indeed, more than the lawyer could well raise: however, he at last consented to pay down 100 *l.* rather than bring himself into fresh inconveniences; which they oblig'd him immediately to send for, first looking over the note, to see that he did not send for a constable instead of the money. Upon the payment, they discharg'd him from his confinement.

Not long after this, our princess was apprehended for stealing a silver tankard in Covent-Garden, and, after examination, committed to Newgate. At the following sessions she was found guilty, and condemn'd, but afterwards repriev'd, and order'd for transportation. This sentence was executed, and she was sent to Jamaica, where she had not been above two years, before she return'd to England again, and set up for a rich heiress. By this means, she got married to a very wealthy apothecary at Westminster, whom she robb'd of above 300 *l.* and then left him.

After this, she took a lodging, in a house where no body liv'd but the landlady, a watchmaker, who was also a lodger, and herself and maid. When she thought her character here pretty well established, she one night invited the watchmaker and her landlady to go with her and see a play, pretending she had a present of some tickets. They consented, and only madam's maid, who was almost as good as herself, was left at home. She, according to agreement, in their absence broke open almost all the locks in the house, stole 200 *l.* in money, and about thirty watches; so that the prize, in all, amounted to about 600 *l.* which she carried to a place before provided, in another part of the town. After the play was over, our Princess invited her companions to drink with her at the Green Dragon tavern in Fleetstreet, where she gave them the slip, and went to her maid.

We now proceed to the catastrophe of this prodigious woman, who, had she been virtuously inclin'd, was capable of being the phœnix of her age; for it was impossible for her not to be admir'd in every thing she said and did. The manner of her last and fatal apprehension, was as follows, we having taken the account from the papers of those times.

One Mr Freeman, a brewer in Southwark, had been robb'd of about 200 *l.* whereupon he went to Mr Lowman, keeper of the Marshalsea, and desired him to search all suspicious places, in order to discover the thieves. One Lancaster was the person most suspected, and while they were searching a house near New Spring-Gardens for him, they spied a gentlewoman, as she seemed to be, walking in the two pair of stairs room in a night-gown: Mr Lowman immediately enters the room, spies three letters on the table, and begins to examine them: madam seems offended with him, and their dispute caused him to look on her so stedfastly that he knew her, call'd her by her name, and carried away both her and her letters.

This was in December 1672, and she was kept close prisoner till the 16th of January following, when she was brought by writ of habeas corpus to the Old-Bailey, and ask'd whether or no she was the woman who usually went by the name of Mary Carleton, to which she answered, that she was the same, the court then demanded the reason of her returning so soon from the transportation she had been sentenced to. Here she made a great many trifling evasions, to gain time, by which means she gave the bench two or three days trouble. At last, when she found nothing else would do, she pleaded her belly, but a jury of matrons being called, they brought her in not quick with child. So that on the last day of the sessions she received sentence of death, in the usual form, with a great deal of intrepidity.

After condemnation she had abundance of visitants, some out of curiosity, others to converse with her, learn her sentiments of futurity, and give her such instructions as were needful. Among the latter, was a gentleman to whom she gave a great many regular responses; in which she discovered herself to be a Roman Catholick, profest her sorrow for her past life, and wish'd she had her days to live over again; she also blam'd the women who were her jury for their verdict, saying, that she believed they could not be sure of what they testify'd, and that they might have given her a little more time.

On the 22d of January, which was the day of her execution, she appeared rather more gay and brisk than ever before. When her irons were taken off, (for she was shackled) she pinn'd the picture of her husband Carleton on her sleeve, and in that manner carried it with her to Tyburn. Seeing the gentleman who had conversed with her, she said to him in French, 'Mon Ami, le bon Dieu vous benisse, my friend, God bless you.' At hearing St Sepulchre's bell toll, she made use of several ejaculations. One Mr Crouch, a friend of hers, rode with her in the cart, to whom she gave at the gallows two popish books, called, *The Key of Paradise*, and *The Manual of Daily Devotion*. At the place of execution she told the people, 'that she had been a very vain woman, and expected to be made a precedent for sin; that tho' the world had condemned her, she had much to say for herself; that she pray'd God to forgive her, as she did her enemies'; and a little more to the same effect. After which, she was turn'd off, in the 38th year of her age, and in the same month she was born in.

Her body was put into a coffin, and decently buried in St Martin's church yard, on which occasion a merry wag wrote this distich.

> The German Princess here, against her Will,
> Lies Underneath, and yet, Oh strange! lies still.

Verses on the German Princess.

I.

> What might our Princess be esteemed,
> If Women all are Wonders deem'd;
> Since, from the same unsounded Cause,
> Of Wonders, she the Wonder was?

II.

> A Woman's Arts, the learn'd pretend,
> No Man alive can comprehend:
> Carleton in wiles, whenever try'd,
> Exceeded all the Sex beside.

III.

> No Woman's Craving can be still'd,
> So Solomon the wise Man held;
> By any single Man he meant;
> Not fifty Carleton could content.

IV.

In Vain her Qualities we trace;
O'er all the Sex she claims a Place;
For all the wondrous Sex combin'd
To call her Wonder of their Kind.

THE LIFE OF
DICK BAUF

This insolent offender was born in the Kingdom of Ireland, but whereabout we could not learn, nor indeed can we find that he knew himself; for his parents being strollers, he was carried at their backs through a great many countries before he came to understanding; so that when he enquired about these matters, they could not recollect in what climate he had first seen the light; only they remember'd that the chamber of his nativity was a gravel pit; that the bed on which his mother was delivered, was a few rushes on the ground, while the heavens were her only canopy; and what the earth round about her produced, all the provisions and ornaments for her lying-in.

At twelve years of age he had the wide world to shift for himself in, his parents being then forced to swing for their lives on a piece of cross timber, where they had the misfortune to have their breath stopp'd. Their crime was only breaking open and rifling a house, and murdering most of the family. Dick was present at the action, and contributed towards it as much as he was able, but found mercy at the assizes on account of his youth. Some say that he was pardoned only on the hard condition of being executioner to his own parents, and that he was at first very unwilling to take away the lives of those that gave him his, but consented, at last, when he found that there was no excuse, that such a worthy family might not be entirely cut off by one single act of justice. 'Tis added, that on the same consideration, his father and mother perswaded him to the action, and gave him their blessing at the hour of their departure, assuring him that they had much rather die by his hands, than by the hands of a stranger; since they were sure of his prayers in their last moments. These words afforded great consolation to young Richard, and enabled him to get thro' the work with a Christian fortitude.

Being now left an orphan, young, helpless, and alone, he determined to look out for some gentleman, whom he might serve in the quality of a skip-kennel, or some handy-craftsman, of whom he might learn a trade, for his support in an honest way. But all his enquiry was in vain; for the lamentable exit of his parents, and the occasion of it being fresh in every one's memory, their infamy rested on him, and there was no man to be found who would receive him into his house. His own barbarity, also, in taking away the lives of his father and mother, contributed not a little to his disgrace. So that, in short, he could not so much as get to be boy in any stable, under the hostler. What a terrible mortification must this be to a lad who had resolved to turn over a new leaf, and not tread in the steps of his forefathers! But there was no helping it, so must either turn rogue for a living, or inevitably starve.

Being as yet unfit to engage in any great and hazardous enterprize, he took up the decent occupation of a pick-pocket, at which he soon became very dextrous, haunting daily all the fairs, markets, and even churches, round the country, and in this manner picking up a very good living; till being often detected, and obliged to go thro' the discipline of the horse-pond, he was obliged to think of some other order of sharpers, in which to get himself entered, being now also grown pretty stout.

There is in Ireland, a sort of men, whom we may properly enough call Satyrs, from their living in woods, and desart places; among these Dick Bauf was next enroll'd. These people never came to any towns, but continue in their private holds, stealing horses, kine, sheep, and all sorts of cattle that came in their way, on which they subsist: as for money, they seldom meet with any, nor, indeed, do they need it, since they have no consolation, but among themselves. But Dick had been used to a more publick course of fife, and therefore this could not please him long; so that he soon became a Cygarek, whose office it is to haunt churches, feasts, and publick assemblies, on purpose to cut off any part of the wearing apparel of the gentry, which they are always sure to sell for ready money, keeping correspondents for that purpose. Bauf had not followed this very long, before he was detected, and severely whipp'd at the cart's arse, thro' the streets of Dublin.

But all these inferior orders soon became tiresome to our adventurer the more, on account of the bad success he met with whilst he was in them. The next, then, therefore, was to get acquainted with a gang of Grumeis, who take their name from the similitude of their practice to that of the young boys who climb up to the tops of the masts at sea, with great activity, and are call'd cats, or grumeis, by the sailors. The thieves that bear this name, are house-breakers, who make use of a ladder of ropes, with hooks in one end of it, by which they easily ascend to the chamber windows, having fastened their ladders with a long pole. These robbers were very common in Dick Bauf's time, and did a world of mischief, both in town and country, doing all with so much expedition, that they more frequently escap'd than other house-breakers, yet commonly with as large booties of gold, silver, linnen, and every thing that came to hand, as any body at all. When they had done their work, their method was to pull a string, which was fastened to the end of the hooks, and so raise them, upon which the ladder fell without leaving any marks behind it.

Dick having been one time upon such an exploit as this, when he had thrown out to his comrades all the money and plate he could find, they treacherously pulled the line before-mention'd, took down the ladder, and made off, leaving him to shift for himself, in revenge for an affront which he had lately put upon some of the company. Now was poor teague almost out of his wits to think how he should make his escape; but necessity is the mother of invention. It was not long before he found an old bed cord, which he ty'd to the window, and so let himself down, cursing and swearing as he went away, at the villainy of his companions, and protesting that it was not safe for a man of honour to keep them company.

He had not got above a mile or two from the place where the robbery was committed, before he heard his gang under a hedge, loading one another with oaths and deprecations about dividing the spoil. It immediately came into his head to be now even with them for the abuse; and he was not at a loss how to go about it. 'O Lord, gentlemen,' says he, 'make the best of your way, for I am pursued by half a dozen men, several of whom are just at my heels. We shall all be taken in two moments, if we stay.' Confusion, and a consciousness of their guilt, would not let them stay to examine the artifice; so that they all ran as fast as they were able, leaving the Devil to take the hindmost, and Dick Bauf to pick up a great part of what they had stollen; with which he made off, mightily pleas'd.

Next he got into a crew of Wool-Drawers, whose trade is to snatch away cloaks, hats, or perukes, from towners; a very sly sort of theft, practis'd only in the night, the greatest part of their cunning lying in the choice of a proper opportunity. They go always in companies, three or four together, about nine or ten at night, most commonly on dark rainy evenings, which are generally the most favourable to their practice. The places they chuse, are dark allies, and passages where a great many people come along, and there is a facility of escaping by a great many ways; which they do to prevent their being surpriz'd by the neighbours, if those that are robb'd should cry out, as they frequently do. These same thieves, too, are accustom'd to go sometimes in lacquey's habits, and, in this manner, to get admittance into masques, balls, or feasts, with pretence to look for their masters. Being enter'd, they find means to lay hold of a cloak or two, or any thing that lies in their way; which they boldly carry out, saluting every body they meet with cap in hand, by this means frequently getting off undiscover'd; the door-keepers seldom suspecting but they are really what they pretend.

But Dick Bauf was at last taken in one of these pranks, also, and burnt in the hand for it at Galway; upon which, he grew weary of the lay. He was, moreover, now a man full grown, very lusty, and able bodied; which determin'd him to take to the highway. He was not long making provision for this new course; and being, in every particular, well accouter'd for it, he proceeded in a most intrepid and insolent manner that ever fellow did. All the four provinces of Ireland were scarce large enough for him to range in, and hardly afforded him occasions enough for him to make proof of his courage so much as he desir'd. Night and day he pursu'd his villainies, and practis'd them on all ranks and degrees; rich and poor, old and young, man, woman, and child, were all the same to him: for he was as impartial as death, and altogether as inexorable; being never soften'd to pity.

One day, meeting with the Earl of Dannegal, in the road between Ballishannon and Sugo, he very boldly order'd the coachman to stop; then riding up to his Lordship, he told him, 'that he humbly craved his pardon for making so free with a peer of the kingdom, as to molest him on the road; but that he had a small petition to present, and he was certain his Lordship had more goodness than to turn away his ears from the cries of the poor and needy'. 'Well,' says the Earl, 'and what is your request?' 'Only,' quoth Dick, 'that you would give me all the money that you have about you at present; which, I think, is a very reasonable demand, considering your Lordship's wealth, and that I never troubled you before.' 'How,' says the peer, 'what are you a highwayman, then?' 'Better words, my Lord,' reply'd Bauf, 'I am only a gentleman freebooter, who live in the manner of our forefathers, before there was any such thing as property in the world. Pray what is your Lordship better than me, or any other man, that such an estate, or such a sum of money must be yours, and it must be death, forsooth, for another to meddle with it? Are we not all the sons of Adam? Did not the Almighty make us all equal in the beginning? Certainly he did. Therefore, dear brother, out of your abundance be pleased to supply my necessity, or I shall serve you as Cain did Abel; play the fratricide upon you.' His Lordship perceiv'd that at this time he was got on the wrong side of the question, there being a pistol cock'd on the other, which is a more powerful argument than any syllogism in the schools. This made him willing to own the fraternity, and, without more a-do, to comply with the request of his necessitous brother, by giving him an hundred and fifty guineas. 'This is like a brother, now,' says Bauf, 'and I shall always look upon you to be one of the best of our whole family.' So he rode off, very well pleas'd with his booty.

He was now so notoriously remarkable for the daily robberies that he committed on the Mount of Barnsmoor, that no person of quality would venture to travel that way without a very large retinue. In a word, he kept his residence in this place, till, by an order of the government, there was a guard-house built on the middle of it; and the regiments lying at Colerain, Londonderry, Belfast, and other garrisons in the North of Ireland, were oblig'd to detach thirty or forty men thither, under a serjeant and a corporal, and to relieve them monthly, on purpose to secure the passengers, who travelled that way, from being interrupted by this audacious robber.

These measures oblig'd him to shift his quarters, and reside about Lorras. Here it was that he one day met General Ingoldsby on the road, with only a groom and a footman, who rode on horseback behind him. Any one will think it was a pretty bold attempt to set even upon these; but this was nothing to him. He bid the old soldier stand and deliver, with as bold a voice as ever he had given the word of command to his men. His Honour, however, thinking it would not be suitable to his coat for him to surrender at once, when the enemy was so much inferior to him in strength, refus'd to obey, and a warm engagement ensu'd, in which Dick got the better. For having several pistols left after he had shot the general's own horse, and kill'd his groom, there was no room for any farther opposition. What he took from this brave commander, was about eighty guineas in money, a gold watch, and a diamond ring; yet he did not get off, according to the proverb, entirely shot free: for the footman discharg'd a pistol through one of his legs; but, in all probability, he had died for it, if his horse had not been very good.

In the end, such grievous complaints of his frequent outrages were made to the government by so many people, that a proclamation was issu'd out for the apprehending him, with the promise of five hundred pounds reward to him that could do the state this signal piece of service: for, in short, he began to be look'd upon as a dangerous person to the whole kingdom. This great sum caus'd abundance of people to look out after him, and, among others, were several who had often had a fellow-feeling with him, by being employ'd to dispose of what he stole. Bauf was so enrag'd when he heard of this, that he vow'd revenge; which he thus executed.

Some of these persons daily travell'd a bye road about business: as he knew their time of passing, he one day way-laid them, and stopp'd them singly, as they came, tying them neck and heels, and putting them into an old barn by the road-side. When he had by this means got nine or ten together, he set the barn on fire, and left them to be consum'd with it; which they all were, without remedy.

This inhuman action was soon discover'd by the persons being miss'd, and the bones that were found in the rubbish; whereupon, finding the country too hot to hold him, he fled in disguise to Donagh-a-dey, took shipping, and escap'd to Port-Patrick in Scotland; from whence he design'd to have gone to France. But lighting into a publick house, where there was a handsome landlady, he got familiar with her, which occasion'd him to stay longer than he intended, and, indeed, too long for him: for the husband, at last, observing the freedom that our rover took with his wife, he caus'd him to be apprehended in a fit of jealousy, having before a suspicion who he was.

When he was carried before a magistrate, all circumstances appear'd against him: so that he was sent back under a strong guard to Ireland, where he was soon known. Being committed to Newgate in Dublin, and shortly afterwards condemn'd; 'tis said, he offered five thousand pounds for a pardon, being worth twice the sum. But all proving ineffectual, he was executed at Dublin on Friday the 15th of May, 1702, aged 29 years. His body was afterwards hang'd in chains, on Barnsmoor-Mount, in the province of Ulster.

THE LIFE OF
COLONEL
JAMES TURNER

T his gentleman was born in the city of Worcester, in the year 1609, of very wealthy parents, who plac'd him with a goldsmith of reputation in London, as soon as of years for a trade. With this man he serv'd his apprenticeship very faithfully, and had the character of being a young man well qualify'd for business. When his father thought proper to put him into trade for himself, he gave him a stock of no less than three thousand pounds, to which he soon added two thousand pounds more by marriage. He had great success in business for some years, and was esteem'd the wealthiest man in his neighbourhood, so that his word would have pass'd for almost any sum.

Mr Turner had always a considerable inclination for pleasure and company, taking peculiar delight in associating himself with the gentlemen who were officers of the city militia. Among these he was complimented with a captain's commission, then a major's, then a lieutenant colonel's, and at last with the command of one of the regiments, in which he continu'd till the unhappy action that brought him to his end was discover'd, to the surprize of all the world.

The Colonel's temper was very generous and noble, which, 'tis thought, in some measure, brought on him that decay of his fortune which he afterwards labour'd under. In his post, particularly, whenever he march'd out with his regiment, he was very liberal in his entertainments, and commonly run himself to four times the expence that was necessary. 'Twas the same on every other occasion; no man was more free with his money, or more ambitious of living in splendor and reputation, than Colonel Turner.

This disposition had with him the same effect as it commonly has with others who ruin themselves by their generosity: he had no notion of retrenching his expences when he perceiv'd his substance waste; but was resolv'd to support himself with the same pomp as usual, however he came by the money. 'Twas easy for such a man to commit a great many little secret actions, that were in themselves dishonourable, before he lost his character, on account of his great business. Several of these things discover'd themselves after he was convicted, which even the persons that were wrong'd did not suspect before. One instance in particular will be well worth relating; and was as follows.

He apply'd himself one day to a merchant, and bought of him as much train-oil and rice, as came to three hundred and sixty pounds, which he promis'd to pay for as soon as the goods were deliver'd. Accordingly the day after he went to the merchant's house, and gave him the full sum in money and notes; for which the merchant wrote a receipt, while it all lay on the desk. Two of Turner's accomplices (for he made use of assistants) came just at this time, and pretended some urgent business with the merchant, and, in short, play'd their part so well, that one of them got off with the greatest part of Turner's payment, while the other kept the innocent man in discourse. Neither of them took any more notice of the Colonel than if they had not known him, nor did the merchant imagine he had any concern in the matter till he was found guilty of another crime, of which take this short account.

There was one Mr Francis Tryon, a great merchant, who liv'd in Lime-Street, whom Colonel Turner knew to be very rich. In order to rob this man, one of the abovemention'd fellows convey'd himself into his cellar in the dusk of the evening, and as soon as Mr Tryon was abed, and as he thought asleep, he let the Colonel in at the door. They went up together to his bed-chamber, bound him, gagg'd him, and us'd him in a very barbarous manner; and then going into his warehouse, they took from thence, a large quantity of diamonds, saphires, rubies, &c. which Turner knew where to find: then they took all the money in the house, which amounted to a very large sum; so that the whole booty was reputed to be the value of five thousand nine hundred and forty six pounds, four shillings, and three pence. They made off with all this quietly. Mr Tryon had a man and a maid-servant, but they both lay abroad this night by permission, of which the Colonel had before receiv'd information.

Strict enquiry was made after the thieves, and all such jewels as were remarkable were particularly describ'd, while Turner thought himself secure in his character, which had so long screen'd him. But some of the things describ'd were seen in his house, and the discoverers were resolv'd to examine further: whereupon the Colonel, his wife, and his three sons, John, William, and Ely, were apprehended, and upon search almost all the jewels were found. There was now no room for evasion; the whole family were carry'd before Sir Thomas Allen, Knight and Alderman, and all committed to Newgate.

At the next sessions they were all indicted for the said robbery; but after a full examination of what evidence they had, and considering what the Colonel himself said in his defence, 'twas thought proper by the court to acquit the wife and sons, and to bring the Colonel in guilty; whereupon the usual sentence of death was pass'd on him, and executed on the twenty first of January, 1662–63; when he was drawn in a cart from Newgate to the end of Lime-Street in Leaden-hall Street, and there hang'd on a gibbet erected for that purpose; being 53 years old.

The Colonel left a paper behind him full of expressions of piety and contrition, too long to be inserted here: we would only observe, that tho' all who knew him, wonder'd at the fact, yet every one believ'd him guilty, because the proofs were so clear.

There was a robbery in his life-time, which no body could then find out; but after his death 'twas generally thought he was the manager. A letter was sent to a wealthy dealer at Chichester, sign'd with the name of a merchant his acquaintance in London, informing him of a profitable purchase in his way, and inviting him to town. The Chichester man had before receiv'd advices of this kind from the same friend, and found them of service, therefore scrupled not, but set out the next day with what money and notes he had in the house; but before he got half way to London, he was robb'd of all by two men in disguise. He soon found his correspondent had not sent to him, and was astonish'd. Col. Turner's death clear'd all, he knowing both their circumstances.

THE LIFE OF
TOM KELSEY

Thomas Kelsey was born in Leather Lane, in the parish of St Andrew's Holborn; but his mother being a Welch woman, and she having an estate of about 40 *l.* per annum, left her by an uncle at Wrexham in Denbighshire, the whole family went down thither to live upon it, which consisted only of the two old people, and this their son.

Tom was from his infancy a stubborn untoward brat, and this temper encreased as he grew up; so that at 14 years of age he was prevail'd on by one Jones, who has since been a victualler in London, to leave his father and come up to town, in order to seek his fortune. Having neither of them any money, they were oblig'd to beg their way along in the best English they were masters of. Going one day to a gentleman's house with their complaint, he took a liking to the boys, and receiv'd them both into his house; Kelsey in the quality of a horse-keeper, and Jones as a falconer. It may be supposed they were both awkward enough in their callings, but Tom's place was the least difficult, so that he kept it the longest, the gentleman being soon weary of his falconer, and glad to send him about his business again.

Kelsey used to tell the following story, as the reason of Jones's discharge; whether it were exactly true or no, there is something pleasant in it. One day the master and man went out a hawking together, and as soon as the master discovered the game, he gave the appointed sign, and Jones, who had the hawk on his fist, let her fly. The poor falcon, without pursuing the game, mounted directly upwards; upon which the gentleman began to be in a terrible passion, not suspecting the cause of her so doing. At last, when he saw no sign of her coming down again, 'I believe,' says he, 'the hawk intends to lodge in the sky to-night.' 'I believe so too,' quoth Jones, 'for she took her night-cap along with her.' The gentleman was not long finding out what this night-cap was; for in a few minutes the bird dropp'd down dead by them with her hood on, having flown upwards till she was quite spent. This not only got Jones a discharge, but procured him a handsome caning into the bargain, which he would have been very willing to have gone without.

Jones's being turned away, while Kelsey was retain'd, was the occasion of breaking off their acquaintance, which probably might save Jones from the gallows; it being very likely that if they had continued together, they would both have shared the same fate; whereas Jones now got a tapster's place in London, and continued ever after in the same business either as a servant or a master. It was not a great while after, before Tom Kelsey was detected in some little pilfering tricks, and turned out of doors after his companion, whom he could not find when he came to London. His being out of place till he could subsist no longer, and his natural inclination to dishonesty, soon brought him forwards in the course of life for which he was afterwards so infamous. He fell into company with thieves, and was as bold and as dextrous in a little time as the best of them, if not even beyond them all.

Going one day by the house of Mr Norton, a silversmith in Burleigh-Street, near Exeter-Change, a couple of his companions came by him like strangers, and one of them snatch'd off his hat, and slung it into the goldsmiths chamber window, which stood open, running away as fast as they could. Tom, who had a look innocent enough to deceive any body, made a sad complaint to Mr Norton, who stood at his door, and saw all that past. It happened that at that time there was no body at home but himself, of which Tom had got intelligence before. 'Poor lad!' says Mr Norton, 'you shall not lose your hat; go up stairs and fetch it yourself, for I cannot leave the shop.' This was just what Tom wanted; he went up and took his hat, and with it a dozen of silver spoons that lay in his way; coming down in a minute, and making a very submissive bow to Mr Norton for his civility, who let him go without suspicion. This prize was divided between him and his two associates, as is common in such like cases.

Tom was not, however, so successful in his villainies, but that he was condemn'd to be hang'd before he was 16 years of age. The fact was breaking open the house of one Mr Johnson, a grocer in the Strand, and stealing from thence two silver tankards, a silver cup, six silver spoons, a silver porringer, and 40 *l.* in money. But he got off this time on account of his youth, and the interest his father made at court; for hearing of his son's condemnation, the old gentleman came directly up to town, and arrived before the day appointed for his execution, procuring a full pardon by the meditation of some powerful friends.

To prevent his following the same courses again, and exposing himself afresh to the sentence of the law, the old gentleman put his son apprentice to a weaver, but before he had served half a year of his time, he ran away from his master, and took to his old courses again. It was his pride, to make all whom he conversed with as bad as himself, an instance of which appeared in what he did by one David Hughes, a cousin of his by the mother's side. This youth going to Kingston assizes along with Tom, a few days after he came to town, he was prevailed upon by him to pick a pocket in the court; in which action being apprehended, he was immediately try'd, and condemned to be hang'd upon a gibbet within sight of the bench, as a terror to others. This week was fatal enough to young Hughes; for he came to London on the Monday, on Tuesday and Wednesday spent and lost 10 *l.* which was all the money he had, along with whores and sharpers, on Thursday in the evening pick'd a pocket, was condemned on Friday morning, and hang'd on Saturday. This was the end of one of Kelsey's hopeful pupils, who had the impudence to boast of it.

Another of the actions of this extravagant, was, his robbing the Earl of Feversham's lodgings. This nobleman was General of the Forces in the reign of King James the Second, and consequently had a centinel always at his door. Tom dress'd himself in a foot soldier's habit one evening, and went up to the fellow who was then on duty, asking him a great many questions, and offering, at last, to make him drink, if he knew where to get a couple of pots of good beer. The soldier told him there was very good a little beyond Catherine-Street, but he durst not leave his post so long as to fetch it. 'Can't I take your place, brother soldier?' quoth Tom, 'I am sure if some body be at the post there can be no danger.' The soldier thank'd him, took the sixpence, and went his way; mean while Tom's associates got into the house, and were rifling it as fast as they could. They had not quite done when the soldier came back; whereupon Tom gave him twopence more, and desired him to get a little tobacco also. While the poor fellow was gone for this, the villains came out, and Tom went with them, carrying off not only above 200 *l.* worth of plate, but even the soldier's musquet. The next day the centinel was call'd to account, and committed to prison. At the ensuing court martial he was ordered to run the gantloop for losing his piece, and then was sent to Newgate, and loaded with irons, on suspicion of being privy to the robbery, where, after nine months confinement, he miserably perished.

Kelsey, after this, broke open the house of the Lady Grace Pierpoint, at Thistleworth, and stole from thence a great many valuable things. But soon after one of his companions impeached him for this fact; whereupon, being informed that the officers were in search after him, he fled to the camp of King William in Flanders. Here he got a considerable booty out of his Majesty's tent, and from other general officers, with which he got to Amsterdam, and sold it to a Jew; whom he also robb'd afterwards, and sold what he had gotten to another Jew at Rotterdam, from whence he re-embark'd for England.

He had not been long returned to his native country, before he was detected in breaking open the house of a linnen-draper in Cheapside, which put a final end to his liberty, tho' not to his villainy: for being sent to Newgate, and having no hopes of ever getting out any more, unless to go to Tyburn, he grew desperate, and resolved to do all the mischief he could there. Mr Goodman, one of the turnkeys of that jayl, being one day drinking in the common side cellar, Kelsey privately stabb'd him into the belly with a knife, of which wound he instantly died. For this murder he received sentence of death at the next sessions in the Old-Bailey, and a gibbet being erected in Newgate-Street, near the prison, he was thereon executed on Friday the 13th of June, 1690, being then no more than 20 years of age. As a terror to the other prisoners who were then in confinement, his body was suffered to hang on the gibbet the space of three hours.

THE LIFE OF
NAN HEREFORD

W hether it be that we entertain a greater regard for the female sex than for the other; or whether the instances of their falling into those sorts of vices that expose them to the cognizance of the law are less frequent, or whatever else may be the cause of it, 'tis certain, that a female offender excites our curiosity more than a male, if she has any way distinguish'd her self in the course of her actions. Some indeed will say, that we need not be at a loss to find the reason of this; because a woman always discovers more art and cunning than a man, when she applies her self to the practice of fraud. We will not dispute any point of honour with the subtil soft fair sex, since 'tis our duty to yield to them, as we are taught by the example of our common father Adam: let it be their finer genius, or whatever else they, or their greatest admirers will call it, that gives 'em this advantage, we must still acknowledge it, and confess that an Anne Bonny, or a Mary Read, are greater names than a Blackbeard, an Avery, or a Roberts; and that the tricks of a German Princess leave stronger impressions than the open robberies of Hind and Du Vall, or the cheats of Morrell.

But not to amuse the reader with a long preface to a short life, we would only observe, that Anne Hereford, the person of whom we are now to write, was one of those women who, in her time, was more famous than almost any one of the male robbers, whose actions have adorn'd, as well as fill'd, this work; which extraordinary reputation (if we may use a word here that is commonly taken in a good sense) was, we believe, chiefly owing to her sex, and the manner in which she imposed on mankind. One instance, out of many, shall suffice to give an idea of her cunning; and one instance of this kind is as good as one thousand, since, however they may be diversify'd by circumstances, all these sort of stratagems tend to one thing, and 'tis easy at the beginning of a story to know where it will end. But first take this short account of her original. She was born at Ipswich in Suffolk, of very honest parents, who both died when she was about seventeen years of age. No sooner was she an orphan than she came up to London, where she got a service, and lived in it above half a year: it was then her misfortune to fall into bad company, who seduced her from her place, and brought her to be a partner with them in their evil courses, which she pursu'd afterwards all the days of her life; taking care still to keep herself genteely, and not to be seen among her associates; by which means she long escap'd unsuspected, and during which time she executed the following piece of invention.

She took very good lodgings in King-Street, Westminster, where she enter-tain'd an experienced old beldam as her assistant, knowing very well, that she could not pursue her enterprizes without help. It was the business of this old woman to enquire about for a rich young novice in that neighbourhood, who might be a proper subject to work on. Upon a diligent search, she found there was a young shopkeeper, by trade an apothecary, who was both rich and cove-tous. These two qualities were look'd upon as a sufficient excuse for their taking him in; for first, as he was so very wealthy, he might spare a few hundred pounds without hurting himself; and then, secondly, his being covetous made it a sort of duty, in their opinion, to take from him what they could use, though he had not the heart to do it. There is a sort of natural antipathy between those free-baters and an avaritious person; whereas, in reality, a robber should at least speak well of a miser, because 'tis through his means that the other often gets so much money at a time. But Nan did not reason in this manner; she used to say ''twas a just judgment upon them for their grievous sins, when any such person was stripp'd of his gold, or, in other words, of his God'.

Nan hept herself up close at home, and the old woman was sent of many an idle errand to the apothecary's shop; one time for pomatum, another time for

117

mithridate, another for diascordium, and so continually for such things as the use of was well known. This frequent coming induced the apothecary to take notice of her, and talk to her in a more free and pleasant manner than at first. She took care to improve those opportunities, which were all she came for, and to run from indifferent things to his domestick affairs; asking him, in particular, 'why he did not marry?' His answer was such as might be expected from a miser, 'that the times were hard, trading dead, and housekeeping expensive'. 'That's true,' said she, 'but a rich wife, man, would make amends for all this.' 'A good one, and a rich one too,' quoth he, 'would be a brave thing indeed: I must confess, I should be glad to embrace such an opportunity of altering my condition.' The old woman had now nothing to do, but to insinuate, that she was certain such fortunes might be had, and raise a curiosity in him of knowing farther what she meant. This part she acted to admiration, till she made the young fellow stark mad to draw the secret from her; and he was almost ready to throw himself at her feet when she told him, 'that there was a young gentlewoman of her acquaintance, who was niece to a very eminent citizen of London, and had two thousand pounds to her portion, lodg'd in her uncle's hands, which must be paid her upon the day of marriage, if demanded.' The next question was, 'how he should get into the young lady's company'. To this 'twas as readily reply'd, 'that her uncle kept a very strict hand over her, and permitted her to go abroad but very seldom; but that she had now and then the liberty of making our old lady a visit, she having been formerly a nurse in her father's family: and every time the poor thing is at my house,' says the crafty old baggage, 'she complains of her uncle's severity, and wishes she could meet with a good opportunity of altering her condition with a man who would use her well, and take her entirely out of the old man's tutelage.' The apothecary was charm'd, and engaged the old dame to do all she could for him.

Having taken down the names both of the uncle and the damsel, he goes the next day into the City and makes inquiry concerning them, with as much care as an old usurer would examine his security before he put out his money. He soon found that there was such a man as had been describ'd, and that he had a niece with two thousand pounds. The old woman had been very exact in these particulars, for fear he should give himself this trouble; which she afterwards wish'd he might, the better to confirm his good opinion of her sincerity. He had no business to enquire any further, than whether or no there were such persons, and such a sum of money;

because he had been before caution'd against letting the uncle see him, or know anything of his design. To be sure he was now very earnest to see his good angel again, as he afterwards call'd her, that they might concert further measures, and that he might engage her more strongly to his interest by a promissory note, to be paid as soon as ever he got the young lady. Our go-between was not long absent from his shop; but when he made his proposal to her, she seem'd more cold than before, and told him, that she would not for the world be concern'd in the match, if he had nothing in view but getting the money: 'However,' said she, 'since I have promised you, I'll bring you together; and if you like her person, and she likes yours, then we will talk further of conditions; for as I am but a poor woman my self, a small gratuity would not be unacceptable, if I do you any service.'

In a few days our apothecary was introduced to the company of Nan Hereford; who receiv'd him like a girl that had never seen a man in her life before; such modesty, such silence, so many blushes, were enough to deceive almost the Devil himself: the interview was but very short; for the lady was afraid of staying long abroad, lest her uncle should be angry. Her coldness made Galen the warmer, till the old woman whisper'd him not to say too much at first, for fear he should spoil all. In a word, Miss went home, without so much as promising him positively that she would endeavour to come again; however, she gave him room to hope a little. The next time the old woman saw our gallant, he renew'd his proposal to her, protested, he liked her choice beyond any woman he had ever seen in his life, and begg'd of her to proceed as vigorously for him as she was able. After a few compliments, a bond was drawn up for an hundred pounds, payable to the old woman on the day of marriage, in case she effected what she had undertaken. He seemed to give this bond more willingly than she receiv'd it, and would almost have doubled it, when, a few days after his angel told him, 'that she had seen Miss, and perceiv'd she entertain'd a good opinion of him; for she had promis'd to come to her house again'.

The next meeting was something longer, and even long enough to finish the whole affair. He told her plainly that he lov'd her, could maintain her handsomly, and would make her his wife, if she pleased, without any further ceremony. The counterfeit fortune seem'd to consent, but withal intimated, that she left her uncle only because he did not use her well, and allow her any money; and that therefore she hoped he would not serve her in the same manner. 'I have been hitherto,' says she, 'kept so short, as not to be allow'd apparel suitable to my condition, and I shall think it hard to be used so by you too: my uncle will suspect some design of leaving him, if I should now press him more than ordinary for a supply, and as I am, I am unfit to appear as your wife. My fortune may be demanded when we are marry'd, and 'tis best not to trouble the old man till all be secure.' Thus she ran on, talking at a distance, but plain enough for him to see what she meant; and it was now proper to try his mettle. If she found him bleed well, as the phrase among these people is, 'twould be worth while to tickle him a little longer, and even marry him, if it were necessary; but otherwise Madam had nothing else to do, but to give him the bag, and look out for fresh sport. The stratagem succeeded beyond her most extravagant expectations; for he fetch'd two hundred and fifty guineas, to give the more signal proofs of his sincerity, and leave her no room to suspect his loving her. All this he threw into her lap, told her he had three times as much more at home, and she should enjoy whatever was in his power to procure.

In a word, they were soon after marry'd, and bedded the same day, because Madam durst not be absent from her uncle's house all night. When he had enjoy'd the darling of his soul, as she now began to be in earnest, he sent her home with a thousand sighs and expressions of fondness; promising to come in a few days, and demand both her and her fortune of her uncle. In the mean while he continued very impatient, till time would allow him in good manners to make his claim; and Madam and her old procuress made off the ground to fresh lodgings, far enough from him, and where he was never like to see her, or hear of her any more.

When three days were over, our apothecary dress'd himself up in his best clothes (which were entirely new on the wedding-day, to answer what his spouse had bought with his money) took a coach, and drove into the City, up to the door of the supposed uncle. He expected a warm reception, and had fortify'd his mind to bear it; so that, when he had knock'd, and was admitted to the old gentleman's presence, he peremptorily said, 'he was come to demand his wife'. 'I know nothing of your wife, nor you neither,' quoth the old man, 'and desire therefore that you'd explain your meaning.' Galen smartly reply'd, 'I mean your niece, Sir, who is my lawful wife.' 'Your wife, man!' said t'other; 'since how long, pray?' The apothecary here named the day and the circumstances, to convince him of the truth of what he said; but the old man told him his niece was not out on the day specify'd, and that he could not comprehend his drift. In short, they came at last to high words; and the apothecary seemed so positive and sincere all the while, that the uncle began to think he had been imposed on; whereupon he ask'd him, 'if he knew his wife when he saw her?' 'I should be glad,' reply'd Mr Gallipor, 'if you would try me.' The old man agreed to send for his niece, and she came accordingly. 'This is none of my wife,' said the disappointed young man. 'But this is my niece though,' quoth the other; 'and all the nieces I have in the world too.' They both stand aghast, and the young lady is as much surprized as they, to hear her self talk'd of by the name of wife, when she was certain she had never had the pleasure of being one. The old man having fully weigh'd the case, 'Friend,' says he, 'be convinc'd that some trick has been plaid you, and be so kind as to relate the particulars of your courtship, and every thing that has pass'd between you.' This was no sooner demanded than consented to; and one particular clear'd up another through the whole course of the affair, till the apothecary was as fully convinc'd as any body that he had met with a couple of sharpers. All he had now to do, was to think of Job, go peaceably home, tell over the money he had left, and advance one penny per shilling on his medicines.

This relation has been somewhat long; but as 'tis the only story in this life 'twill be the more excusable. We shall now conclude what we have to say of this criminal in as few words possible. After this adventure Nan grew enamour'd of one Kirkham a player, who consented to live with her. To maintain their just extravagancies, she went a shop-lifting, and he on the highway. He had the fortune to be taken on his first progress, and hang'd for what he had done in good time; but Nan continued her occupation for six years longer, stealing from mercers, linnen-drapers, and lace-men, as much goods as were suppos'd to be worth above four thousand pounds. However, at last, she also was detected, at a linnen-draper's shop in Cornhill, as she was endeavouring to secure a piece of muslin, after she had come to the shop in a chair, with two or three footmen at her heels. Before the sessions, 'tis said, she offer'd an hundred guineas to prevent her adversary's appearing against her; but in vain, for he was resolv'd to prosecute her to the utmost. She also attempted to set Newgate on fire, for which she was very heavily fetter'd and hand-cuff'd. Being condemn'd at the Old-Bailey, she was executed before the prison she had endeavour'd to destroy, on Monday, the twenty second day of December, in the Year 1960, aged twenty eight years. Her body was given to the surgeons for a skeleton.

THE LIFE OF
MOLL JONES

Mary Jones was born in Chancery-Lane, where her parents lived in a great deal of credit. She was brought up to the making hoods and scarves at the New-Exchange in the Strand. She married an apprentice, whom she loved extremely, and whose extravagancies were thought to be the first occasion of her taking to a dishonest course of life; for as he was not in a capacity to get any money himself, she was willing to do any thing in order to furnish him with whatever he wanted; being fond of having him always appear like a gentleman. The first species of thieving she took to, was picking of pockets.

One day meeting, near Rosamond's-Pond, in St James's Park, with one Mr Price, a milliner, keeping shop in the same Exchange in which she was bred, Moll pretended to ask him some questions about Mrs Zouch, a servant of his, who had murder'd her bastard-child; whereupon he pull'd out a tin trumpet, which he usually carry'd in his pocket to hold to his ear, being so very deaf that he could not hear otherwise. Whilst he was earnestly hearkening to what Moll said to him thro' this vehicle, she pick'd a purse out of his breeches, in which were fifteen guineas and a broad piece. Mr Price never miss'd it, till he came home, and then where to find her he could not tell.

Shortly after this, she was apprehended for picking the pocket of one Mr Jacob Delasay, a Jew, who was chocolate-maker to King James II and King William III and lived over-against York-Buildings in the Strand. For this fact she was committed to Newgate, and burnt in the hand; which punishment making her out of conceit with the trade of diving or filing, she turn'd shop-lift, in which she was very successful for three or four years; at the end of which, privately stealing half a dozen pair of silk stockings from one Mr Wansel, a hosier in Exeter-Change, she was detected in her very committing the theft, by one Smith a victualler, at the Rose and Crown ale-house, over against the little Savoy-Gate in the Strand, who was buying a pair of stockings there at the same time. This Smith being a constable, seized her, and carrying her before Justice Brydal, he committed her to Newgate, after which she was burnt in the hand again.

Once more Moll obtaining her liberty, she was resolv'd to be reveng'd on Smith the constable, at whose house she had spent a pretty deal of money, for discovering her in thieving; therefore knowing this victualler to be very vain-glorious, as well as covetous, usually boasting of his friends in the country, and his wealth at home, she found thereby that he had some relations about Ludlow, in the confines of Shropshire and Herefordshire, which gave her opportunity to put this trick upon him.

In a summer evening, something late, a rogue of her acquaintance, booted and spurr'd, with a horse in his hand, and covered with dust, came along the Strand, and very solicitously and hastily enquired out for Mr Smith, and by his neighbours was informed which was his house. The fellow follow'd their direction; yet like an ignorant countryman that dared not to go one step without new directions in the wood of this great town, he kept the same gaping enquiry in his country tone, where Mr Smith dwelt. The people thought the fellow mad; but it prepared Mr Smith, with very great solemnity, to receive this importunate visitant. Being come to his door, he with some earnestness and elevation of voice, demands which in his house? Smith gravely answer'd beyond the question, 'I am the master, for want of a better: what would you please to have with me?'

Our impostor, upon this, tells him, 'that if he be the gentleman, he hath some news out of the country, which most nearly concerns him, having come on purpose to be the first messenger of such glad tidings'. 'Pray, Sir, come in,' quoth Smith, 'you are very heartily welcome; pray how do all our friends in the country?'

'Very well,' quoth the rogue, 'except your uncle that is dead; who we hope is best of all. A little before his death, he made his will, and, Sir, hath made you his heir, and left you all his personal estate besides, save a few legacies. To-day he is to be bury'd by some of his kindred; but before I came away, knowing my deceased master your uncle's mind, I took an inventory of all the goods, and lock'd up all his bonds and other writings, and the money and plate, in one of the great chests, and have brought the key along with me, which I here present you with.'

To have seen the perplexed looks of this ale-draper, which he labour'd to frame to a countenance of grief, (but could not for his more prevalent joys which visibly appear'd) would have made a man split his sides with laughing. At length, after a deep sigh, and a few ejaculations on the certainty of death, he unriddled his face, and very heartily welcom'd the fellow, brought him into his kitchen, and cramm'd his guts with good victuals and drink, commanding his wife to make him what cheer she could, since there was no recalling the dead, though he was a dear uncle, and the very best of friends.

During this preparation, the fellow stands at some distance, plucks off his hat, and so keeps it, and much ado there was to persuade him to be cover'd; then he desired his new master's favour, that he might continue the bailiff and steward of his lands; to which Smith readily assented, fore-praising his honesty and faithfulness. After supper, they resum'd the discourse, with which Smith was much delighted. Then they began to consider of their journey, the expedition whereof this fellow very much urged, in regard of those poor kindred of his uncle's, who, no doubt, would make havock of those goods which were left about the house, and perchance might venture upon the locks, and seize the rest; whereupon all haste was used to begin the journey; but Smith would not disgrace himself among his kindred, and therefore would stay till he had provided himself and his wife with new mourning cloaths, and things suitable to his new fortunes, with a black suit and cloak for the man, who was to attend them into the country, and bring them to this inheritance.

When these were ready, they set forward, the victualler having discharged his man's horse-hire, and other expences, besides diet and lodging, during his stay in London. Upon the road he was very officiously waited upon by this new servant the first four days journey, lodging the last night, as this impostor said, within ten miles of the place whither they were to go: but early in the morning up gets the spark, saddles his horse with the portmanteau and his mourning in it, and away he gallops by another road, leaving his master to find out the utopia of his great windfall; who arising, and missing his guide and servant, that was lost beyond all enquiry, began to suspect the cheat; yet covetousness prevailing against reason, he resolv'd to pursue the adventure; and having the town in mind, which he was inform'd was no farther than ten miles off, he rode thither, where he could hear of no such man, nor no such matter.

Vex'd, and yet asham'd to enquire any farther, or to make a discovery of his own folly, poor Nick and Froth and his doxy turn'd their horses heads, and sorrowfully departed, cursing the hour they ever saw this cheating rogue; and to add to their misfortunes, their money was drawn very low, so that they were forced to make long journies and short meals in their way homewards; and at last, to keep themselves, were fain to part with their horses at St Alban's, whom their hard travel and harder feeding had brought down to a third of the price they cost them in London. After this on foot, weary'd and wasted with vexation, they at last arrived at London, and in the evening crept into their house to avoid the laughter of their neighbours, among whom, before their setting out, they had nois'd their sudden wealth; the defeat whereof at length coming to their knowledge, never was poor man so flouted and jeer'd as he was for many years after.

But Moll did not very long outlive this piece of revenge; for still following the art and mystery of shoplifting, she was apprehended for privately stealing a piece of sattin out of a mercer's shop on Ludgate-Hill, whither she went in a very splendid equipage, and personated the late Dutchess of Norfolk, to avoid suspicion of her dishonesty; but her graceless grace being sent to Newgate, and condemn'd for her life at the Old Bailey, she was hang'd at Tyburn in the twenty fifth year of her age, on Friday the eighteenth day of December, in the year 1691.

THE LIFE OF
TOM TAYLOR

A t the same time with Moll Jones was executed Tom Taylor, a parson's son, born at Colchester in Essex; who accustoming himself to gaming from twelve years of age, was so addicted to idleness, that he would not be brought up to any honest employment. Farthermore, rejecting the good counsel of his parents, and joining himself to bad company, he soon got into a gang of pick-pockets, with whom he often went out to learn their evil profession, and find the ready way to the gallows. Going once, with three or four of these diving sparks, to Guildford, a market town in Surrey, where there was next day a fair to be kept, fearing to be discover'd in that concourse of so many people, they resolv'd to do their business that very evening, when the people were very busy in fitting up their stalls, and some little trading was stirring besides. Their first consultation was how to draw the folks together to make one jobb of it, which was agreed on in this manner. Tom Taylor pretending to be an ignorant clown, got his head into the pillory, which was elevated near the market house, as if he had only a mind to be laugh'd at. The noise thereof causing the whole town to run together to see this spectacle, his companions so ply'd their work, while the people gaz'd, laugh'd, and star'd, that they left but few of them any money in their pockets. Nay, the very keeper of the pillory, who was as well pleas'd at this curious sight as any body, was serv'd in the same manner with the rest.

Tom seeing the work was done, and having the sign given him that his comrades were departing, came down from his wooden machine; whereupon the company dispers'd themselves. A little while after, some of them clapping their hands into their pockets, they cry'd out with one voice, that their pockets were pick'd, while in the confusion Tom slunk away to his companions, who were out of the reach of apprehension.

At last, Taylor being pretty expert at picking of pockets, he set up for himself; and one day going to the playhouse in Drury-Lane, very well dress'd he seated himself by a gentleman in the pit, whose pocket he pick'd of about forty guineas, and went clean off. This good success tempted Tom to go thither the next day, in a different suit of cloaths, when perceiving the same gentleman in the pit, whose pocket he had pick'd but the day before, he takes his seat by him again. The gentleman was so sharp, as to know his face again, for all his change of apparel, though he seem'd to take no notice of him; whereupon putting a great quantity of guineas into the pocket next Tom, it was not long before he fell to diving for them. The gentleman had sew'd fishing hooks all round the mouth of that pocket, and our gudgeon venturing too deep, by unconscionably plunging down to the very bottom, his hand was caught, and held so fast, that he could no manner of way disentangle it.

Tom angled up and down in the pocket for near a quarter of an hour, the gentleman all the while feeling his struggling to get his hand out, took no notice, till at last Tom very courteously pulling off his hat, quoth he, 'Sir, by a mistake, I have somehow put my hand into your pocket, instead of my own.' The gentleman, without making any noise, arose and went to the Rose-Tavern, at the corner of Bridget-Street, and Tom along with him, with his hand in his pocket, where it remain'd till he had sent for some of his cronies, who paid down eighty guineas to get the gudgeon out of this dry pond. However, the gentleman being not altogether contented with this double satisfaction for his loss, he most unmercifully caned him; and then turning him over to the mob, they as unmercifully pump'd him, and duck'd him in a horse-pond, and after that so cruelly us'd him, that they broke one of his legs and an arm.

Tom meeting with such bad usage in his first setting up for himself, he was so much out of conceit with the trade of picking pockets, that he left it quite off, and follow'd house-breaking; in which kind of villany he was so notorious, that he had committed above sixty felonies and burglaries only in the county of Middlesex, in less than fourteen months. He reign'd eight years in his crimes; but at length setting a barn on fire betwixt Brentford and Austirly, a little village lying about a mile north from that town, while the servants came from the dwelling house to quench it, he ran up into a chamber, pretending to help to preserve the goods, but ran away with a trunk, in which was a great deal of plate, and an hundred and forty pounds in money. He was apprehended before he got to Hammersmith, where being carry'd before a magistrate, he was committed to Newgate; and receiving sentence of death at the Old Baily, when about twenty nine years of age: he was hang'd at Tyburn on Friday the eighteenth day of December, in the year 1691, as before mention'd. Where he said he had been addicted to swearing, drunkenness, whoredom, and all other sins whatever, excepting murder.

On the same day, besides these two, suffer'd, 1. One William Horsey, for the horrid murder of two men, one of which was his particular friend; 2. William Smith, a vintner, for felony; 3. Mary Motte, for the barbarous murder of her male bastard child, by putting it up in a basket, and exposing it in a gutter, till it was starv'd; 4. John Barret, a furrier's son, who was put apprentice to a clothier, but serving only four years of his time, and getting into bad company, he committed a burglary, which brought him to this shameful death; 5. William Good, for robbing a gentleman in Hackney Fields of a silver-hilted sword, a gold watch, and twenty eight guineas; 6. Richard Johnson, for committing several most notorious robberies in and about the cities of London and Westminster, and other places in the county of Middlesex; 7. Anne Miller, for felony and burglary; 8 and 9, Edward Booth, and Humphrey Malice, and last of whom was a gardener at Westminster, for robbing a gentleman in Chelsea Fields of a silver snuff-box, a gold watch, a periwig, a beaver-hat, a pair of stone buckles set in silver, and twenty four shillings in money. 10. A glazier living in Exeter-Street, for committing several notorious robberies on the highway, to the great astonishment of all his neighbours, among whom he seem'd to carry a very civil and honest correspondence, and devoutly exclaim'd against all manner of vice; but as the old proverb is, 'The still sow drinks all the draught'.

THE LIFE OF
GEORGE SEAGER

T he following account was sent in a letter from a gentleman in London to his friend in the country, in the year 1697.

SIR,

I Have no great Inclination to tell Stories, which perhaps is nothing but the Effect of an ill-grounded Vanity, that makes me prefer the expressing of what I imagine, to the relating of what I have seen. The Profession of a Story-Teller sits but aukwardly upon young People, and is down-right Weakness in old Men. When our Wit is not arrived to its due Vigor, or when it begins to decline, we then take a Pleasure in telling what does not put us to any great Expence of Thought. However, in Compliance with your Request I will for once renounce the Pleasure which I generally take in my own Imagination, to relate the unaccountable Actions of George Seager, who was lately executed here.

This notorious Fellow, aged twenty six Years at the Time of his Death, was born at Portsmouth in Hampshire, where his Father and Mother dying, his Sister took Care of him for a while; but she not being able to support herself, left him to the Parish to keep him, the Overseers whereof placed him out to spin Pack-Thread. After two Years he left that Employment, and went to a Silk Throwster for a Year and half; when running away from his Master, he took bad Courses, as being addicted to Gaming, Swearing, Drunkenness, and Theft; but a Gang of the *Ruby* Man of War pressing him, he went on board that Ship to Sea, where robbing the Seamens Chests, he was often whipp'd at the Cap stern, put in the Bilboes, and once Keel-haul'd. Keel-hauling a Man is tying a Rope round his Middle, to which two other Ropes are so fasten'd, that carrying him to the End of the Main-Yard-Arm on the Starboard-side of the Ship, he is flung from thence into the Water, and hauled under the Ship by a Man standing on the Main-Yard-Arm on the Larboard-side, where a Gun is fired over the Criminal's Head as he is drawing up. However, as no Punishment would deter him from pilfering, the Captain of the Ship, rather than be plagued with him, put him ashore at Plymouth, from whence he begg'd his Way to Portsmouth, where he listed himself into Johnny Gibson's Regiment, to whom he was a continual Plague.

The first Time he mounted the Guard, being put Centry on the Ramparts, and ordered by the Corporal not to let the grand Rounds pass without challenging, he said, he would take Care of them, imagining that if he challenged them he must fight them too. So the grand Rounds going about at Twelve at Night, with Johnny Gibson at the Head of them, Seager, who had got a whole Hatful of Stones by him, because he chose to fight at a Distance cries out; 'Who comes there?' Being told, they were the grand Rounds; 'Oh! D—mn ye,' quoth George, 'the grand Rounds are ye? Have at you then; for I have waited for you this Hour and above.' So pelting them with Stones as fast as he could fling, the grand Rounds could not pass any farther, till they called out to the Captain of Lamport Guard, who sent the Corporal to relieve him, in order to his being examin'd; but Johnny Gibson finding him to be a raw Soldier, who had never been upon Duty before, he escaped any Punishment inflicted on Offenders by Martial Law.

Another Time, some arch Soldier putting a Whisp of Hay into the Mouth of the Wooden Horse, which stands at the End of the Parade by the Main-Guard House, Johnny Gibson espying it, quoth he, 'Ise warrant him an honest Fellow, who was so kind as to give my Horse some Hay; gin Ise ken who it was, Ise give him Sax-pence to drink.' George standing by the

Governor when he said so, quoth he, 'It was I, Sir, who gave your Horse that Hay,' Said Johnny then, 'Ise vow it was well done of thee, and there is Sax-pence for thy Pains; but as you was so civil as to feed my Horse, you ought to ride him to Water too.' So commanding him presently to be mounted on it, with a fifty Pounds Weight at his Feet, he there sate for an Hour, cursing Johnny's Civility to him to the very Pit of Hell.

But not long after this Riding-Bou, George standing Centry one Night at Johnny's Door, as he was coming homewards to his House, quoth he, 'Who comes there?' Johnny Gibson the Governor reply'd, 'A Friend, Lad.'— 'What Friend? Stand, Sir.—' Quoth Johnny, 'Ise am the Governor,' George reply'd, 'I don't know that; therefore stand off, till I call the Corporal, or else I'll shoot you.' Johnny would fain have press'd upon his Post; but when he saw himself frustrated in his Design, quoth he, 'Ise see, honest Friend, that ye know yer Duty, therefore ye need no call the Corporal, there's a Shilling for ye; and if ye'r hungry, ye may gang into my Kitchen and fill yer Belly, and in the mean Time Ise will stand for ye.' George refused his Favour several Times; but when Johnny as often promised him upon his Word and Honour, that not the least Harm should come to him for leaving his Post, he gave him his Musquet, and went into his Kitchen. When he had fill'd his Belly, he went out by a backward Door to the Guard-House, where being several Soldiers playing at Cards, he put in among them. While he was here the Corporal espying him, 'Ha, ha,' quoth he, 'how a Pox came you here from your Post already?' George reply'd, 'Don't you trouble yourself about that, I have got one there to stand for me.'

The Corporal said no more to him then; but about an Hour and a half afterwards going to relieve the Centries, when he came to George's Post, he was much surpriz'd to see Johnny walking there with a Musquet on his Shoulders, who cry'd out, 'Come, mauke Haste Mon, and relieve me, for it is a vary cold Night; but, by my Sol, Ise will never stond for any Knave agen, till he gang to fill his Belly; however, Ise shall ken that ill faud Loon another Time from a black Sheep.' Some Time after, George being in Johnny's own Company, and standing another Time Centry at his Door, wanting Shoes, he ask'd him for a Pair. Quoth Johnny, 'Hast thou ever a Piece of Chalk about thee?' George told him, 'Yes'; and giving him a Piece, with which he drew out a pair of Shoes on the Centry-Box, quoth he, 'There's a Pair for thee.' George could not well tell what to say to him; but as soon as Johnny went in a-doors, he draws out a Man standing Centry on the Centry-Box, and went off from his Post. Afterwards, the Governor coming out, and seeing what George, who was not there, had done, he presently went to the Guard-House to see for him; but finding none of the Gentleman, he sent a Corporal with a File of Musqueteers to look for him. After long searching about the Town, they found him playing at All-Fours in an Ale-House, and brought him Prisoner to Johnny, who demanding how his Impudence could be so great as to quit his Post before he was reliev'd, he said, 'He had left a Man to do his Duty'. 'Yes,' quoth Johnny, 'a Man chalk'd out for me.' 'Why,' replies George, 'I thought a Centry chalk'd out for you, would do as well as a Pair of Shoes for me.' But, to be short, Johnny committed him to the Hole, where living only upon the Allowance of Bread and Water for fourteen Days, he was then brought forth, and ran the Gauntloop six Times thro' the whole Regiment.

After this George had also ran the Gauntloop several Times for robbing the Soldiers Barracks of Victuals, Linnen, or any Thing else that he could find; but no Punishment deterring him from his pilfering Tricks, he was in a Draught sent over to Flanders, where going one Day into a great Church in Brussels, he espy'd a Capuchin-Fryar confessing a young Woman in a very private Place; and as soon as the good old Father had given Absolution to his Penitentiary, he made up to him under Pretence of confessing his Sins; for, as it happen'd, the Fryar was an Englishman. But, instead of confessing his manifold Crimes, his Intention was to commit more; for, pulling a Pistol out of his Pocket, and clapping it to his Breast, quoth he, 'Reverend Father, I perceived the young Gentlewoman, whom you just now confess'd, gave you something; but let it be more or less, unless you surrender it to me, who have most Need of it, I will shoot you thro' the Heart, altho' I was sure to be hang'd this very Moment for it.'

The Fryar being much surprized at these dangerous Words, and deeming Life sweet, he gave him what he had of his Female Penitentiary, which was two Louis d' Ors; then binding him Hand and Foot in a Corner adjacent to his Confession-Box, he went away; and that same Day, deserting his Regiment, made the best of his Way for England, where he committed several most notorious Burglaries in the Cities of London and Westminster, and the Out-Parts thereof; but at last being apprehended, and sent to Newgate, for breaking open the House of the Lord Cutts, and taking thence Plate and fine Linnen valued at Two Hundred and forty Pounds, he was hang'd at Tyburn, on Wednesday, the Twenty seventh Day of January, in the Year 1696–97.

Thus have I given you all the Account I could collect, of a Man, whose Life you were so desirous to be acquainted with; there is nothing very remarkable in his Actions, but his being your Countryman is a sufficient Excuse for your Curiosity.

I am, SIR, Yours, etc.

We may add by way of postscript to the foregoing letter, that at the same time and place were executed the following Criminals, *viz*. 1. Joseph Potter, aged twenty seven years, and born in Southwark; who running away from King William's service at sea, broke open the Lady Auverguerque's house, and took from thence one hundred and thirty pounds in money, which he consumed in less than a week; and when he came to the tree, such was his impudence as to say, 'I must needs own that I have brought my hogs to a fair market, but what care I for hanging, since a short life well spent is better than a long one!'

2. Benjamin Ellison, aged twenty five years, and born at Wapping, was condemn'd for breaking open the house of the Earl of Albemarle, and taking thence some jewels, and a gold watch of great value; but he was not much concerned at his untimely end; for, instead of repenting, he said, 'If I now was to live my life over again, I would be no other trade but a thief; because he has no sooner done his work, but he is paid for his labour.'

3. James Ayres, aged thirty years, and born in Scotland, was condemn'd for committing several most notorious robberies on the highway; and being come to the place of execution, and espying a country fellow gazing earnestly upon him, quoth he, pointing at the same time towards him, 'I have got one half-crown in my breeches still; and believing you to be out of business, I will give it you with all my heart, to take but one turn for me for half an hour: and let me tell you, a crown an hour is good pay for any working man in England.'

THE LIFE OF
HARMAN
STRODTMAN

The following account was taken in writing from the criminal's own
mouth, the day before he was executed at Tyburn, which was on
Wednesday the 18th day of June, 1701. The relation seems to be made
with so much sincerity, that we thought it best to use his own words, in which
he has express'd his case, and given us a sketch of his life, as briefly, and yet as
fully as can be expected.

In the year 1683, or a little before, I was born at Revel in Liefland, and had
the happiness to come of a good family; my parents being persons of some
account in the world, and also godly and religious people, who took great care
of my education.

About the year 1694, my father sent me to school to Lubeck, where I continued
till Michaelmas, 1698. From thence I went to Hamburgh, and stay'd there till I set
out for England. I arriv'd at London the 18th day of March following, together
with one Peter Wolter, who came with me from my native place. We were both
bound apprentice to Mr Stein and Mr Dorien, merchants and partners in London.

Peter Wolter and myself having been fellow-travellers, and being now fellow-prentices, we liv'd for some time very friendly and lovingly together, till about August last, when his sister was married to Mr Dorien, one of our masters. Then he began to be so proud, and so very domineering over me, and abusive to me, that I could not bear it. We had several fallings-out, and he did twice beat me; once before the maids of the house in the kitchen, and at another time in the compting-house; and did, besides that, often complain and tell tales of me to my masters; thereby raising their displeasure against me, and creating me their ill-will; so that they kept me close at home, and would not give me the same liberty which my fellow-apprentice, and myself before, had, of going abroad sometimes for recreation. Upon this account I conceived an implacable hatred against him, and the Devil put it into my heart to be reveng'd on him at any rate.

First I design'd to do it by poison, having to that purpose mixt some mercury with a certain white powder, which he had always in a glass in the chamber, and of which he us'd to take a dose very often, for the scurvy. But it being then winter-time (I think the latter end of December or beginning of January) I found he had left off taking his powder; and so I might wait long enough before I could see the effects of my poison, if I stay'd till the time he was to take that powder again. Therefore I thought of another way to dispatch him, and this was by stabbing him.

On Good-Friday morning, my masters sending me on an errand, I took from thence opportunity to go to Greenwich, from whence not returning till the Thursday following, my masters were so very angry with me, that they bid me be gone. Upon this I went away, and took lodgings in Moor-fields: and two days after I took other lodgings at the sign of the Sun, an ale-house in Queen-Street, in London.

Now I had a key of the fore-door of my master's house, which I got made for me a long time before Christmas, by that which was my masters; and this was for my private use, that I might, unknown to my masters, go in and out at any time when I had a mind to it; but at last the Devil taught me another use of this key; for by the help of it I came to my masters house on Saturday, about half an hour past eight at night; and being got in, I went up two pair of stairs, and having got into an empty room, adjoining to Peter Wolter's chamber, I shut myself in there, and some time after fell asleep.

About twelve a clock being awake, after I had been some time hearkening, perceiving all was very quiet in the house, I went down to a room one pair of stairs, where a tinder-box lay, and having lighted a candle, enter'd the compting-house, and there took out several notes and bills, and some money too. Then I went up again two pair of stairs, carrying with me a certain piece of wood, wherewith they us'd to beat tobacco, which I found in my chamber. When I was got up stairs, I sprang into Peter Wolter's room, and coming to his bed-side, open'd the curtains, and with my tobacco beater knock'd him on the head, giving him four or five blows on the left side of it, and another on the right. Thus it was that I most barbarously murder'd this poor creature, whom I intended, had this fail'd, to have shot to death; having brought with me two pistols, ready charged, for that wicked purpose.

When I perceiv'd Peter Wolter was quite dead, I proceeded to search his breeches, and chest of drawers, and took a note of twenty pounds, with some money, out of his pocket; which money, with that I had taken in the compting-house, amounted to eight or nine pounds. Then I pack'd up some of his linnen and woollen clothes, and having made a bundle of them, went down with it one pair of stairs, and out of a window there, threw it into the next house, where no body dwelt. Then I went up stairs again, and having cut my candle in two, both pieces being lighted, I set one in the chest of drawers, and the other on a chair, close by the bed-curtains, intending to have burnt the house, in order to conceal, by this heinous fact, the other two of theft and murder, which, thro' the instigation of the Devil, I had now most barbarously committed. Then I went thro' a window, out of the house, into that where I had flung the bundle; and staying there till about five in the morning, went away with the bundle, and what else I had taken, to my lodgings in Queen-Street, where I put on clean clothes, and then went to the Swedes Church in Trinity-Lane.

The next day, being the second Monday after Easter, I went to a goldsmith, one that I knew, in Lombard-Street, where I found my Master Stein, with another gentleman. My master ask'd me, whether I would go willingly to his house, or be carried thither by two porters: I said I would go. So, after some questions about the horrid facts I had committed at his house, and my denying of them, I was search'd, and the bill of twenty pounds, which was in the deceased's pocket, was found upon me.

Then my master asking me where I lay, I told him in Moor-Fields; so we went thither, and came to my former lodgings, but the people of the house told him, I did not lie there now. By this my master finding that I was unwilling to let him know where I had lain, or how I had dispos'd of the things which I had stoll'n out of his house, he promis'd me, that if I would confess, no harm should come to me; for he would take care to send me presently beyond seas. Upon this I freely told him the truth; where I lay, and where those goods of his were, as we were walking together. So he presently took a coach, and carried me first to my lodgings in Queen-Street, where he received the bills, clothes, money, and all that I had thus stollen, and then he carried me to Sir Humphry Edwin; who, upon his examination of me, and my own confession of all these facts, did most justly commit me to Newgate; where I must leave it to others to relate how I behaved myself during my confinement.

I have freely given this true and impartial account of myself, and my sinful actions, to the world, that all men, both young and old, might take warning by me, who once little thought I should ever be capable of committing such foul and enormous crimes. And now I am going to leave this world for ever, before I have lived long enough in it (as being but about eighteen years of age) to know either it or myself: but I thank the divine Grace, that has open'd my eyes, and set me in a clearer light, by which I am come within sight and apprehension of better things. Let me therefore, for once and ever, advise all men to be warn'd by my fall, and take great care to their ways, that they do not stumble upon the snares of Satan, as I have done; for perhaps all may not have the same divine mercy and help given them for their recovery, as I have had; for which I love and praise my great maker and redeemer, and will adore him to all eternity.

137

THE LIFE OF
MOLL RABY

We have chosen this offender's most usual name to distinguish her by, tho' like the rest of her calling, she had almost as many names as the fabulous Hydra had heads. She was born in the parish of St Martin's in the Fields, and took betimes to ill courses, in which she continued till her death. Madam Ogle was not more dextrous at bilking hackney coaches, than Moll Raby at bilking her lodging, in which species of fraud her talent originally lay, and at which she had more success than at any thing else she undertook. We will give an account of her first exploit this way, as a specimen of the rest.

This adventure was at a house in Great Russel-Street, by Bloomsbury-Square; where passing for a great fortune, who was oblig'd to leave the country by reason of the importunate troublesommess of a great many suitors, she was entertain'd with all the civility imaginable: this seeming honest creature, who was a saint without, but a devil within, continued there about a fortnight, to encrease her character, making a very good appearance as to her habit, for she had a talley-man in every quarter of the town. At last, understanding one day that all the family was to take their pleasure as to morrow, at Richmond, she resolved to take this opportunity; and when they were all absent, excepting the maid, she desired her to call a porter, and gave him a sham bill drawn on a banker in Lombard-Street, for one hundred and fifty pounds, which she desired might be all in gold; but fearing such a quantity of money might be a temptation to make the porter dishonest, she privately requested the maid to go along with him, and she, in the mean time, would take care of the house. The poor maid, thinking no harm, went with the porter to Lombard-Street, where they were stopp'd for a couple of cheats; but they alledging their innocency, and proving from whence they came, a messenger was sent home with them, who found it to be a trick put upon the servant to rob the house; for before she came back, Moll Raby was gone off with above eighty pounds in money, one hundred and sixty pounds worth of plate, and several other things of a considerable value.

For offences of this nature, she was thrice burnt in the hand, after which she marry'd one Humphry Jackson, a butcher, who was taught by her to leave off his trade, and go upon the pad in the day time, while she went upon the buttock and twang by night; which is picking up a cull or spark, whom pretending she would not expose her face in a publick-house, she takes into some dark alley, where, whilst the decoy'd fool is fumbling with his breeches down, she picks his fob or pocket, of his watch or money, and giving a sort of a hem as a signal she hath succeeded in her design, the fellow with whom she keeps company, blundering up in the dark, knocks down the gallant, and carries off the prize.

But after the death of this husband, Moll turn'd arrant thief, and in the first exploit she then went upon, she had like to come scurvily off; the adventure was this: going upon the night-sneak, (as the phrase of these people is) she found a door half open, in Downing-Street at Westminster, where stealing softly up stairs into a great bed chamber, and hiding herself under the bed, she had not been there above an hour, before a couple of footmen brought candles into the room, whilst the maid, with great diligence, was laying the cloth for supper. The table being furnish'd with two or three dishes of meat, five or six persons sat down, besides the children that were in the house; which so affrighted Moll, that she verily thought, that if their voices and the noise of the children had not hinder'd them, they might have heard her very joints smite one against another, and the teeth chatter in her head. But what was worst of all, there being a little spaniel running about to gnaw the bones that fell from the table, and one of the children having thrown him a bone, a cat that watch'd under the table, being

139

more nimble, catch'd it, and ran with it under the bed, where Moll lay incognito; the dog snarling and striving to take the bone from her, the cat so well us'd her claws to defend her prize, that having given the buffer, (that is their canting name for a dog) two or three scratches on the nose, there began so great a skirmish betwixt them, that, to allay the hurly burly, one of the servants took a fire shovel out of the chimney, and flung it so furiously under the bed, that it gave Moll a blow on the nose and forehead, that stunn'd her for near half an hour. The cat rush'd out as quick as lightning, but the dog stay'd behind, barking and grinning with such fury, that neither her fawning nor threatning could quiet him, till one of the servants flung a firefork at him, which chas'd him from under the bed, but gave her another unlucky blow cross the jaws. At length, supper was ended, but the dog still growling in the room, the fear of his betraying her, rais'd such a sudden loosness in her, that she could by no means avoid discharging herself, which made such a great stink, that it offended the people, who, supposing it to be the dog, they turn'd him out, and not long after they all withdrew themselves; when Moll coming from under the bed, she wrapt the sheets up in the quilt, and sneaking down stairs, she made off the ground as fast as she could.

Another time Moll Raby being drinking at an alehouse in Wapping, she observed the woman of the house, who was sleeping by the fire-side, to have a good pearl necklace about her neck, at which her mouth immediately water'd, and which she thus secured. Having drank a pot of drink with a consort which she had in her company, she sent the maid down in the cellar again to fill the pot, and in the mean time cut off the necklace with a pair of scissars, and taking the pearls off the string, swallowed them. Before they had made an end of that pot of drink, the woman awaking, she miss'd her necklace, for which she made a great outcry, and charged Moll and her comrade with it, but they stood upon their innocency, and going into a private room, stript themselves, when nothing being being found upon them, the woman thought her accusation might be false, and so was forced to lose her necklace without being able to suspect in what manner.

Mary Raby, alias Rogers, alias Jackson, alias Brown, was, at last, condemned for a burglary, committed in the house of the Lady Cavendish, in Soho-Square, the 3d of March, 1702–3, upon the information of two villains, namely, Arthur Chambers and Joseph Hatfield, who made themselves evidences against her. At the place of execution, at Tyburn, on Wednesday the 3d of November, 1703, she said she was thirty years of age, that she was well brought up at first, and knew good things, but did not practise them, having given up herself to all manner of wickedness and vice, such as whoredom, adultery, and unjust doings. As for the fact she stood condemn'd for, she only own'd so much, and no more of it, than this. That some part of the goods stollen out of that lady's house, was brought to hers, in the Spring Garden, where she then liv'd, she understood, the next day after the robbery was committed, and not before, whose goods they were.

She farther said, That she had a husband, she thought, in Ireland, if still alive, but she was not certain of it, because it was now six years since he left her. However, she was very sorry she had defiled his bed, and wish'd he was present, that she might desire him to forgive her that injury. She begg'd also pardon of all the world in general, for the scandalous, impious, and wicked life she had lived: and she pray'd, that all wicked persons, especially those she had been concerned with, would take warning by her; and that they might have grace so to reform and amend their lives betimes, never to be overtaken in their sins. Before she was turn'd off, she was again press'd to speak the whole, in relation to the fact she was now to die for, she persisted in what she had said before about it: but still own'd she had been a very great sinner, as being one that was guilty of Sabbath-breaking, swearing, drinking, lewdness, buying, receiving, and disposing of stollen goods, and harbouring of ill people.

As an Appendix to the life of Moll Raby, we shall add some account of Moll Hawkins, from her living with a fellow of that name, who was a most notorious pick-pocket, was condemn'd on the 3d of March, 1702–3, for privately stealing goods out of the shop of Mrs Hobday, in Pater Noster-Row. She having been repriev'd for nine months, upon the account of her being then found quick with child, tho' she was not, she was now call'd down to her former judgment. When she came to the place of execution at Tyburn, on Wednesday the 22d of December, 1703, she said she was about twenty six years of age, born in the parish of St Giles's in the Fields; that she served three years apprenticeship to a button-maker in Maiden-Lane, by Covent Garden, and followed that employ-ment for some years after; but withal gave way at the same time to those ill practices which were now the cause of her death.

Before this Moll Hawkins projected shoplifting, she went upon the question lay, which is putting herself into a good handsome dress, like some exchange girl, and then taking an empty bandbox in her hand, and passing for a milliner's or sempstress's apprentice, she goes early to a person of qualitys house, and knocking at the door, asks the servant if the lady is stirring yet; for if she was, she had brought home, according to order, the sute of knots, (or what else the Devil puts in her head) which her ladyship had bespoke over night; while the servant goes up stairs to acquaint the lady with this message, the custom is in the mean time to rob the house, and go away without an answer. Thus she one day served the Lady Arabella Howard, living in Soho Square, when the maid went up stairs to acquaint her ladyship that a gentlewomen waited below with some gloves and fans, Moll Hawkins took the opportunity of carrying away above fifty pounds worth of plate, which stood on a side-board in the parlour, to be clean'd against dinner time.

THE LIFE OF
TOM SHARP

Thomas Sharp was born of very honest parents at Rygate in Surrey, where he served his time to a glover: but he had not been long out of his apprenticeship, ere, by the influence of bad company, he was so harden'd in villainy, as not to be reclaim'd either by wholsom advice, threats, or the examples of his companions, who were executed before him. Nothing could put an end to his roguery, but the halter that put an end to his life.

To prove that this fellow was not only Sharp by name, but also sharp by nature, we need only relate the following adventure. Dressing himself one day in an old sute of black clothes, and an old tatter'd canonical gown, he went to an eminent tavern in the city, where at that time was kept a great feast of the clergymen, and humbly begg'd one of the drawers to acquaint some of the ministers above stairs, that a poor scholar was waiting below, who crav'd their charity. Accordingly the drawer acquainted one of the divines, that there was a poor scholar below in a parson's habit. The gentleman going down, and commiserating his seeming poverty, introduc'd him into the company of all the clergymen, who made him eat and drink very plentifully, and gather'd him betwixt four and five pounds, which he thankfully put into his pocket. One of the divines then, after asking pardon for making so free, desired to know of him at what university he was bred. Tom Sharp told them, he was never bred at any. 'Can you speak Greek?' the divine ask'd again. 'No,' replied Tom. 'Nor Latin?' the divine ask'd. 'No, Sir,' said Tom. 'Can you write then,' quoth the divine? 'No, nor read neither,' replied Tom. At which they fell a laughing, and said, 'he was a poor scholar indeed'. 'Then I have not deceived you gentlemen,' quoth Tom and so he brush'd off with their charitable benevolence, as thinking himself not fit company for such learned sophisters.

This poor scholar afterwards using the Vine alehouse at Charing Cross, which was then kept by a rich old man, who knew not that he was a thief, he brought several of his gang there once a week, to keep a sort of a club up one pair of stairs, with a design to rob the victualler. Accordingly, they had several times struck all the doors above stairs with a dub, that is, a pick-lock, but could never light on his mammon; whereupon, one night, Tom Sharp puts the candle to the old rotten hangings that were in the club-room, and setting them in a blaze, he and his company cried out 'Fire'. The alarm brings up the old man in the trice, who in a great fright ran up to secure his money: Tom runs softly after him at a distance, to espy where his hoard was, and in the mean time, his associates, with two or three pails of water, having quench'd the flame, which had done no great damage, the old man, at the news, return'd down with a great deal of joy, leaving his money where it was before. With this information, the night following, Tom and two of his companions having a great supper there, with each his lass, they took the opportunity of taking away 500 pounds in money; which, when the old cove miss'd, he was ready to hang himself in is own garters.

His chiefest dexterity lay in robbing waggons, which, in their canting language, they call tumblers. They who follow this sort of thieving, do generally wait in a dark morning, in the roads betwixt London and Bow, Black-heath, Newington, Islington, Highgate, Kensington Gravel-Pits, or Knightsbridge, and going in at the tail of a waggon, they take out packs of linnen or woollen cloth, boxes, trunks, or other goods. One time above the rest, Tom Sharp and his accomplices following a waggon along Tyburn Road to St Giles's Pound, they had no conveniency at all of entering it, by reason a man drove the team before, and the master and his son, a lad of about thirteen years of age, rid behind on one horse. Still they follow'd the waggon 'till it came just under Newgate, when Tom Sharp, who was a lusty hail fellow, snatching the boy off the horse, he ran down the Old Bailey with him under his arms, at which the father cry'd out to his man to stop the waggon, for a rogue had stolen away his son; so whilst the master rid after Tom Sharp, and the man run after his master, one of Tom's comrades slipt two pieces of woollen cloth out of the waggon. The old man got his son again, for Tom dropp'd him at the Sessions-House Gate.

Under this sort of thieving is also comprehended the robbing of coaches in the night time in London, by cutting off trunks and boxes which are tied sometimes behind them; and also the chiving bags or portmanteaus from behind horses, that is cutting them off; for chive, among thieves, signifies a knife. One night Tom Sharp, and another like himself, following a man on horse-back quite from Charing-Cross beyond the Royal-Exchange, they had no opportunity of getting his portmanteau, because he held one hand on it all the way; but coming just under Aldgate, acute Mr Sharp took the man a grievous rap over the knuckles, crying out at the same time, 'What a pox, will you ride over people?' So whilst the fellow clapt his fingers to his mouth, to suck them for ease, Tom's comrade cut off the portmanteau, in which was good linnen, and other things of value, which pretty well made amends for the long fatigue they had after him and his prancer, as they call a horse.

For offences of this nature, Tom Sharp was in Newgate no less than eighteen times before the last fatal time. Take the following description of that prison, as this fellow deliver'd it to some of his friends, in his half-comic, half-tragic strain.

''Tis a dwelling in more than Cimmerian darkness, an habitation of misery, a confus'd chaos, without any distinction, a bottomless pit of violence, and a Tower of Babel, where are all speakers, and no hearers. There is mingling the noble with the ignoble, the rich with the poor, the wife with the ignorant, and the debtors with the worst of malefactors. It is the grave of gentility, the banishment of courtesy, the poison of honour, the centre of infamy, the paradise of cousenage, the hell of tribulation, the treasure of despair, the refuge of vengeance, and den of foxes. There he that yesterday was great, to-day is mean; he that was well fed abroad, there starves; he that was richly clad, is stark naked; he that commanded, obeys; and he that lay in a good bed, is forc'd to rest himself on the hard boards, or cold stones. There civility is metamorphos'd into insolence, courage into subtilty, modesty into boldness, knowledge into ignorance, and order into confusion: there one weeps, whilst another sings; one prays, whilst another swears; one goes out,

145

another comes in; one is condemn'd, another absolved; and in fine, one shall hardly find two persons of one mind and exercise. There hunger is their appetite; their times of meals, always when they get any thing to eat; their table, the floor; their sauce, the filthy stinks of their wards; and their musick, nothing but snoring, sneezing, and belching. The hangings of their chambers are ever in mourning, adorn'd with large borders of cobwebs; their seats the ground; and they live apostolically; that is, without scrip, without staff, and without shoes. Many of their collars are edg'd with a piece of peeping linnen, to represent a neck-cloth, but indeed it is only the forlorn relicks of their shirts crawling out at their necks; and some of the prisoners have their appointed hours, wherein they fight their bodily enemies, and evermore obtain the victory, by continually bearing in triumph the blood of the vermin they destroy on their nails. In a word, sighs are their chief air, coldness their comfort, despair their food, rattling of chains their musick, and death and damnation their sole expectation; whilst a turnkey, with the grim aspect of his countenance, makes them tremble with fear of a new matyrdom; tho' the insulting rascal, in the height of his pride, need not screw his ill-favour'd face to a

frown, because he knows not how to look otherwise; which so dejects the spirits of those poor imprison'd slaves, who fear him, that the condition of their looks seems to implore his smiles; tho' his flinty heart having renounc'd any remorse, casts a defiance in their sad and piteous faces . . .'

This may suffice for a specimen of Tom's eloquence. We shall now proceed to relate some more of his adventures.

Going one day into Godlington's coffee-house, formerly at the corner of Parker's-Lane, in Drury-Lane, and sitting down at a common table, as the room is to all comers, a little after came in one of his comrades, and sat himself down too. Tom Sharp at the same time was looking on a curious gold medal, which he had sharp'd somewhere, and an attorney of New-Inn, sitting opposite to him, he desir'd the favour of looking on't; which being granted him, and the gentleman having view'd and commended it for a choice piece, his comrade, whom he seem'd not to know there, must needs have a sight of it too from the attorney; who thinking no harm, gave it into his hands. After he had fairly look'd on it a while, he as fairly march'd off with it: Tom Sharp saw him, but would not in the least take notice thereof, as knowing where to find him; and all this while the gentleman imagin'd nothing but that the right owner had received it again.

A little while after Tom Sharp demanded courteously his medal, excusing the gentleman's detention thereof upon the account of forgetfulness. The gentleman starting, replied, 'Sir, I thought you had it long since.' He told him, he had it not, and as he deliver'd it unto him, he should require it from no other person. They came to high words, the gentleman pish'd at it, and in the conclusion, bade Tom take his course; and so he did; for having first took witness of the standers by, he su'd him, and recover'd the value of the medal twice over.

Another time Tom Sharp, being very well dress'd, he went to one Counsellor Manning's chambers in Gray's-Inn, and demanded a hundred pounds which he had lent him on a bond. The barrister was surpriz'd at his demand, as not knowing him; but looking on the bond, his hand was so exactly counterfeited, that he could not in a manner deny it to be his own writing: however, as he knew his circumstances were such, that he never was in any necessity of borrowing so much money of any man, and that therefore he could not be indebted in any such sum, upon the account of borrowing, he told Tom he would not pay a hundred pounds in his own wrong. Hereupon Tom taking his leave, told him he must expect speedy trouble.

Mr Manning expecting to be arrested, sent for another barrister, to whom opening the matter, they concluded it was a forg'd bond; whereupon Mr Manning's counsel got a general release forg'd for the payment of this hundred pounds. When issue was join'd, and the cause came to be try'd before the Lord Chief Justice Holt, the witnesses to Tom Sharp's bond swore so heartily to his lending of the money to the defendant, that he was in a very fair way of being cast; till Mr Manning's counsel moving the court in behalf on his client, acquainted his Lordship, that they did not deny the having borrow'd a hundred pounds of the plaintiff, but it had been paid above three months. 'Three months' (quoth his Lordship) 'and why did not the defendant take up his bond, or see it cancell'd?' To this his counsel reply'd, that when they paid the money the bond could not be found, whereupon the defendant took a general release for payment thereof; which being produc'd in court, and two knights of the post swearing to it, the plaintiff was cast. This put Tom Sharp into a great passion, so that he cry'd to his companions, as he was coming through Westminster-Hall, 'Were ever such rogues seen in this world before, to swear they paid that which they never borrow'd?'

147

This fellow's inclination to wickedness was so strong, that it did not stop its career in such crimes, which could only be punish'd with a fine and pillory; but being a man of an undaunted mind in acting any sort of villainy, he was often wont to say, that that man deserv'd not the fruition of the least happiness here, that would not, rather than go without it, venture his neck. Thus sin, if it be dress'd up in specious pretences, may be entertain'd as a companion; but when it appears in its own shape, it cannot but strike horror into the soul of any, if not really stupify'd, as Tom Sharp was, who, to maintain himself in an idle course of life, would perpetrate any thing.

Among many other arts, peculiar to persons of his profession, Tom learn'd that of making black dogs, which are shillings, or other pieces of money, made only of pewter, double wash'd; by means of which he maintain'd himself for some time. It may not be amiss to observe here, that what the professors of this hellish art call George Plateroon, is all copper within, with only a thin plate about it; and what they call compositum, is a mix'd metal, which will both touch and cut, but not endure the fiery test. Tom had not been a great while at the trade of coining, before several of his gang were apprehended, and sent post to the gallows for their wicked ingenuity, which oblig'd him to employ all the powers of his wit and invention, in the search of something else that might conduce to supply him in his manifold extravagancies.

In the next place he went to picking of pockets, at which being detected, he was committed to New-Prison; where having a great many loose women coming after him, who supply'd him with a great deal of money, he had all the privilege imaginable in the jail; and going to take his trail at Hicks's-Hall for his fact, one John Lee, a turnkey, conducting him thither, gave him the liberty of being shav'd by the way in a barber's shop. The keeper having also a pretty long beard, quoth Tom Sharp, 'Come, we are time enough yet, sit down, and I'll pay for taking your beard off too.' Whilst he was trimming, Tom talk'd one thing or other to hold him in discourse, till at last the barber cry'd, 'Shut your eyes, or else my ball will offend 'em.' The man did as he was bid, and Tom took this occasion to slip out, the barber not taking him for a prisoner, and hid himself in an alehouse hard by. The turnkey not hearing him talk, open'd his eyes, and not seeing him in the shop, rose up so hastily, that he overthrew cut-beard, bason, water, and all upon him, and ran out into the street with the barber's cloth about him, and napkin on his head. The people seeing him thus, with the froth about his face, concluded him mad, and as he ran gave him the way. The barber, with his razor in his hand, ran after the turnkey, crying, 'Stop thief, stop thief'; but he never minding the outcry, still ran staring up and down, as if his wits had lately stolen away from him, and he was in pursuit of them. Some durst not stop him, and others would not; till the barber seiz'd him at last, and getting his cloth and napkin from him, made him pay sixpence besides for being but half shav'd, while Tom in the time of this hurly-burly, got clear off.

Being afraid of being apprehended for this escape, he was obliged to lie incognito in a garret in St Andrew's-Street, by the Seven-dials, where also dwelling in the same house one Baynham, a poor illiterate taylor, who was lately turn'd an astrologer, and had a mighty great conceit of his own natural parts, which were very extraordinary in ordinary things, they became intimately acquainted one with another; and hearing this star-gazer often wish he could speak Arabic, for the understanding Albumazar, Messahalah, Abdilazus, Ulugh Beighi, and other authors, who had written on the art of astrology in that language, Tom Sharp pretended he had that tongue as perfect as his own, and would teach it him in three month for forty shillings, one half in hand, and the other when he had perform'd his bargain. Baynham was very glad of this opportunity, and giving him twenty shillings, he was to procure Erpenius's Arabic grammar, which he understood no more than a wild Indian did Welsh or Irish. Tom proceeded with teaching his pupil a great many canting words, telling him *Autem* was Arabic for a church; *Borde*, a shilling; *Buffer*, a dog; *Belly-cheat*, an apron; *Cokir*, a liar; *Cuffin*, a man; *Canke*, dumb; *Cannakin*, the plague; *Deusse-avil*, the country; *Ferme*, a hole; *Flag*, a groat; *Glymmer*, a fire; *Gar*, a lip; *Gybe*, a pass; *Harmanback*, a constable; *Jigger*, a door; *Kinchin*, a child; *Libege*, a bed: *Make*, a half-penny; *Nab*, a hat; *Prat*, a thigh; *Quarron*, a body; *Ruffin*, the Devil; *Swag*, a shop; *Slat*, a half-crown; *Trin*, the gallows; *Win*, a penny; *Yarum*, milk; and abundance more to the same purpose.

With this jargon, and meer gibberish, invented by villains to shroud their wicked intentions from the knowledge of honest people, he deluded the cunning man, who being an apt scholar, could in less than four and twenty hours, very significantly express himself, and tell the meaning of 'Bite the Peter or Roger'; 'Tip me my earnest'; 'Pike on the leen'; 'Plant your whids'; 'Stow your whids'; 'The mort tipp'd me a wink'; 'Tip the Cole to Adam Tyler', and so forth; all which Tom made him believe were terms belonging to the art of astrology, and signified Sol is in Opposition to Luna; Saturn in Conjunction with Mars; Venus is Ascendant in the cusp of the Ninth House; Mercury is in Quartile to Jupiter, the Moon is got into Aquarius; the Sun and Venus are come to a Trine; the Sun will suffer a great Eclipse, and the like. They went on in this manner for two or three days, when Tom absconding from his lodging, not one digit of his body was to be seen ever after. Thus he trick'd the poor astrologer, as nicely as he had the daughter of James Gardiner a printer, out of above fifty shillings, in telling her five or six years before, that she should have a husband in a short time, and the poor creature was not married at the time of Tom's adventure.

Afterwards Tom Sharp equipping himself in a cloak, he went to the Portuguese chapel in Lincolns-Inn-Fields, and privately threw a paper of lamp-black into the holy water, plac'd by the door, having first changed the silver bason for a pewter one, which he had under his cloak. Soon after the priest came out and crossed himself, and having said a short ejaculation to himself, he look'd towards his bigotted congregation, to bless them with a *pax vobiscum*, but when he saw them all have black crosses on their foreheads, and the people also saw one on his, there was such staring one upon the other, as if they would have star'd thro' one another. At length they found they were impos'd upon by some heretick, who was got far enough off before now; whereupon, highly resenting the prophanation of that which they thought sufficient proof against the D—l, and all his works, they presently went to cursing of him with their greatest anathema of bell, book, and candle; but Tom being ready curs'd to their hands, their revenge did him no injury at all.

Tom's last fact was shooting a watchman, who oppos'd him to breaking open a shoe-maker's shop at the corner of Great Wild-Street, facing up Great Queen-Street. He was apprehended and condemn'd for this murder; but such was his impiety, whilst under sentence of death, that instead of thanking such who had so much Christianity in 'em as to bid him prepare for his latter end, he would bid them not to trouble his head with the idle whimsies of Heaven and Hell, for he was more a man than to dread or believe any such matter after this life. But when he came to the place of execution, which was at the end of Long Acre in Drury-Lane, and the halter was put about his neck, he then chang'd his tone, and began to call out for mercy, with such a sorrowful voice, which could not but awake the most lethargick conscience that ever the Devil lull'd asleep. One there might plainly see by the deluge of tears which fell from his eyes, what convulsion-fits his poor soul suffer'd, whilst his own mouth confess'd how grievously his afflicted spirits were stretch'd on the rack of black despair. Now was the time that the voluminous registers of his ill conscience, which formerly lay clasp'd in some unsearch'd corner of his memory, were laid open before him; and the Devil, who hitherto gave him the lessening end of the perspective-glass to survey his licentious courses, turn'd the magnifying end to his eye, which made him implore Heaven for a gracious pardon of his manifold transgressions. In this manner he was turn'd off the cart on Friday the twenty second day of September, 1704, aged twenty nine years.

THE LIFE OF
ANN HARRIS

Ann Harris, alias Sarah Davies, alias Thorn, alias Gothorn, was born of honest but poor parents, in the parish of St Giles without Cripplegate; but being debauch'd by one James Wadsworth, she soon abandoned all manner of goodness. This Wadsworth was otherwise call'd Jemmy the Mouth among his companions. He was hang'd for felony and burglary at Tyburn, in the twenty fourth year of his age, on Friday the twenty fourth of September, 1702. She lived next with one William Pulman, otherwise call'd Norwich Will from the place of his birth, who also made his exit at Hyde-Park Corner on Friday the ninth of March 1704–5, aged twenty six years, for robbing one Mr Joseph Edwards on the highway, of a pair of leather bags, a shirt, two neckcloths, two pocket-books, twenty five guineas, a half broad piece of gold, and four pounds in silver.

Now Nan being twice left a hempen widow in less than three years, she had learn'd in that time to be as vicious as the very worst of her sex, and was so absolutely enslav'd to all manner of wickedness thro' custom and opportunity, that good admonitions could work no good effects upon her. Her inclination was entirely averse to honesty, as appears by the following example.

She went one day to a mercer's shop on Ludgate-Hill, in a hackney coach, very finely dress'd, with a pretended footman waiting on her; where looking of several rich pieces of silk and velvet, she bargained for as much as came to two hundred and odd pounds; which being more money than she had about her, she desired the mercer to go along with her to her house, and she would pay him all in ready specie. They putting the goods into the hackney coach which brought her thither, the mercer and she stept in, and rid with all speed to Dr Adams, who kept a mad house at Fulham; where being enter'd, and telling the doctor this was the gentleman of whom she had spoken to him in the morning, he, and three or four lusty fellows, set upon the mercer like so many merciless bailiffs on a poor prisoner; one taking him by the arms, another by the middle, another by the legs; which rustical usage made the poor man ask the meaning thereof, and bawl out for two hundred and odd pounds. 'Ay, ay,' quoth the doctor, 'the poor gentleman's very bad indeed; he's raving mad, tie him quickly down in that chair, and presently shave his head.'

All the while they were lathering and shaving him, his cry was still for either goods or money; which made the doctor say, 'Pray, Madam, see how his lunacy makes him talk at random!' She, shaking her head, replied, 'True, Sir; but is there any hopes of his recovery?' To which the doctor answer'd, 'You must know, Madam, that there are three kinds of frenzies, according to the three internal senses of imagination, cogitation, and memory, which may be severally hurt: for some are frantick, which can judge rightly of those things that they see, as touching common sense and imagination; and yet in cogitation and fantasy they err from natural judgment. Then some others being frantick, err in imagination; and there are some frantick, who do err both in sense and cogitation; that is, both in imagination and reason, and do therewith also lose their memory, which is the worst of all frenzies; and this it is which afflicts this unhappy gentleman: but I doubt not of making him *compos mentis* again in less than a month.'

While the doctor was setting forth the difference of madness, the mercer was struggling and raving like a madman indeed; and when he saw Nan give the doctor five guineas, with all giving him a strict charge to take great care of her husband and he should want for no encouragement, he cried out, 'She's a lying b—h, she's none of my wife; my wife's at home in Ludgate-Street; stop her, stop her, stop her, she has cheated me of my silk and velvet. I am not mad, I am not mad, but a parcel of rogues here will make me run out of my senses.' Quoth Dr Adams then to his men, 'Poor gentleman! he's very bad indeed; we must bleed him too, and give him a strong clyster at night; confine him to a room where there's no light at all, and bind him fast down hand and feet in his straw; and for one week give him nothing but water-gruel, with little or no bread in it; but the week after, if his distemper decreases, we may venture to give him a little ptisan broth boil'd with some husk'd barley.' The mercer hearing these directions, cried out, 'I'll have none of my blood taken from me, I have had enough taken from me already without paying for; I want no clyster, I tell you I am in my right senses; I'll have none of your gruel and Devil's broth; what cheat me and starve me too! No, no, I am not lunatick.' Quoth the doctor, 'You shall not be starv'd, Sir; what diet I prescribe now, is to restore you to your health again.' 'To health,' said the mercer again, 'I think you are going to take it from me, as the whore has my goods.'

But all the mercer's talking was to no purpose; for Nan being gone off with her booty, he was hurried to his dark room; where, being bound down to his bed, a clyster was applied to him much against his will. However, he obtain'd his liberty in less than four days; for Nan Harris sending a penny-post letter to his wife, which inform'd her where her husband was, she, and some friends, went with all speed to Dr Adams's, in whose house they found the poor mercer almost mad indeed, for the loss of his goods and freedom too; so they brought him home; but the doctor never saw nor heard of Nan Harris any more.

I think those who would arrive to as much perfection as they are capable of enjoying here, must as well know bad, that they may avoid or shun it, as the good, which they ought rather to embrace; therefore to procure the reformation of others, by the wicked examples of such whom the sword of justice has cut off for their heinous enormities, I shall relate another memorable prank play'd by Nan Harris.

She going once to Dr Case, student in physick and astrology, when he liv'd in Black-Friers she was no sooner introduc'd into his presence, with also one Charles Moore, but she thus declar'd the cause of her waiting on him. 'Sir, the report of your great experience in your practice hath brought me hither, humbly imploring your assistance, and that instantly, if you have any respect to the preservation of life: the trouble I shall put you to shall be gratefully recompenced to the utmost of my ability.' The doctor then inquiring of her, who it was, and what manner of distemper the person labour'd under, she told him, ''Twas her husband, who being very drunk last night, came to a sad mischance in coming down a pair of stairs; but looking upon the doctor to be a wise man, she would give him leave to tell what his ail might be, and for that purpose had brought his water.' Dr Case smelling by her former words, what might afflict her husband, he put the water into an urinal, and after well shaking it for about a minute, quoth he, 'Good woman, your husband hath terribly bruised himself by falling down a pair of stairs.' 'Ay' (replied Nan) ''tis realy true, Sir, what you say; I see, Sir, your knowledge is infallible; but now, Sir, comes the difficulty, can you tell me how many stairs he fell down?'

Here the doctor was put to a *Ne plus ultra*; however, to save his credit as well as he could, he takes the urinal into his hand again, and shaking it somewhat longer than before, quoth he, 'Your husband fell down all the stairs.' 'Nay' (reply'd Nan) 'there you are out, Sir, for he fell down but half the stairs.' The doctor being now somewhat abashed at his false guessing, and shaking the urinal again, quoth he to Nan, 'Is here all your husband's water?' Said Nan, dropping a fine courtesy at the same time, 'No, Sir, there's but half his water.' The doctor then, who was a mighty cholerick man, being in a great passion, cry'd, 'A pox on you, your bringing but half his water, made me imagine your husband fell down all the stairs, when if you had brought all his water, I could easily have told you, that he had fell down but half the stairs.'

155

Nan upon this excusing her ignorance, she desired his advice for the speedy cure of her husband's bruises, and whilst the doctor was writing a receipt for her, pulling a cord out of her pocket, with a noose, she and her spark came behind him, and nimbly clapping it over his head, they acted the part of a Turkish mute on a bashaw; for having almost strangled him with several sudden jerks, they went away with a silver tankard and cup, leaving our old friend in a sad case indeed, till he came to himself again, which was not in half an hour; in which time the booty was divided betwixt Nan and Charles Moore.

This Moore was an infamous rogue, who, for breaking open the house of Sir John Buckworth, Bart. was executed on Friday, Sept. 27 1707 at Tyburn, where he told the ordinary of Newgate, that if he had known when he was try'd, that he should have dy'd, he would have hang'd one or two with him for a fancy; for then he would have made some discovery of persons concern'd with him in thieving, but now he was resolv'd to make none.

Thus far have we proceeded on Nan's wicked crimes, to deter others from the like practices; because nothing renders man or woman more contemned and hated, than when their actions only tend to irregularity: we have only to add, that biding adieu to every thing that looked like virtue, she drove a great trade among goldsmiths, to whose shops often going to buy gold rings, she only cheapen'd till she had the opportunity of stealing one or two; which she did by means of a little ale held in a spoon over the fire, till it congeal'd thick like a syrup, for by rubbing some of this on the palm of her hands, any light thing would stick to it, without the least suspicion at all. She was as well known among the mercers, lacemen, and linnen-drapers, on Ludgate-Hill, Cheapside, or Fleet-Street, as that notorious shoplift Isabel Thomas, who was condemned for the same crimes.

But at last she was apprehended for her pranks, and being so often burnt in the face, that there was no more room left for the hangman to stigmatize her, the court thought fit to condemn her for privately stealing a piece of printed callico out of the shop of one Mr John Andrews. Then to evade their sentence, she pleaded her belly, and that she might succeed, used the old stratagem of drinking new ale very plentifully, to make her swell, cramming a pillow under her petti-coats to make her look big. Having matrons of her own profession ready at hand, who, right or wrong, bring in their wicked companions quick with child, to the great impediment of justice, her sentence was respited. But tho' she had the good luck to impose thus on the bench after she was condemn'd, yet at the end of nine months (all which time she was not wanting to procure a pregnancy, if all the men in the gaol could have done it for her, but they work'd in vain) she was call'd down to her former judgment, and hang'd in the twentieth year of her age, at Tyburn, on Friday July the thirteenth.

THE LIFE OF

ANN HOLLAND

This was her right name, tho' she went by the names of Andrews, Charlton, Edwards, Goddard, and Jackson. This practice, is very usual with thieves, because falling oftentimes into hands of justice, and being often convicted of crimes, yet thereby it appears sometimes, that when they are arraign'd at the bar again, that is the first time that they have been taken, and the first crime whereof they have ever been accus'd: moreover, if they should happen to be cast, people, by not knowing their right names, cannot say the son or daughter of such a man or woman is to be whipp'd, burnt, or hang'd on such a day of the month, in such a year; from whence would proceed more sorrow to them that suffer'd, as well as disgrace to their parents. For this reason an alias is prefix'd to several names, when such persons are indicted, as we have observed before, whose delight is to be gentlemen and gentlewomen without rents, to have other folks goods for their own, and dispose of them at their own will and pleasure, without costing them any more than the pains of stealing them.

As to Anne Holland, her usual way of thieving was what they call the service-lay, which was hiring herself for a servant in any good family, and then, as opportunity serv'd she robb'd them.

Thus living once with a Master Taylor, in York-Buildings in the Strand, her mistress was but just gone to a christening, when her master came home booted and spurr'd out of the country, and going up into his chamber, where she was making his bed, he had a great mind to try his manhood with her, and accordingly threw her on her back. Nan made a great resistance, and would not grant him his desire without he pull'd off his boots. He consented, and at his command she pluck'd one off; but whilst she was pulling off the other, somebody knocking opportunely at the door, she ran down stairs, taking a silver tankard off the window, which would hold two quarts, saying, she must draw some beer, for she was very dry. She not returning presently, poor Stitch was swearing, and staring, and bawling, for his maid Nan to pull off his t'other boot, which was half on and half off; but being extraordinary strait, he could neither get his leg farther in nor out. And there he might remain 'till doomsday for Nan, for she was gone far enough off with the wedge, that's to say, the plate, which she had converted into another shape and fashion in a short time.

Another time Nan having been at a fair in the country, as she was coming up to London, she lay at Uxbridge, where being a good pair of Holland sheets to the bed, she was so industrious as to sit up most part of the night, and make her a couple of good smocks out of one of them; so in the morning, putting the other sheet double towards the head of the bed, she came down stairs to breakfast. In the interim, the mistress sent up her maid to see if the sheets were there, who turning the single sheet a little down as it lay folded, she came and whisper'd in her mistress's ear, that the sheets were both there; so Nan discharging her reckoning, she brought more shifts to town than she carried out with her; and truly she had a pretty many before, or else she could not have liv'd as she did for some years.

This unfortunate creature, at her first launching out into the region of vice, was a very personable young woman, being clear-skinn'd, well shap'd, having a sharp piercing eye, a proportionable face, and exceeding small hand; which natural gifts serv'd rather to make her miserable than happy; for several lewd fellows flocking about her, like so many ravens about a piece of carrion, to enter her under Cupid's banner, and obtaining their ends, she soon commenc'd, and took degrees, in all manner of debauchery; for if once a woman passes the bounds of modesty, she seldom stops till she hath arriv'd to the very height of impudence.

However, it was her fortune to light on a good husband; for one Mr French, a comb-maker, living formerly on Snow-hill, taking a fancy to her in a coffee-house, where she was a servant till she had an opportunity to rob her master, such was his affection, without in the least knowing she had been debauch'd, that he married her, and was better satisfy'd with his matching with her who had nothing, than many are with wives of great portions. But the comb-maker's joys were soon vanish'd, for his spouse being brought to bed of a girl within six months after Hymen had join'd them together, it bred such a great confusion betwixt them, that there was scarce any thing in the kitchen, or other part of the house, which they did not continually fling at one another's heads. Whereupon her husband confessing a judgment to a friend in whom he could confide, all his goods were presently seiz'd, and she turn'd out of house and home, to the great satisfaction of Mr French, who shortly after went to Ireland, and there died.

Nan Holland being thus metamorphos'd from a house-keeper to a vagabond, she was oblig'd to shift among the wicked for a livelihood; and to give her what was her due, tho' she was but young, yet could she cant tolerably well, wheedle most cunningly, lie confoundedly, swear desperately, pick a pocket dexterously, dissemble undiscernably, drink and smoke everlastingly, whore insatiably, and brazen out all her actions impudently.

A little after this disaster, she was married to one James Wilson, an eminent highwayman, very expert in his occupation, for he never was without false beards, vizards, patches, wens, or mufflers, to disguise the natural phisiognomy of his face. He knew how to give the watch-word for his comrades to fall on their prey; how to direct them to make their boots dirty, as if they had rid many miles, when they were not far from their private place of rendezvous; and how to cut the girths and bridles of them whom they rob, and bind 'em fast in a wood, or some other obscure place. But these pernicious actions justly bringing him to be hang'd in a little time, at Maidstone in Kent, Nan was left a hempen widow, and forc'd to shift for herself again.

After this loss of a good husband, Nan Holland being well apparell'd, she, in company with one Tristram Savage, who had lain under a fine for crying the scurrilous pamphlet, entitled, *The Black List*, about streets, a long time in Newgate, where they became first acquainted, went to Dr Trotter in Moor-fields, to have her nativity calculated. When they were admitted into the

J. Nicholls delin.

Parr Sc.

Nan. Holland and Tristram Savage Robbing Dr. Trotter in Moorfields.

conjuror's presence, who took them to be both of the female sex, because Savage was also dress'd in women's clothes, and being inform'd by Nan what she came about, he presently drew a scheme of the twelve houses, and filling them with the insignificant characters of the signs, planets, and aspects, display'd about the time and place of her birth in the middle of them, the following jargon.

That the Sun being upon the cusp of the tenth House, and Saturn within it, but five degrees from the cusp, it denoted a fit of sickness, which would shortly afflict her; but then Mercury being in the eleventh House, just in the beginning of Sagittarius, near Aldebaran, and but six degrees from the body of Saturn, in a mundane square to the Moon and Mars, it signified her speedy recovery from it. Again, Cancer being in a zodiacal trine to the Sun, Saturn, and Mercury, she might depend upon having a good husband in a short time; and moreover, it was a sure sign, that he who married her should be a very rich and thriving man.

Thus having gone through this astrological cant, quoth Tristram Savage to Doctor Trotter, 'Can you tell me, Sir, what I think?' The Conjuror replied, with a surly countenance, 'It is none of my profession to tell peoples thoughts.' 'Why then' (said Savage) 'I'll shew 'em you.' Whereupon pulling a pistol out of his pocket, and clapping it to the doctor's breast, he swore he was a dead man, if he made but the least outcry; which so surpriz'd him, that, trembling like an aspen leaf, he submitted to whatever they desir'd. So whilst Nan was busy in tying him neck and heels, Savage stood over him with a penknife in one hand, and his pop, (that's what they call any thing of a gun) in t'other; still swearing, that if he did but whimper, his present punishment should be either the blade of his penknife thrust into his wind-pipe, or else a brace of balls convey'd thro' his guts. To be still more sure of the conjuror's not cackling, they gagg'd him, and then rifling his pockets, they found a gold watch, twenty guineas, and a silver tobacco-box, which they carry'd away, besides taking two good rings off his finger.

After these good customers were gone, the conjurer began to make what noise he could for relief, by rowling about the floor like a porpoise in a great storm, and kicking on the boards with such violence, that the servants verily thought there was a combat indeed betwixt their master and the Devil. But when they went up stairs, and found him ty'd and gagg'd, they were in no small astonishment; and quickly loosing him, he told them how he was robb'd; whereupon they made quick pursuit after Nan Holland, and the other offender, but to no purpose, for they were got out of their reach, and the knowledge of all the stars.

Altho' she had receiv'd mercy once before, yet she took no warning thereby, but when at liberty still pursued her old courses, which in 1705 brought her to Tyburn; where, instead of imploring for mercy from above, she cry'd out upon the hard heart of her judge, and the rigor of the laws; also cursing the hangman; but forgetting to repent of the fact which brought her into the executioner's hands, and would, unrepented of, deliver her soul into the far less merciful hands of another hereafter.

THE LIFE OF
JACK GOODWIN

When silver tankards were more in vogue in the alehouses than they are at present, this fellow going into one to drink, he call'd for a tankard of ale, which being brought, he drank it off, and having cut out the bottom of it, paid the victualler for his liquor, who seeing the tankard on the table, had no suspicion that any damage had been done it. But shortly after some other company came in, and the tapster running into the cellar to fill them that tankard, which Mr Goodwin had been fingering, the fellow wonder'd to see the cock run and the tankard never the fuller, whereupon, turning it up, he could find no more bottom in it, than mariners can in the ocean.

Another time Jack Goodwin being in the country, as far as Durham, and destitute of money, he happen'd to meet with another idle companion, with whom he made a bargain to beg their way up to London; and in order to excite people's pity the more, his new companion was to act the part of a blind man, and he was to be his guide, instead of a dog and a bell. So getting a penny-worth of searing wax, with which taylors sear the edges of silks and slight stuffs, Jack Goodwin mollifying it over a candle, he dawb'd his comrade's eye-lids therewith, insomuch that he could not open them.

Our couple thus proceeding on their journey, they had by their cruizing or begging thro' the countries pick'd up about the sum of four pounds sixteen shillings, by that time they had got up to Ware: next making the best of their way up to London, within ten or eleven miles of the same, being to cross a small brook over a narrow wooden bridge, with a rail but on one side of it, for the conveniency of foot passengers, when they were upon it, Goodwin threw his blind comrade into the water, where he stood up to the neck, but moving neither one way nor t'other, for fear of being drowned. In the mean time his guide made straight to London. Soon afterwards some passengers coming by, who took pity on the fellow, as supposing him to be really blind, they help'd him out of the brook, and setting him on terra firma, he presently, by their directions, arrived at a house, where getting some warm water, he wash'd his eye lids; which being then open'd, he march'd after his fellow-traveller to London, where he might hunt about long enough before he found him out, for Jack was got into some ill house or another, where he was as safe as a thief in a mill.

The Duke of Bedford being visiting a person of quality one night very late, whilst the footmen were gone to drink at some adjacent boozing-ken, or alehouse, the coachman was taking a nap on his box; and Jack Goodwin coming by at the same time with some of his thieving cronies, they took the two hind wheels off the coach, and supported it up with two pieces of wood, which they got out of a house which was building hard by. So having carried them away, His Grace not long after going into his coach, and the footmen getting up behind in a hurry, no sooner did the horses begin to draw, but down fell His Grace, footmen and all; who looking to see how the accident came, they found the hind wheels were stollen; whereupon the Duke was oblig'd to go home in a hackney coach.

This John Goodwin, alias Plump, was condemned when he was but eleven years of age, for picking a merchant's pocket of one hundred and fifty guineas, and was afterwards several times in great danger of his life, before justice took hold of him in earnest.

At last, committing a burglary in company with another, when he was but eighteen years of age, he was apprehended and carried before Sir Thomas Stamp, knight and alderman of London; where, after he was examin'd, being searched, several cords were found in his pocket; upon which, his Worship asking Goodwin what trade he was, he reply'd, 'A taylor': then Sir Thomas taking up the cords, and looking very wistly on them, quoth he, 'You use methinks, very big thread.' 'Yes, Sir, (said Goodwin) 'for it is generally coarse work which I'm employ'd about.'

Next searching his comrade, Henry Williams, a pistol was found loaded in his bosom; upon which Sir Thomas asking what trade he was, he reply'd, 'A taylor too': 'What both taylors' (said his Worship) 'and pray what implement is this belonging to your trade?' Quoth Williams, 'That pistol, Sir, is my needle-case.'

To conclude, Sir Thomas was so astonish'd at their impudence, that he immediately made their mittimus for Newgate, and being try'd at Justice-Hall in the Old-Bailey, they were both condemned to die, and soon after executed at Tyburn, in company with Chambers, Morris, &c.

165

THE LIFE OF
WILL ELBY

This noted malefactor was born at Deptford, in the county of Kent, of very honest parents, who bound him apprentice to a blockmaker at Rotherhithe; but he was no sooner out of his time, than instead of setting up, or working for himself, he went rambling abroad, and delighting in bad company, he soon grew in love with their vices. He went first of all upon the waterpad, which is, going on night with a boat on board any ship, or other vessel lying down the river of Thames, and finding therein no persons to watch the same, or else catching the watch asleep, break open the padlocks of the cabbins or hatches, and rob 'em.

William Elby, alias Dun, having been like to suffer twice or thrice for this sort of robbery, he kept company with several notorious house-breakers; particularly with one Peter Bennet, alias Peter Flower, but commonly called French Peter, from the place of his birth, as being born at Niort, in the province of Poictou in France. This fellow, in the 25th year of his age, was hang'd at Tyburn, on Wednesday the 25th of October, 1704.

Elby had also broke open several houses with one Samuel Scotland, a gardiner, who was condemned for 23 fellonies and burglaries, and hang'd for them on Wednesday the 30th of December, 1702, at Tyburn; where pulling off his shoes, and flinging 'em among the spectators, he said, 'My father and mother often told me that I should die with my shoes on, but you may all see that now I have made them both liars.' This impudent speech has been used by more than one.

At the same time with Scotland, was one John Goffe executed there, with whom, and some others, Will Elby having taken a house in Boswel Court, in Cary-Street, near Lincolns-Inn-fields, in the name of a lady whose steward Goffe pretended to be, he had the key thereof delivered to him; then he went to several goldsmiths about town, and telling them a plausible story, that his lady wanted several pieces of plate, as silver tasters, spoons, forks, and cups, they, by his appointment, brought what he bespoke, to this empty house, where they expected to be paid for their goods.

But when these tradesmen came thither, and were one after another let in by a genteel sort of a fellow, with a green apron ty'd before him like a butler, and introduc'd into a back parlour, they found no other furniture but about half a dozen rogues, who clapt pistols to their breasts, and told them, they were certainly dead men, unless they quietly parted with their plate. Whereupon, life being sweet, they surrender'd, as they came one after another, what they had, and suffer'd themselves to be ty'd hand and foot into the bargain, and thrown into a cellar, where they were found by a porter's wife, to whom Goffe (who lost his life for this fact) had given the key of the street door, with orders to make a fire in the house; tho' when she went into the cellar for coals, she perceived nothing there to burn but three goldsmiths, who, by this means, escap'd perishing by hunger and cold.

Again, William Elby had committed many burglaries with one James Hacket, a taylor's son, living in Exeter Street, behind Exeter-Change, in the Strand, who was hang'd when 24 years of age, at Tyburn, on Friday the 6th of June, 1707, for breaking and robbing the houses of Mr Churchill, Mr Battersby, Mr Hays, and Mrs Yalden. Moreover, he had done a few felonies and burglaries, with one Toothless Tom, so call'd, from having most of his teeth knock'd out, by a person whose pocket he was once attempting to pick, in St Margaret's church, at Westminster; and who was hang'd in the 23d year of his age, at Tyburn, on Wednesday the 22d of March, 1703–4,

Will Elby was once concerned with one John Estrick, in robbing his master, Thomas Glover, Esq; at Hackney, of as much plate as came to eighty pounds, for which, one Susannah Barnwell an honest servant, was wrongfully accus'd, and turn'd out of her service; but when Estrick shortly after came to be hang'd for other crimes, at Tyburn, on Wednesday the 10th of March, 1702–3, he there confess'd his coming to that untimely end, was occasioned by John Prosser, his brother in-law, and the day before he suffer'd death, sent the following letter, to his former master Thomas Glover, Esq.

March the 9th, 1702–3

SIR,

I heartily beg God's Pardon for all my Sins, and ask you forgiveness for the Damage I have done you. But as I am a dying Man, Susan knows nothing of your Plate, tho' I falsely accused her of it, God forgive me!

JOHN ESTRICK.

Afterwards he went upon the foot-pad, with one William Stanley, a shoe-maker, who having robb'd two men in Stepney fields, from one of whom he had taken a watch, the person who lost it, put next day an advertisement thereof, in the *London Gazette*; and not long after, Will Stanley, going to pawn it to Mr Chambers, a pawnbroker, living at the corner of Blackmore-Street, in Drury-Lane, he, knowing it to be that described in the news-papers, went to stop him, but then running out of his shop as fast as he could along Drury Lane, and being pursu'd by some who cry'd 'Stop Thief', one John Elliot, a watchman, going then on his duty, and endeavouring to seize Stanley, he ran him thro' the body with his sword, so that he dy'd on the spot; and the murderer was hang'd for it in the 28th year of his age, at Tyburn, on Wednesday the 26th of January, 1703–4.

But tho' Elby had seen so many terrible examples of his wicked companions being cut off before, yet taking no warning thereby, he rather grew more harden'd in his sins, and never thought justice would overtake him. He and his associates one evening, meeting with young Pontack, the famous mutton chop seller, by Christ Church Hospital, as coming from Newington they leaped unawares upon him, out of a ditch, and having first taken fourteen or fifteen shillings in money from him, they then striped him stark naked; then tying his hands behind him, they hung 5 or 6 mutton chops, which they had bought for supper, about his neck, and sent him home; saying at the same time, 'Since your impudence assumes a French name, to put off boil'd mutton and broth, our justice directs us to send you home in a French fashion; that is to say, without shoes or any thing else.'

Will Elby never pretended to be an artist at picking pockets; nevertheless, when Mr Thomas a shoemaker, being drinking at the Dog tavern in Newgate Street, laid a wager that he would defie the best pick pocket in the world to get his money from him, he was selected to manage Crispin, who, to secure a mark'd guinea which he was to lose, had put it in his mouth. So following him from place to place, till he came into the piazza's in Covent Garden, Will Elby pull'd a hankerchief out of his pocket, in which was some old shillings, and dropping the money, a mob came presently round him, among whom was Mr Thomas, to help him to pick up his money. Afterwards the rabble asking Will whether he had all? he said, 'I have all my money, thank you, except a guinea mark'd so and so, which I fancy the gentleman there' [pointing to the shoemaker] has in his mouth, by what I perceive of him.' Whereupon, the vindictive mob searching the shoe-makers mouth by force, and finding such a guinea there as Elby described, they did not only give it him, but had like to have knock'd Mr Thomas on the head; who return'd back strait to the Dog tavern, where the guinea was got before him, and he was well laugh'd at besides, for losing a wager of two guineas more.

169

But once this fellow meeting with one Lieutenant Job Lord, as he was coming from Chelsea, he attempted to rob him, at first the lieutenant was at a loss whether he should stand on his own defence, or no, as imputing the resistance would turn to no better account than of one pyrate fighting another, when nothing is got betwixt them but blows and empty barrels; but rather than lose what he had, he engag'd the foot-pad, and obtaining the victory, give him several cuts over the head; and then tying him neck and heels, did not only take about eighteen guineas from him, but left him there bound to assault the next passenger which came that way.

After this great malefactor received this mischance, being very poor a long time, he was so prophane as to say to some of his comrades, that he would sell himself to the Devil for money, who (as wicked as they were) exhorted him to the contrary, telling him, that wizards and witches were never rich, when they had any familiarity with infernal powers; but he said, 'I am resolved to do it, to better advantage.'

Being in a little time after in Newgate again, and one Sunday up at chapel, when several strangers were there, to hear a sermon preached to some condemned persons, among whom was a country farmer; as the bumpkin was leaning against the wooden grates, thro' which the felons peep, like the Lions in the Tower, and taking a nap with the high stiff collar of his wastecoat unbuttoned, Elby was so dextrous as take off a cheat which he wore in the room of a shirt, from under all his cloaths, which was not missed at all by the country hick, till he came home, and then he swore and raved like a mad man, to think which way he should lose that, without losing his coat and wastecoat.

Anoher time Elby, and some as good as himself at roguery, being at Bartholomew Fair, where, among the crowd, a country fellow on horseback was staring at a merry andrew playing his tricks, two of them supporting the saddle on their shoulders, Elby privately cut the girts and bridle, and led away the horse unperceived, so that the mob dispersing, after the fool had diverted them a little from the gallery of the booth, the country fellow tumbled down in the dirt, in a great surprize at the loss of his fellow-creature, and was obliged to go home to Enfield a-foot.

Mr Abel, that had once the honour to sing before the King of Poland's bear, keeping a consort of vocal and instrumental musick in York Buildings, Will Elby, who had been a thief a long time, and was resolved to be one till he dy'd, being well dressed in an embroidered coat, and a long wig, and getting admittance gratis, among the quality there, (for now a-days a mere mountebank, or a player, the two worst professions upon earth, in his laced sute, shall be more respected than a gentle-man of merit, in one that is out of fashion) whilst the people were in the height of their jollity and pastime, he privately stole above half a score gold watches, which he carried clear off, without seeing the conclusion of the musical entertainment.

But, at last, this base villain, tho' he had receiv'd both the sentence of the law, and the mercy of his prince before, breaking open the dwelling house of Mr James Barry, at Fulham, and killing therein his servant, Nicholas Hatfield, he was committed to Newgate. Whilst sentence of death was passing on him at the Sessions-House, in the Old Bailey, his impudence was so great, as to curse the whole bench; nor was his ill behaviour less remarkable under condemnation, when, being perswaded to discover his accomplice or accomplices in the said murder, he said, 'that if any one should ask him again, any such question, he would presently knock him down'. In this resolution he continued till he was executed, and hang'd in chains at Fulham, in the county of Middlesex, on Saturday the 13th of September, 1707, aged 32 years.

THE LIFE OF
DICK LOW

This person took to thieving in his minority, and was become very expert in it at the age when others usually begin. One time when he was about 11 or 12 years old, creeping privately in an evening behind a goldsmith's compter in Cheapside, the goldsmith comes from a back room, and goes himself behind the compter; insomuch that Dick Low had no opportunity of going out invisible; whereupon he cries, 'Whoop, whoop'. At this the goldsmith cry'd, 'Hey, hey, is this a place to play at whooper's hide? Get you gone, you young rogue, and play in the streets.' But Dick yet lying still, cry'd again, 'Whoop, whoop'; which made the goldsmith in a great passion cry, 'Get you gone, Sirrah, or I'll whoop you with a good cane, if you want to play here.' Whereupon Dick went away with a bag of fifty pound, which the goldsmith miss'd next day.

But as he grew up in years, his stature made him past those exercises which they call the morning, noon, or night sneak, which is privately sneaking into houses at any of those times, and carrying off what next comes to hand; for all's fish that comes to net with them, who are term'd Saint Peter's children, as having every finger a fish-hook. He went also upon other lays, such as taking lobs from behind ratlers; that is to say, trunks or boxes from behind coaches; and upon the mill, which is breaking open houses in the night; for which purpose they have their tinder-boxes, matches, flints, steels, dark-lanthorns, bags, cords, betties, and chissels to wrench. This was then the manner, but at present they have a new way, of using a large turning gimlet or orgor, with which boring holes thro' a wooden window, they presently with a knife cut out a hole big enough to put in their hand to unbolt it; whereby an honest man is soon undone by these sly rascals, who call themselves prigs, which, in their canting language, denotes a thief. As for the religion of these people, they term themselves but half Christians, because of the two principal commandments they keep but one, which is to love God, but in no case their neighbour, from whom it is their livelihood to steal. These thieves have a quick eye to take hold on all advantages of obtaining an unlawful prize; and highwaymen have commonly their spies in all fairs, markets, and inns, who view all that go and come, and learn what money they carry, how much, where they leave it, and in what hands, whereby they for whom they spy may be masters of it.

When Richard Low was a foot soldier in Flanders, he and his comrade being one day very peckish, and meeting with a Boor in Ghent, loaded with capons, partridges, and hens, they struck up a bargain with him for half of them, which Dick's comrade carry'd off, whilst he was fumbling and pulling out all his things in his pockets to find out his money. His coin amounting to nothing answerable to the poultry he had bought, he order'd the Boor to follow him, 'till at length he brought him into a cloyster of Capuchin fryers, where some of them were confessing folks; then he told the Boor, that the provision he had bought of him was for this house, and a certain Father, who was there confessing, was the Superior, to whom he would go, and acquaint his Reverence that he must pay him. Accordingly going up to the confessor, and privately putting sixpence in his hand, he whisper'd him in the ear, saying, 'Reverend Father, this honest country man here is a particular acquaintance of mine, who's come hither to be confess'd; but living six miles off, and business requiring him home this evening, I beseech you to be so kind as to confess him as soon as you can.'

The good Father, oblig'd by the alms given aforehand, promis'd him, that when he had ended the penitent's confession whom he had at his feet, he should dispatch him presently; and at the same time calling to the Boor, quoth, Dick, 'Go not hence and the Father will perform what you want presently.'

So Dick going after his comrade, when the aforesaid penitent had made an end of his Canterbury story to the priest, the spiritual juggler called the clown to him, who stood bolt upright, looking very wishfully on the confessor, to see if he put his hand in his pocket to pay him. The Father Confessor look'd as wishfully on the Boor, to see him stand with so little devotion to be confess'd; but imputing the cause thereof to his simplicity, he bids him kneel, which the clown did with some reluctancy, as thinking it to be an insulting ceremony for a man to kneel to receive his own money. However, obeying the order with grumbling, the priest bids him make the sign of the cross; at which the Boor being out of patience, believing the confessor to be out of his wits, he chatter'd, and rav'd, and swore like a mad man, which made the confessor imagine the Boor was possess'd with the Devil. Upon this he put his hempen girdle about the poor fellow's neck, and making the sign of the cross over his head, began to conjure him, by saying some devout prayers. This made the man so mad indeed, that he tore off the confessor's habiliments, and throwing him down on the ground, demanded loudly his money for the poultry.

This rustical usage made the Father suppose he had the Devil himself to deal with; so that with a weak and affrighted voice, he began to commend himself to all the saints in the almanack for their assistance; and at the clamour and noise that was betwixt him and the priest, the whole convent of friers came out in procession with crosses and hallow'd lights in their hands, and casting holy water about on every side, as believing there was a legion of devils in their chapel. But the Boor still crying out for his money for his poultry, the prior made a strict enquiry into the matter, and found some knave had impos'd on the fellow, who had no other satisfaction, than that of the convent's cursing him that had cheated the Boor, by bell, book, and candle.

In a short time Dick came home again, and there being one Mr Pemmell, an apothecary, living in Drury Lane, it was his misfortune to have a wife who kept company with one Davis a glazier; but bad circumstances obliging him to fly for sanctury to Thornbury in Gloucestershire, his Madona was in great want of another gallant. However, she being naturally prone to liberality, and always extravagantly rewarding kindnesses of this nature, it was not long 'ere a particular acquaintance of her's undertook to supply her with a new lover, which was Dick.

As soon as he was introduced into the company of the apothecary's wife, she took a huge fancy to him; for he behaved himself so pleasantly, and his caresses

173

were so agreeable, that his mistress esteemed herself the happiest woman in the world, in the enjoyment of a person so facetious, and accomplished with all the mysteries of love. Whenever he came to her house, which was always when her husband was from home, she entertained him with such an unreserved freeness, that she concealed nothing from her spark, that might either please his fancy or curiosity. But one day opening a chest of drawers to take out somewhat, Dick espy'd a couple of bags of money, at which his mouth instantly water'd; for altho' his mistress told him, that as long as one penny was in them, his pockets should never be unfurnished, yet he wanted to be master of them presently; and indeed it was not long before he had them at his command; for business requiring the apothecary in the country for about a week, Dick then lay in his house at rack and manger; and having two other rogues like himself at a great supper prepared for them there, they began about 12 of the clock at night, to declare their intention with sword and pistol, saying, that whoever presumed to speak but one word, suffered present death.

To work they now went, gagging and tying first the procurer. In the mean time the apothecary's wife seeing how her friend was served, she fell on her knees, and heartily beseeched them not to use her so. Quoth Dick, 'No, no, Madam, we'll only tie your hands, lest you should ungag that serious, and now silent, bawd there.'

After she was secured, they went down into the kitchen, and gagg'd and ty'd the maid and apprentice; then rifling the house, they carry'd away two hundred and fifty pounds, and some plate, to a considerable value. But Dick thinking it unmannerly to go away without saying any thing, he went to his late beloved mistress, and giving her a Judas kiss, quoth he, 'Dear Madam, farewell, and when I am gone, say, I've done more than ever your husband did; for I've bound you to be constant now.'

After this, Dick Low going one morning into the Rose and Crown alehouse, kept by one Mr Nayland, in Clare-Court, in Drury-Lane, he desired a private room, by reason he had some company coming to him about some business. A private room was shew'd him, and a double pot of drink brought with a silver cup to drink out of; and being alone, the man of the house sate with him chatting, till they were both weary. At last, Nayland was wanted by other company, and whilst he was gone out, Dick having with some soft wax, fasten'd the bottom of the cup under the board of the table, which was covered with a carpet hanging somewhat down all round it, he came to the bar, saying, 'I see my company will not come, therefore I'll stay no longer.' Then paying his reckoning, and the man of the house going into the room to bring away the pot and the cup (which first he could find, but not the other high nor low) he charges Dick, who had not yet received his change, with down-right theft. The one curs'd and swore he had it not, and the other swore and curs'd he had it, so that between them both, they were ready to swear the house down about their ears.

Dick was then searched, and though nothing was found about him, yet Nayland swore still he must have the cup, or else know of the going of it; therefore he should pay for the loss. But Dick standing as stifly upon his reputation, which was never worth any thing, he insisted he had it not, nor knew any thing of its being gone; whereupon, a constable being fetch'd, he was carry'd before Justice Negus, where the loser making his complaint as truly the matter was, and Dick Low alledging his innocency, the magistrate was in a quandary how to do justice: 'For,' quoth he to the complainant, 'here's a cup lost, and the prisoner doth not deny but he had it; but then it was missed whilst he was in the house, and he searched without finding any thing about him; besides, he had no body with him, therefore it could not be convey'd away by confederacy; so unless you'll lay point-blank felony to his charge, I can do no otherwise than discharge him.'

Then the victualler, who was an Irishman, reply'd, 'Tish fery true, Shir, what you shay, but by my shalvashion, rader dan he should go without hanging, I will shwear twenty felonies against him, or any ting elsh what your Worship pleash to command me, for I love to oblige any shivel shentleman as you be.' 'Indeed,' said the justice, 'you will not oblige me in hanging a man wrongfully.' In a word, there being no plain proof to justify that Dick Low either had the cup, or convey'd it away to another, and it being plain that he was charg'd in custody before ever he went out of the house, he came off with flying colours, and soon sent another of his clan to fetch off the cup, by going to drink in the same room, and removing it from under the table into his breeches without any suspicion, paying for his liquor, and fairly returning that cup that was brought to him.

This fellow, when he was but seven or eight years old, was one of those urchins, whom a rogue habited like a porter, carrying on his shoulders in a great basket, he would, as any gentleman came by him in an evening, put out his hand, and snatch off his hat or periwig, and sometimes both; which would make the person robbed, look and stare about like any wild man, and swear to think what should become of them, for he could have no mistrust of the porter with the load on his back, who would still keep going on, as if he knew nothing of the matter.

But when Dick was grown too big for this unlawful exercise, he industriously apply'ed himself to picking of pockets; and one day, he and two others of that profession, having been eight or nine miles in the country, where they were so extravagant as to spend all their money, as they were coming into Hammersmith, they bethought themselves on the following stratagem to get more before they entered London. Two of them acted the parts of drunken men in the town, reeling, tumbling, and abusing several people; who, believing them to be really drunk, let them pass on without much interruption. Hereupon, their sober companion Dick Low, seeing no body would take them up, he was resolv'd to do it himself; so meeting them, as if by chance, they gave him the jostle; which not taking so patiently as the others had done, he not only had high words with them, but from words they fell to blows. At last, two being against one, it was thought unequal, and they having been abusive to others, a great company was assembled, and among them the constable, who seizing on all three, carried them before a justice, who hearing the matter, and finding by the testimony of the people who went with them, that only the two who were drunk were wholly to blame, his Worship ordered them to be set in the stocks for two hours, and discharged Dick Low.

This order was obey'd, and the delinquents were presently put into the stocks, where they behaved themselves so pleasantly in foolish discourse, that a great number of people hovered about them; the mean time Dick was not idle, for he made such havock among their pockets, that in the two hours time they were in the stocks, he had gain'd about eight pounds by the frolick; then coming to London, they fell into hard drinking like so many drunken Germans; but in the midst of their cups, they had civility, every now and then, to drink the health of all them by whom they had fared the better.

This fellow, tho' he was not above 25 years of age, when he was hang'd at Tyburn, with Jack Hall and Stephen Bunce, in 1707, had reigned long in his villany; and the fortunate success which he had had in his manifold sins, made him only repent that he had practis'd them no sooner.

THE LIFE OF
JACK HALL

This most notorious villain, was bred a thief from his mother's womb; and there is no sort of theft, but what he was expert in, as breaking open houses, going on the foot-pad, shop-lifting, or pilfering any small matter that lies in the way; nay, if it was but mops and pails; the 'drag', which is, having a hook fastened to the end of a stick, with which they drag any thing out of a shop window in a dark evening; and 'filing a cly', which is picking pockets of watches, money, books, or handkerchiefs. To this end he used to haunt churches, fairs, markets, publick assemblies, shows, and be very busy about the play-house. And he that performs this last part of thieving, commonly gives what he takes to another; that in case he should be found with his hand in any man's pocket, he might prove his innocency, by having nothing about him, but what he can justify to be his own.

Jack Hall was as dextrous in picking a pocket, as ever he was in sweeping a chimney; for on a market day once in Smithfield, a grasier having received some money for his cattle, and put it into his coat pocket in a bag, this nimble spark, to whose fingers any thing stuck like birdlime, observing the same, he soon became master of it, and brought it to his comrades that were drinking at an alehouse hard by; and to shew his farther dexterity in filing a cly, emptying the bag, he untruss'd a point in it, and finding out the man, who was still in the market selling off the rest of his cattle, he put it into his pocket again. A little after which, a person coming to the farmer for some money, he went with him to his inn, and pulling out his bag, and putting therein his hand for money to pay the creditor, he eagerly plucked it out in a sad stinking pickle, swearing, 'that he had thirty pounds in his bag but just now. But, woundkins, it was now turned to a T—d'.

Another time, meeting with a man who knew what profession he was of, he said to Jack, 'I wonder how people can have their pockets picked? For I am sure no body could ever pick mine.' Quoth Jack, 'If you will lay a wager of ten shillings, to be spent here for the good of the house, your pocket shall be picked in Westminster-Hall, by to-morrow noon if you'll be there.' The stakes on both sides were laid down in the hands of the people of the house; and the person who defy'd having his pocket picked, went next morning to Westminster-Hall, which being vacation time, there was no body in it but two little boys whipping a top, who every two or three times as the man passed by 'em blew quills of lice

upon his cloaths, and then cry'd out to him, 'O! Sir, you are all lousy!' He perceiving it, desired the boys to pick them off, which office they performed with great assiduousness, till one of them pick'd his pocket of a purse, with some certain pieces of silver, which he had lain he would not lose.

The boys then carry'd the prize to Jack Hall and the man having walked in Westminster-Hall his appointed time, he went to the people in whose hands the stakes were deposited, to claim his money; but Jack Hall being there at the same time, told him, he had lost the wager, because his purse was there before him; so giving it him again, he was in a great surprize, to think how he should come by it; which being told him, they had the wager spent with great satisfaction on both sides.

Jack Hall having a design once to rob a great merchant in the City of London, he went oftentimes hankering about his house, but could never effect it; whereupon he bethought himself of this stratagem: he was to be put into a pack done up like a bale; and by the contrivance of his comrade, who was very well apparell'd, he was to be laid into this merchant's house in the evening, as so much silk, which he was to see next morning, and to buy off his hands, in case they agreed.

Accordingly this bale full of iniquity, wedg'd inwardly on all sides with coarse cloth and fustian, was laid up in the warehouse. Night being come, and the apprentices weary, two of them, whilst their master was at supper, went to rest themselves, and by accident lay along on this bale, which was plac'd by some others; insomuch that the extream anguish of their weight being very heavy upon Jack Hall, he could scarce fetch his breath. Upon this, he drew out a sharp knife, and making a great hole in the fillet of the bale, he also made a deep wound in the buttocks of him that lay most upon it, which made him rise, and roar out, his fellow-apprentice had killed him. Running out to his master in the agony, his fellow-apprentice followed him, and was innocently secur'd, till a farther examination of the matter. In the mean while Jack Hall made his escape out of a window, with only taking two pieces of velvet along with him.

At the same time the merchant seeing his apprentice in a very bloody condition, and fearing, if the bale of silk he lay on should be spoilt with the blood, he must be forced to pay whatever price was required, he ran presently into the warehouse to prevent any damage coming to it, where finding it mightily shrunk in its bulk, it rais'd some suspicion of roguery in him; for opening it, he found therein nothing of value, then searching about his warehouse, and missing the two pieces of velvet, he plainly perceived some rogue had been pack'd up in the bale, with an intent to rob his house when he and his family were in bed; whereupon, the accus'd apprentice was set at liberty, and a surgeon fetched for the wounded one, who cost his master above five pounds before he was well.

He was also very good for the 'lob', which is thus: going with a consort into any shop to change a pistole or guinea, and having about half of his change, cries the consort, 'What need you to change? I have silver enough to defray our charges where we are going.' Upon this, the other throws the money back again into the money box; but with such dexterity, that he has one of the pieces, whether shilling or half crown, sticking in the palm of his hand, which he carries clean off, without any suspicion of fraud. Again, he was very expert at the 'whalebone-lay', which is, having a thin piece of whalebone daubed at the end with birdlime, with which, going into a shop with a pretence to buy something, they make the shop-keeper, by wanting this and that thing, to turn his back often; and then take the opportunity of putting the whalebone, so daubed with birdlime, into the tell of the compter, which brings up any single piece of money that sticks to it. After which, to give no mistrust, they buy some small matter, and pay the man with a pig of his own sow.

The year before Jack Hall, the chimney-sweeper, was hang'd, having committed sacrilege at Bristol, in robbing Ratcliff-Church in that city, he made the best of his way for London; where after a little while, his extravagancies reducing him to the want of money again, in order to recruit his pockets, he went with some of his wicked associates, upon the 'running-smobble', which is this: one of them goes into a shop, and pretending to be drunk, after some troublesome behaviour, he puts the candles out, and taking away whatever comes first to hand, he runs off, whilst another flings handfuls of dirt and nastiness into the mouth and face of the person that cries out 'Stop Thief', which putting him or her into a sudden surprize, it gives them an opportunity of going off without apprehending.

One time Jack Hall being drest like a gentleman, (tho' you must suppose, like Æsop's crow, he was decked in other people's plumes) and sitting on a bench in the Mall in St James's Park, a Life-Guard man, and one Mr Knight an attorney, living in Shandois-Street, near Covent-Garden, meeting one another just by the place where Jack sate, after some complements were passed between them, the lawyer invited the Life-Guard man, whom he had not seen a long time before, to dine with him at his house the next day, for he should be very welcome, and any friend that he should bring along with him. The Life-Guard man promis'd he would be sure to wait upon him; but asking his friend whether he liv'd in the same place still, 'Yes, yes,' (quoth the Lawyer) 'I still live within three doors of the Feathers alehouse in Shandois Street.' They then parted; and now Jack Hall's wits were on the tenters for making some advantage by this invitation which he had heard given: so the next day, above an hour before the time, when hungry mortals whet their knives on thresholds, and the soles of shoes, he was lurking thereabouts, and at last, setting his eyes on the Life-Guard man, whom he knew again, he was no sooner entred into his friend's house, but Jack was at his heels, and entred also with him, with as much confidence as if he had been an acquaintance of the lawyer. There were above half a score gentlemen and gentlewomen, among whom he sate down, and soon after, dinner being set on the table, with great variety of dainties, the strange gentleman, Jack Hall, did eat as heartily, and talk as boldly, as any there.

All the while the Life-Guard man took him to be one of the inviter's acquaintance, and the inviter suppos'd him to be the Life-Guard man's friend; but in the end, he prov'd to be neither of their friends, especially the lawyer's; for waiting his opportunity, he went to the side board, which stood in a convenient place, and putting a dozen of silver spoons, and as many silver forks, into his pockets, he walk'd off incognito. The Life-Guard man, soon after, miss'd Jack, and the lawyer miss'd his friend's friend, as he thought him; but it was not much longer 'ere the spoons and forks were missing, and altho' strict search was made for them, yet were they not found. None but the friend, or he that was thought so on both sides, being missing, the lawyer asked the Life-Guard man for him; but the Life-Guard man telling the lawyer he was none of his friend or acquaintance, it was concluded, *nemine contradicente*, that the absent person was the rogue that had converted the lawyer's plate to his own use.

Another time, Jack Hall being very well dress'd, and pretending to be a country gentleman, he took lodgings at the house of one Dogget, a Quaker, and button-seller, living in Burleigh-Street, in the Strand, where he behaved himself very soberly till an opportunity offered to out-wit the Quaker, who thought it no harm to outwit every body. For the key of his chamber being left one day in the door, he took the impression of it in clay, and had another made by it; a little after which, old Dogget and his wife going to their country-house, for two or three days, leaving none at home, but a wanton kinswoman, an apprentice, and maid, Jack in the mean time had the conveniency of entring their bed-chamber, when all in the house were in bed, and opening a trunk he took out above eighty pounds in money and plate, and opening the street door went off with it. But when the old folks came home again, and found what had happen'd, the house was all in an uproar; there was powerful 'holding forth' by the man, who storm'd and rav'd, and fell a kicking the trunk about like a foot-ball, which he did with a great deal more ease than he could when it was full.

After this exploit, Jack Hall, Stephen Bunce, and Dick Low, going upon an enterprize at Hackney, about 12 of the clock at night, they, by the help of their betties and short crows, made a forcible entry into the house of one Clare, a baker, whose journey-man being ty'd neck and heels they threw him into the kneading-trough, and the apprentice with him. Jack Hall stood centry over them, with a great old rusty back-sword, which he found in the kitchen, and swearing with a great grace, that their heads, both went off as round as a hoop, if they offered to stir or budge. In the mean time Dick Low and Stephen Bunce, went up to Mr Clare's room, whom they found in bed with his wife, and ty'd and gagg'd the old folks, without any consideration of their age, which had left them but few teeth, to barricade their gums from the injury they might receive from those ugly instruments that stretched their mouths asunder.

Finding not so much as they expected, the old man they ungagged again, to bring to a confession where he hoarded his money; but extorting nothing out of him, Jack Hall being then come up to them, for fear they should sink upon him, which is an usual thing among thieves, to cheat one another, he took up in his arms the old man's grand-daughter, about six years old, lying in a trundle-bed by him, and said, 'D—n me, if I won't bake the child presently in a pye, and eat it, if the old rogue will not be civil.' These scaring words made Mr Clare beg heartily that they should not hurt the child, and he would discover what he had; so fetching, by his order, a little iron-bound chest from under the bed, and unlocking it, they took what was in it, which was about eighty pounds; then obscuring their dark lanthorns, they bid the baker good night, and commanded him to return them thanks that they spared his ears, which is against the law for any of their occupation to wear.

Another time Jack Hall going to one Mr Aspin, a robe-maker, living in Portugal-Street, by Lincolns-Inn back-gate, he pretended that he had occasion for a gown for his brother, who was a parson in the country, but he would have a very good one, though it cost him the more money. 'I can furnish you with all sorts and sizes,' said Mr Aspin; and thereupon fetch'd several, and shew'd him. Jack turn'd many of them over, but still desired to see better. At length one was brought which he seem'd to like; but, said he to the robe-maker, 'I doubt it is too short? T'other said he did not doubt but it was long enough in all conscience'; and thereupon he was for trying of it upon Jack, who said, 'Alas! there will be no certain measure by me, for my brother is taller than I am by the head and shoulders; but as he is a man about your pitch, I desire the favour of you to put it upon yourself, and then I shall guess the better whether it is long enough or no.'

Mr Aspin, to satisfy his customer, did so; but as he was putting it on, Jack took up a barrister's gown, and shew'd him a fair pair of heels. Mr Aspin, without putting off the gown, pursu'd him; in the mean time two of his companions, who laid perdue, acted their parts; for Stephen Bunce went into the shop, and taking the next parcel of goods which came to hand, he marched off. And Dick Low, fearing that if the shop-keeper kept his pace he might overtake Jack Hall, having placed himself in the way on purpose, catches hold on Mr Aspin, and says, 'O! dear, Doctor Cross, who thought of seeing you? I am glad I have met you with all my heart: but pray, Sir, what makes you run in this distracted manner about the streets?' 'Pish,' (quoth Mr Aspin) let me go, I am no parson, you are mistaken in the man, for I am running after a rogue that has robb'd me.' Then Dick Low reply'd, but still holding him, 'I beg your pardon, Sir, for my mistake, for you are as like my friend Doctor Cross, as ever I saw two men in my life like one another.'

Letting him go at last, Jack before now was turn'd the corner of a street or two, and was quite out of sight. By this time also several of the neighbours being gathered together, they were in an admiration to see old Aspin in a canonical habit; some saying, 'Surely he was not going to christen his own child himself, which his maid Betty lay in with!' whilst others perswaded him to go home, and put off the gown, and then make an enquiry after the thief, since he was at present got clear away. Mr Aspin took their advice; but when he came to his shop, he found a second loss, which made him more angry than before, and swear, that the fellow that met him, might well call him Doctor Cross, for d—n him if he had not all the crosses in the world come upon him at once.

This most notorious malefactor thought it no injustice to rob every body; and all his vices, whatever deformity the eye of the world apprehended to be in them, his unaccountable wickedness look'd upon as no less excellent than the most absolute of all virtues. But his villainy being so unparellel'd, that justice was obliged to unsheath her sword against him, a shameful catastrophe put an end to his wicked crimes in the year 1707, when he deservedly suffered death at Tyburn, with his companions Low and Bunce.

THE LIFE OF
MADAM
CHURCHILL

Deborah Churchill, alias Miller, was born within six miles of the city of Norwich, in the county of Norfolk, of worthy honest parents, who gave her very good education, and brought her up in her younger years in the ways of religion and good manners; but she had wickedly thrown off all those good things, which were endeavoured to be fixed in her, and abandoned herself to all manner of filthiness and uncleanness, which afterwards proved her shame and ruin. She was first married to one John Churchill, an ensign in Major General Faringdon's regiment; by whose name she commonly went, but seldom by her second husband's who, two or three years before her misfortunes, was married to her in the Fleet prison, upon agreement first made between them both, that they should not live together, nor have any thing to do with each other. Which agreement was strictly performed; and so she continued freely to keep company with one Hunt a Life-Guard man, as she had begun to do in her former husband's time.

She had liv'd with the aforesaid bully Hunt for seven years together, in a lascivious and adulterous manner, which broke her first husband's heart, by whom she had two children surviving at the time of her unfortunate death. She had liv'd also in incontinency about three months, with one Thomas Smith, a cooper, who was hanged at Tyburn, on Friday the 16th day of December, 1709, for breaking open and robbing the house of the Right Honourable the Earl of Westmorland; at which time were likewise hanged Aaron Jones and Joseph Wells, for the murder of one Mr Lamas near Marybone.

This noted jilt bore a great sway in Drury-Lane, as in taking tribute of all new whores who presumed to walk there at night, to venture their souls, if men would their bodies, for the small price of two-pence wet, and two-pence dry. She was here a common strumpet, and prostituted herself to all comers and goers, whose pockets she constantly pick'd. An instance of her manner, was what she did with one Mr Jeffery W——, a bookseller, living lately in St Paul's Church-Yard, from whom taking a pocket-book, in which were several notes and bills of value, Hunt her bully, went the next day to his shop, and returning the pocket-book to him, said, 'By this I understand you have been more familiar with my wife than became you; but take notice, I shall require satisfaction for the affront, or otherwise take what follows.' The bookseller being conscious of what was laid to his charge, rather than the scandal should come to his wife's ears, to whom he was newly married, he gave him ten guineas, with a promise of paying him thirty more the next day. But in the mean time acquainting a book-binder, living in Little-Britain, with the matter, knowing the world pretty well, met Hunt at the place where Mr W—— was to give him thirty guineas, and threatning to secure him with a constable, the sharper was forced not only to surrender his pretensions to the thirty guineas, but to return the former ten, for fear of being carry'd before his betters.

As she was once going thro' Cheapside, upon the buttock and file, she pick'd up a linnen-draper living in Cornhill who being as sharp as she, he found he had lost his watch in the tavern where they were drinking, which was at the Three Tuns in Newgate-Street, and charged her with it. She deny'd it stifly, neither could it be found upon her, tho' the maids of the house had stript her stark naked. But the linnen-draper swearing point-blank that she had it, and sending for a constable to secure her, she discovered the watch, which was hid in the bottom of a leather chair; whereupon she was committed to Wood-Street compter.

But the abovesaid linnen-draper never appearing against Madam Churchill, when under confinement, she was at last discharged; but had not long enjoy'd her liberty before she was committed to New-Prison, for picking a gentleman's

185

pocket of a purse, wherein was an hundred and four guineas. Whilst she was there, she seemed to be really a pious woman; but only her religion was of five or six colours; for this day she would pray that God would turn the heart of her adversary, and to-morrow curse the time that ever she saw him.

She at last got out of this mansion of sorrow also, but soon forgetting her afflictions, she pursued her wickedness continually, till she had been sent no less than 20 times to Clerkenwell Bridewell; where receiving the correction of the house every time, by being whipt, and kept to beating hemp from morning till night, for the small allowance of so much bread and water, which will but just keep life and soul together, she commonly came out like a skeleton, and walked as if her limbs had been ty'd together with packthread; yet let what punishment would light on this common strumpet, she was no changling, for as soon as she was out of gaol, she was still running into greater evils, by deluding, if possible, all mankind.

One night picking up one William Fowler, a barber, living in Bull-Inn-Court, in the Strand, and carrying him to her lodging in Castle-Street, behind the north side of Long-Acre, they went to bed, where the amorous folly of these two lovers consisted, no doubt, more of action than expression: but in the height of these enjoyments, bully Hunt unexpectedly came home, and knocking hard at the door, startled our two inamorato's who were more strictly entangled in each others arms, than Mars was by Vulcan's crafty net, when entwin'd in amorous folds with the Cyprian goddess. In the mean time Deb. Churchill, being otherwise employ'd than to come out of a warm bed, and endanger the catching of cold, was as mute as a fish; neither could she in reason make answer to the disturber of her joys, till the business she was about was consummated.

But bully Rock, impatient of delay, repeating his strokes on the harmless door, Madam found herself constrained to demand 'who was there?' tho' in words imperfect, as one waked out of a profound sleep. Knowing the voice, upon reply, she capitulated with Hunt, till she might hide her cully, for whom there was no other refuge but crawling under the bed; where being secured, she jumped out, and in great haste ran to the door, speaking as she was wont, 'Oh! my soul! Oh thou most welcome man to me alive': when in herself she thought, 'What envious devil has brought thee hither at this juncture to disturb my pleasure?'

The bully thus entered, began to salute her in his usual language, 'You whore, you bitch, what rogue have you got in bed with you now?' But finding no body there, he kicked her about the room like a foot ball, saying again, 'Where have you hid the scoundrel, that durst presume to bestow a citizen's fate upon my honour, in making me a cuckold?' Then drawing his sword, quoth he, 'I've not killed a man this great while, but by G—d I'll send one out of the world now.' So thrusting his sword under the bed, poor Tonsor began to cry out for quarter; at the same time creeping out of his nest so extreamly powder'd with dust and feathers, that bully Hunt taking him rather for a devil than a man, the fright he was in gave the as much frighted cut-beard the favourable opportunity of making his escape out of the house, with only the loss of his breeches, in which was a good silver watch, and about four pound in money. But for this trick he swore, 'he would never go a whoring again', which was as dangerous as trusting his arms in the throat of a lyon, or his purse with a highwayman.

Now after Madam Churchill had reign'd a long time in her wickedness, as she was coming one night along Drury-Lane, in company with Richard Hunt, William Lewis, and John Boy, they took an occasion to fall out with one Martin Were, and she aggravating the quarrel, by bidding them sacrifice the man, they killed him between King's-Head Court and Vinegar-Yard. The three men who committed this murder made their escape; but she being apprehended as an accessary therein, was sent to Newgate, and shortly after condemned for it on the 26th of February, 1707–8.

After sentence of death was passed on her, her execution was respited, by virtue of a reprieve given her, upon the account of her being thought to be with child; which she pretended to be, in hopes it might be a means to save her life, or at least put off her death for a time. But when she had lain under condemnation almost ten months, and was found not to be with child, she was called to her former judgment. Then being convey'd in a coach to Tyburn, on Friday the 17th of December, 1708, she was there hang'd in the 31st year of her age. But, before she was turn'd off, she desired all the spectators to pray for her, and that God would be pleas'd to be merciful to her poor soul: moreover, calling to one she call'd nurse, an apple-woman's daughter in Drury-Lane, she earnestly begg'd of her to take care of her poor children, for whom she seemed to be very much concerned. These were her last words, which she spoke in the cart, into which she was put as soon as she came to the place of execution.

THE LIFE OF
HARVEY
HUTCHINS

T his malefactor, Harvey Hutchins, was born of honest parents, his father being a sword-blade-maker by trade; who, when this unhappy son came to be about fourteen years of age, put him apprentice to a silver-smith in Shrewsbury; but pilfering very often from his master, he had him sent at last, to Shrewsbury gaol.

In this prison the young lad came acquainted with some London thieves, who, occupying their calling in the county of Salop, they were also committed to the same jail; where Hutchins hearing them tell of the several notable and ingenious robberies that were committed in and about London, by some of the chief masters of their profession, he was resolved to make the best of his way thither after he obtained his liberty.

About three or four months after his confinement, came the assizes; when being try'd, and whipt at the cart's arse, upon his friends paying his fees, he got his enlargement and came up to Islington, where he lurk'd about the town, and took up his lodging in a barn. But his mind still ran upon the ingenuity of the topping thieves in London, particularly one Constantine, who, for the fine stories he had heard told of him, he admired above the rest. At last he moves into the great metropolis, where getting acquainted with some young pick-pockets, he enquired among them for this Constantine, who told him he might be found at one Snotty-Nose Hill's who kept the Dog-Tavern in Newgate-Street.

The young Salopian being overjoyed he had found out where Mr Constantine used, one evening he goes to the Dog-Tavern to enquire, saying, after his country dialect or tone, 'he had vary ennest busness wod him'. The drawer presently went up stairs to Mr Constantine, who was then drinking with a great many of his thieving fraternity, and acquaints him, 'that there was a young country lad below wanted earnestly to speak with him'. Quoth Constantine, 'With me? D—n me, I don't know any country lad. What is he? Perhaps he's sent for some trepan; prithee go down and ask him his business.' The drawer comes to the country lad, asking, 'what he would have with Mr Constantine, and he would go up and tell him'. Young Shropshire told him, 'No hearm, but his busness wes such, that mornt tol it to eny buddy bot hemself.'

The drawer returns again with this message, and Constantine wondring who this lad should be, ordered him to be brought up to the stairs head, where coming out to him, quoth he, 'Do you want me, lad?'; he reply'd 'Yes, Mester, vor I am come abive a hundered moiles to zee you.' Said Constantine, 'What is your business with me?' He answered, 'Vy, Mester, I heve ben in Shrewsbury joil, vere haring a grot morny vine stories of you, by zum gentlemen that vare prosners with me, I am come up to London on porpus to beand myself prontice to yow.' Hereupon, Constantine could not forbear smiling at the lad's fancy, and taking him into the room, where he repeated the story to his company, it caused a great deal of laughter among them.

He gives the boy sixpence, and a glass or two of wine, and bade him 'be sure to come to him at the same place about seven the next night, and he would take him upon liking, and according as he found him tractable, diligent, and acute in his business, he would take him apprentice'. The boy overjoyed at this good fortune (as he unhappily thought it) took his leave, and, according to order, was next night at the Dog-Tavern punctually at the hour appointed, where his master Constantine was ready to go with him upon a trial of skill; which was this. Constantine having stole a silver tankard, about three months before, out of an alehouse in Cheapside he had, nevertheless, been there in disguise several times after; and observing much plate still in use about the house, he told the

189

boy the story going along the street, and promised him, that if he could carry off another clean, and bring it to him at a certain house in White-Chapel, he would certainly take him apprentice, and make a man of him when he was out of his apprenticeship; at the same time intimating to him, that the house was just before him where he was going to drink.

The boy took his story right, but just as his master was come to the house, pulling him by the sleeve, quoth he, 'Mester, Mester, can yow ran well?' 'Yes,' (reply'd his master,) 'as well as most men in England; I have often out-ran hundreds together before now.' 'Weel then,' (said the boy) 'if you can ran well, ne'er fear but we'll hove a tonkad.'

Into the house Constantine goes first, and calling for a room, the boy followed him to the bar, as his servant, and with a low voice asked the man of the house, 'if he did not lose a silver tankard about three months ago?' 'Yes,' reply'd he; which Constantine over hearing, took as fast as he could to his heels, the boy at the same time crying out, 'That was the man that stole it.' Upon which the victualler, and the servants, ran presently out in pursuit of him, but to no purpose, for he was got out of sight in an instant, and in the mean time the boy took another silver tankard out of the bar, and got safely to the place appointed by his master; who no sooner saw him, but he fell a cursing, and damning, and sinking, at him, like a madman, for putting him into such bodily fear, withal telling him, 'that if he had been taken, he should have been certainly hang'd by the best neck he had; but,' quoth he, 'Sirrah, have you got a tankard?' 'Yes,' reply'd the boy, and taking it from under his coat, gave it him; saying at the same time, 'Mester, if yow hed not virst asor'd me thet yow cud ran well, I wud a gut et sum uddar vay.'

A little after this running bout, young Harvey and his master going through Denmark Court in the Strand, they espy'd a silver tankard, cup, salver, and some spoons and forks, lying on a side-board in the parlour of one William Bunworth, a school-master; at which Constantine's mouth watering, quoth he to his apprentice, who was now bound to him for three years, 'Is there no possibility, Harvey, of getting that plate, whilst that damn'd maid is in the parlour?' 'Yes, Mester,' quoth he, 'if you will carry me up to the mester of the school, and pretending I am a noughty boy, give hem sumthing to whop me, and then var menaging the maud, I'll leve that to yow, Mester.'

Accordingly they both went up stairs without asking any questions, and coming into the school, Constantine, who was drest much like a gentleman, with his long tail wig, and sword by his side, address'd himself to the school-master, saying, 'Sir, I have got an unlucky rogue of a boy here for a servant, who is the saddest dog as ever was known for going of an errand; for send him but to the next door and he will stay two or three hours before he returns with an answer: I have try'd fair means, and foul means with him, and yet all will not do; wherefore, I humbly beg the favour of you to do so much as give him a good whipping, and next week I shall send him to school to you, to be instructed in writing and casting accompts, for I would fain have the rascal come to good if I could.' At the same time he slipt a crown-piece into Bunworth's hand, who being such a miserly covetous fellow, that he would never marry for fear of bringing a charge of children on him, he was overjoyed at so large a gift for doing so small a piece of service.

Immediately the school-master takes Harvey to task, who began to set up his pipes, and cry'd heartily; but all to no purpose; one of the lustiest boys in the school was call'd out to hoist him, who getting him on his back, the master handsomely flank'd him. In the mean time Constantine went down stairs, desiring him before to send his boy after him, as soon as he had given him correction. Then approaching the maid with fair words, he gave her a shilling, to fetch a pint of sack for him and her master, who was just upon coming down to him upon some business that was betwixt them. The poor servant mistrusting no harm, takes the shilling, and went for the wine; in the mean time he went off with all the plate, and presently came down Harvey and went after him.

In less than four or five minutes, school being done, down comes Bunworth himself, and seeing the maid coming in at the street-door with a pint of wine in her hand, quoth he, 'Who is that for, Mary?' She told him, the gentleman that was just now with him, ordered her to fetch it. Quoth he, 'A very generous civil gentleman, I vow; he gave me a crown but for whipping that unlucky rogue of his, who, according to the character of him, is, indeed, a very naughty boy.' Said the maid again, 'Ay, but Sir, where is all the plate that was on the sideboard here just now?' 'Plate!' quoth Bunworth, 'what plate? I saw no plate.' Away they both went searching the closet, and every hole and corner of the house, but not finding it, Bunworth cries out, 'Ruin'd and undone for ever! I'm robb'd, I'm robb'd! Oh! that damn'd son of a whore of a gentleman, whilst I was whipping his unlucky son of a whore his boy, he has whipt away all my plate. Thieves! Thieves!' At this uproar all the neighbours came into assist him, thinking they were then in the house; but, indeed, the thieves were farther a field, without doubt making merry over their booty, whilst poor Bunworth was damning and sinking himself to the pit of hell for his loss, which he did not long survive, for within a little while after he died with mere vexation and grief.

In fine, Harvey very truly and honestly served out his time with his master, when setting up for himself, he had very pretty business in house-breaking, and liv'd very creditably and handsomly among those of his profession, for about nine years, in and about the cities of London and Westminster, and in that time had often paid scot and lot to Newgate, and other jails about town; but at last being apprehended for breaking open a Jew's house at Dukes-Place, and robbing it of above four hundred pounds in money and plate, he was hang'd at Tyburn in 1704, aged twenty six years.

THE LIFE OF
TOM MARSH

This fellow being one who, (like all other rogues) employ'd his wits in all manner of villany, to support himself in the pursuit of his unlawful appetites, he one while used an alehouse in Leicester Fields, the man whereof having a very handsome wife to sit in the bar, she brought a great many customers, who were in hopes of qualifying her husband for horn fair. But the hostess being as cunning as her guests, she would not be like a glove, for every one's drawing on; for if she had any gallants, it was her resolution that they should be of the best, and those she counted so, who had the most money in their pockets. Her carriage in all company seemed to be varnished with a very great modesty; but it was only counterfeited, for several having laid seige to the fortress of her chastity, she had surrendered it for the presents of fine hoods, scarves, gloves, rings, or other such womanish toys.

Among the crowd of this woman's admirers, was Thomas Marsh, who discovering his flaming passion to her, she as soon made him sensible by what means he must cool it, which was, by giving her a silk night-gown; so, after promising her one, they parted, and he went home, to contrive how to be as good as his word, whilst the other found out a way to procure her husband's absence for a night or two. This she accomplished by sending him fifteen miles off, to Watford in Hertfordshire, to see her mother, who then lay a dying.

In the mean time Tom finding the strength of his pocket was not sufficient to accomplish his promise, he supply'd that defect by this stratagem: visiting a woman of his particular acquaintance, who had then lately stolen a very rich gown (namely Eleanor Jackson, alias Scotch Nell, who was since hang'd at Tyburn, for stealing a calicoe petticoat from one Mrs Margaret Stephens) and acquainting her with his design, which was more than mere love, as you will find by the sequel of the story, he beg'd the favour of her to lend it him, to facilitate his intention. Accordingly she did as he desired, upon assurance that he would see it forth coming; then sending it by a porter to the victualler's wife, she accepted it and the following letter, with a smiling countenance.

> MY DEAR,
>
> HAVING sent you a Gown by the Bearer, this is also to acquaint you, that I must die or see you To-day. Never Man lov'd to such a Degree as I do; but it is true, never Man lov'd so amiable a Creature. You may be sure of my Company at the Time appointed. If I had a thousand Lives, I would expose them all for so dear a Blessing. How long will this Day seem to me! How many tiresome Minutes am I to pass, before that I arrive at that which is the Perfection of my Happiness! Thus dearly Love will make us pay for his Joy! But I shall owe him the more, if in this Time of my Pennance I can prevail upon you to believe that never Man deserved more to possess you! I shall give a Proof of it, and if you give all your Heart, I'll venture for mine.
>
> Your humble Servant,
>
> THO. MARSH

Towards the evening this passionate lover paid her a visit, being very merry at her house till late at night, when preparing for bed, they took up some good liquors, as cyder, stout, and brandy, to enjoy themselves in private; but Tom had put a small dose of laudanum into his beloved's cup, which made her, after but one enjoyment, fall so fast asleep, that you might as well awake the dead as her ladyship. Now Tom, thinking it was good to make hay while the sun shin'd, took three gold rings off her fingers; then taking the keys of a chest of drawers out of her pocket, he rifled them of the best of her cloaths, and forty pounds in money; which bundling up in his friend's gown, he left Madam Nick-and-Froth to retrieve her loss by the old way of scoring two for one.

After this he cheated the country up and down, by pretending to be a disbanded soldier, or shipwreck'd seaman; for which purpose he made false passes, and counterfeited their seals, after this manner. Going to three or four magistrates, and procuring their warrants, signed and sealed, by swearing the peace against Tom a Nokes, or Jack a Stiles, he would take a piece of clay, which being rubb'd with a bit of butter, that it might not stick to the wax, the impression thereon would come off very clean; then dry it very hard, and it gives the same impression on wax. But Tom being once detected in this sort of forgery, he was whipt at Tuttle-Fields Bridewell; a place where all the senses of a man may enjoy a peculiar pleasure; by seeing nothing but the marks of poverty, smelling the fragrant odour of that commodity, which they often beat for their own destruction, hearing the harmonious noise made with beetle and punny, tasting water without adulteration, and feeling a good bull's pizzle in case they won't work.

Once Tom Marsh lodging at one Mr Bennet's house near Mutton-Lane, who and his wife were strong Presbyterians, he seemed to be a precisian too, which made his landlord and landlady have a great respect for their seemingly serious lodger. Tom made use of their good opinion, and one Sunday in the evening, coming home from a meeting-house, he sat down by the fire, in a very devout sort of a posture, as having his glove on his head, and arms a-cross; then desiring the old people to fetch him a Bible, they, glad to see him in this godly frame of mind, brought him one presently. Taking it in his hand, he pitch'd on that chapter of the Gospel, which tells the evangelical story of our Saviour's bidding the lame man take up his bed and walk, which he read with a great emphasis; and afterwards going to his repose, he, very early in the morning, bundled up his bed, which flinging out of the window, he carried clean away.

About noon the landlord's daughter going to make Tom's bed, she came down in a great agony to her mother; to whom telling what had happen'd, she made as terrible an outcry of her loss, in the neighbourhood, as the people did of the wild Irish coming hither, a little before the Prince of Orange arriv'd at London; but her husband being a moderate man, and, for his profession, a merry

195

one too, he bade her be quiet, because Tom had been so civil as to prove over night by scripture, that he ought to walk away with it.

This wicked person was born near Ludlow in Shropshire, a mason by trade, and coming up to London, married a very honest woman, by whom he left a girl behind him; but being of an idle lazy disposition, he took to ill courses, and had not only been whipt at the cart's tail, for stealing lead off St Paul's Cathedral, but for a trespass, in entring a man's yard, with a design to rob him, he was also fin'd twenty pounds, and committed to Newgate till he paid the sum, where he remained 4 years, except some little time when he broke out, which he did twice, but was both times soon retaken, and punish'd with hand-cuffs, the neck-collar, and double irons.

Whilst he was under confinement, he had a child by one Elizabeth Key, a notorious whore, a prisoner in the same gaol for debt, whom, as being of a fickle or rather lustful temper, he slighted, for the sake of Jane Hays, another prisoner there for debt. It was not long after his correspondence with the last, that he got his fine remitted, and obtain'd his liberty. But he did not enjoy it long; for committing a burglary at Hampstead, he was committed to Newgate again, and on the 20th of December, 1710, hang'd at Tyburn, where he confessed 'twas he murdered the farmer at Shipperton, in the county of Middlesex, and not Mr Charles Dean the attorney, who, a little before was wrongfully executed for it, at that same time that one Mr Crouch was try'd on the same account at Justice-Hall in the Old-Bailey, but was honourably acquitted.

THE LIFE OF
TOM GERRARD

O f all the two hundred and forty two malefactors, which were executed at Tyburn, and elsewhere in and about London, from the beginning of Sir Thomas Abney's mayoralty, to the end of Sir Richard Hoare's, this Thomas Gerrard was not, for the short time he triumphed in his villany, inferior to any of them for wickedness. He was born in the parish of St Giles's in the Fields, of good and honest parents, who kept the Red Lion Inn, in Holborn. Having some small education bestowed on him, he was, when about sixteen years of age, put apprentice to a poulterer in Clare Market, where he serv'd part of his time; but being addicted to ill company, so as wholly leading a loose and idle life, it drew him into many streights and inconveniencies, which to repair he took to the trade of thieving, following it for a considerable time, whereby he had often been in Newgate, and was condemn'd once before he committed the fact for which he at last suffer'd death.

Whenever he was out of a jail, never vessel without sails, or without anchor or rudder, was more driven and toss'd by the waves, than his thoughts were on robbing all he could, which made him a profess'd master in all manner of roguery.

One time Gerrard having committed a great robbery in London, fearing to be apprehended for it, he stole a horse worth above thirty pounds, and rid into

Lincolnshire; where lying at a bye inn within a mile of Grantham, and espying a very large punch-bowl, made of a new fashion'd mixt metal resembling plate, brought to some company, he suppos'd it to be realy silver, and by its bigness to be worth near sixty pounds. Then going to bed, and observing this bowl to be lock'd up in a closet in the room where he lay, he broke it open in the dead of the night, and privately carried off the imaginary plate, without his horse, to Newark upon Trent; where being made sensible 'twas not silver, he threw it into the river, but damn'd himself to the very pit of hell, for being such a fool as to leave a horse of a considerable value, for a bargain not worth twenty shillings. However, to be reveng'd on the people, who had got sufficiently by his covetousness, he went, about a month after, to the house, when 'twas late at night, and setting fire to it burnt it down to the ground in less than two hours; and by this villainous action ruin'd a whole family at once.

This base offender had a dog that he had learnt to pick pockets as well as the best artist whatever of that profession; but after the untimely end of his master seeking out for another, who should he pitch upon, but Dr B— the Presbyterian parson, on whom he mightily fawn'd; and being a pretty dog, as handsome as any Bolonese, he was lik'd by that reverend gentleman, who made very much of him, till one day going thro' Newgate-Street, whilst he went into a tobacconist's shop to buy some tobacco, his new dog in the mean time ran into Newgate Market, and fetch'd him a purse, in which was betwixt thirty and forty shillings, which he receiv'd without asking any questions. Presently the old doctor stepping somewhere else, the dog ran again to Newgate Market, and fetch'd him another purse, with much such another sum of money, and gave him that too. The doctor looking now on his dog to be a great offender in that kind, as soon as he came home he call'd this criminal to justice, and very fairly hang'd the poor cur, for fear he should at last pick pockets in his meeting house.

Tho' house-breaking was the chief villany which Tom Gerrard went upon, yet sometimes he counterfeited bank-notes, exchequer-bills, malt tickets, bills of sale, or seamens tickets, sign'd with any intricate hand. By these cheating tricks he had once got so much money by him, that being able to put fifty pounds into the hands of one Mr Thornicraft, a goldsmith in the Strand, he went, with another of his accomplices, to the Cross-Keys tavern, at the corner of Henrietta-Street, in Covent-Garden, and sending for one Mr Blake an upholsterer, he made a bargain with him for as many goods as came to about the abovementioned sum, asking him at the same time, if he would accept a bill drawn upon Mr Thornicraft for the money.

The upholsterer knowing the goldsmith to be a very honest man, accepted it, and going with Gerrard's friend to the shop, he found it acceptable there. Then returning back to the tavern again, the person who was along with the poor tradesman gave his wicked comrade a wrong bill, whilst he seemingly began to beat down the price of the goods for which he had bargain'd, by pretending he had over-bad himself. In the mean time the other went to the goldsmith's with the right bill, and receiv'd the money. At last Gerrard and the upholsterer agreed together, and a couple of porters were sent to carry away the goods, for which he gave him the false bill, as he found to his cost, when he went to Mr Thornicraft, who had paid the fifty pounds above an hour before he came, to the man who had been with him there before, to see if the former bill was good. Thus we may see that the ways of cheating honest people are infinite.

A certain prophane gentleman in Leicester-Fields having a parrot, which he taught more to swear and curse than any thing else, one day it happen'd that Tom Gerrard sneaking about dinner time into the parlour where Poll was hanging in a cage, he went to the side-board and took off several pieces of plate; but the parrot having an eye upon him, she set up her throat, and fell a scream-ing out, 'Thieves, G—d d—n you, Thieves, Thieves, by G—d, make haste.' This uproar quickly alarm'd the servants, who running to see the cause of Poll's swea-ring and cursing after this manner, they apprehended Tom Gerrard, on whom they found half a dozen silver spoons, and as many forks of the same metal; for which he was burnt in the hand.

He was much addicted to drunkenness, being so often disguis'd with drink, that many have thought his father got him when he was drunk, as one may suppose his mother was when she brought him forth. Whenever liquor depriv'd him of his senses, he valued not upon what villainous enterprizes he went, for then nothing came amiss to him; and he was not sober when he acted his last part of roguery on this terrestrial stage, which was breaking open a house in company with another, and robbing it, as it appeared on his trial, which is as follows.

Thomas Gerrard, and Tobias Tanner, were both indicted for breaking open the dwelling house of William Gardiner, in the night-time, and taking from thence eight dozen pair of worsted stockings, value ten pounds, and eight pound weight of thread, twenty five shillings, with other things of value, the goods of the said William Gardiner, on the 10th of August, 1710. It appeared that the prosecutor about midnight, on the date aforesaid, was knock'd up by the watch, and found his house broke open, and his goods gone. To fix it upon the prisoners, one John Audrey, a person concern'd with them, deposed, that himself, with the prisoners, and a person not taken, broke into the prosecutor's shop, thro' the brick work, under the window, about twelve at night, took away the goods, and sold them to Mat. Bunch, for three pounds six shillings, which was equally divided amongst them. Gerrard, upon his trial, confess'd the fact; but the evidence being not strong enough against Tanner, he was acquitted.

By this and other examples, the good effects of the late Act of Parliament against house-breakers, have visibly appeared in the many sessions held since: it hath contributed so much toward suppressing some of the most noted gangs of that kind, that most of the greatest masters in villany have been justly cut off by the evidence of their own companions.

Whilst this wicked wretch lay under condemnation in the condemn'd hold in Newgate, by the application of some neighbours and friends of his father's, who went to Windsor in his behalf, a reprieve was procur'd for him, which he first obtain'd under pretence that he could make great discoveries of unlawful practices, to the great benefit of several of Her Majesty's subjects, who had greatly suffered by thieves; but the time being elaps'd, wherein he was to perform this promise, and no progress made therein, he was call'd down to his former judgment, and accordingly ordered for execution, which he suffered at Tyburn, on Wednesday the 24th of August, 1711, aged twenty four years.

'Tis very proper to observe here, that as soon as word was brought that the cart wherein he rid to the gallows, was coming by his father's door, his poor mother ran distracted, at the sorrowful news of her son's disaster.

THE LIFE OF
DAVY MORGAN

O f all the villains which have been obnoxious to the civiliz'd part of mankind, Davy Morgan was as great as any living in the last or present age. He was born at Brecknock, the chief town in Brecknockshire, in South-Wales, from whence he came up to London in the quality of a servingman to a Welsh knight, when about 18 years of age; but as young as he was, he quickly learnt to rob his master of money and clothes to the value of above 150 pounds, and then ran away from his service.

Being now his own master, the company he kept were none of the best, for they were all the greatest housebreakers, pick pockets, and shoplifters, both in town and country; by whose conversation becoming as wicked as the best of them, he had not long turn'd thief before he broke open the house of a Venetian ambassador in Pall-Mall, and robb'd him of above two hundred pounds worth of plate, for which being shortly after apprehended, he was committed to the Gate-House at Westminster.

The following description, or rather character, of that prison, cannot be disagreeable in this place.

In this gaol, when prisoners are disposed to drink, the industry of man teaches 'em to make a pit in the top of their hats, and to drink in 'em more grease than water. If there be found among them a pot or kettle, it hath been used in the most base offices, serving for a piss-pot, for a flagon, for an oil-pot, or bason. As for napkins the prisoners here take their shirts, or the outside of their breeches; and for a tablecloth the wrong side of an old thread-bare cloak. In their garments they keep a great uniformity, going all of 'em clothed after the manner of penitentiaries in Lent, all black enough, but most sadly rented and torn. So great simplicity is among 'em that they cover their body with one only shirt, whereof many times they have no more than the sleeves, and they never leave it off till it can go alone. If Momus should come into that prison, he could find nothing to reprove them for, because one may see them to the very intrails. Combs, tooth-pickers, wastballs, handkerchiefs, and brushes, are utterly banished from this place. Here they spend most of their time in exercising themselves on divers instruments of musick, having the itch for the mistress of their recreation. This gaol is reckon'd the wicket-door of Hell; and tho' a prisoner should enter there fuller and richer than the Queen of Sheba when she visited King Solomon, yet should he come forth more lank, more dry, and more feeble, than the seven lean kine which Pharaoh saw once in his dreams.

After Davy Morgan had procured his liberty again, he broke one night into the house of Doctor Titus Oats in Ax Yard, in Westminster, and stood centinel over that reverend divine, whilst his comrades rifled most of the rooms; and then tying him neck and heels, after the same manner as they do a soldier, with a couple of muskets which they found in the kitchen, Davy very sorely gagg'd him, saying, 'that if his mouth had been so well cramm'd but a few years ago, he had not swore so many mens lives away for pastime'.

Another time getting into a gaming-house, frequented much by Bully Dawson, and perceiving he had won a great deal of money, he requested the favour of speaking a word or two with in the next room: Dawson taking him to be some chub or cully, went along with him, where shutting the door, Davy pulls out a pistol, which presenting to his breast, quoth he, 'I want money, Sir, upon a very extraordinary occasion, therefore deliver what you have without any resistance, for if you make but the least noise soever, I'll shoot you thro' the heart, tho' I were sure to die on the spot.' Bully Dawson being strangely surpriz'd at these words, and dreading what a desperate man might do in his rage, gave him all his money, which was about eighteen guineas. Then tying him hand and foot, Davy went about his business. By that time the Bully thought this bold robber was gone, calling out for help, several sharping gamesters came out of the gaming-room to him, and untying him, ask'd, 'how that adventure came to pass?' Which Dawson resolving, thro' several vollies of loud oaths, they fell a laughing heartily at him, and cry'd, 'Dawson, 'twas a fair nick.'

At last, Davy Morgan having committed a great robbery in London, in breaking open a Jew's house in Dukes-Place, and taking from thence above two thousand pounds in gold, he fled into Wales; and in Presteen in Radnorshire, did not only rob the church of its Communion plate, but also broke open the house of one Edward Williams, whom he barbarously murdered; but being apprehended at Bristol, and sent to gaol in the county where he committed this most barbarous crime, he was executed at Presteen, in April 1712, aged 43 years, and hanged in chains.

Now this notorious offender being hanged on a gibbet, for an example to others, it happened to be within a mile of a place where a very honest man lived, whose wife had been his strumpet; and she was resolved one evening (in remembrance of what had formerly past between them) to make his corps a visit as he hung on the gallows. To that end going all alone, she came near the gibbet in a very melancholly and lamenting manner; where being come, and beholding the dead corps waving in the air, she stood still, looking stedfastly on it.

It happened at the same time that a country traveller, who was a footman, and whose journey was intended towards that town from whence this woman came, being alone, and darkness overtaking him, he grew doubtful of the way, and fearful of being robb'd, and therefore he retir'd out of the road, and lay close under the gibbet, still listening if any passenger went by to direct him in his way, and secure him by his company. This person was unseen by this night-visitant, who thinking none had been there but the dead corps, accosted it after this manner: 'Ah! poor Davy, how sadly art thou expos'd to all the infelicities of wind and weather? How oft have you and I enjoyed sweet pleasure in each others arms, and then gone from our place of meeting both together? and must I now part with thee here, and so go home without thee?'

At these words the traveller starting up in haste, 'No, by no means,' quoth he, 'I shall be glad of your company': and with that made towards her with what speed he could; but away runs the woman, thinking her old companion had just dropp'd down from the gibbet, and followed her. The man unwiling to be left alone he knew not where, followed her hard, crying out, 'Stay for me, stay for me'; but the faster he called, the faster she ran. Fear added to the haste of both; down they tumbled often, but as soon got up again; still she fled, and still he pursued her: but contrary was the issue of their fears; for she never looked back till she came to her own house; where finding the doors open, and her husband set at supper, she ran in with so much violence, that she tumbled her husband, and his stool down one way, and the table and the meat another way; so that her husband, frighted as well as she, ask'd her what the pox she ailed, and whether she had brought the Devil to her tail. But she was so much frighted, that it was long eer she could make him any answer, or come to her right senses; and then she told him she was sadly fear'd by the Devil's running after her as she came home. But the poor traveller, when he found himself near the town, slackened his pace, and so went quietly to an inn, and there related the whole story. If this fright, and the shame that followed it, made this lewd woman to see the foulness of her sin, and brought her to repentance, perhaps it was the best nights work that she ever made.

204

This Davy Morgan was a great comrade of John Winteringham, who was born at Pomfret in Yorkshire; but for robbing the lodgings of his master, Thomas Wynn, Esq; of a great many valuable goods, and his master's landlord, Mr James Montjoy, of a great quantity of plate, was executed at Tyburn, on Wednesday the 10th of March, 1713–14, aged 25 years.

THE LIVES OF
CHRISTOPHER DICKSON, JOHN GIBSON, AND CHARLES WEYMOUTH

C hristopher Dickson, the first of these malefactors, aged 22 years, was born at White-Chapel, where he served five years apprenticeship with a baker, and then by consent, parted with him. Afterwards he was journeyman to another baker, but staid not long there, before bad company drew him away, and seduced him to follow wicked courses. The chief persons who led him astray, were John Gibson and Charles Weymouth; the first of whom aged twenty years, was born at Newcastle under Line, in Staffordshire, and was a sea faring man; and the other aged twenty five years, born at Redriff, had also been brought up to the sea, and served the Queen on board some of her men of war, for several years off and on.

When these wicked wretches first launched out into the ocean of iniquity, they met a poor old man going to Brentford Market, whom they assaulted on the highway; but finding nothing about him but an old pair of spectacles, Kit Dickson took them away for madness: the old man begging hard for them said, 'Gentlemen, pray be so kind as to return me my spectacles; for they are but little worth to you, and very serviceable to me, as fitting very well my age, which is above threescore years.' But Dickson swearing heartily at him, because he had no money, told him, he would not part with them, till Jack Gibson said to his comrade, 'Prithee, Dickson, give the poor old fellow his spectacles; for if we follow this trade, we may assure ourselves, we shall never reach his years, to make any use of them'; whereupon Dickson returned the old man his spectacles again.

One morning before break of day, these sparks lying perdue for a prey, where was a dead horse flea'd in a field, they threw the carcass cross the road; and a little after a country fellow riding before it was light, a full gallop, and not perceiving the obstacle laid in his way, down fell his horse, and flung him into a ditch. In the mean time, these acute rogues coming to his assistance, they very kindly helped him out of the mire; but for civility-money, they took three pounds odd money of him, and bound him both hand and foot, whilst his horse was run quite away. Some short time after it being broad day, some passengers came by, to whom the country fellow crying out for relief, they went and unbound him; and when he was on his legs again, and saw the flea'd horse lying in the road, quoth he, 'Gads bleed, such rogues as these were never heard of before, for they have stolen the very skin off of the horse I rid on.' Then going home on foot, where he found the horse was got before him, quoth he to his wife and servants, 'Gads bleed, how came Dobbin alive again? I'm sure it can't be him, it must be the Devil in his shape; for my horse was killed and flea'd not above three or four hours ago, by a parcel of rogues that robbed me of all the money I had about me.' And ever after, let his wife and servants say what they would to the contrary, they could never persuade him that it was the same horse he rid out with.

Another time these accomplished villains riding into the country, they there killed an ox, and cuting off three of its feet, about the same length that neats feet are usually sold at market, they put them into their portmanteaus, which were only stuff'd with straw. Then going to an inn in Faringdon in Berkshire, they called for a very plentiful supper, and went up to their chamber, in which was two beds. But before they turned into bed, they cramm'd the straw which they had in their portmanteaus up the chimney, and then filled them again with two good pair of Holland sheets, three pillowbiers, two pair of callico window curtains, one fine blanket, and a very good quilt, and then went to their repose.

In the morning our adventurers lying very late, the chamberlain having the curiosity of going softly up stairs to see whether they were stirring, and peeping thro' the keyhole of the door, against which one of the beds was placed, he perceived three cloven feet, which they had tied to their feet, dangling out at the bed's foot. At this sight running down stairs again very much affrighted, (for his hair stood on end, and the sweat ran down his face in drops as big as pease) quoth he to his master and mistress, 'The three strangers that came hither last night, are three devils; nay, I'm sure they must be devils, for I saw their cloven feet.'

The master not believing this relation without ocular inspection himself, away he crept softly up stairs, and peeping thro' the keyhole too, he no sooner saw the black cloven feet hanging out at the bed's foot, but he ran down stairs faster than he went up, and told his wife, that it was true what the chamberlain said, furthermore adding, 'I am ruined and undone; for if it should be known that so many devils haunt my house, I shall never have a customer come to it again; and how to be rid of those devils I can't tell.'

The inn-keeper's wife being much startled at what her husband said, after some short pause on the matter, quoth she, 'My dear, I would have you go and fetch the parson of the parish hither presently, and see if he can rid the house of these infernal guests, by laying them.' Accordingly the parson was fetched, who positively assured them over a pint of sack, that he would soon send them all to Hell again, their proper place of rendezvous, in spite of their teeth.

The parson now softly creeping up stairs to behold them, he no sooner saw their cloven feet too, but he ran down again in as great precipitation as the inn-keeper and chamberlain had done before him, saying, 'Indeed, neighbours, them guests in that room are certainly all devils; therefore the only advice I can give you is this, that when their devilships are pleased to come down, you must give them very good words, and take not one farthing for what they have had for themselves or for their horses.'

The inn-keeper and his wife promis'd to observe his direction, altho' their reckoning came to above a guinea; and at last the devils coming down into the kitchen, where they called for a good breakfast, they demanded what was to pay? Quoth the host, 'Not one farthing, gentlemen: you are kindly welcome, without paying any thing.' They still insisted upon paying their reckoning; but when they found that their landlord and landlady would not take any money, they took horse and rid strait towards London. Afterwards the chamberlain going to take the linnen off the bed, and finding it ready took to his hands, with divers other things, as above specified, he acquainted his master thereof, who said, 'Why then I'm come off better still; for considering they were thieving devils, 'tis very well they did not take the house away with them; but I hope I shall never be troubled with such guests again.' And indeed he had his desire, for it was their intention not to trouble him any more.

At length the Devil indeed having left these sham devils in the lurch, they were met with at last, and sent to Newgate; and at Justice-Hall in the Old-Bailey, were indicted upon three special indictments, for assaulting and robbing John Edwards, Thomas Blake, and Samuel Slap, on the Queen's highway.

To all these indictments Weymouth pleaded guilty; and the other two putting themselves upon their trial, it was proved, that the several persons robb'd, coming to town to sell cattle, staid to drink at the Anchor and Hope at Stepney, where the prisoners were, with others of their gang; and staying till near ten o'clock at night, as they were coming over the fields, were set upon; and they robbed Edwards of a hat, value four shillings, eleven shillings in money, and a pocket-book; Blake of fourteen shillings in money, a pocket-book, a pair of scissars, and a buckle; and Slap of twenty shillings in money, and a hat. Edwards having a stick in his hand, oppos'd them, and defended himself as long as he could; but they beat him so very barbarously, that he was in danger of his life, and could not appear against them.

William James one of their accomplices, being sworn, depos'd, that he and the prisoners, and Charles Wade, and Henry Thompson, not taken, being at the Anchor and Hope in Stepney, were told by a woman, that there were three men had money; whereupon they went to the sign of the World's End, and stay'd till they came out, and then followed and robbed them: the evidence being so very plain, the jury found them guilty.

When these criminals were under sentence of death, they whistled and play'd at cards, till the very day before they were to die; when reflecting on the past follies of their ill spent lives, they then began to bewail their misfortunes; before this they were so little concerned for the dreadful circumstances in which they lay, that instead of preparing themselves for their latter end, they only sung and damn'd. Weymouth particularly declared, that his coming to an untimely end, was occasion'd by his keeping company with an old bawd in Grays-Inn-Lane, of whom, and all others of that profession, he gave the following character.

They are the refuse and sink of all human society, who having pass'd thro' all the degrees of wickedness with their own bodies, and finding they are incapable of acting any farther wickedness themselves, do (when they are grown old) become the Devil's factors, and tempt others to do that which they are now unable to perform, and thereby do what in them lies to take the Devil's work out of his hands, their whole business being to involve others in the same damnation with themselves. These, wherever they are found, are the very pests and plagues of a nation, and above all other offenders, deserve to be made examples of publick justice.

209

On Wednesday the 10th of March, 1713–14, they were convey'd up Tyburn Road. At the same time suffered death with them, Alexander Petre, for privately stealing a great quantity of copper, of the value of twenty pounds, out of the warehouse of one Mr Thomas Chambers. He readily confess'd that he was guilty of the fact; but said, that one Powel, the evidence against him, was the person that enticed him to the commission of that crime. He was twenty two years of age, born at Newcastle upon Tine, in the county of Northumberland; his calling a sailor, having for twelve years been employ'd on board several of Her Majesty's men of war; and the last of them on board which he serv'd was the *New Advice*, a fourth rate. And also Samuel Denny, alias Appleby, was hanged on the same day, for stealing a gelding from Mr John Scagg, and robbing him of twenty seven shillings in money, on the Queen's highway; he was twenty three years of age, born at Braintree in Essex, and a wheelwright by his trade; but had served four years as a private centinel in the army, which being a soldier was the occasion of his taking to ill courses.

JACK COLLINGS, KIT MOOR, AND DANIEL HUGHES

J ack Collings, alias John Collinson, was born of mean parents at Faustone, near Hull in Yorkshire, and being brought up to no trade, he had been a footman to several gentlemen, both in the country, and here in London; where he was some time a coachman to one Colonel Kendal. This gentleman sending Jack to sell a pair of coach-horses, because they were not well match'd, Jack obey'd his master's orders, and ran away with the money. Afterwards his master taking him, he committed him to the Marshal's in the Savoy, from whence he sent him for a soldier into Flanders, but quickly deserting his colours, he came into England again, where being much addicted to keep company with lewd women, he got sadly pox'd.

Getting himself cur'd, when the apothecary brought in the bill, which came to forty eight shillings and four-pence, Jack swore it was a very unconscionable bill, and if he would not be contented with a groat, he would never pay him a farthing. The apothecary swore and curs'd like a madman, saying, he would never take that, and away he flounc'd out of the room in a great passion: but on the stairs pausing to himself, and considering it was better to take that groat than to lose all, he went up again, saying, 'Come, Sir, since you'll pay me no more, let's see that groat.' So having given Jack a receipt in full of all accounts, when he was going out of the room again, quoth he, 'Let me be D——n'd, Sir, if I have got any more than one poor two-pence halfpenny by you.' Jack thinking the profit large, and it being towards evening, he follow'd the apothecary towards the Halfway House betwixt London and Hampstead, where a good opportunity favouring his design, he commanded Galen to stand and deliver, or else he would shoot him thro' the head. Jack's orders being obey'd, he did not only take his groat from him again, but also robb'd him of a good silver watch, and twenty four shillings.

In this exploit he had like to have been taken, and made his escape so narrowly, that being afraid to go on the foot-pad again, he follow'd house-breaking altogether, in which he was successful for many years; but betwixt while he was a soldier for six years, and attain'd to the office of a serjeant in Colonel Wing's regiment. However, being not satisfied with his station, he still pursued unlawful courses then too, even to the time that he was disbanded; and then keeping company with an ill woman, he car'd not whom he wrong'd to support her; and yet that same strumpet, whom he maintain'd by hazarding his neck, was a witness against him for his life, as it appears in his trial, which is partly thus:

He was indicted for breaking the house of John Halloway, and stealing thence two exchequer notes, value a hundred pounds each, one hundred thirty seven pounds ten shillings in money, and one hundred ninety four pounds in gold. It appear'd by the evidence, that Mr Halloway being at London, the prisoner was at his house at Chelsea, to intreat his favour for a ticket of re-entrance into the Royal Hospital there, and Mrs Halloway permitted him to go up stairs; and the money and bills being in a closet in the room, he found an opportunity to break it open, and carry them off.

The woman he kept company with swore, that going to look for him, she met him in a coach, and upbraiding him for riding so, while she wanted, he gave her money to pay off her lodging, and bid her do it, and come to him again; which she did; and she saw a great bag of money in the coach, which he told her was worth six hundred pounds, and that he had it out of the prosecutor's closet.

They then went to a lodging at Wapping, and he bought her clothes, and himself a coat and wig to disguise him.

Mrs Griffin, their landlady at Wapping, depos'd, that the prisoner and the witness having taken a lodging at her house, she suspected them to be loose people; and that the prisoner having sent her man to borrow the *Gazette*, he look'd upon it, and laid it down, saying, 'there was nothing in it', and so went up stairs; and that causing her man to look over the *Gazette*, she found the prisoner describ'd, and so got a constable and secur'd him.

He had seventy pounds seventeen shillings found upon him when taken, and twenty two guineas and a half, and a broad piece. He own'd to the constable who took him, he had robb'd Mr Halloway, but did not say of so much as was mention'd in the indictment. The fact being plainly prov'd upon him, he was found guilty.

He was also a second time indicted for robbing Mr James Boyce on the Queen's highway, of a silver watch, value three pounds, and ten shillings in money.

Mr Boyce depos'd, that coming out of Bedfordshire in a coach, the prisoner set upon him on this side Kentish-town, about three of the clock in the afternoon; and after he had got his watch and money, ask'd him for his green purse; and he telling him he had none, he made him turn his pockets out, and pull off his gloves, to shew he had no rings.

The prisoner call'd some witnesses to prove he was at another place when that was done, but none appearing, he was found guilty too of that indictment, and hang'd at Tyburn, on Wednesday the 10th of March, 1714, aged 42 years.

On the same day were also executed two other house-breakers, namely, Kit Moor, and Daniel Hughes.

———

Christopher Moor, the first of these, aged 20 years, born in the parish of St Giles's in the Fields, for the most part of his life had been a tapster in some victualling houses in and about London; he confess'd that a little before that, he one night robb'd a house in Grey-Fryers, near Christ's-Hospital, by lifting up a sash window, and entring the parlour; that he took from thence six silver tea-spoons, and a strainer, with a silk handkerchief ell-wide, which he sold for three shillings; and as for the plate, that he sold it with a larger parcel, (amounting to a hundred ounces) for four shillings an ounce. Farthermore he said, that he had wrong'd one Mr Johnson, a working silversmith, by swearing falsly heretofore that he had bought of him, and one Roderick Audrey, another most notorious rogue, some plate that he had stolen out of the Lady Edwin's house. But the fact for which he was condemn'd to die, was for a burglary committed in breaking open the house of one Mr Tho. Wright, in the night, and taking thence a pair of silver branches, and eight tea-spoons, two tea-pots, a lamp, and a large quantity of other plate. He would not discover where it might be found, that the right owner might have it again; for when he was press'd by the ordinary of Newgate to make a discovery thereof if he could, he did not so much alledge his incapacity, as he plainly shew'd his un-willingness of doing it; saying, 'that tho' he could do it, yet he would make no such discovery, if he was sure to be d—n'd for it'.

Daniel Hughes, the other person, aged but sixteen years, born at Gravesend in the county of Kent, was brought up to the sea, and condemn'd for the same fact with Kit Moor; and such was their impudence to the very last, that when they went into the cart, which was to carry them to the place of execution, they were no sooner ty'd to the copses, but they pull'd off their shoes, and flinging them among the spectators, repeated this common speech of such wretches: 'Our parents often said we should die on a fish day, and with our shoes on; but tho' the former part of their prediction is true, yet we will make them all liars in the latter part if it.'

It is to be observ'd, that tho' the ages of these two unfortunate lads together made but 36 years, yet they were as vicious as more noted rogues, taking pride in all manner of lasciviousness, Sabbath-breaking, drunkenness, swearing, cursing, gaming, and all sorts of vices whatever. They had committed between them above 50 burglaries in London, Westminster, and Southwark. In fine, the obstinacy of the two young malefactors in their iniquity, and their impudent behaviour towards all who came to see them, was scarce ever parallel'd; so that it was very requisite justice should lay hold of them, and prevent their doing further mischief.

THE LIFE OF
ELEONOR
SYMPSON

Eleonor Sympson was born of very honest parents, at Henly upon Thames, in Oxfordshire. She laid a bastard, got on her by the clerk of the parish, to her own father, who was a farmer; for which piece of impudence being turned out of doors, she came up to London, and turned common whore. Whilst she continued this wicked course of life, she picked up late one night a linnen-draper, to whom pretending so great modesty and bashfulness, that she was asham'd to go with a man into a tavern or an alehouse, they at last agreed to go into a dark alley.

Here, whilst the cully was feeling what gender she was of, she in the mean time was feeling for his watch, which privately drawing half way out of his fob, quoth she, 'The watch is coming Sir.' He being eager on the game of high gammer cook, cry'd, 'D—n the watch, I don't value the watch of a farthing.' At last, when she had got the watch out of his fob indeed, and transported it into her own pocket, she said again, 'Pray, dear Sir, make haste, for I vow the watch is just here.' He still not apprehending her meaning, reply'd again, 'D—n the watch, I tell you I don't value the watch of a farthing.'

The sport being over, they parted, but he had not gone far, when beginning to have a thought about him, he felt for his watch, and finding it out of its precincts, he made all the haste he could after his mistress, and overtaking her in St Martins-Lane, charged her with a constable, who committed her to the Round-House all night.

Next morning the linnen-draper appeared against her at St Martin's vestry, where charging her upon oath, before the justices, of her robbing him of his watch, quoth one of the old mumpsimusses, 'Well, Mrs Jelliver, what have you to say for yourself now? you see the fact is sworn possitively against you.' Mrs Jelliver, as he called her, dropping a very fine courtesy, and looking as demure as a whore at a christening, said in her defence, 'That going home last night to my lodging, that gentleman there, who is my accuser, did so far prevail with me as to be naught with him in a dark alley, and whilst he was jumbling me up against a wall, Sirs, to pass the time away, I play'd with his watch, which being half way out of his fob, I told him, let him deny it if he can, that the watch was coming, whereupon he reply'd, D—n the watch, he did not value the watch of a farthing; nay, when I had the watch quite out of his fob, and had put it into my own pocket, at the same time pointing to it, and plainly telling him the watch was here, still he was so eager at his work, that he said again, D—n the watch, I tell you I don't value it of a farthing; so thinking it of more consequence than that comes to, I was carrying it home for my own use, but since he requires it again, here it is gentlemen, and I freely return it him again with all my heart.' At this confession, the justices were all ready to split their sides with laughing; and making the complainant give his mistress a guinea for his folly, he had his watch again, and she being discharged, went about her business.

Another time Sympson being pick'd up by a couple of captains in the Coldstream, or second regiment of foot guards, they carried her to Rigby's ordinary, at the Roe Buck in Suffolk Street, where having a good supper, and being also much elevated with wine, they began to act several beastialities upon her; but she made them pay for their frolick in the end; for having drank them to such a pitch, that they both fell into a sound sleep upon the floor, honest Smypson began to dive into their fobs and pockets, whence she took a couple of gold watches, two purses of guineas, some silver, two gold snuff-boxes, two diamond rings off their fingers, broke the silver hilts off their swords, then sh—t—g in both their perukes, which she clapt on their heads again, she went off without saying so much as a word to any body. When they awoke, and found their loss, what vollies of oaths and curses flew about the room, like peals of great ordnance! There was striving betwixt them, who should swear the fastest; but all to no purpose; the whore being gone they knew not whether, they were forced to be contented with their calamity; and what was worse too, to pay a reckoning of four pounds into the bargain.

One time Nell meeting a butcher's son of Clare Market, who was a J— in the same county, he being dispos'd to have a game at tricke-tracke with her, (for you must know, that by his father's trade, he was given to the flesh) she takes him into Pissing-Alley, in Holywell-Street, otherwise called the backside of St Clements in the Strand, so eminently noted for taylors selling there their cabbage. No sooner were they arrived into that dark hole, so fit for fornication and adultery, but as he was lugging out his dagger, to whip her thro' the beard, she at the same time lugged out his silver hilted sword from his side, which he never paid for to this day, and cry'd, 'Pray Sir, don't play the Spaniard upon me, to use both spado and rapier upon me at once; I shall never be able to bear it.' The J— who was a man of no great metal at the best, reply'd, 'My dear, I'll use you gently,' and immediately, (being dead drunk) he fell down on his arse. Hereupon Nell takes up her coats, stops his mouth with her T—y M—y, and pisses down his throat. His W— now fancying himself in a tavern, and taking nell's warm water for mull'd wine, he said, he was very well satisfied, and would pay the reckoning next day to a farthing, and so fell asleep, while Nell carried off his sword, wig, and hat, and left him there wallowing in Sir Reverence, urine, and other nastiness, till somebody that came by carried him to the place of his habitation, laid him upon a butcher's block, and left him to shift for himself.

Now it happening to be about one of the clock on a Saturday morning, the butcher who owned the block was drinking at an adjacent alehouse. Whilst he was there, a calf newly killed, but not drest, was stolen from before his shop; which missing, he fell a swearing and staring like a devil for his loss, and called out to the man that was then putting out the stands and sheds against the market-people came, and ask'd him if he knew any thing of his calf. 'D—n me,' reply'd the fellow, 'can't you see? why it lies upon your block there.' 'By G—,' quoth he, 'so it does; well, Jack, I beg your pardon, for I did not see it till you told me.' So taking out his knife, and whetting it on his steel, quoth he, 'Prithee Jack come hither, and lend me a hand to lift him on one of the hooks, to flay him.'

The butcher was briskly whetting his knife still, and did not mind what his calf was made of, till Jack coming to assist him, finding it was somewhat of a man, said to him, 'Master, this is J— such a one, 'tis no calf; but yet, Sir, as his flesh may be a novelty, I don't know but it may fetch a penny in the pound more than the best mutton in the market, considering he has fed himself a long time upon laced mutton, and will to his dying day, if he can have it gratis; for he never loved to pay for any thing in his life, unless needs must, when the Devil drives.' The butcher seeing his mistake, kicks him off of the block, but was bound over for it next day, and had he not have made up his W—p's loss, by Nell, he had certainly been prosecuted for the robbery.

But a little after this exploit, Sympson finding that her tail brought her not the coming-in she expected, though she was a tolerable handsome woman, and a good tongue pad, she was resolved to try what her hands could do. The first experiment she made this way, was at a certain mercer's in Bedford-Street; whither going in a chair very well dress'd, with a couple of sham footmen attending her, in good liveries, when she came into the shop, she called for several pieces of silk to look on. In the mean time an apple pasty coming in for the family, she seemed on a sudden to be taken very ill, and withdrew from the place where she was, to the farther end of the shop, and sat at the end of a counter, under which was a great deal of rich silks.

Her footman taking the hint of her illness, told the journeyman, there happening then to be none but him, that they believed their lady (who past for the Countess of Colrain) being newly married, longed for some of the apple pasty just then come in, for she was mighty apt to long of late for any thing that was good. The journeyman pitying her condition, presently ran up stairs, and acquainted his master and mistress of the matter. They were mightily concerned at it; but before they came down, she gave her two footmen six whole pieces of silk, who put them into the chair, the chairmen not supposing any otherwise than that the suppos'd lady had bought it.

When the mercer and his wife came down, they invited her up stairs, which kindness, after some seeming reluctancy, she accepted of, eat very heartily of the pye, as she might have done of other varieties which were there, but she refused them. When she had done, she returned them many thanks, invited them to her lodgings in St James's-Square, and for their extraordinary civility, promis'd to lay out five or six hundred pounds with them, before she and her lord went to Ireland.

When she came down stairs, she laid out four or five guineas, and pitched upon other silks, to the value of one hundred and twenty pounds, which ordering to be brought to her house as aforesaid in the evening, (because she was going then to pay a visit to the Dutchess of Somerset at Northumberland House at Charing Cross,) she then took chair, and went off. But within a few hours afterwards, the silks she had stol'n being miss'd, there was a great outcry, the mercer swearing that the longing lady had long'd for more than she could eat; which proved as he said, for going to enquire after her in St James's-Square, there was no finding the Lady Colrain, nor any thing like it.

Another time she went to a linnen-draper's shop in Cornhill, attended with a couple of footmen behind a hired chariot; who knocking at the door with an authority, for it was then about eight or nine at night in winter time, the journeyman opened it, and gave admission to this suppos'd person of quality, and her attendants, whom she pretended to feud to a couple of merchants by the East-India-House. Being shew'd several parcels of the finest muslins, she pitched

upon as much as came to eighty pounds, when pulling out a purse, in which she had not above twenty guineas, and perhaps most of them counters, quoth she, 'Upon my word, Sir, I have less money about me than I thought for, so I cannot pay what I have agreed for; therefore I beg the favour of you to let your young lad, your apprentice here, just step to Mr such a one, my banker, in Lombard-Street, and telling him you are come from the Countess of Colrain, desire him to pay you one hundred pounds upon sight of this note.'

Away goes the apprentice with the note, and in came her two footmen, who presently knocking down the journeyman, stunn'd him to that degree, that they carried off above two hundred pounds worth of muslin into the chariot, and went off with it, before the other could recover himself. After above a quarter of an hour, calling down his master, he told him of the disaster, and wondering the apprentice did not come back in above an hour's time, at last a messenger was sent from the banker, at whose house they found the lad charged with a constable, for bringing a forg'd note. But when the master came in his behalf, and told how the matter was, to his loss of above two hundred pounds, he was discharged.

But not long after this notorious robbery, Sympson was taken in the act of shoplifting at Sturbridge Fair, and was committed to Cambridge gaol, and the assizes following being try'd, she received sentence of death; whereupon she pleaded her belly, and a jury of matrons being impannell'd, as is usual on such occasions, she was brought in quick with child; and was really so; for she was brought to bed of a girl before the assizes following; when being called down to her former judgment, she was hanged at Cambridge, upon Saturday the 19th of July 1714, aged twenty eight years.

THE LIFE OF
RHODERICK
AUDREY

To give an exact character of this malefactor, would require a very curious pen; for he was so dextrous in thieving, that he seemed to be begotten by some thief, and so he came an acute villain into the world. He could scarce speak plain when he began to practice the taking of what was none of his own; and so improved himself in the art and mystery of thieving, that he was hanged a little after he was turned his teens.

'Tis true he had two elder brothers, who envied his acuteness in villany, and as they had the priority of birth, so they thought it their birth-right to exceed the youngest, in what brought them to the gallows. One of these made himself an evidence against his own brother, to save himself from swinging. We must own they left nothing unattempted to claim a superiority over Rhoderick, in the faculty of thieving, as robbing friend or foe; but the greatest of their exploits was only for pots, or tubs of butter, pieces, not flitches of bacon, wet linnen, and old cloaths, whereas the other scorned to meddle with not any thing unless plate or money.

When the young one, who is the subject of this discourse, began first to launch abroad in the world, he was (tho' his friends could bestow neither writing nor reading upon him) so ripe-witted in roguery, that none of his years could match him; he had not seen nine when he was a great proficient in iniquity; and was so successful in his designs, that with the decoy of a sparrow, he got above two hundred pounds in less then a twelvemonth. His way was as follows.

He'd go to Chelsea, or Hampstead, or Bow, or Lambeth, East, West, North, or South, for he was never out of his road, and carrying a sparrow along with him, would be playing about a house, where he saw a side-board of plate in the parlour, or any other good moveable, learning, the bird to climb the ladder, or fly to hat. If the sashes were open, or the street-door, he would throw in his sparrow; then following it to catch it again, he stole away the plate, and left the sparrow to answer for his master's conduct. But if he was seen by any body in the house before he had finished his work, it was a very plausible pretence that his design was no other than running after his bird, as honest children will do in such cases; and he being also in a state of infancy in a manner, the people that so caught him, did no otherwise than let him go about his business; nay sometimes were so kind, as to help him to catch it: as it was impossible at such times for him to carry away the whole plate-fleet at once, nevertheless he commonly oblig'd those that helped him with the taking away a silver spoon, a fork, or some such little thing.

In this manner he was successful for some time, having bit a great many in Kensington-Square, as well as at Fulham, Highgate, Islington, Hackney, and other country villages about London; till he was so well known at catching sparrows, that they would as often catch him, and send him to fly his sparrows in Bridewell. Here he had been so often used to punny and block, that it hardened him in audaciousness; for when he was from working on hemp, that precious commodity by which he died, he still went on daily in his pernicious courses. He would do nothing in a morning; saying, there was nothing to be got then but a few tea spoons, and china ware: nor would he often go abroad by night, because then parlour-shutters being clapp'd up, prevented his seeing what house could furnish him with a parcel of plate to his mind. His hunting about for a prey was always about dinner-time; not but that he would go out morning and evening, if a blow was set him; that is to say, if any of his society gave him intelligence, that then there was an opportunity of taking a quantity of wedge, which in the thieves language is silver.

Whenever his money was gone he still went upon fresh exploits, till all the country towns and villages within ten miles about London, were sensible, that the boy who play'd with the sparrow was a thief. Yet tho' he was often sent to New Prison, and the Gatehouse at Westminster, the justices took so much pity on his tender years, as not to commit him to Newgate, for fear of his being spoilt, tho' he was already spoilt to their hands. This favour still encouraged Rhoderick in his villany, till at last he was committed to Newgate, whither he went twenty times afterwards, and being try'd upon a matter of petit-larceny, for which the jury found him guilty of ten-pence, he flung from the bar a shilling to the judge, desiring his Lordship to give him two-pence for his change; which piece of impudence caused him to be so well flaug'd, that he never valued whipping at the cart's arse ever after.

Playing his pranks on t'other side the water in Surrey, he, with one Jacob Letherton, who was also hanged, was committed to the Marshalsea Prison in Southwark, from whence by a writ of habeas corpus, being removed upon a sham robbery charged against them on this side the water, and no person appearing against them, they had the good luck to procure their enlargement: for these younkers were not so extravagant, but they deposited a little cash against a rainy day, in the hands of an old tutor of thieves, keeping a publick house not far from White Chapel church, or else they had been sent out of the land of the living some years before they did make their last exit at Tyburn.

To hard drinking he was not much addicted; but for gaming and whoring he was a little devil; 'tis said he had (as little, and as young as he was) a wife too, who nick-nam'd him Man Tod. Her own name, before she wedded with him, was Kate Smith, the daughter of a hawker, born in St Giles's parish, where she got a great deal of money, by pretending to be a sempstress. Under this cover going with an empty band-box in her hands early in a morning to any gentleman's house, and knocking at the door, she would impudently ask the servant that open'd it, whether the lady is stirring, for she had brought such a parcel of lace or muslin, as her ladyship had bespoke of her over night. The servant perhaps innocently brings her into the parlour to tarry, till he or she goes up to acquaint the lady of the sham sempstress waiting below; who before she receives an answer from above, rifles parlour and closets of what she can find fit for her turn, and marches off. But this manner of thieving has been described before.

But to return again to Kate's pretended husband Audrey. As he was one day about dinner-time, walking with another thro' Soho-Square, espying a great parcel of plate in a remote room of a person of quality's house, his mouth so watered at the glittering sight, that he could not pass by it with a safe conscience; and holding a council with his comrade about it, he thought it impracticable to attempt the taking of it. However, young Audrey would not acquiesce to his opinion; have it he would: so desiring his faint hearted comrade, who wore a green apron, to lend it him, he presently steps to an oil shop, buys two or three balls of whiting, returns to the house he was resolved to attack, and getting upon the rails, falls to cleaning the windows with the whiting, and a foul hankerchief, with as good an assurance as if he had been the butler, or some other servant belonging to the family. He was mighty handy about his work, lifting the sashes up and down, and going in and out to clean them, without any suspicion of people going by, who could have no mistrust of his not dwelling there; till at last he cleaned the side-board of all the plate, which he brought away in his apron, to the value of eighty pounds.

Another time young Audrey going thro' Golden Square, in company with the aforesaid companion, and seeing a great many silver forks and spoons, with other pieces of plate, lying on the dresser under a kitchen window, he and his comrade fell a playing at pitch and hussel just against it; and at last letting a halfpenny rowl down the window, Audrey was climbing over the rails to go down after it, at which the cook-maid scolded and told him he should not come down, nor have what was fell down; and he on the other side, begged and pray'd for it, and still made the best of his way downwards, till the fiery cook-maid fell into such a passion, that she run up stairs in a great fury to beat him. In the mean time Audrey's comrade put a stick he had in his hand through the knocker of the door, so that with all her pulling, and locking and unlocking, as thinking some fault was in the lock, she could not open it.

Whilst she was in this fatigue, Audrey was not idle, for he got the plate out of the kitchen window, saying, when he came out, 'you B B B Bitch,' (for he much stuttered) 'I have got it and no thanks to you'; which made her reply (though she knew not what he had got) in a prophetical manner, 'Ay, you young impudent Rogue, I'll warrant you I shall see you hanged.' But whether she did or not, I can't tell: however, if she did not, a great many hundreds did for her; and must needs say, that he went very decently to the gallows; being in a white waistcoat, clean napkin, white gloves, and having an orange in one hand, but no book in the other; though a great many who could read no more than he, when they went to be hanged would have a book, to seem either learned or devout.

He would often upbraid his two brothers with the meanness of their spirits, in stealing such trifling matters, which were not worth taking the pains of carrying away; telling them, they were only fit to rob orchards, roosts, and sties, of their fruit, pullen, and pigs, at which they were pretty expert; especially his brother John; who being a tapster some small time at Highgate, one day an ancient widow in the town, that had newly had a sow pigg'd, in a field not far from the cottage where she dwelt, Jack Audrey happening to come by with some puppies in his lap, which he was sent to drown, spy'd the sow and her young ones in the ditch, to which he repaired, and for his three puppies which he left, takes as many of the pigs away with him to a private place in Cane Wood, where Jack, as often as he could in a day, constantly resorted, and fed them with milk, which he had learned to milk from the cows that were feeding there by, into his hat, till he had brought them up to some three weeks growth, still cutting their hoofs to the very quick, so that they could not run thence. Being not found out, no more talk was had in Highgate, and thereabouts, than of the strange and prodigious birth of this sow, every one thinking that she had littered one half pigs, and the other puppies, which was universally look'd on as very ominous of some ensuing disaster; nor was the same unriddled, till Jack having one day liberty given him to go to London, was catched driving them up to town.

But as young Rhoderick, for roguery, carried the bell from either of his brothers Jack or Will, we shall still trace his life. After the facts above related, stealing a box, and plate, and money, out of a house in Red-Lyon-Square, he was taken in the fact, and committed to Newgate; and when brought on his trial for the same, was burnt in the hand, and ordered to hard labour for two years, in Bridewell in Clerkenwell. Here he had not been above six months of his time, before Richard Keele, William Lowther, and Charles Houghton, were also committed for two years, and being shew'd by young Audrey where the keeper's arms were, the three abovesaid persons attempted to break into the room where they lay, but were prevented in their design. Nevertheless they made a riot, in which Charles Houghton was killed on the spot, Keele lost one of his eyes, and Lowther was desperately wounded in the back. On the keeper's side, one Perry, his turnkey, and sutler to the prison, was stabb'd thro' the heart with a penknife. Whilst this engagement lasted, of which we have before given some account, young Audrey broke into the deceased turnkey's chamber, from whence he stole twenty pounds, and then found a way to break out of Bridewell; making way also for eighteen or twenty more, who followed their leader; but were as soon retaken, excepting him, who shulk'd about four or five months before he was apprehended, and that upon acting a fresh piece of villany.

Being now committed to Newgate for his last time, his thoughts were employ'd how to break out there too; using some few stratagems, but he was unsuccessful in all his attempts. Here his chief diversion was eating instead of fasting, drinking instead of sober living, gaming instead of saving what he had, whoring instead of preserving his health, swearing instead of praying, and damning himself instead of making a due preparation for his latter end.

When he came before the bench again, they knew him very well by his impudence, of which he had a good stock; and being found guilty of stealing, after his late breaking out of Bridewell, a great quantity of plate, sentence of death was past on him.

Whilst he was in the condemn'd hold, he was no changling; for thinking little of being hang'd, he was very rude, hindering other prisoners that were under the same unhappy circumstances, and would have employed the short time appointed for them to live, to the best advantage, by performing the laudable exercises of devotion. But yet he had so much grace in him, as to own the sentence past upon him was just, and confess'd above a hundred robberies in particular that he had committed; besides acknowledging his commission of as many more, which he could not call to mind where. What he stole was (as abovesaid) plate and money, to the value of two thousand pounds at times; but so profuse had he been with it, that he had scarce money to buy him a coffin.

At last the fatal day was come, in the year 1714 when he was to go from hence, and be no more seen; then being convey'd in a cart, unpitied by all honest people, to Tyburn, he seem'd very loth to die; but no reprieve coming, which he expected to the last, in consideration of his youth, he departed to the tune of a penitential psalm, being no more than 16 years of age.

THE LIFE OF
WILL CHANCE

William Chance was born of mean parents, near Colchester in Essex, by whom he had not the least learning at all bestow'd upon him, tho' he was from his very infancy a child that shew'd a promising genius.

When he came to be about sixteen years of age, he was put out apprentice by the parish to a weaver, where he was so unlucky, that at three years end his master gave him his indentures, and sent him packing; when to support himself, he took to thieving.

He was so good a proficient in the art of taking what was not his own, that a gentleman who took a great fancy to his archness, often invited him to dine with him at his table; and one day above the rest, after dinner, said, 'Will, if thou wilt this night steal the bed I lie upon out of my chamber, I'll give thee five guineas, on the word of a gentleman.' Will accepted the proposal, and left the gentleman without giving him time to reply.

A doctor of physick died some days before at Colchester, and was buried there in St Mary's church-yard; Will goes in the dead of night, takes the dead body by the heels, and throwing it upon his back, walked gently on towards the gentleman's house unobserved, and mounting a ladder, which he purposely contrived to stand at one corner, very fairly began to untile that part of the house over the chamber where the gentleman lay. Scarce was a hole made in the roof of the house, when Will let fall the doctor thro'.

The noise surpriz'd the gentleman to be sure, and hearing no one stir, he rises out of his bed, and by the help of a candle, that was burning in the chimney, plainly discover'd, as he thought, the body of Will on the floor, who he imagin'd had broken his neck by the fall. This gave him no small uneasiness, and made him lament his curiosity; then calling to one of his men, in whom he could safely confide, quoth he, 'See here, Tom, what a strange thing has happen'd, Will. Chance, whom I have so often entertain'd, has attempted to break into my house to rob me, but in the attempt has broke his neck. I have that pity for his misfortune, that to hide his death from the world, you and I, Tom, will take the pains privately to bury him; the church-yard is near at hand, and before break of day we can dig a shallow grave and throw him into it.'

The man, in compliance to his master's pleasure, consented; so wrapping the body up in an old blanket, away they trudged to the church-yard, where finding a grave ready made to their hands, they flung their load into (tho' unknown to them) its proper place. In the mean time Will. Chance got into the house, and carried off his bed; which when they return'd, put them into a worse fright than before, as supposing Will's ghost had, in their absence, play'd the thief, to be reveng'd for the sudden loss of its earthly tabernacle. But their admiration was more rais'd the next day, when he came *in propria persona*, to demand the five guineas, according to promise. At first the gentleman would not believe his own eyes, 'till feeling it was flesh and blood, and being acquainted with his whole stratagem, he accordingly paid him five guineas.

Shortly after this adventure, surprising Sir Jonathan Thornicroft, Bart. he unawares knock'd him off his horse, and rifled him of a diamond ring worth 120 pounds, a gold watch worth 50 pounds, and 290 guineas. A great noise of this robbery being made all over the country, with the promise of a reward of 100 pounds for any that could discover this bold robber, Will fled to a rich uncle's at Thetford to lie there incognito, till this hubbub was all over. His uncle was a grazier, who caress'd and receiv'd him with all the tokens of respect that could possibly be shown a near relation. While he was here he bargain'd with his uncle for 20 oxen, signing an obligation for the money, which he promis'd to pay within a month or two; then taking leave of his uncle, he hired one to drive the oxen to Norwich. After two or three months were expired, the old gentleman not hearing from him, turns to his writings, where he found the nest, but the birds flown; for Will had temper'd the ink with saltpetre, and other corrosive ingredients, which eat thro' the paper. This startled the old man so that he suddenly took pen in hand, and writ a very severe letter to his kinsman, threatening him with a course of law.

He pretended to be greatly concern'd at the matter, the better to maintain his uncle's esteem, cries out whore first, and summon'd his uncle to appear at the assizes at Norwich; having in the mean time suborn'd a false witness or two, to give evidence to a forg'd paper, wherein his uncle was found to confess himself indebted to his father, in the sum of 600 pounds, payable, in case of his decease, to this his unlucky son. The usual hand and mark of the uncle was artificially counterfeited, with a different ink from the body of the obligation, both temper'd with soot, to make them seem of such standing as the date would require. Besides this, he had also forg'd a certain discharge, the tenor whereof was, that he had receiv'd 20 oxen for 200 pounds of the said six hundred.

This acquittance was cunningly seal'd up, and sent to a countryman near Colchester, whom he had also hir'd to be an assistant; and he deliver'd it to the uncle, in the presence of the court. Will, so soon as he saw him begin to open it, pray'd the court to examine his papers, which they did, and the discharge made so much for him, that judgment was pass'd in his favour, and the defendant constrain'd not only to renounce his pretence, but also condemn'd to pay the remainder of the sum that was mention'd in the obligation, which was four hundred pounds.

At last having exhausted all his ill-got money upon drinking, gaming, and whoring, he betakes himself to house-breaking, for which he had been twice committed to Newgate, and try'd at the Old-Bailey, but had the good luck to escape hanging, because the witnesses were defective in their evidence. This success in his roguery did so harden him, that there was scarce a gaol throughout London but what he was more than once a tenant in. He was once condemn'd at Hertford assizes for the foot-pad, but his time not being yet come he was repriev'd, and after an imprisonment of two years and a half, he pleaded his pardon granted by Queen Anne, and obtained his liberty once more. But not making good use of his freedom, and the royal mercy he received, he pursued his old courses, and went upon the foot-pad, till he and another being apprehended for robbing a gentleman near Paddington, of a silver hilted sword, and forty two shillings in money, they were committed to Newgate, where his comrade making himself an evidence, to secure his own neck, Will was convicted and received sentence of death.

Whilst he was in the condemned hold, he was at first very profligate, swearing, cursing, drinking, singing, and dancing, to the great hindrance of the other condemned malefactors from their devotion: but when the dead warrant was brought to the Lodge of Newgate, his countenance changed at the fatal news, and he began to employ the little time he was to live in serious meditations of his approaching end, which was on Wednesday, the 21st of April, 1715, when he was hanged at Tyburn aged thirty five years.

THE LIFE OF

JAMES

FILEWOOD

This fellow was often called Vilet, tho' Filewood was his right name. He was born of honest parents, in the parish of St Peters Cornhill. His father was a poulterer; which occupation he, and two or three other brothers, pretended originally to follow; but finding that the fiddling work of scalding, picking, and gutting cocks and hens, and other poultry, was not so beneficial as picking pockets, they took up that employment, as knowing there was their ready money as soon as they had done their work.

When this fellow suffered death, 'twas thought there were some of his brothers who deserved it more, one of them having been formerly condemn'd, gave proof that the mercy was ill bestowed, for he lived to do a great deal of mischief; and another of them had been at Old Bridewell by Fleet-Ditch, where he was two years at hard labour; which going hard against the grain, he and some others mutiny'd, with a design to break out; but the keepers and Bluecoat Boys soon quelled them. And in this rash attempt, one Isaac Rag, a prisoner then with him, and who was afterwards an evidence against White, and another person hanged with him, for the horrid murder of Mrs Knap in Jockey-Fields, had one of his eyes shot out.

But to return to James Filewood. As soon as he had lifted himself under the banners of wickedness, he first went a 'clouting', that is, picking handkerchiefs out of pockets: in which having pretty well improved himself, after often being duck'd in a horse-pond, or pumped, he next ventured to pick pockets and fobs of money and watches. To which purpose, he always gave his constant attendance at the King's going to the Parliament-House, the Lord-Mayor's Show, the artillery men making a mock fight, entries of ambassadors, Bartholomew and Southwark Fairs, Drury-Lane and Lincolns-Inn play-houses, or any other place where a great concourse of people is drawn together upon any occasions; and to be sure he never miss'd going on Sundays to church, tho' it was more to serve the Devil, than that omnipotent majesty, to whose honour and glory the house of prayer is erected; and here he would, as well as pick pockets, change an old hat or two for a new one.

In the late Queen's reign, Vilet being try'd at the assizes at Oxford, for a matter in which he was allowed the benefit of clergy, being put to read his neck verse, a student standing at the bar, took so much compassion as to instruct him. The words were 'Lord have mercy upon us': so he held the book, and the scholar bid him say after him: 'O Lord,' says the scholar; 'O Lord,' says Vilet; and his thumb being upon the other part of it, the scholar said, 'Take away thy thumb'; says Vilet then, 'O Lord, take away thy thumb'. Quoth the judge, '*Legit, aut non legit, ut clericus?*' And he that was appointed to answer, being pleas'd to favour the criminal, reply'd. '*Legit ut clericus*'; by which means he saved his neck this time.

One day this Vilet meeting with another of his own profession, named Clark, 'Come Clark,' quoth he, 'since we have so happily stumbled upon one another, let us take a pint together.' 'A match,' says the other; so they went into a tavern in Holborn. But drinking about for a while, when they came to examine their pockets, they found themselves deceived, one thinking the one had, and the other thinking the other had, money enough to defray the reckoning, when indeed both of them could make not above a groat. 'Hang it then,' (said the inviter) 'we had as good be in for a great deal as a little.' So they called lustily till it came to five or six shillings, then looking out at the window, as if they had been viewing the descent, says one to the other, 'I have it now.' Upon that, knocking, and desiring to speak with the master, up he came. 'Sir,' says Vilet, 'we came hither about a mathematical business, to measure from your window to the ground: I have laid upon 13 foot my friend on 13 foot 9 inches, and you are to be judge that I slip not this line' (which was packthread upon a piece of brass, which joyners and carpenters use in mensuration) 'till he goes down, to see whether from this knot,' (shewing it him) 'which is just so much, it reaches to the ground.' The vintner was content. The other sharper being below in the street, cry'd, 'It did not reach by eleven inches.' 'Pray, Sir,' said Vilet to the vintner, 'hold it here till I step down and see; for I won't believe him.' So down he went, telling the drawer he'd paid his master, and away they both scoured, leaving the string for the reckoning.

Once Jemmy Vilet having stolen an alarum watch, stifly denied it before the Justice, so that upon the slender evidence he was discharged; but before he got out of his Worship's presence, the alarum went, and he was ordered to be brought back again, and searched; at which he cry'd out, 'What devilish luck have I, that I should so easily baffle both Justice and constable, and yet am trapanned by the watch!' But for all his jesting, the Justice was in such good earnest now, that he committed him to Newgate, and had he not so far made it up with the prosecutor to throw in a Bill of Ignoramus at sessions, he might have perhaps been hanged then.

Once Vilet having been at some country fairs, he got a pretty deal of money; but falling into play with a shoemaker at Lincoln, it was his misfortune to lose it, cloaths and all. Crispin gave him his old cloaths, and his leather apron, and when he departed from Lincoln, was so civil, as to put twenty shillings into his pockets to bear his charges. With this he sets out to travel, and coming to a lone inn betwixt Grantham and Stamford, he puts in there, and spending four or five shillings, the people provided him a good lodging, and Jemmy went to bed betimes. It so fell out, that they had several guests came to the inn, which took up all their lodgings, so that a parson coming in very late, they had no room for him. The parson rather than go farther, chose to accept of a bedfellow; but there was none cared to be disturbed at that time of night but Vilet whom they took for a shoemaker, and who was well enough pleased with the honour of having such a bedfellow.

Matters being thus accomodated, and the parson a-bed, he soon fell asleep, and slept very heartily, being tired with the fatigue of his days journey; but Vilet having slept well before, had no mind to sleep any more that night, but lay awake meditating mischief; and seeing the parson had a great deal of money in his pockets, which he pulled out to pay for a pot of beer which he called for to make his bedfellow drink, he was contriving how to change breeches with him, well knowing his own pockets were but thin lin'd with that precious metal. After having resolved what he would do, he gets up at the dawning of the day, and puts on not only the parson's breeches, but also all his sacerdotal garments, finding they fitted him very well; and being rigg'd in those sacred habiliments, down stairs he goes very softly, and calls the hostler, bidding him bring his boots, and make ready his horse.

Now the hostler, not in the least mistrusting, but that Vilet being in that dress, was really the parson, brought him his boots, and ask'd him what corn he must have? He told him half a peck of oats, which was accordingly given him; and Vilet was very uneasy till the horse had eat them; but in the mean time, that he might be the sooner ready to go, he called to pay; and was answered he had paid all last night but for his horse. The horse having eat up his corn he was very much in haste to be gone; but the hostler asking what it was a clock by his watch, which he saw the parson pull out the night before, it put Vilet to a little stand, not having so far examin'd his pockets as to know whether he had or no, and therefore being loath to make a vain essay, he answered that his watch was down, and so got upon his horse, and giving the hostler a shilling, rid away as fast as he could; and it being summer weather, he had a long day before him. After he had rid a considerable way, he examines his pockets, and finds in them six guineas, four pounds odd money in silver, and a very good watch; and having found himself so well provided, he rid away the more merrily, resolving to live well as long as that lasted.

But let us return to the true parson, whom he left fast asleep in his bed, about seven in the morning, it being in June, the parson awakes, and going to bid his bedfellow good morrow, he soon found not only that the bird was flown, but also that he had flown away with his feathers; for he saw nothing there but some old cloaths, which he suppos'd belonged to his bedfellow; whereupon he calls for somebody to come up; but the servants, who supposed it to be only the shoemaker, ask'd him, what a pox ail'd him to make such a noise, and bid him be quiet, or else they'd make him quiet. This vex'd the parson, and made him knock the harder; till the chamberlain came up, and threatened to thrash his sides, if so be he would not be quiet.

The minister wondring at this rude treatment, ask'd, 'where was his cloaths?' The chamberlain still taking him for St Hugh, reply'd, 'Where the plague should

233

they be but upon the chair, where you left them? Who the Devil do ye think would meddle with your cloaths? They an't so much worth I'm sure, you need not fear any body's stealing them.' 'The man's mad, I think,' replies the parson: 'Do ye know who ye speak to?' 'Speak to,' says the fellow; 'Yes, sure, I think I do.' 'If you did, you'd use better words,' says the parson. 'Better words,' says the man; 'my words are good enough for a drunken shoemaker.' 'Shoemaker!' says the parson; 'I am no shoemaker, I am the minister that came in here last night.' 'The Devil you are,' replies the chamberlain, 'I am sure the minister went away soon after three a clock this morning.' With that the minister gets out of bed in his shirt, and taking hold of the chamberlain, 'Sirrah,' says he, 'bring me my cloaths, and my money, and my watch, or I'll break your neck down stairs.' With this noise and scuffle comes up the master of the inn, and some other of the servants; who presently knew that was none of him whom they took for a shoemaker; and upon a little enquiry into the matter, found that St Hugh had made an exchange with the parson. Whereupon the master of the inn furnished him with a suit of his own, and money to bear his charges, till they could hear what became of the thief.

234

He was at length taken in picking a pocket, and tho' the value he took from the person did not come to ten shillings, yet he was convicted thereof; and likewise upon another indictment preferred against him by Mrs Frances Baldock, for snatching from her a pocket valued at one shilling, and in which were twelve guineas and two pistoles. For these facts he received sentence of death at Justice-Hall in the Old-Bailey; but no report being immediately given in to the King of the malefactors condemned the sessions he was try'd, he remained in the condemned hold till another sessions; when the dead warrant being signed for eight criminals, he was one among them appointed for death; and accordingly on the 31st of October, 1718, he took shipping at Newgate, sailed with a fair wind up Holborn river, and striking against the rock of St Giles's, was cast away at Tyburn, in the 27th year of his age.

Tho' many are the examples made in a year of such wicked wretches, yet hanging being an easy death, or as the thieves themselves call it' 'half an hours pastime', they no more dread the gallows, than they do the perpetrating a murder to screen their villany from the knowledge of justice. 'Tis true, we have that merciful compassion in Great-Britain, towards offending persons, as not to

put them to any exquisite torment; but if thieves were to be all severely puni-
shed in this nation, I believe the terror and fear thereof, would make fewer than
there now are. I do not presume to direct the Parliament what laws they shall
enact for the punishment of thieves of any kind; but in my opinion, if those
offenders were to be sent, during life, to dig in the lead mines in Cornwall, or
the coal-pits at Newcastle, that perpetual labour they would count worse than
hanging.

235

THE LIVES OF
WILLIAM WARD, SAMUEL LYNN, RALPH EMMERY, ROBERT VICKERS, JOHN PRIOR, AND FRANCIS PARQUET

As all these malefactors were executed at the same time, and as we have not many particulars to relate of any one of them, we thought it best to put them all into one chapter.

William Ward was born at Drydocking in the county of Norfolk. When he was but three years old, his parents removed from thence to the city of Norwich. His father who was a mill-wright by trade, made him, when capable, to work with him in that occupation: afterwards he came up to London, where he married a very honest woman, and at Bow, and other places thereabouts, followed the business he was brought up to; but unhappily falling into ill company, he was too easily seduced to follow their bad examples. The first fact he committed, was the taking off from a hackney-coach standing at the Four Swans-Inn door within Bishops-Gate, a portmanteau corded under the coach-man's seat, in which there was a gold watch and chain, cloaths, and several other things of value, which were sold together for fourteen guineas, and shared between him and two others concerned with him in that fact: however, the right owner had them again for twenty one guineas.

Another time Will Ward riding thro' Holborn in a hackney-coach, and espying a porter with a great trunk on his back, bids the coachman stop, and call the porter to him; accordingly the man of carriage comes, to whom giving a shilling to step just by of an errand, he bade him lay his load into the coach, of which he would take care. No sooner was the porter gone, but Ward calls to the coachman again, who was feeding his horses, and bids him drive to such a place, where the porter (he said) was to meet him. He is driven to an alehouse in Lutener's-Lane, which harbours all sorts of villains; where opening the trunk to find what prize he had got, he found therein about eighty pounds in money, besides a great quantity of rich cloaths, both woollen and linnen; in the mean time the porter was making a great outcry all thro' Holborn for his loss, but all to no purpose, for the owner of the trunk sued his sureties, which all ticket-porters give, and they again su'd the porter, who was put in gaol for his folly.

Not long after, Ward committed another robbery at the Four Swans-Inn in Bishopsgate-Street, taking from another hackney coach a portmanteau trunk, but being presently stopped and seized with it, was carried to the Poultry Compter, from whence he was committed to Newgate, so that he had no opportunity to know what was in it. At the sessions held at the Old-Bailey in October 1718, he was try'd for it, and found guilty of his last fact; which proving but a single felony, he was thereupon only ordered for transportation; but whilst he lay under confinement he was convicted upon two other indictments. First for breaking open the house of Thomas Lane, and stealing ten pounds weight of tea, on the 12th of April 1717; and secondly, for a burglary committed by him and Samuel Lynn hereafter mentioned in the house of Mr Julian Bailey, in the parish of St Giles's Cripplegate, from whence they took divers pieces of plate to the value of forty pounds, on the 24th of July, 1717, and on Monday the 16th of February 1718–19, he was executed, being twenty two years of age, at Tyburn, where he confess'd that about a twelve-month before then, he and Sam Lynn took from off a coach standing at the Spread Eagle Inn in Gracechurch-Street a portmanteau with goods in it, belonging to Dr Tilburg; and had also been concerned together in several other facts, but could not particularly recollect themselves about them.

Samuel Lynn was born at Brampton in Norfolk, and for some time lived at a neighbouring town called Sherington. When he was young, his father (a grocer and tallow-chandler) removed to the city of Norwich, where he was bound apprentice to him, and afterwards wrought journey-work there, and then came up to London, where falling into ill company, he soon took to picking of pockets, for which he was brought to justice; particularly for picking the pocket of the Lady Dorcas Roberts, from whom he took a green silk purse with three guineas, and sixteen shillings in it, on the 16th of March, 1713–14, and a little after was try'd and received sentence of death for the same, but afterwards received the King's gracious Pardon, and pleaded it at the Old Bailey on the 16th of August 1715, the conditions of that pardon (which he did not observe) being, that he should transport himself within six months out of His Majesty's dominions in Europe; but wanting grace to improve this mercy, he not only fell in again among his wicked acquaintance, but returned to his former trade of thieving, till he was condemned for the same fact as Ward abovementioned, and at the same time hanged at Tyburn; aged 19 years.

Ralph Emmery, was executed at the same time, for a murder and robbery committed by him on the body of Nathaniel Asser, on the 28th of June, 1718. He was born in Old Street, in the parish of St Giles's Cripplegate. He was a parish-boy, and bound for nine years to a cane-chair maker, whom he served faithfully all that time, which when expired he followed that business for himself, going about the streets to get mending work of that sort, whereby he got a livelyhood. The murder he stood condemned for, was committed in Stepney Fields, in company with William Audley, and Sarah Brown, executed some time before. Emmery took out of the deceased's pocket a pocket-book, and some coffee; however, he deny'd the bloody fact, saying, that he never was guilty of any murder, but could not justify himself in other matters, for he had lived a long time in fornication and adultery, had been a prophane swearer, a vile drunkard, and all along neglected the service of God; that he had abandoned himself to a sinful course of life, and for six years past made it his common practice to pick pockets, that for these and the like wicked facts he was committed once to the gaol in White-Chapel, and six times to Newgate; that he had took several trials, been thrice whipt, and sent twice to Bridewell, but none of those corrections working any reformation in him, he still pursued his wicked course of life.

The abovesaid Ralph Emmery had likewise been upon the foot-pad, and with two others meeting just upon the close of the evening with a non-juring parson just beyond the Halfway House to Hampstead, one of them justled the honest doctor, which the other two perceiving, they seem'd to take the doctor's part, saying, 'go along with us, Sir, for that's some rogue without doubt'. So these two rogues went scolding along with the single rogue, getting the doctor betwixt 'em to protect him from robbing, till coming to a ditch Emmery pushes the doctor into it, takes his hat off his head, and runs away with it. 'Look you there now,' said the other two, 'did we not tell you before that he was a rogue; we hope you'll be pleased to bestow something on us for conducting you hither.' The doctor did not at all like his guardians, and indeed he had no reason, for taking his peruke, coat, and sword, from him, they search'd his breeches, in which finding about eight shillings, they then left him to get out of the ditch.

239

John Prior was born at Caisoo in Bedfordshire; of such poor parents, that they could not bestow any education upon him, insomuch that he could neither write nor read; for a livelihood he follow'd husbandry in the country, but leaving both husbandry and country, he came up to London about the beginning of the year 1716, and listed himself in the second regiment of foot-guards, soon after which giving way to a lewd life, he committed several most notorious robberies on the foot-pad, at many country places about the cities of London and Westminster.

He was at last condemn'd for the following robberies on the highway, with Robert Vickers and Francis Parquot: first, for assaulting and robbing William Spinnage, Gent. and taking from him a purse with fourteen guineas, and a half guinea, a watch, value eight pounds, and other things, as he was riding in a hackney coach in Farringdon Lane, near Hornsey, on the eighteenth of August

1718. Next for a like Assault and Robbery by them jointly committed on the person of George Floyer Esq; on horseback, near Tottenham Court, in the parish of St. Pancras, from whom they took a pair of pistols, value forty shillings, and a gelding, value thirty pounds, on the eighteenth of September following. And lastly, for such another Assault and Robbery, which the said Prior and Vickers committed on Mr William Squire, who was by them roughly handled, and threaten'd to be kill'd (besides their taking from him five guineas, a watch with a chain and seal, and ten shillings in silver, near the Turnpike at Tottenham without any regard to the said Mr Squire's character, being one of his Majesty's messengers. After his condemnation he was very impudent in the condemn'd hold, and was in great hopes of a reprieve, but he was nevertheless hang'd at Tyburn on Monday the sixteenth of February beforemention'd, aged 34 years.

Robert Vickers, hang'd also at the same time, aged twenty three years, was born at Nethercot in Warwickshire, and when but very young going from thence to Westbury in Buckinghamshire, he was there bound apprentice to a baker. When his time was expired he came up to London, and was journeyman to a baker in Cow-Cross, and afterwards to another in Golden Lane, in the Parish of St Giles's Cripplegate. But he growing weary of his employment, listed himself in the second Regiment of Foot Guards, where he had not been very long before he began to be loose, and follow ill courses, especially going on the foot-pad.

The first person whom he attack'd in this manner was a certain Irish barrister of the King's-Bench Walks in the Temple, who was very well known for his not taking the oaths to the then present government. This lawyer Vickers meeting one night walking from Mary le-bone, cross the Fields towards Southampton House, he did not only take what Money he had, but also stript him to his shirt, which dawbing all over with dirt in a pond, he put it on the lawyer, saying, that now be looked something like a limb of the law, since he was in black. Then tying him neck and heels, he left him there to ponder till next morning, on Wingate's Statutes, Coke upon Littleton, Magna Charta, old Plowden, Levine's Reports, and other musty Authors of the Law.

Francis Parquot, hang'd also with the abovementioned malefactors, aged thirty years, was born in France, at a seaport town call'd Marines, near Rochel. When he was about fifteen years old he came into England, where he lived three years with a French jeweller. Then leaving his master he went to the city of Bath, and there kept a shop for some time; but being in debt, was forced to leave that place, and come up to London, where he privately follow'd his occupation, till falling into ill company, he betook himself to house-breaking, which he follow'd till his acquaintance with Prior and Vickers brought him to share their fates.

THE LIVES OF JOHN TRIPPUCK THE GOLDEN TINMAN, ROBERT CANE, THOMAS CHARNOCK, AND RICHARD SHEPHERD

The first of these offenders had been an old sinner, and had acquir'd the nick name of the Golden Tinman, in the same manner as a former practitioner in his wretched calling, did that of the Golden Farmer. Trippuck had robbed alone and in company for a considerable space, till his character was grown very notorious. Some short time before his being taking up for this last offence, he had by dint of money and interest procured a pardon. However, venturing on the fact which brought him to death, the person injured soon seized him, and being inexorable in his prosecution, Trippuck was cast and received sentence. But having still some money, he did not lose all hope of a reprieve, but kept up his spirits, by flattering himself with his life being preserved, till within a very few days of execution. If the ordinary spoke to him of the affairs of his soul, Trippuck immediately cut him short with, 'D'ye believe I can obtain a pardon?' 'I don't know that indeed,' says the doctor, 'But you know one counseller such a one,' says Trippuck, 'prithee make use of your interest with him, and see whether you can get him to serve me, I'll not be ungrateful Doctor.'

The ordinary was almost at his wits end with this sort of cross purposes; however, he went on to exhort him to think of the great work he had to do, and entreated him to consider the nature of that repentance, which must attone for all his numerous offences. Trippuck upon this, opened his breast, and shewed him a great number of scars, amongst which were two very large ones, out of which he said two musquet bullets had been extracted. 'And will not these, good Doctor,' quoth he, 'and the vast pains I have endured in their cure, in some sort lessen the heinousness of the facts I may have committed.' 'No,' said the ordinary, 'what evils have fallen upon you in such expeditions you have drawn upon yourself, and are not to imagine that these will in any degree, make amends for the multitude of your offences. You had much better clear your conscience, by a full and ingenious confession of your crimes, and prepare in earnest for another world, since I dare assure you, you need no hopes of staying in this.'

Trippuck as soon as he found the ordinary was in the right, and that all expectation of a reprieve or pardon were totally in vain, began, as most of those sort of people do, to lose much of that stubborness, they mistake for courage; he now felt all the terrors of an awakened conscience, and therefore persisted no longer in denying the crime for which he died; tho' at first he declared it altogether a falshood, and Constable his companion had deny'd it even to death.

It had been reported, that this Trippuck was the man who killed Mr Hull towards the end of the summer before on Black Heath; but when this story reached his ears, he declar'd it was an utter falsity, repeating this assertion to the ordinary a few moments before his being turned off; pointing to the rope about him, said, 'As you see this instrument of death about me, what I say is the real truth.' He died at last with all outward signs of penitence.

Richard Cane was a young man, of about twenty two years of age, at the time he suffered. Having a tollerable genius when a youth, his friends put him apprentice twice; but to no purpose; for having got rambling notions in his head, he would needs go to sea: there too but for his own unhappy temper he might have done well, for the ship of war in which he sailed, was so fortunate as to take, after eight hours sharp engagement, a Spanish vessel, of an immense value, but the large share he got here did him little service: Richard as soon as he came home made a quick hand of it, and when the usual train of sensual delights, which pass for pleasures in low life, had exhausted him to the last farthing, necessity, and the desire of still indulging his vices, made him fall into the worst, and most unlawful methods, to obtain the means by which he might pursue them.

Sometime after this, the unhappy man of whom we are speaking, fell in love with a virtuous young woman, who lived with her mother, a poor well-meaning creature, utterly ignorant of Cane's behaviour, or that he had ever committed any crimes punishable by law. The girl, as such silly people are wont, yielded quickly to marriage, which was to be consummated privately, because Cane's relations were not to be disobliged, who it seems did not think him totally ruined, while he escaped matrimony. But the unhappy youth not having money enough to procure a license, and being ashamed to put the expense on the woman and her mother, in a fit of amorous distraction, he went out from them one evening, and meeting a man somewhat fuddled in the street, he threw him down, and took away his hat and coat. The fellow was not so drunk, but that he cried out, and people coming to his assistance, Cane was immediately apprehended; and so this fact, instead of raising him money enough to be married, brought him to death in the most ignominious way.

While he lay in Newgate, the miserable young creature who was to have been his wife, came constantly after him to cry with him, and deplore their mutual misfortunes, which were encreased by the girl's mother falling sick, and being confined to her bed through grief for her design'd son in-law's sad fate. When the day of his suffering drew on, this unhappy man composed himself to submit to it with great serenity: he prosessed abundance of contrition for the wickedness of his former life, and lamented with much tenderness those evils he had brought upon the girl and her mother. The softness of his temper, and the steady affection he had for the maid, contributed to make his exit much pity'd; which happened at Tyburn in the 22d year of his age. He left a paper behind him, which he also read at the tree, containing a confession of his crime, a vindication of his sweetheart's character, and a profession of his faith, and universal charity.

Richard Shepherd was born of very honest and reputable parents in the city of Oxford, who were careful in giving him a suitable education, which he through the wickedness of his future life utterly forgot, insomuch, that he knew scarce the Creed and Lord's Prayer, at the time he had most need of them. When he grew a tollerable big lad, his friends put him out apprentice to a butcher, where having served a great part of his time, he fell in love with a young country lass hard by; and his passion growing outragious, he attacked her with all the amorous strains of gallantry he was able. The hearts of young uneducated wenches, like unfortify'd towns, make little resistance when once besieged, and therefore Shepherd had no great difficulty in making a conquest. However the girl insisted on honourable terms, and unfortunately for the poor fellow they were married before his time was out. 'An error in conduct, which in low life is seldom retrieved'.

It happened so here; Shepherd's master was not long before he discovered this wedding; he thereupon gave the poor fellow so much trouble, that he was as last forced to give him forty shillings down, and a bond for twenty eight pounds more; which having totally ruined him, Dick fell unhappily into the way of dishonest company, who soon drew him into their manner of gaining money, and supplying his necessities at the hazard both of his conscience, and his neck. He became an expert proficient, yet could never acquire any thing considerable thereby, but was continually embroiled and in debt; his wife bringing in every year a child, contributing not a little thereto.

When he first began his robberies, he went on house breaking, and committed several facts in the city of Oxford itself; but those things not being so easily concealed there, as at London, report quickly began to grow very loud about him, and Dick was forced to make shift with pilfering in other places, in which he was so unlucky, that the second or third fact he committed in Hertfordshire, he was detected and seized, and at the next assizes capitally convicted; yet his friends out of compassion to his youth, and in hopes he might be sufficiently check'd by so narrow an escape from the gallows, procured him first a reprieve and then a pardon.

But this proximity to death made little impression on his heart, which is too often the fault of persons, who receive mercy, and have too little grace to make use of it. Dick, partly driven by necessity (for few people cared after his release, to employ him) partly through the instigations of his own wicked heart, went again upon the old trade, for which he was so lately like to have suffered; but thieving was still an unfortunate profession to him. He soon after fell again into the hands of justice, from whence he escaped by impeaching Allen and Chambers, two of his accomplices, and so evaded Tyburn a second time; yet all this signified nothing to him, for as soon as at home, he was at work in his old way, till apprehended and executed for his wickedness.

No unhappy criminal had ever more warning than Shepherd, of his approaching miserable fate, if he would have suffered any thing to have detered him; but alas! what are advices, what are terrors, what even the sight of death itself, to souls hardened in sin, and consciences so feared as his. He was taken up, carried before Col. Ellis and committed to Newprison for a capital offence. He had not remained there long, before he wrote the Col. a letter, in which (provided he were admitted an evidence) he offered to make large discoveries. His offers were accepted, and both convicted capitally at the Old-Bailey, by him, were executed at Tyburn; whither Shepherd quickly followed them.

Shepherd had picked up while in Newgate, a thoughtless resolution as to dying, not uncommon to old malefactors, who having been often condemned, grow at last hardened to the gallows. When he was exhorted to think seriously of making his peace with God, he replied, It was done, and he was sure of going to Heaven.

Thomas Charnock, executed with these, was a young man well and religiously educated. He had by his friends been placed in the house of a very eminent trader, and being seduced by ill company, yielded to a desire of making a shew in the world; and in order to it, robbed his master's accompting-house; which fact made him indeed conspicuous, but in a very indifferent manner from what he had flattered himself with. They died tolerably submissive and penitent; this last malefactor especially, who had rational ideas of religion. The day of their execution was January the 29th, 1719–20.

THE HISTORY OF
THE WALTHAM BLACKS, AND THEIR TRANSACTIONS, TO THE DEATH OF RICHARD PARVIN, EDWARD ELLIOT, ROBERT KINGSHELL, HENRY MARSHAL, JOHN AND EDWARD PINK, AND JAMES ANSEL, ALIAS PHILIPS, AT TYBURN, WHOSE LIVES ARE ALSO INCLUDED

S uch is the unaccountable folly which reigns in too great a part of the human species, that by their own ill deeds, they make such laws necessary for the security of mens persons and properties, as would otherwise appear cruel and inhuman; and doubtless, those laws which we esteem barbarous in other nations, and even some which appear so, tho' anciently practiced in our own, had their rise from the same cause. I am led to this observation, from the folly which certain persons were guilty of, in making small insurrections for the sake only of getting a few deer; and going on, because they found the lenity of the laws could not punish them at present, untill they grew to that height as to ride in armed troops, blacked and disguised, in order the more to terrify those whom they assaulted; and where ever they were denied what they thought proper to demand, whether venison, wine, money, or other necessaries for their debauched feasts, they would by letters threaten to plunder and destroy with fire and sword, whomsoever they thought proper. These villanies being carried on with a high hand for some time, in the year 1722 and 1723, their insolence grew at last so intollerable, as to oblige the legislature to make a new law against all who thus went armed and disguised, and associated themselves together by the name of Blacks, or entered into any other confederacies to support and assist one another in doing injuries and violencies to the persons and properties of the King's subjects.

By this law it was enacted, 'That after the first Day of June, 1723, whatever Persons armed with offensive Weapons, and having their Faces Black'd, or went otherwise Disguised, should appear in any Forest Park, or Grounds enclos'd with any Wall or Fence, wherein Deer were kept, or any Warren where Hares or Conies are kept, or in any Highway, Heath, or Down, or unlawfully Hunt, Kill, or Steal, any Red or Fallow Deer, or rob any Warren, or steal Fish out of any Pond, or maliciously break down the Head of any Fish-pond, or kill or wound Cattle, or set Fire to any House or Out-House, Stack, &c. or cut down, or any other ways destroy Trees planted for Shelter or Profit, or should maliciously shoot at any Person, or send a Letter, demanding Money or other valuable Things, or should rescue any Person in Custody of an Officer, for any such Offences, or by Gift or Promise, procure any one to join with them, should be deemed Guilty of Felony without Benefit of Clergy, and suffer Pains of Death as Felons so convicted.'

Nor was even this thought sufficient to remedy those evils, which the idle follies of some rash persons had brought about, but a retrospect was also, by the same act, had to offences heretofore committed, and all persons who had committed any crimes punishable by this act, after the second of February, 1722, were commanded to render themselves before the 24th of July, 1723, to some Justice of his Majesty's Court of King's Bench, or to some Justice of the Peace for the county where they lived, and there make a full and exact confession of the crimes of such a nature which they had committed, the times when, the places where, and persons with whom; together with an account of such person's places of abode, as had with them been guilty as aforesaid, in order to their being thereupon apprehended and brought to judgment according to law, on pain of being deemed felons, without benefit of the clergy, and suffering accordingly. But they were entitled to a free pardon and forgiveness, in case that before the 24th of July they surrendered and made such discovery. Justices of Peace by the said Act, were required on any information being made before them, by one or more credible persons, against any person charged with any of the offences aforesaid, to transmit it under their hands and seals, to one of His Majesty's principle Secretary's of State, who by the same Act was required to lay such information and return before His Majesty in Council; whereupon, an order was to issue for the person so charged, to surrender within forty days, and in case he refused or neglected to surrender within that time, then from the day in which the forty days were elaps'd, he was to be deemed as a felon convict, and execution might be awarded as attainted of felony by a verdict. Every person also who after the time appointed for the surrender of the person, should conceal, aid, or succour him, knowing the circumstances in which he then stood, should suffer death as a felon, without benefit of the clergy. And that people might the more readily hazard their persons for the apprehending such offenders, it was likewise enacted, that if any person should be wounded so as to lose an eye, or the use of any limb, in endeavouring to take persons charged with the commission of crimes within this law, then on a certificate from the Justices of the Peace, of his being so wounded, the sheriff of the county was commanded within thirty days after the sight of such certificate, to pay the said wounded person 50 *l.* under pain of forfeiting 100 *l.* on failure thereof; and in case any person should be killed in seizing such persons as aforesaid, then the said 50 *l.* was to be paid to the executors of the person so killed.

249

It cannot seem strange, that in consequence of so extraordinary an act of the legislature, many of these presumptuous and silly people should be apprehended; and a considerable number of them, having upon their apprehension been committed to Winchester gaol, seven of them were, by habeas corpus, removed to the greater solemnity of their trial to Newgate, and for their offences brought up and arraign'd at the King's Bench Bar, Westminster; and were convicted on full evidence, all of them of felony, and three of murder. We shall inform you, one by one, of what has come to our knowledge in relation to their crimes, and the manner and circumstances with which they were committed.

———

Richard Parvin was master of a publick-house at Portsmouth, a man of a dull and flegmatick disposition, who continually denied his having been in any manner concerned with these people, though the evidence against him at his trial, was as full and as direct as possibly could have been expected, and he himself evidently proved to have been upon the spot, when the violences committed by the other prisoners were transacted. In answer to this, he said, 'that he was not with them, tho' indeed he was upon the forest'; for which he gave this reason: he had, he said, a very handsome young wench who lived with him, and for that reason being admired by many of his customers, she took it in her head one day to run away; he hearing that she had fled cross the forest, pursued her, and in that pursuit, calling at the house of Mr Parford, who keeps an alehouse on the forest, this landlord, it seems, who was an evidence against the other Blacks, took him into the number, tho' as he said, he could fully have cleared himself, if he had had any money to have sent for witnesses out of Berkshire; but the mayor of Portsmouth, seizing as soon as he was apprehended, on all his goods, put his family into great distress, and whether he could have found them or no, hindred his being able to produce any witnesses at his trial. He persevered in these professions of his innocency to the very last, still hoping for a reprieve, and not only feeding himself with such expectations while in prison, but also gaz'd earnestly when at the tree, in hopes that a pardon would be brought him, till the cart drew away, and extinguished life and the desire of life together.

———

250

Edward Elliot, a boy of about seventeen years of age, whose father was a taylor, at a village between Petsworth and Guilford, was the next who received sentence of death with Parvin. The account he gave of his coming into this society, has something in it very odd, and which gives a fuller idea of the strange whims which possessed these people. The boy said, that about a year before his being apprehended, thirty or forty men met him in the county of Surrey, and hurried him away; he who appeared to be the chief of them, telling him that he enlisted him for the service of the king of the Blacks; in pursuance of which he was to disguise his face, obey orders of whatsoever kind they were, such as breaking down fish ponds, burning woods, shooting deer, taking also an oath to be true to them, or they by their art magick would turn him into a beast, and as such make him carry their burthens, and live like a horse upon grass and water. And he said also, that in the space of time he continued with them, he saw several of their experiments of their witch-craft; for that once when two men had offended them, by refusing to comply in taking their oath, and obeying their orders, they caused them immediately to be blindfolded, and stopping them in holes of the earth up to their chin, ran at them as if they had been dogs, bellowing and barking as it were in their ears; and when they had plagued them a while in this ridiculous manner, took them out, and bid them remember how they offended any of the Black nation again, for if they did, they should not escape so well as they had at present. He had seen them also, he said, oblige carters to drive a good way out of the road, and carry whatsoever venison or other thing they had plundered, to the places where they would have them: moreover, that the men were generally so frighted with their usage, and so terrified with the oaths they were obliged to swear, that they seldom complained, or even spoke of their bondage.

As to the fact for which they died, Elliot gave this account: 'that in the morn. when that fact, for which he died, was committed, Marshal, Kingshel, and four others came to him and persuaded him to go to Farnham-holt, and that he need not fear disobliging any gentlemen in the country, some of whom were very kind to this Elliot: they persuaded him that certain persons of fortune were concerned with them, and would bear him harmless if he would go. He owned that at last he consented to go with them, but trembled all the way; insomuch, that he could hardly reach the Holt, while they were engaged in the business for which they came, *viz.* killing the deer. The keepers,' he said, 'came upon him, for he was wandered a considerable way from his companions after a fawn, which he intended to send as a present to a young woman at Guilford; him therefore they quickly seized and bound, and leaving him in that condition, went in search of the rest of his associates. It was not long before they came up with them; the keepers were six, the Blacks were seven in number; they fell warmly to it with quarter-staffs; the keepers unwilling to have lives taken away, advised them to retire; but upon their refusing, and Marshall's firing a gun, by which one of the keepers belonging to the Lady How was slain, they discharged a blunderbuss and shattered the thigh of one Barber amongst the Blacks, upon which three of his associates ran away, and the two others, Marshal and Kingshell, were likewise taken, and so the fray for the present ended. Elliot lay bound all the while within hearing, and in the greatest agonies imaginable, at the consideration that whatever blood was spilt, he should be as much answerable for it as those who shed it; in which he was not mistaken; for the keepers returning after the fight was over, carried him away bound, and he never had his fetters off after, till the morning of his execution. He behaved himself very soberly, quietly, and with much seeming penitence and contrition; he owned the justice of the law in punishing him, and said, 'he more especially deserved to suffer, since at the time of the committing this fact, he was servant to a widow lady, where he wanted nothing to make him happy or easy.'

252

Robert Kingshell was 26 years old, lived in the same house with his parents, being apprentice to his brother a shoemaker. His parents were very watchful over his behaviour, and sought by every method to prevent his talking ill courses, or being guilty of any debauchery whatever. The night before this unhappy accident fell out, as he and the rest of the family were sleeping in their beds, Barber made a signal at his chamber window, it being then about eleven a clock: Kingshell upon this, arose and got softly out of the window; Barber took him upon his horse, and away they went to the Holt, twelve miles distant, calling in their way upon Henry Marshal, Elliot, and the rest of their accomplices. He said it was eight a clock in the morning before the keepers attacked them; he owned they bid them retire, and that he himself told them they would, provided the bound man (Elliot) was released, and deliver'd into their hands; but that proposition being refus'd, the fight presently grew warm. Barber's thigh was broke, and Marshal killed the keeper with a shot. Being thereupon very hard pressed, three of their companions ran away, leaving him and Marshal to fight it out, Elliot being already taken, and Barber disabled. It was not long before they were in the same unhappy condition with their companions. From the time of their being apprehended, Kingshell laid aside all hopes of life, and applyed himself with great fervency and devotion, to enable him in what alone remained for him to do, *viz.* dying decently.

Henry Marshal, about thirty six years of sge, the unfortunate person by whose hand the murther was committed, seem'd to be the least sensible of the evils he had done of any, such was the pleasure of Almighty God, that till the day before his execution, he neither had his senses, nor the use of his speech: when he recovered it, and a clergyman represented to him the horrid crime of which he had been guilty, he was so far from shewing any deep sense of the crime of shedding innocent blood, that he made light of it, and said, 'sure he might stand upon his own defence, and was not bound to run away and leave his companions in danger.' This was the language he talked for the space of twenty four hours before his death, when he enjoyed the use of speech; and so far was he from thanking those who charitably offered him their admonitions, that he said, he had not forgot himself, but had already taken care of what he thought necessary for his soul; however, he did not attempt in the least to prevaricate, but fairly acknowledged that he committed the fact for which he died, tho' nothing could oblige him to speak of it in a manner as if he was sorry for, or repented of it, farther than for having occasioned his own misfortunes. So strong is the prejudice which vulgar minds may acquire, by often repeating to themselves certain positions, however ridiculous or false, that a man had a right to imbrue his hands in the blood of another, who was in the execution of his office, and endeavouring him in the commission of an illegal act.

253

These of whom we have last spoken, were altogether concerned in the aforemention'd fact, which was attended with murder. But we are now to speak of the rest, who were concerned in the felony only, for which they with the abovemention'd Parvin suffered. Of these there were two brothers, whose names were John and Edward Pink, carters in Portsmouth, and always accounted honest and industrious fellows, before this accident happened. They did not, however, deny their being guilty, but on the contrary, ingeniously confessed the truth of what was sworn, and mentioned some other circumstances than had been produced at the trial, which attended their committing it. They said that they met Parvin's house-keeper upon the road, that they forced her to cut the throat of a deer which they had just taken upon Bear Forest, gave her a dagger, which they forced her to wear, and to ride cross legg'd with pistols before her. In this dress they brought her to Parvin's house upon the forest, where they dined upon a haunch of venison, feasted merrily, and after dinner sent out two of their companions to kill more deer; not in the King's Forest, but in Waltham Chace, belonging to the Bishop of Winchester: one of these two persons they called their king, and the other they called lyon: neither of these two brothers objected any thing, either to the truth of the evidence given against, or the justice of that sentence passed upon them; only one insinuated that the evidence would not have been so strong against him and Ansel, if it had not been for running away with the witness's wife, which so provok'd him that they were sure they should not escape when he was admitted a witness. These, like the rest, were hard to be persuaded that the things they had committed were any crimes in the eyes of God, and said, deer were wild beast, and they did not see why the poor had not as good a right to them as the rich: however, as the law condemned them to suffer, they were bound to submit; and in consequence of that notion, they behaved themselves very orderly, decently, and quietly, while under sentence.

James Ansel, alias Stephen Philips, the seventh and last of these unhappy persons, was a man addicted to a worse and more profligate life than any of the rest had ever been; for he had held no settled employment, but had been a loose disorderly person, concerned in all sorts of wickedness for many years, both at Portsmouth, Guilford, and other country towns, as well as at London. Deer were not the only things that he had dealt in; stealing, robbing on the highway, had been formerly his employment; and in becoming a Black, he did not, as the others, ascend in wickedness, but came down on the contrary a step lower: yet this criminal, as his offences were greater, so his sense of them was much stronger than in any of the rest, excepting Kingshell, for he gave over all manner of hopes of life, and all concerns about it as soon as he was taken; yet even he had no notion of making discoveries, unless they might be beneficial to himself; and though he owned the knowledge of twenty persons who were notorious offenders in the same kind, he absolutely refused to name them, since such naming would not procure himself a pardon. Talking to him of the duty of doing justice, was beating the air: he said he thought there was no justice in taking away other peoples lives, unless it was to save his own; yet no sooner was he taxed about his own going on the highway than he confessed it, and said, he knew very well bills would have been preferred against him at Guilford assizes, in case he had got off at the King's-Bench, but that he did not greatly value them: for tho' formerly he had been guilty of some facts in that way, yet they could not all now be proved; and he should have found it no difficult matter to have demonstrated it of those then charged upon him, of which he was not really guilty, but owed his being thought so to a profligate course of life he had for some time led, and his aversion to all honest employments. As bold as the whole gang of these fellows appeared, yet what with sickness, what with the apprehension of death, they were so terrified, that not one of 'em but Ansel, alias Philips, was able to stand up, or speak, at the place of execution; many who saw 'em there, affirming, that some of them were dead even before they were turned off.

As an appendix to the melancholly history of these seven unhappy persons, we will add part of a letter written at that time by a gentleman of Essex, to his friend in London, containing a more particular account of the humour of these people than we have seen any where else.

A Letter to Mr. C. D. in London.

DEAR SIR,

You cannot but have heard of the Waltham Blacks, as they are called, a set of whimsical merry Fellows, that are so mad to run the greatest

255

Hazards for the Sake of a haunch of Venison, and passing a jolly Evening together. For my Part, I took the Stories of them for Fables, till Experience taught me the contrary, by the Adventure I am going to relate to you.

To begin then, my Horse got some Way a Stone in his Foot; so that finding it impossible to get him along, I was glad to take up at a little blind Ale-House, which I perceived had a Yard and Stable behind it. The Man of the House received me very civily, but when I ask'd him whether I could lodge there that Night, he told me No, he had no room. I desired him then to put something to my Horse's Foot, and let me sit up all Night: The Man made me no Answer; but when we came into the House together, the Wife dealt more roughly and more freely with me, that truly I neither could nor should stay there, and was for hurrying her Husband to get my Horse out: However, on putting a Crown into her Hand, and promising her another for my Lodging, she at last told me that there was indeed a little Bed above Stairs, on which she would order a clean Pair of Sheets to be put; for she was persuaded I was more of a Gentleman than to take any Notice of what I saw passed there. This made me more uneasy than I was before: I concluded now I was got among a den of Highwaymen, and expected nothing less than to be robbed and have my Throat cut; however, finding there was no Remedy, I even set myself down, and endeavoured to be as easy as I could.

By this Time it was very dark, and I heard three or four Horsemen alight, and lead their Horses into the Yard. As the Men where coming into the Room where I was, I overheard my Landlord say, Indeed Brother you need not be uneasy, I am positive the Gentleman's a Man of Honour. To which I heard another Voice reply, What good could our Death do to any Stranger? Faith I don't apprehend half the Danger you do: I dare say the Gentleman would be glad of our Companies, and we should be pleas'd with his, come, hang Fear, I'll lead the Way. So said, so done, in they came, Five of them, all disguis'd so effectually, that unless it were in the same Disguise, I should not be able to distinguish any one of them. Down they sat and he who was constituted their Captain *pro hac Vice*, accosted me with great Civility, and asked me 'If I would honour them with my Company at Supper.' I did not yet guess the Profession of my new Acquaintance: But supposing my Landlord would not suffer either a Robbery or a Murder in his own House, by Degrees my Mind grew perfectly easy.

About Ten a Clock, I heard a very great Noise of Horses, and soon after of Mens Feet trampling in a Room over my Head: Then my Landlord came down and informed us, Supper was just ready to go upon the Table. Upon this, we were all desired to walk up; and he, whom I before called the Captain, presented me with a humorous kind of Ceremony to a Man more disguis'd than the rest, who sat at the upper End of the Table, telling me at the same Time, he hoped I would not refuse to pay my Respects to Prince Oroonoko King of the Blacks. It then immediately struck into my Head, who those worthy Persons were, and I called myself a thousand Blockheads in my Mind for not finding it out before; but the Hurry of Things, or to speak the Truth, the Fear I was in, prevented my judging, even from the most evident Signs.

As soon as our aukward Ceremonies was over, Supper was brought in: It consisted of eighteen Dishes of Venison in every Shape, roasted, boiled with Broth, hashed Collups, Pasties, Umble Pies, and a large Haunch in the Middle larded. The Table we sat at was very large, and the Company in all twenty one Persons; at each of our Elbows there was set a Bottle of Claret; and the Man and Woman of the House sat down at the lower End. Two or three of the Fellows had good natural Voices, and so the Evening was spent as merily, as the Rakes pass theirs at the King's Arms, or the City Apprentices at Sadler's Wells. About Two the Company seemed inclined to break up, having first assured me that they should take my Company as a Favour any Thursday Evening, if I came that Way.

Before I conclude my Epistle, it is fit I should inform you, that they did me the Honour, of acquainting me with those Rules by which their Society was govern'd. Their Black Prince assured me that their Government was perfectly Monarchial, and that when upon Expeditions, he had an absolute Command; But in the time of Peace (continued he) and at the Table, I condescend to eat and drink familiarly with my

257

Subjects as Friends. We admit no Man into our Society, 'till he has been twice drunk with us, that we may be perfectly acquainted with his Temper, but if the Person who sues to be admitted, declares solemnly he was not drunk in his Life, this Rule is dispensed with, and the Person is only bound to converse with us a Month. As soon as we have determined to admit him, he is to equip himself with a good Mare or Gelding, a Brace of Pistols, and a Gun to lye on the Saddle Bow; then he is sworn upon the Horns over the Chimney; and having a new Name conferred by the Society, is thereby entered upon the Roll, and from that Day foreward, considered as lawful Member.

He went on with abundance more of their wise Institutions which are not of Consequence enough to tell you: In the Morning having given my Landlady the other Crown Piece, I speeded directly home, as much in Amaze at the new People I had discovered, as the Duke of Alva's Huntsman when they found an undiscovered Nation in Spain, by following their Master's Hawk over the Mountains. Pray, in Return let me see if all your London Rambles can produce such another Adventure.

I am yours, &c.

Before we leave these people we think it proper to acquaint our readers, that their folly was not to be extinguished by a single execution; there were a great many young fellows of the same stamp, who were fools enough to forfeit their lives upon the same occasion. However, the humour did not run very long; tho' some of them were impudent enough to murther a keeper or two afterwards, in the space of a twelvemonth, the whole nation of the Blacks was extinguished, and these country rakes were contented to play the fool upon easier terms. The last blood that was shed on either side, being that of a keeper's son at Old Windsor, whom some of these wise people fired at as he look'd out of the window.

A special assizes was held at Reading, before three of his Majesty's judges, to try the persons concern'd in this murther, and several others. Four men were capitally convicted and executed; several others were ordered for transportation, and in short this was the decisive stroke which put a period to their whimsical monarchy. The men that were hang'd, like those abovementioned, were so weak with lying in prison, that one of them was borne between two to the Town-Hall, and carry'd upon the hangman's back into the cart that convey'd him to the tree. The rest were not in a much better condition.

259

THE LIFE OF

JOSEPH BLAKE, ALIAS BLUESKIN

As there is impudence and wickedness enough in the lives of most publick malefactors, to make persons of a sober education and behaviour, wonder at the depravity of human nature; so there are sometimes superlative rogues, who as far exceed the ordinary class of rogues, as they do honest people; and whenever such a monster as this appears in the world, there are enough fools to make such a noise about his conduct, as to invite others to imitate the obstinacy of his deportment, thro' that false love of fame, which influences those wretches. Amongst the number of these, Joseph Blake, better known by his nick name of Blueskin, always deserves to be remembred, as one who studiously took the paths of infamy, in order to become famous.

By birth he was a native of this City of London; his parents being persons in tollerable circumstances, kept him six years at school, where he did not learn half so much from his master, as he did evil from his school-fellow William Blewit, from whose lessons he copied so well, that all his education signified nothing. He absolutely refusing, when he came from school, to go to any employment, but on the contrary set up for a robber when he was scarce seventeen; but from that time to the day of his death, was unsuccessful in all his undertakings, hardly ever committing the most trivial fact, but he experienced for it, either the humanity of the mob, or of the keepers of Bridewell, out of which, or some other prison, he could hardly keep his feet for a month together.

He fell into the gang of Lock, Wilkinson, Carrick, Lincoln, and Daniel Carrol. And being one night out with this gang, they robb'd one Mr Clark of eight shillings, and a silver hilted sword, just as candles were going to be lighted. A woman looking accidentally out of a window, perceived it, and cry'd out 'Thieves': Wilkinson fired a pistol at her, which (very luckily) upon her drawing in her head graz'd upon the stone of the window, and did no other mischief. Blake was also in the company of the same gang, when they attack'd Captain Langley at the corner of Hide Park Road, as he was going to the camp; but the captain behaved himself so well, that notwithstanding they shot several times thro' and thro' his coat, yet they were not able to rob him. Not long after this, Wilkinson being apprehended, impeached a large number of persons, and with them, Blake and Lock. Lock hereupon made a fuller discovery than the other before Justice Blakerby, in which information there was contained no less than seventy robberies, upon which he also was admitted a witness; and having nam'd Wilkinson, Lincoln, Carrick and Carrol, with himself, to have been the five persons who murder'd Peter Martin the Chelsea Pensioner, by the Park Wall. Wilkinson thereupon was apprehended, tried, and convicted, notwithstanding the information he had before given, which was thereby totally set aside.

Blake himself also became now an evidence against the rest of his companions, and discovered about a dozen robberies which they had committed, amongst these there was a one very remarkable one. Two gentlemen in hunting caps were together in a chariot on the Hampstead-Road, from whom they took two gold watches, rings seals and other things to a considerable value, and Junks, alias Levee, laid his pistol down by the gentlemen all the while he search'd them, yet they wanted either the courage or the presence of mind, to seize it and prevent their losing things of so great value. Not long after this Oakly, Junks, and this Blake, stopp'd a single man with a link before him in Fig-Lane, and he not surrendering so easily as they expected, Junks and Oakey beat him over the head with their pistols, and then left him wounded in a terrible condition, taking from him one guinea and one penny. A very short time after this, Junks Oakey, and Flood, were apprehended and executed, for robbing Colonel Cope and Mr Young of that very watch, for which Carrick and Malony had been before executed, Joseph Blake being the evidence against them.

After this hanging work of his companions, he thought himself not only entitled to liberty but reward: therein however he was mightily mistaken, for not having surrendered willingly and quietly, but being taken after long resistance and when he was much wounded, there did not seem to be the least foundation for this confident demand. He remained still a prisoner in the Woodstreet compter, obstinately refusing to be transported for seven years, 'till at last procuring two men to be bound for his good behaviour, he was carried before a worthy alderman of the City and there discharged. At which time, some-body there present asking how long time might be given him, before they should see him again at the Old-Bailey? A gentleman made answer, in about three sessions, in which time it seems he guessed very right; for the third sessions from thence, Blake was indeed brought to the bar.

For no sooner was he at liberty but he was employed in robbing; and having picked up Jack Shepherd for a companion, they went out together to search for prey in the fields. Near the Half Way House to Hampstead, they met with one Pargitar, pretty much in liquor, whom immediately Blake knock'd down into the ditch, where he must inevitably have perished, if John Shepherd had not kept his head above the mud with great difficulty. For this fact the next sessions after it happened, the two brothers (Brightwells) in the Guards were tried; and if a number of men had not sworn them to have been upon duty at the time the robbery was committed, they had certainly been convicted, the evidence of the prosecuter being direct and full. The elder Brightwell died in a week after he was released from his confinement, and so did not live to see his innocence fully clear'd by the confession of Blake.

A very short space after this Blake and his companion Shepherd, committed the burglary together in the house of Mr Kneebone, where Shepherd getting into the house, let in Blake at the back door and carry'd off goods to a considerable value. For this, both Shepherd and he were apprehended; and the sessions before Blake was convicted, his companion received sentence of death; but at the time Blake was taken up, had made his escape out of the condemned hold.

He behaved with great impudence at his trial, and when he found nothing would save him, he took the advantage of Jonathan Wild's coming to speak with him, to cut the said Wild's throat, a large gash from the ear beyond the windpipe; of which wound Wild languished a long time, and happy had it been for him if Blake's wound had proved fatal, for then Jonathan had escaped death by a more dishonourable wound in the throat, than that of a penknife: but the number of his crimes, and the spleen of his enemies procured him a worse fate. Whatever Wild might deserve of others, he seems to have merited better usage from this Blake; for while he continued a prisoner in the compter, Jonathan was at the expence of curing a wound he had received, allowed him three shillings and six-pence a week, and after his last misfortune promised him a good coffin, actually furnished him with money to support him in Newgate, and several good books, if he would have made any use of them: but because he freely declared to Blueskin, there was no hopes of getting him transported, the bloody villain determined to take away his life, and was so far from shewing any signs of remorse, when he was brought up again to Newgate, that he declared if he had thought of it before, he would have provided such a knife as should have cut off his head.

At the time that he received sentence, there was a woman also condemned, and they being placed as usual, in what is called the Bail Dock at the Old-Bailey, Blake offered such rudeness to the woman, that she cried out and alarmed the whole bench. All the time he lay under condemnation, he appeared utterly thoughtless and insensible of his approaching fate. Tho' from the cutting of Wild's throat, and some other barbarities of the same nature, he acquired amongst the mob the character of a brave fellow; yet he was in himself but a mean spirited timorous man, and never exerted himself, but either thro' fury or dispair. He wept much at the chapel before he was to die; and tho' he drank deeply to drive away fear, yet at the place of execution he wept again, trembled, and shewed all the signs of a timorous confusion, as well he might, who had lived wickedly, and trifled with his repentance to the grave. There was nothing in his person extraordinary; a dapper, well set fellow, of great strength, and great cruelty; equally detested by the sober part of the world, for the audacious wickedness of his behaviour, and despised by his companions for the villanies he committed even against them. He was executed in the 28th year of his age, on the 11th of November, 1724.

Shepherd in the Stone Room in Newgate.

THE LIFE OF
JOHN SHEPHERD

A mongst the prodigies of ingenious wickedness and artful mischief, which have surprized the world in our time, perhaps none has made so great a noise as John Shepherd, the malefactor of whom we are now going to speak. His father's name was Thomas Shepherd, who was by trade a carpenter, and liv'd in Spittle-Fields; a man of an extraordinary good character, and who took all the care his narrow circumstance would allow, that his family might be brought up in the fear of God, and in just notions of their duty towards their neighbour; yet he was so unhappy in his children, that both this son John and another took to ill courses, and both in their turns were convicted at the bar in the Old-Bailey.

After the father's death, his widow did all she could to get this unfortunate son of hers admitted into Christ's Hospital, but failing of that, she got him bread up at a scool in Bishopsgate-Street, where he learned to read, and might in all probability have got a good education, if he had not been too soon removed, being put out to the trade of a cane-chair-maker. His master us'd him very well, and probably he might have liv'd honestly with him but he dying in a short time afterwards Shepherd was put to another, a much younger man, who used him so harshly, that in a little time he ran away from him. He was then put to another master, one Mr Wood in Witch-Street, from whose kindness and of Mr Kneebone's, whom he robbed, he was taught to write, and had many other favours done him by that gentleman, whom he so ungreatfully treated. But good usuage or bad was grown all alike to him now; he had given himself up to the sensual pleasures of low life, drinking all day, and getting to some impudent strumpet at night.

Amongst the chief of his mistresses there was one Elizabeth Lion, commonly calld Edgeworth Bess; the impudence of whose behaviour was shocking even to the greatest part of Shepherd's companions; but it seems charm'd him so much, that he suffered her for a while to direct him in every thing; and she was the first who engaged him in taking base methods to obtain money wherewith to purchase baser pleasures. This Lion was a large masculine woman, and Shepherd a very little slight-limb'd lad; so that whenever he had been drinking and came to her quarrelsome, Bess often beat him into better temper, though Shepherd upon other occasions manifested his wanting neither courage nor strength. Repeated quarrels however between Shepherd and his mistress as it does with people of better rank, created such a coldness, and at last a seperation.

The creature he picked out to supply the place of Betty Lion, was one Mrs Maggott, a woman somewhat less boisterous in her temper, but full as wicked: she had a very great contempt for Shepherd, and only made use of him to go and steal money, or what might yield money, for her to spend in company that she lik'd better. One night when Shepherd came to her, and told her he had pawn'd the last thing he had for half a crown, 'Prithee,' says she, 'don't tell me such melancholly stories, but think how you may get more money: I have been in White-horse Yard this afternoon; there's a piece-broker there worth a great deal of money, he keeps his cash in a drawer under the compter; and there's abundance of good things in his shop that would be fit for me to wear'; a word you know to the wise is enough; 'let me see now how soon you'll put me in possession of them.' This had the effect that she desired; Shepherd left her about one o'clock in the morning, went to the house she talked of, took up the cellar window bars, and from thence entered the shop, which he plundered of money and goods to the amount of 22 *l.* and brought it to his doxy the same day before she was stirring, who appeared thereupon very well satisfied with his diligence, and helped him in a short time to squander what he had so dearly earned.

He still attained some affection for his old favourite Bess Lyon, who being taken up for some of her tricks, was committed to St Giles's Round-house, where Shepherd going to see her, broke the doors open, beat the keeper, and like a true knight errant, set his distressed paramour at liberty; which heroick act got him so much reputation amongst the ladies in Drury-Lane, that there was no body of his profession so much esteemed by them as John Shepherd. His brother Thomas, who was himself in tollerable estimation with that debauch'd part of the sex, now importun'd some of them to speak to his brother John to lend him a little money, and for the future allow him to go out a robbing with him. To both these propositions, Jack, being a kind brother, consented at the first word, and from thence forward the two brothers were always of one party.

In about three weeks after their coming together, they broke open a linnen-draper's shop, near Clare Market, where the brothers made good use of their time; for they were not in the house above a quarter of an hour, before they made shift to strip it of 50 *l*. But the younger brother acting impudently in disposing of some of the goods, he was detected and apprehended, upon which the first thing he did was to impeach his brother, and as many of his confederates as he could. Jack was very quickly apprehended upon his brother's information, and committed by Justice Parry to the Round-house, for farther examination; but instead of waiting for that, he began to examine, as well as he could, the strength of the place of his confinement; which being much too weak for a fellow of his capacity, he marched off before night, and committed a robbery into the bargain; vowing to be revenged on Tom who had so basely behaved himself (as Jack phrased it) toward so good a brother.

That information going off, Jack went on in his old way as usual. One day he and J. Benson being in Leicester Fields, Benson attempted to get a gentleman's watch; but missing his pull, the gentleman perceived it, and rais'd a mob, where Shepherd passing briskly to save his companion, was apprehended in his stead, and being carried before Justice Walters, was committed to New-Prison, where the first sight he saw, was his old companion Bess Lion, who had found her way thither upon a like errand. Jack, who now saw himself beset with danger, began to exert all his little cunning, which was indeed his master-piece. He applied himself first to Benson's friends, who were in good circumstances, hoping by their meditation to make the matter up; but in this he miscarried. Then he

267

attempted a slight information; but the Justice to whom he sent it, perceiving how trivial a thing it was, and guessing well at the drift thereof, refused it. Shepherd was now driven to his last shift, when Bess Lion and he laid their heads together how to break out; which they effected by force, and got safe off to one of Bess Lions old lodgings, where she kept him secret for some time, frightening him with stories of great searches being made after him, in order to detain him from conversing with any other woman.

But Jack being not naturally timorous, and having a strong inclination to to be out again in his old way with his companions, it was not long before he gave her the slip, and lodged himself with another of his female acquaintance, in a little bye court near the Strand. Here one Charles Grace desired to become an associate with him. Jack was very ready to take any young fellow in as a partner of his villanies; especially as Grace told him that his reason for doing such things, was to keep a beautiful woman without the knowledge of his relations. Shepherd and he getting the acquaintance of one Anthony Lamb, an apprentice to Mr Carter, near St Clements church, they inveigled the young man to consent to let them in to rob his master's house. He accordingly perform'd it, and they took from Mr Barton, who lodged there, to a very considerable value. But Grace and Shepherd quarrelling about the division, Shepherd wounded Grace in a violent manner, and on his quarrel betraying one another, Grace and Lamb were taken. But the misfortune of poor Lamb, who had been drawn in, so far prevailed upon several gentlemen who knew him, that they not only prevailed to have his sentence mitigated to transportation, but also furnished him with necessaries, and procured an order, that on his arrival there he should not be sold, as the other felons were, but that he should be left at liberty to provide for himself as well as he could.

It seems that Shepherd's gang, which consisted of himself, his brother Tom, Joseph Blake, alias Blueskin, Charles Grace, and James Sikes, whom his companions called Hell and Fury not knowing how to dispose of the goods they had taken, made use of William Field for that purpose, whom Shepherd in his ludicrous stile, us'd to characterize thus; that he was a fellow wicked enough to do any thing, but his want of courage permitted him to do nothing but carry on the trade he did; which was that of selling stolen goods when put into his hands. But Blake and Shepherd finding Field sometimes delatory, not thinking it always safe to trust him, they resolved to hire a warehouse and lodge their goods there; which accordingly they did near the Horse-Ferry in Westminster. There they plac'd what they took out of Mr Kneebone's house, and the goods made a great shew there, whence the people in the neighbourhood really took them for honest persons, who had so great wholesale business on their hands as occasion'd their taking a place there which lay convenient for the water. Field however importun'd them, having got scent they had such a warehouse, that he might go and see the goods, pretending that he had it just now in his power to sell them at a very great price: they accordingly carried him thither and shewed him the things. Two or three days afterwards, Field, tho' he had not courage to rob any body else, ventured however, to break open the warehouse, and took every rag that had been lodged there.

Not long after, Shepherd was apprehended for robbing Mr Kneebone, and tried at the next sessions at the Old-Bailey. His appearance there was very mean, and all the defence he pretended to make, was, that Jonathan Wild had helped to dispose of part of the goods, and he thought that it was very hard that he should not share in the punishment. The court took little notice of so insignificant a plea, and sentence being passed upon him, he hardly made a sensible petition for the favour of the court in the report; but behav'd throughout as a person either stupid or foolish; so far was he from appearing in any degree likely to make the noise he afterwards did.

When put into the condemned hold, he prevailed upon one Fowls, who was also under sentence, to lift him up to the iron spikes placed over the door which looks into the lodge, a woman of a large make attending without, and two others standing behind her in riding hoods. Jack no sooner got his head and shoulders thro' between the iron spikes, than by a sudden spring his body followed with ease; and the women taking him down gently, he was, without suspicion of the keepers, (tho' some of them was drinking at the upper end of the lodge) convey'd safely out of the lodge door, when soon getting a hackney coach, he went clear off before there was the least notice of his escape; which, when it was known, very much surprized the keepers, who never dreamt of an attempt of that kind before.

As soon as John breathed the fresh air, he went again briskly to his old employment; and the first thing he did was to find out one Page, a butcher of his acquaintance in Clare-Market, who dres'd him up in one of his frocks, and then went with him upon the business of raising money. No sooner had they set out, but Shepherd remembring one Mr Martin's a watch maker, near the Castle Tavern in Fleet-Street, and the situation of the shop, he prevailed upon his companion to go thither, and screwing a gimlet fast into the post at the door, they tied the knocker of the door thereto with a string, and then boldly breaking the glasses, snatched three watches before a boy that was in the shop could open the door, and marched clear off; Shepherd having the impudence upon this occasion, to pass underneath Newgate.

However, he did not long enjoy his liberty, for stroling about Finchly Common, he was apprehended and committed to Newgate; and was put immediately in the Stone Room, where they loaded him with a heavy pair of irons, and then stapled him fast down to the floor. He being left there alone in the sessions time, most of the people of the gaol then attending at the Old-Bailey, he with a crooked nail opened the lock, and by that means got rid of his chain, and went directly to the chimney in the room; where, with incessant working, he got out a couple of stones, and by that means entered a room called the Red Room, where no body had been lodged for a considerable time. Here he threw down a door, which one would have thought impossible to have been mov'd by the strength of a man though with ever so much noise. From hence with a great deal to do, he forced his passage into the chapel, there he broke a spike off the door, forcing open by its help four other doors. Getting at last upon the leads, he from thence descended gently, by the help of the blanket on which he lay, (for which he went back thro' the whole prison) upon the leads of Mr Bird a turner, next door to Newgate, and looking in at the garret window, saw the maid going to bed. As soon as he thought she was asleep, he stepp'd down stairs, went thro' the shop, opened the door, then into the street, leaving the door open behind him.

In the morning when the keepers were in search after him, hearing of this circumstance by the watchman, they were then perfectly satisfied of the method by which he went off: however, they were obliged to publish a reward, and make the strictest enquiry after him some foolish people having propagated a report, that he had not got out without connivance. In the mean while Shepherd found it a very difficult thing to get rid of his irons, having been obliged to lurk about and lye hid near a village not far from town, 'till with much ado he procured a hammer and took them off. He was no sooner freed from the incumbrance that remained upon him but he came privately into the town and that night robbed Mr Rawlin's house a pawn-broker in Drury-Lane. Here he got a very large booty, and amongst other things a very handsome black suit of cloaths and a gold watch. Being dressed with these he carried the rest of the foods and valuable effects to two women, one of whom was a poor young creature whom Shepherd had seduced, and who was imprisoned on this account.

No sooner had he taken care of the booty, but he went amongst his companions, the pick-pockets and whores in Drury Lane and Clare Market; where being accidentally espied fudling at a little brandy-shop, by a boy belonging to an alehouse who knew him very well, the lad immediately gave information; upon which he was apprehended, and re-conducted with a vast mob to his old Mansion-House of Newgate, being so much intoxicated with liquor, that he hardly was sensible of his miserable fate. They now took effectual care to prevent a third escape, never suffering him to be alone a moment, which as it put the keepers to great expence, they took care to pay themselves with the money they took of all who came to see him.

In this last confinement it was that Mr Shepherd and his adventures became the sole topick of conversation about town: numbers flocked daily to behold him; and he, far from being displeased at being made a spectacle of, entertained all who came with the greatest gaiety that could be. He acquainted them with all his adventures, related each of his robberies in the most ludicrous manner, and endeavoured to set off every circumstance of his flagitious life, as well as his capacity would give him leave; which, to say truth, was excellent at cunning, and buffoonery, and nothing else. Nor were the crowds of people on this occasion, that throng'd to Newgate, made up of the dregs of the people only, for then there would have been no wonder; but instead of that, persons of the first distinction, and not a few even dignified with titles. 'Tis certain that the noise made about him, and this curiosity of persons of so high a rank was a very great misfortune to the poor wretch himself; who from these circumstances began to conceive grand ideas of himself, as well as strong hopes of pardon; which encouraged him to play over all his airs, and divert as many as thought it worth their while, by their presence, to prevent a dying man from considering his latter end. Yet when Shepherd came up to chapel, it was observed that all his gaiety was laid aside, and he both heard and assisted with great attention at divine service; tho' upon other occasions he as much as he could avoided religious discourse; and depending upon the petitions he had made to several noblemen to interceed with the King for mercy, he seemed rather to aim at diverting his time till he receiv'd a pardon, than to improve the few days he had to prepare himself for his last.

On the 10th of November, 1724, Shepherd was by *certiorari* removed to the Bar of Court of King's Bench at Westminster; an affidavit being made, that he was the same John Shepherd mentioned in the record of conviction before read. Mr Justice Powis awarded judgment against him, and a rule was made for his execution on the 16th.

Such was the unaccountable fondness this criminal had for life, and so unwilling was he to lose all hopes of preserving it, that he fram'd in his mind all resolutions of cutting the rope when he should be bound in the cart, thinking thereby to get amongst the crowd, and so into Lincoln's-Inn-Fields, and from thence to the Thames. For this purpose he had provided a knife, which was with great difficulty taken from him, by Mr Watson who was to attend him to death. Nay, his hopes were carried even beyond hanging; for when he spoke to a person to whom he gave what money he had remaining, out of the large presents he had received from those who came to divert themselves at Shepherd's Show, or Newgate Fair, he most earnestly entreated him, that as soon as possible his body might be taken out of the hearse which was provided for him, put into a warm bed, and, if it were possible, some blood taken from him; for he was in great hopes he might be brought to life again; but if he was not, he desired him to defray the expences of his funeral, and return the overplus to his poor mother. Then he resumed his usual discourse about his robberies, and in the last moments of his life endeavoured to divert himself from the thoughts of death. Yet so uncertain and various was he in his behaviour, that he told one whom he had a great desire to see the morning he died, that he had then as much satisfaction to his heart, as if he was going to enjoy two hundred pounds per annum.

At the place of execution, to which he was convey'd in a cart, with iron handcuffs on, he behaved himself very gravely; confessing his robbing Mr Philips and Mrs Cook, but denying that Joseph Blake and he had William Field in their company when they broke open the house of Mr Kneebone. After this he submitted to his fate on the 16th of November, 1724, much pitied by the mob.

THE LIFE OF
LEWIS
HOUSSART

A s there is not any crime more shocking to human nature, or more contrary to all laws human and divine, than murder, so perhaps there have been few murders, in these last years committed, accompanied with more odd circumstances than that for which this criminal suffered.

Lewis Houssart was born at Sedan, a town in Champaigne, in the kingdom of France; his own paper says, 'that he was bred a surgeon, and qualified for that business'; however that were, he was here no better than a penny barber, only that he let blood, and thereby got a little money. As to the other circumstances of his life, all we shall say of him is, that while his wife Anne Rondeau was living, he married another woman, and the night of the marriage, before sitting down to supper, he went out a little space. During the interval between that and his coming in, it was judged from the circumstances, that he cut the poor woman's throat, who was his first wife, with a razor. For this being apprehended he was tried at the Old-Bailey; but for want of proof sufficient was acquitted. Not long after he was indicted for bigamy; upon which indictment, scarce making any defence, he was found guilty. He said thereupon, 'that he did not trouble himself to preserve so much as his reputation in this respect, for in the first place he knew they were resolved to convict him, and in the next place his first wife was a Socinian, an irrational creature, entitled to the advantages of no nation nor people, because she was no Christian; and accordingly the Scripture says, with such a one have no conversation, no, not so much as to eat with them.' An Appeal was then lodg'd against him by Solomon Rondeau, brother and heir to Anne his wife; yet that appearing to be defective, it was quash'd, and he charged upon another; whereunto joining issue upon six points, they came to be tried at the Old-Bailey; where the following circumstances appeared upon the trial.

That at the time he was at supper at his new wife's house, he started on a sudden, looked agast, and seemed to be very much frighted. A little boy deposed, that the prisoner gave him money to go to his own house in a little court, and fetch the mother of the deceased Anne Rondeau to a gentleman who would be at such a place and stay for her. When the mother returned from that place, and found no-body wanting her, or that had wanted her, she was very much out of humour at the boy's calling her; but that quickly gave way to the surprize of finding her daughter murder'd as soon as she enter'd the room. This boy who called her was very young; yet out of a number of persons that were in Newgate,

he singled out Lewis Houssart, and declared that he was the man who gave him money to go for old Mistress Rondeau. Upon this and several other corroborating proofs the jury found him guilty: upon which he arraigned the Justice of the court, declaring, that he was innocent, and that they might punish him if they would, but they could not make him guilty; and much more to the like effect. But the court was not troubled at that; and he scarce endeavoured to make any other defence.

While in the condemn'd-hole, amongst the rest of the criminals, he behaved himself in a very odd manner, insisted upon it that he was innocent of the fact laid to his charge, and threw out most opprobrious language against the court that condemn'd him; and when he was advised to lay aside such heats of passionate expressions, he said, 'he was sorry he did not more fully expose the British Justice upon the spot at the Old-Bailey, and that now, since they had tied up his hands from acting, he would at least have satisfaction in saying what he pleased.'

When this Houssart was first apprehended he appeared to be very much affected with his condition, was continually reading good books, praying and meditating, and shewing the utmost signs of a heart full of concern, and under the greatest emotions; but after he had been once acquitted, it made a thorough change in his temper: he quite laid aside all his former gravity, and gave way, on the contrary, to a very extraordinary spirit of obstinacy and unbelief. He puzzled himself continually, and if Mr Deval, who was then under sentence, would have given leave, would have puzzled him too, as to the doctrines of a future state, and an identical resurrection of the body, saying, he could not be persuaded of the truth thereof in a literal sense. But Mr Deval, after he had answered as well as he could these objections once, refused to hearken a second time to any such discourses, and was obliged to have recourse to harsh language, to oblige him to desist. In the mean while his brother came over from Holland, on the news of this dreadful misfortune, and went to make him a visit in the place of his confinement; where going to condole with him on the weight of his misfortunes, instead of receiving the kindness of his brother in the manner it deserved, Houssart began to make light of the affair, and treated the death of his wife and his own confinement in such a manner, that his brother leaving him abruptly, went back to Holland, more shocked at the brutality of his behaviour, than grieved for the misfortune which had befallen him.

It being a considerable space of time that Houssart lay in confinement in Newgate, and even in the condemn'd-hole, he had there of course abundance of companions; but of them all he affected none so much as John Shepherd, with whom he had abundance of merry, and even loose, discourses; once particularly, when the sparks flew very quick out of the charcoal fire, he said to Shepherd, 'See, see! I wish there were so many bullets that might beat the prison down about our ears; and then I might die like Sampson.'

It was near a month before he was called up to receive sentence; after which he made no scruple of saying, that since they had found him guilty of throat-cutting, he would verify their judgment by cutting his own throat. Upon which when some, who were in the same sad state with himself, objected to him how great a crime self-murder was, he immediately made answer, he was satisfied it was no crime at all: and upon this he fell to arguing in favour of the mortality of the soul, as if certain that it died with the body, endeavouring to cover his opinions with false glosses on that text in Genesis, wherein it is said, 'That God breathed into Man a living Soul'; from whence he would have inferr'd, 'that when a man ceased to live, he totally lost that soul'; and when it was asked of him, where then it went, he said, 'he did not know, nor did it much concern him.'

275

The standers by, who, notwithstanding their profligate course of life, had a natural abhorrence of this theoretical impiety, reproved him in very sharp terms, for making use of such expressions; upon which he replied, 'Ay! would you have me believe all the strange notions that are taught by the parsons? that the Devil is a real thing? that our good God punishes souls for ever and ever? that Hell is full of flames from material fire; and that this body of mine shall feel it? Well, you may believe it if you please, but it is so with me that I cannot.'

Sometimes, however, he would lay aside these sceptical opinions for a time, talk in another strain, and appear mightily concerned at the misfortunes he had drawn upon his second wife and child: he would then speak of Providence, and the decrees of God, with much seeming submission, would own that he had been guilty of many and grievous offences, and say, 'that the punishment of God was just, and desired the prayers of the minister of the place, and those that were about him.'

When he reflected on the grief it would give his father, who was near 90 years old, to hear of his misfortunes, he was seen to shed tears; but as soon as these thoughts were a little out of his head, he resumed his former temper, and was continually asking questions in relation to the truth of the Gospel dispensation, and the doctrines therein taught of rewards and punishments after this life. Being a Frenchman, and not perfectly versed in our language, a minister, of the Reformed Church of that nation, was prevailed upon to attend him. Houssart received him with tolerable civility, seemed pleased that he should pray by him, but industriously waved all discourses of his guilt, and even fell out into violent passions, if a confession was pressed upon him as a duty. In this strange way he consumed the time allowed him to prepare for another world.

The evening before his execution, the Foreign Minister, and he whose duty it was to attend him, both waited upon him at night, in order to discourse with him, on those strange notions he had of the mortality of the soul, and a total cessation of being after this life; but when they came to speak to him to this purpose, he said, 'they might spare themselves any arguments upon that head, for he believed a God and a Resurrection as firmly as they did.' They then discoursed to him of the nature of a sufficient repentance, and of the duty incumbent upon him to confess that great crime for which he was condemned, and thereby give Glory unto God. He fell at this into his old temper, and said with some passion, 'If you will pray with me, I'll thank you, and pray with you as long as you please; but if you come only to torture me of my guilt, I desire you would let me alone altogether.'

His lawyers having pretty well instructed him in the nature of an Appeal, and he coming thereby to know that he was now under sentence of death at the suit of the subject, and not of the King, he was very assiduous to learn where it was he was to apply for a reprieve: but finding it was the relations of his deceased wife from whom he was to expect it, he laid aside all those hopes, rightly conceiving it a thing impossible to prevail upon people to spare his life, who had almost undone themselves in prosecuting him.

In the morning of the day of execution he was very much disturbed at being refused the Sacrament, which, as the minister told him, could not be given him without his confession: yet this did not prevail; he said, 'he would die then without receiving it.' A French minister having before said to him, 'Lewis Houssart, since you are condemned on full evidence, I must inform you, that if you persist in this denial, you can look for nothing but to be d—,' Houssart replied, 'You must look for damnation yourself, for judging me guilty, when you know nothing of the matter.' This confused frame of mind he continued in, till he entered the cart for his execution, persisting all the way he went in like declarations of innocence, tho' sometimes intermixed with short prayers to God to forgive his manifold sins and offences.

At the place of execution he turned very pale, and grew very sick. The ministers told him, they would not pray by him, unless he would confess the murder for which he died; whereupon he said, 'he was very sorry for that; but if they would not pray by him he could not help it; he would not confess what he was totally ignorant of.' He persisted even at the moment of being tied up; and when such exhortations were again repeated, he said, 'Pray do not torment me! Pray cease troubling of me! I tell you I will not make myself worse than I am.' And so saying, he gave up the ghost, without any private prayer when left alone, or calling upon God or Christ to receive his spirit: he delivered however a paper, a copy of which follows; from whence our readers will receive a more exact idea of the man than from any picture we can draw.

> I Lovi Houssart am 40 Years old, and was born in Sedan, a Town in
> Campaigne near Boullonois. I have left France above 14 Years. I was

Apprentice to a Surgeon at Amsterdam, and after Examination was allowed by the College to be qualified for that Business; so that I intended to go on board a Ship as Surgeon; but I could never have my Health at Sea. I dwelt sometime at Maestrickt in the Dutch Brabant, where my aged Father and Mother now dwell. I travelled thro' Holland, and was in almost every Town. My two Sisters are in France, and also many of my Relations; for the Earth has scarce any Family more numerous than ours. Seven or eight Years I have been in London, and here I met with Anne Rondeau, who was born at the same Village with me, and therefore I loved her. After I had left her, she wrote to me, and said, She would reveal a Secret; and she told me, She had not been chaste, and the Consequence of it was upon her. Upon which I gave her my best Help and Assistance. Since she is dead, I hope her Soul is happy.

THE LIFE OF
JONATHAN
WILD

J onathan Wild was the son of mean parents, but honest and industrious; their family consisted of three sons and two daughters, whom they maintained in the best manner they could from their joint labours, he as a carpenter, and she by selling fruit in Wolverhampton Market in Staffordshire. Jonathan was the eldest of the sons, and having receiv'd as good an education as his father's circumstances would allow him, he was put out an apprentice in Birmingham. He served his time with much fidelity, and came up to town in the service of a gentleman of the long robe, about the year, 1704, or a little later. But not liking his service, he quitted it, and retired again to his old employment in the country, where he continued to work diligently for some time.

At last growing sick of labour, and still entertaining a desire of tasting the pleasures of London, thither he came a second time and worked journey-work at the trade he was bred. But this not producing money enough, to support those expences his love of pleasure threw him into, he got pretty deeply in debt, was suddenly arrested, and thrown into Wood-Street compter. Having no friends to do any thing for him, he liv'd very hardly there, scarce getting bread enough to support him from the charity allowed to prisoners, and what little services he could render to prisoners of the better sort in the gaol. However, as no man wanted address less than Jonathan, so no body could have employed it more properly than he did upon this occasion, for he got so much into the favour of the keepers, that they quickly permitted him the liberty of the gate, and he thereby got some little matter for going of errands. This set him above the very pinch of want, and that was all; but his fidelity and industry in these mean employments procured him such esteem amongst those in power there, that they soon appointed him an under keeper to those disorderly persons who were brought in every night.

Jonathan now came into a comfortable subsistance, having learnt how to get money of such people, by putting them into the road of getting liberty for themselves. Here he met with a lady, who went by the name of Mary Milliner, and who soon taught him how to gain yet much greater sums than in his way of life, by methods which he till then never heard of. By the help of this woman, he grew acquainted with all the notorious gangs of loose persons within the bills of mortality, and was perfectly vers'd in the manner by which they carried on their schemes: he knew where and how their enterprizes were to be gone upon, and what manner they disposed of their ill got goods, and having always an intrieguing head, he set up for a director amongst them, and soon became so useful, that tho' he never went out with any of them, yet he got more money by their crimes, than if he had been a partner therein, which upon one pretence or other, he always declined.

It must be observ'd that anciently when a thief had got his booty, there were multitudes of people ready to help him off, with his effects without any more to do; but this method being totally destroyed, by an Act passed in the reign of King William, by which it was made felony for any person to buy goods stolen, knowing them to be so, there were few or no receivers to be met with; those that still carried on the trade, taking exorbitant sums for their own profit, and leaving those who had run the hazard of their necks in obtaining them, the least share in the plunder. This had like to have brought the thieving trade to nought; but Jonathan quickly put things again in order, and gave new life to the practitioners in the several branches of stealing. The method he took was this.

As soon as any considerable robbery was committed, and Jonathan received intelligence by whom, he immediately went to the thieves, and enquired how the thing was done, where the persons lived who were injured, and what the booty consisted in that was taken away: then pretending to chide 'em for their wickedness, and exhorting them to live honestly for the future, he gave it them as his advice, to lodge what they had taken in a proper place which he appointed, and promis'd to take some measures for their security, by getting the people to give them somewhat to have their goods restored them again. Having thus wheedled those who had committed a robbery, into a compliance with his measures, his next business was to divide the goods into several parcels, and cause them to be sent to different places, always avoiding taking them into his own hands. Things being in this position, Jonathan and Mrs Milliner went to the persons who were robbed, and after condoling the misfortune, pretended that they had some acquaintance with a broker, to whom certain goods were brought, some of which they suspected to be stolen; and hearing that the person to whom they thus applied had been robb'd, they said, they thought it the duty of one honest body to another, to inform them thereof, and to enquire what goods they were they lost, in order to discover whether those they spoke of were the same or no. People who have had such losses, are always ready to hearken to any thing that has a tendency towards recovering their goods: Jonathan or his mistress therefore, had no great difficulty in making people listen to such terms. In a day or two therefore they were sure to come again, with intelligence that they had found part of the things, and provided no body was brought into trouble, and the broker had something in consideration of his care, they might be had again.

This practice of Jonathan's, if well considered, carries in it a great deal of policy. For first it seemed a very honest act to prevail on evil persons to restore the goods which they had stole; and then 'twas a great benefit to those who were robb'd, to have their goods again upon a reasonable premium; Jonathan all the while taking apparently nothing, his advantage arising out of the gratuity left with the broker and out of what he had bargained to give the thief; who also found his advantage in it, the rewards being very near as large as the price given by receivers, since receiving became so dangerous, and affording a certain security into the bargain. With respect to Jonathan, the contrivance placed him in safety from all the laws then in being, so that in a short time he began to give himself out for a person who made it his business to procure stolen goods to their right owners. When he first did this, he acted with so much art, that he not only acquired a very great reputation, not only from those who dealt with him, but even from people of higher station, who observing the industry with which he prosecuted malefactors, took him for a friend of justice, and such afforded him countenance. Certain it is, that he brought more villains to the gallows, than perhaps any man ever did, and so sensible was he of the necessity there was for him to act in this manner, that he constantly hung up two or three of his clients in a twelvemonth, that he might keep up that character to which he had attained; and so indefatigable was he in the pursuit of those he endeavoured to apprehend, that in all his course of acting, never so much as one single man escaped him.

When this practice of Jonathan's became noted, it produced not only much discourse, but some enquiries into his behaviour. Jonathan foresaw this, and in order to invade any ill consequence he put on upon such occasions, an air of gravity, and complained of the evil disposition of the times, which would not omit a man to serve his neighbours and his country without censure: 'For do I not,' quoth he, 'do the greatest good, when I persuade people who have deprived others of their properties, to restore them again for a reasonable consideration: and the villains whom I have brought to suffer punishment? Do not their deaths shew how much use I am of to the country? Why then should people asperse me?' Besides these professions of honesty, two great things there were which contributed to his preservation, and they were these. First, the great readiness the government always shews in detecting persons guilty of capital offences; in which case 'tis common to offer not only pardon, but rewards, to persons guilty, provided they make discoveries; and this Jonathan was so sensible of, that he did not only screen himself behind the lenity of the supreme power, but made use of it also as a sort of authority taking upon him the character of a sort of a minister of justice; which assumed character of his, however ill founded, prov'd of great advantage to him in the course of his life. The other point, which contributed to keep him from any prosecutions, was the great willingness of people, who had been robbed, to recover their goods, so that provided for a small matter, they could regain things very considerable, they were so far from taking pains to bring the offenders to justice, that they thought the premium a cheap price to get off. Thus by the rigour of the magistrate and the lenity of the subject, Jonathan claim'd constant employment; and, according as the case required, the poor thieves were either truss'd up to satisfy the just vengeance of the one, or protected and encouraged, to satisfy the demands of the other. Perhaps in all histories there is not an instance of a man who thus openly dallied with the laws, and play'd even with capital punishment. If any title can be devised suitable to Jonathan's character, it must be that of Director General of the United Forces of Highwaymen, House-breakers, Foot-Pads, Pick-Pockets and Private Thieves. Now the maxims by which he supported himself in this dangerous capacity, were these. In the first place he continually exhorted the plunderers to let him know punctually what goods they at any time took, by which means he had it in his power to give a direct answer to those who came to make enquiries. If they complied faithfully with his instructions, he was a certain protector on all occasions, and sometimes had interest enough to procure them liberty when apprehended. But if they pretended to become independent and despise his rules, or if they threw out any threatning speeches against their companions, or grumbled at the compositions he made for them, in such cases as these, Wild took the first opportunity of putting them into the information of some of his creatures, or the first fresh fact they committed, he immediately set out to apprehend them and laboured so indefatigable therein, that they never escaped him. Thus he not only procured the reward for himself, but also gain'd an opportunity of pretending, that he not only restored goods to the right owners, but also apprehended the thief as often as it was in his power. In those steps of his business which were most hazardous, Wild made the people themselves take the first steps, by publishing advertisements of things lost and directing them to be brought to Mr Wild, who was impowered to receive them, and pay such a reward as the person that lost them thought fit to offer. Wild in this capacity appeared no otherwise than as a person on whose honour the injured people could rely. After he had gone on in this trade, for about ten years with success, he began to lay aside much of his former caution, taking a larger house in the Great Old-Bailey, than that in which he formerly lived, giving the woman, whom he called his wife, abundance of fine things, and keeping an open office for restoring stolen goods. His fame at last came to that height, that persons of the highest qualities would condescend to make use of his abilities, when at any instalation, publick entry, or some other great solemnity, they had the misfortune of losing their watches, jewels or other things, of real or imaginary value. But as his method of treating those who applied to him for his assistance has been much represented, we shall next give an exact and impartial account thereof.

In the first place, when a person was introduced to Mr Wild's office, it was hinted to him, that a crown must be deposited by way of fee for his advice. When this was complied with, a large book was brought out: then the looser was examin'd with much formality, as to the time, place, and manner, wherein the goods became missing; and then was dismissed with a promise of careful enquiries being made, and of hearing more concerning them in a day or two. Wild had not the least occasion for these queries, but to amuse the persons he asked; for he knew beforehand all the circumstances of the robbery much better than they did; nay, perhaps had the very goods in house when the folks came first to enquire for them. When, according to his appointment, the enquirer came the second time Jonathan took care by a new scene to amuse him: he was told that Mr Wild had indeed made enquiries, but was very sorry to communicate the event of them; for the thief, who was a bold impudent fellow, rejected with scorn the offer which had been made him, pretending he could sell the goods at a double price; and, in short, would not hear a word of restitution unless upon better terms: 'But,' says Jonathan, 'if I can but come to the speech of him I don't doubt bringing him to reason.' At length, after one or two more attendances, Mr Wild gave the definitive answer, 'that provided no questions were ask'd, and you gave so much money to the porter who brought them you might have your things returned at such an hour precisely.' This was transacted with an outward appearance of friendship on his side, and with great seeming frankness and generosity; but when you come to the last article, *viz*. what Mr Wild expected for his trouble, then an air of coldness was put on, and he answered with equal pride and indifference, 'that what he did was purely from a principle of doing good; as to a gratuity for the trouble he had taken, he left it totally to yourself, you might do in it what you thought fit.' And even when money was presented to him, he received it with the same negligent grace, always putting you in mind that it was your own act, and that he took it as a great favour, and not as a reward.

Thus by this dexterity in his management, he fenced himself against the rigour of the law, in the midst of these notorious transgressions of it: for what could be imputed to Mr Wild? He neither saw the thief, who took away your goods, nor received them after they were taken: the method he pursued was neither dishonest nor illegal, if you would believe his account on it, and no other than his account of it could be gotten. Had he continued satisfied with this way of dealing, in all human probability he might have gone to his grave in peace: but he was greedy, and instead of keeping constant to this safe method, came at last to take the goods into his own custody, giving those that stole them what he thought proper, and then making such a bargain with the loser as he was able to bring him up to, sending the porter himself, and taking without ceremony whatever money had been given him. But as this happened only in the two last years of his life, it is fit we should give some instances of his behaviour before.

A gentleman who dealt in silks near Covent-Garden, had a piece of extraordinary rich damask, bespoke of him on purpose for the birth-day suit of a certain duke; and the lace-man having brought such trimming as was proper for it; the mercer had made the whole up in a parcel, tied it at each end with blue ribband, sealed with great exactness, and placed on one end of the compter, in expectation of his Grace's servant, who he knew was directed to call for it in the afternoon. Accordingly the fellow came; but when the mercer went to deliver him the goods, the piece was gone, and no account could possibly be had of it. As the master had been all day in the shop, so there was no pretence of charging any thing, either upon the carelessness or dishonesty of servants. After an hour's freting therefore, seeing no other remedy, he e'en determined to go and communicate his loss to Mr Wild, in hopes of receiving some benefit by his assistance; the loss consisting not so much in the value of the things, as in the disappointment it would be to the birth-day. Upon this consideration a hackney-coach was immediately called, and away he was ordered to drive directly to Jonathan's house in the Old Baily. As soon as he came into the room, and had acquainted Mr Wild with his business, the usual deposite of a crown being made, and the common questions of how, when and where, having been ask'd, the mercer, being very impatient, said with some kind of heat, 'Mr Wild, tell me in a few words, if it be in your power to serve me; if it is, I have thirty guineas here ready to lay down; but if you expect that I should dance attendance for a week or two, I assure you I shall not be willing to part with above half the money.' 'Good Sir,' replyed Mr Wild, 'have a little more consideration: I am no thief Sir, nor receiver of stolen goods; so that if you don't think fit to give me time to enquire, you must e'en take what measures you please.'

When the mercer found he was like to be left without any hopes, he began to talk in a milder strain, and with abundance of intreaties fell to persuading

Jonathan to think of some method to serve him, and that immediately. Wild stepped out a minute or two and as soon as he came back, told the gentleman, 'it was not in his power to serve him in such a hurry, if at all: however, in a day or two he might be able to give him some answer?' The mercer insisted, that a day or two would lessen the value of the goods one half to him; and Jonathan insisted as peremptorily, that it was not in his power to do any thing sooner. At last a servant came in a hurry, and told Mr Wild, there was a gentleman below desired to speak with him. Jonathan bowed, begged the gentleman's pardon, and told him, 'he would wait on him again in one minute'. In about five minutes he returned with a very smiling countenance; and turning to the gentleman, said, 'I protest Sir, you are the luckiest man I ever knew; I spoke to one of my people just now to go to a house where I knew some lifters resort, and directed him to talk of your robbery, and to say, you had been with me and offered thirty guineas for the things again. This story has had its effect, and if you go directly home, I fancy you'll hear more news of it than I am able to tell you. But pray, Sir, remember that the thirty guineas was your own offer, you are at free liberty to give them, or let them alone; 'tis nothing to me, though I have done all for you in my power of gratuity.'

Away went the mercer, wondering where this affair would end; but as he walked up Southampton-Street, a fellow overtook him, patted him on the shoulder, delivered him the bundle unopened, and told him the price was twenty guineas. The mercer paid it him directly, and returning to Jonathan in half an hour's time, begged him to accept of the ten guineas he had saved him for his pains. Jonathan told him, 'that he had saved him nothing, but supposed that the people thought twenty enough, considering that they were now pretty safe from prosecution.' The mercer still pressed the ten guineas upon Jonathan, who after taking them out of his hand, returned him five of them, and assured him, 'there was more than enough'; adding, ''Tis satisfaction enough Sir, to an honest man, that he is able to procure people their goods again.' This was a remarkable instance of his moderation he sometimes practised, the better to conceal his villanies. We will add another story, no less extraordinary.

A lady whose husband was out of the kingdom, and who had sent for her over-draughts for her assistance, to the amount of between fifteen hundred and two thousand pound, lost the pocket book in which they were contained, between Bucklers-bury and the Magpye-Alehouse in Leadenhall-Street, where the merchant lived upon whom they were drawn. She, however, went to the gentleman, and he advised her to go directly to Mr Jonathan Wild. Accordingly to Jonathan she came, deposited the crown, and answered the questions she ask'd him. Jonathan then told her that in an hour or two's time, possibly some of his people might hear who it was that had pick'd her pocket. The lady was vehement in her desires to have it again, and for that purpose went so far at last as to offer an hundred guineas. Wild upon that made answer, 'Though they are of much greater value to you, Madam, yet they cannot be worth any thing like it to them; therefore keep your own council, say nothing in the hearing of my people, and I'll give the best directions I am able for the recovery of your notes; in the mean while, if you will go to any tavern near, and endeavour to eat a bit of dinner, I will bring you an answer before the cloth is taken away.' She said she was unacquainted with any house thereabouts; upon which Mr Wild named the Baptist-Head. The lady would not be satisfied unless Mr Wild promised to eat with her: he at last complied, and she ordered a fowl and sausages at the house he had appointed. She waited there about three quarters of an hour, when Mr Wild came over and told her he had heard news of her book, desired her to tell out ten guineas upon the table in case she should have occasion for them, and as the cook came up to acquaint her that the fowl was ready, Jonathan begged she would just step down and see whether there was any woman waiting at his door. The lady without minding the mystery, did as he desired her, and perceiving a woman in a scarlet riding-hood walk twice or thrice by Mr Wild's house, her curiosity prompted her to go near her; but recollecting she had left the gold upon the table up stairs, she went and snatched it up without saying a word to Jonathan, and then running down again, went towards the woman in a red hood, who was still walking before his door. It seems she had guess'd right; for no sooner did she approach towards her, but the woman came directly up to her, and presenting her her pocket-book desired she would open it and see that all was safe: the lady did so, and answering, 'it was all right', the woman in the red riding-hood said, 'Here's another little note for you, Madam': upon which she gave her a little billet, on the out-side of which was wrote ten guineas. The lady delivered her the money immediately, adding also a piece for herself; then she returned with a great deal of joy to Mr Wild, and told him, 'she had got her book, and would now eat her dinner heartily'.

When the things were taken away, she thought it was time to go to the merchants, who probably now was returned from Change; but first thought it necessary to make Mr Wild an handsome present; for which purpose, putting her hand in her pocket, she with great surprize found her green purse gone, in which was the remainder of fifty guineas she had borrowed of the merchant in the morning; upon this she look'd very much confus'd, but did not speak a word. Jonathan perceived it, and ask'd her, 'if she was not well'. 'I am tollerable in health, Sir,' answered she, 'but amaz'd that the woman took but ten guineas for the book, and at the same time picked my pocket of thirty nine.' Mr Wild hereupon appeared in as great a confusion as the lady, and said, 'he hoped she was not in earnest; but if it were so, begged her not to disturb herself, for she should not lose one farthing.' Upon this, Jonathan begging her to sit still, stepped over to his own house, and gave, as may be supposed, necessary directions; for in less than half an hour, a little Jew, that Wild kept, bolted into the room, and told him the woman was taken, and on the point of going to the compter. 'You shall see, Madam,' (replied Jonathan, turning to the lady) 'what exemplary punishment

I'll make of this infamous woman.' Then turning himself to the Jew, 'Abraham,' (says he) 'was the green purse of money taken about her?' 'Yes, Sir,' (replied his agent). 'O la!' (then said the lady) 'I'll take the purse with all my heart; I would not prosecute the poor wretch for the world.' 'Would not you so, Madam,' (replied Wild)? 'well then, we'll see what's to be done.' Upon this he first whisper'd his emissary, and then dispatched him. He was no sooner gone, than, upon Jonathan's saying the lady would be too late at the merchant's, they took coach, and stopped over-against the compter gate by Stocks-Market. The lady wonder'd at all this, but by that time they had been in a tavern there a very little space, back comes Jonathan's emissary, with the green purse and the gold in it. 'She says, Sir,' (said the fellow to Wild) 'she has only broke a guinea of the money for garnish and wine, and here's all the rest of it.' 'Very well' (says Jonathan) 'give it to the lady. Will you please to tell it, Madam?' The lady accordingly did, and found there were forty-nine guineas. 'Bless me!' (says she) 'I think the woman's bewitch'd; she has sent me ten guineas more than I should have had.' 'No Madam,' (replied Wild) 'she has sent you the ten guineas back again, which she receiv'd for the book: I never suffer any such practices in my way; I obliged her therefore to give up the money she had taken as well as that she had stoln.' The lady was so much confounded at these unaccountable incidents, that she scarce knew what she did; at last recollecting herself, 'Well, Mr Wild,' (say she) 'then I think the least I can do is to oblige you to accept of those ten guineas.' 'No,' (replied he) 'nor of ten farthings; I scorn all actions of such a sort as much as any man of quality in the kingdom: all the reward I desire, Madam, is, that you will acknowledge I have acted like an honest man, and a man of honour.' He had scarce pronounced these words, before he rose up, made her a bow, and went immediately down stairs. We shall add but one more relation of this sort, and then go on with the series of our history.

There came a little boy with viols to sell in a basket, to a surgeon's shop; it was in the winter, when one day afer he had sold the bottles that were wanted, the boy complained he was almost chill'd to death with cold, and almost starved for want of victuals. The surgeon's maid, in compassion to the child, who was not above nine or ten years old, took him into the kitchen, and gave him a porringer of milk and bread, with a lump or two of sugar in it. The boy eat a little of it; then said, he had enough, gave her a thousand blessings, and marched off with a silver spoon, and a pair of forceps of the same metal, which lay in the shop as he passed through. The instrument was first missed, and the search after it occasioned their missing the spoon; yet no body suspected any thing of the boy, though they had all seen him in the kitchen.

The gentleman of the house, however, having some knowledge of Wild, and not living far from the Old-Bailey, went immediately to him for his advice. Jonathan called for a bottle of white wine, and ordered it to be mull'd. The gentleman knowing the custom of his house, laid down the crown, and was going on to tell him the manner in which the things were missed, but Mr Wild soon cut him short, by saying, 'Sir, step into the next room a moment, here's a lady, coming hither: you may depend upon my doing any thing that is in my power; and presently we'll talk the thing over at leisure.' The gentleman went into the room where he was directed, and saw, with no little wonder, his forceps and silver spoons lying upon the table. He had hardly took them up to look at them, before Jonathan entered, 'So Sir,' said he, 'I suppose you have no farther occasion for my assistance.' 'Yes indeed I have,' said the surgeon, 'there are a great many servants in our family, and some of them will certainly be blamed for this transaction, so that I am under a necessity of begging, that you will let me know how they were stolen?' 'I believe the thief is not far off,' quoth Jonathan, 'and if you'll give me your word he shall come to no harm, I'll produce him immediately.' The gentleman readily condescended to this proposition, and Mr Wild stepping out for a minute or two, brought in the young viol merchant in his hand. 'Here Sir,' says Wild, 'do you know this hopeful youth.' 'Yes,' answered the surgeon, 'but I could never have dreamt that a creature so little as he, could have had so much wickedness in him: however, as I have given you my word, and as I have had my things again, I will not only pass by his robbing me, but if he will bring me bottles again, I shall make use of him as I used to do.' 'I believe you may,' added Jonathan, 'when he ventures into your house again.' But it seems he was herein mistaken, for in less than a week afterwards the boy had the impudence to come and offer his viols again; upon which the gentleman not only bought of him as usual, but ordered two quarts of milk to be set on the fire, put into it two ounces of glister sugar, crumm'd it with a couple of penny bricks, and obliged this nimble fingur'd youth to eat it every drop up before he went out of the kitchen door; and then, without farther correction, hurried him about his business.

This was the channel in which Jonathan's business usually ran, till he became at last so very notorious, that an Act of Parliament passed, levelled directly against such practices, whereby persons who took money for the recovery of stolen goods, and did actually recover such goods without apprehending the felon, should be deemed guilty of felony in the same degree with those who committed the robbery. After this became a law, a certain honourable person sent to Jonathan to warn him of going on any longer at his old rate, for that it was now become a capital crime, and if he was apprehended for it, he could expect no mercy. Jonathan received the reproof with abundance of thankfulness and submission, but never altered the manner of his behaviour in the least, but on the contrary, did it more openly and publickly than ever. Indeed, to compensate for this, he seemed to double his diligence in apprehending thieves, and brought the most notorious amongst them to the gallows, even tho' he himself had bred them up in their art.

Of these none was so open and apparent a case as that of Blake, alias Blueskin. This fellow had from a child been under the tuition of Mr Wild, who paid for the curing his wounds whilst he was in the compter, allowed him three shillings and six pence a week for his subsistence, and afforded his help to get him out at last; yet soon after this he abandoned him to his own conduct, and in a short space caused him to be apprehended for breaking open the house of Mr Kneebone, which brought him to the gallows. When this fellow came to be tried, Mr Wild assured him, that his body should be handsomely interred in a good coffin at his own expence. This was strange comfort, and such as by no means suited with Blueskin; who insisted peremptorily upon a transportation pardon, which he said he was sure Jonathan had interest enough to procure for him: but upon Wild's assuring him that he had not, and that it was in vain for him to flatter himself with such hopes, Blueskin was at last in such a passion, that though this discourse happened in the presence of the court then sitting, Blake could not forbear taking revenge for what he took to be an insult on him; and therefore clap'd one hand under Jonathan's chin, and with the other cut him a large gash a-cross the throat, which every body at the time it was done judged mortal. Jonathan was carried off, all covered with blood; and though at the time he professed the greatest resentment for such base usage, affirming that he had never deserved to be so treated; yet when he afterwards came to be under sentence of death himself, he regretted prodigiously the escape he then made, often wishing that Blake had put an end to his life, rather than left him to so ignominious a fate. Indeed it was not Blake alone, who had entertained notions of putting him to death; he had disobliged almost the whole group of villains, and there were numbers of them who had taken it into their heads to deprive him of life. His escapes in the apprehending such persons were sometimes very narrow, having received wounds in almost every part of his body, had his skull twice fractured, and his whole constitution so broken by these accidents, and the great fatigue he went through, that when he fell under the misfortunes which brought him to his death, he was scarce able to stand upright, and never in a condition to go to chappel.

291

But we have broke a little into the thread of our history, and must therefore go back, in order to trace the causes which brought on Jonathan's last adventures, and finally his violent death, which we shall now relate in the clearest and concisest manner that the thing will allow.

The practices of this criminal continued long after the Act of Parliament, and that in so notorious a manner at last, that the magistrates of London and Middlesex thought themselves obliged to take notice of him. This occasioned a warrant to be granted against him, by a Worshipful Alderman of the City; upon which Mr Wild being apprehended somewhere near Woodstreet, he was carried into the Rose spunging-house. While he waited the leisure of the magistrate who was to examine him, the crowd was very great; whereupon with his wonted hypocrisy he harangued them to this purpose. 'I wonder, good people, what it is you would see? I am a poor honest man, who have done all I could to serve people when they have had the misfortune to lose their goods by the villainy of thieves: I have contributed more than any one man living, to bringing the most daring and notorious malefactors to justice: yet now by the malice of my enemies, you see I am in custody, and am going before a magistrate, who I hope will do me justice. Why should you insult me therefore? I don't know that I ever injured any of you: let me intreat you, as you see me lame in body, and inflicted in mind, not to make me more uneasy than I can bear. If I have offended against the law it will punish me, but it gives you no right to use me ill, unheard and unconvicted.' The people of the house, and the compter officers, by this time, had pretty well cleared the place; upon which he began to compose himself, and desired them to get a coach to the door, for that he was unable to walk. About an hour after, he was carried before a Justice and examined, and thereupon immediately committed to Newgate. He laid there a considerable time before he was tried; at last he was convicted capitally, upon the following fact.

He was indicted on the afore-mentioned statute, for receiving money for the restoring stolen goods, without apprehending the persons by whom they were stolen. In order to support this charge, the Prosecutrix, Catharine Stephens, deposed as follows: 'on the 22d of January, I had two persons, came into my shop under pretence of buying some lace; they were so difficult that I had none below would please them; so leaving my daughter in the shop, I stepped up stairs and brought down another box; we could not agree about the price, and so they went away together. In about half an hour after, I missed a tin box of lace that I valued at fifty pound. The same night I went to Jonathan Wild's house, but not meeting with him at home, I advertised the lace that I had lost, with a reward of fifteen guineas, and no questions ask'd: but hearing nothing of it, I went to Jonathan's house again, and then met with him at home: he desired me to give him a description of the persons that I suspected, which I did, as near as I could; and then he told me, "that he would make enquiry," and bid me "call again in two or three days." I did so, and then he said, "That he had heard something of my lace, and expected to know more of the matter in a very little time." I came to him again on that day he was apprehended, and told him, that tho' I had advertiz'd but fifteen guineas reward, yet I would give twenty or twenty five guineas, rather than not have my goods. "Don't be in such a hurry," (says Jonathan) "I don't know but I may help you to it for less; and if I can I will: the persons that have it are gone out of town, I shall set them to quarrelling about it, and then I shall get it the cheaper." On the 10th of March he sent me word, "that if I could come to him in Newgate, and bring ten guineas in my pocket, he would help me to the lace." I went; he desired me to call a porter; but I not knowing where to find one he sent a person who brought one that appeared to be a ticket-porter: the prisoner gave me a letter, which he said was sent him as a direction where to go for the lace; but I could not read, and so I delivered it to the porter. Then he desired me to give the porter the ten guineas, or else (he said) the persons that had the lace would not deliver it. I gave the porter the money; he went away and in a little time returned, and brought me a box that was sealed up, but not the box that was lost. I opened it, and found all my lace but one piece. "Now Mr Wild," (says I) "what must you have for your trouble?" "Not a farthing," (says he) "not a farthing for me: I don't do these things for worldly interest, but only for the good of poor people that have met with misfortunes. As for the piece of lace that is missing, I hope to get it you e'er it be long; and I don't know but that I may help you not only to your money again, but to the thief too; and if I can, as you are a good woman, and a widow and a Christian, I desire nothing of you but your prayers, and for them I shall be thankful. I have a great many enemies, and God knows what may be the consequence of this imprisonment.'"

293

The fact suggested in the indictment was undoubtedly fully proved by this deposition; and tho' it happened in Newgate, and after his confinement, yet it still continued as much a crime as if it had been done before. The law therefore condemned him upon it. But if he had even escaped this, there were other facts of a like nature, which inevitably would have destroyed him; for the last years of his life, instead of growing more prudent, he became less so; and the blunders he committed were very little like the behaviour of Jonathan, in the first years of his practice. When he was brought up to the bar to receive sentence, he appeared to be very much dejected, and when the usual question was proposed to him, 'What have you to say why judgment of death should not pass upon you?' he spoke with a very feeble voice in the following terms.

'My Lord, I hope I may even in the sad condition in which I stand, pretend to some little merit in respect to the service I have done my country, in delivering it from some of the greatest pests with which it was ever troubled. My Lord, I have brought many bold and daring malefactors to just punishment, even at the hazard of my own life, my body being coverd with scars I received in these undertakings. I presume, my Lord, to say, I have some merit, because at the time the things were done, they were esteemed meritorious by the Government; and therefore I hope, my Lord, some compassion may be shewn on the score of those services. I submit myself wholly to His Majesty's mercy, and humbly beg a favourable report of my case.'

When Sir William Thompson pronounced sentence of death, he spoke particularly to Wild, put him in mind of those cautions he had recieved of going on in practices, rendered capital by a law, made on purpose for preventing that infamous trade of becoming broker for felony, and standing in the middle between the felon and the person injured, in order to receive a premium for redress. And when he had properly stated the nature and aggravations of his crime, he exhorted him to make a better use of that small portion of time, which the tenderness of the law of England allowed sinners for repentance, and desired he would remember this admonition, though he had slighted others; as to the report, he told him, he might depend on justice, and ought not to hope for more.

Under conviction, no man who appeared upon other occasions to have so much courage, ever shewed so little. When clergymen took the pains to visit him, and instruct him in those duties which it became a dying man to practice, though he heard them without interruption, yet he heard them coldly, and was continually suggesting scruples and doubts about a future state, and putting frequent cases of the reasonableness and lawfulness of suicide, where an ignominious death was inevitably, and the thing was perpetrated only to avoid shame. He was more especially swayed to such notions, he pretended, from the examples of the famous heroes of antiquity; who, to avoid dishonourable treatment, had given themselves a speedy death. As such discourses were what took up most of the time between his sentence and death, so they occasioned some very useful lectures upon this head, from the charitable divines who visited him. One letter was written to him by a learned person, of which a copy has been preferred. 'Tis an excellent piece, but too long to be inserted.

Jonathan pretended to be overcome with these reasons, but it plainly appeared that in this he was an hypocrite; for the day before his execution, not withstanding the keepers had the strictest eye on him imaginable, some-body conveyed to him a bottle of liquid laudanum, of which haven taken a very large quantity, he hoped it would prevent his dying at the gallows. But as he had not been sparing in the dose, so the largeness of it made a speedy alteration in him, which being perceived by his fellow prisoners, seeing he could not keep open his eyes at the time the prayers were said, they walked him about; which first made him sweat exceedingly, and then very sick: at last he vomited, and they continuing still to lead him, he threw the greatest part of the laudanum off from his stomach. He continued notwithstanding that, very drowsy, stupid, and unable to do anything but gasp out his breath. He went to execution in a cart, and the people, instead of expressing any compassion, threw stones and dirt all the way he went along, reviling and cursing him to the last, and plainly shewing by their behaviour, how much his crimes had made him abhorred. When he arrived at Tyburn, having gathered a little strength, (nature recovering from the convulsions into which the laudanum had thrown him) the executioner told him, 'he might take what time he pleased to prepare for death'; he therefore sat down in the cart for some small time, during which the people were so uneasy, that they called out incessantly to the executioner to dispatch him, and at last threatned to tear him in pieces, if he did not tie him up immediately. Such a furious spirit was hardly ever discovered in the populace, who generally behold even the stroke of justice with tears; but so far were they from it in this case, that had a reprieve really come, 'tis highly questionable whether the prisoner could ever have been brought back safety.

Before we part with Mr Wild, 'tis requisite to say something of his wives. His first was a poor honest woman, who contented herself to live at Woolverhampton, with the son she had by him, without ever putting him to any trouble, or endeavouring to take upon her the title of Madam Wild, which his last wife did with the greatest affection. The next was the aforementioned Mrs Milliner, with whom he continued in very great intimacy after they liv'd seperately, and by her

Jonathan Wild going to the Place of Execution.

means he first carried on the trade of detecting stolen goods. The third was one Betty Man, a woman of the town in her younger years, but so suddenly struck with the horrour of her offences, that on the persuasion of a Romish priest she turn'd Papist, and appearing exceedingly devout and thoroughly penitent for all her sins. Wild even retained such an impression of the sanctity of this woman, that he ordered his body to be buried next hers in Pancras church-yard; which his friends saw accordingly performed, about two a-clock in the morning after his execution. The next of Mr Wild's sultana's was Sarah Perrin, alias Graystone, who surviv'd him. The fifth was Judith Nunn, by whom he had a daughter, who at the time of his decease might be about ten years old, both mother and daughter being then living. The sixth and last was the celebrated Madam Wild: this remarkable damsel before her first marriage was known by the name of Mary Brown, afterwards by that of Mrs Dean, being wife to Skull Dean, who was executed about the year 1716 or 1717 for house-breaking. Some people have reported that Jonathan was accessary to the hanging him, merely for the sake of the reward, and the opportunity of taking his relict; who, whatever regard she might have for her first husband, is currently reported to have been so much affected with the misfor- tunes of the latter, that she twice attempted to make away with herself after she had the news of his being under sentence. By this last lady he left no children, and but two by his three other wives, who were living at the time of his decease.

As to the person of this man, it was homely to the greatest degree; there being something remarkably villainous in his face, which nature had imprinted in stronger terms, than perhaps she ever did upon any other. However, he was strong and active, a fellow of prodigious boldness and resolution, which made the pusillanimity shewn at his death more remarkable. He was not at all shy in owning his profession, but on the contrary bragged of it upon all occasions; into which perhaps he was led by that ridiculous respect which was paid him, and the meanness of spirit some persons of distinction were guilty of in talking to him freely. Common report has swelled the number of malefactors executed thro' his means, to no less than one hundred and twenty: certain it is, that they were very numerous, as well in reality as his own reckoning. It has been said that there was a considerable sum of money due to him for his share in the apprehension of several felons at the very time of this death, which happened on Monday the 24th of May, 1725, he being then about 42 years of age.

Burnworth, Blewit, &c. Who Murdered Ball at his House in
the Mint.

THE LIVES OF
EDWARD BURNWORTH, ALIAS FRAZIER, WILLIAM BLEWIT, THOMAS BERRY, EMANUEL DICKENSON, WILLIAM MARJORAM, JOHN HIGGS, &C.

E dward Burnworth, alias Frazier, was the extraordinary person who framed a project for bringing rapine into method, and bounding even the practice of licentiousness within some kind of order. It may seem reasonable therefore to begin with his life, preferable to the rest, and in so doing, we must inform our readers, that his father was by trade a painter, though so low in his circumstances, as to be able to afford his son but a very mean education. However, he gave him as much as would have been sufficient for him in that trade to which he bound him apprentice, *viz.* a buckle-maker in Grub-Street, where for some time Edward lived honestly and much in the favour of his master; but his father dying, and his unhappy mother being reduced into very narrow circumstances, restraint grew uneasy to him, and the weight of a parent's authority being lost, he began to associate himself with those incorrigible vagrants, who frequent the ring at Moorfields, and from idleness and debauchery, go on in a very swift progression to robbery and picking of pockets. Edward was active in his person, and enterprizing in his genius; he soon distinguished himself in cudgel-playing, and such other Moorfields exercises, as qualify a man first for the road, and then for the gallows. The mob who frequented this place, where one Frazier kept the ring, were so highly pleased with Burnworth's performances, that they thought nothing could express their applause so much as conferring on him the title of young Frazier. This agreeing with the ferocity of his disposition, made him so vain thereof, that quitting his own name, he chose to go by this, and accordingly was called so by all his companions.

Burnworth's grand associates were these, William Blewit, Emanuel Dickenson, Thomas Berry, John Legee, William Marjoram, John Higgs, John Wilson, John Mason, Thomas Mekins, William Gillingham, John Barton, William Swift, and some others that is not material here to mention. At first they contented themselves with picking of pockets, and other exercises in the lowest class of thieving, in which, however, they did more mischief than any gang which had been before them for twenty years. They rose afterwards to exploits of a more hazardous nature, *viz.* snatching womens pockets, swords, hats, &c. The useful places for their carrying on such infamous practices, being about the Royal Exchange, Cheapside, St Paul's church yard, Fleet-Street, the Strand, and Charing-Cross. Here they stuck a good while, nor is it probable they would ever have risen higher if Burnworth their captain had not been detected in an affair of this kind, and committed to Bridewell, from whence he was removed to New Prison, where he projected an escape, which he put in execution. During this imprisonment, instead of reflecting on his evil course of life, he meditated only how to engage his companions in attempts of a higher nature, and considering how large a circle he had of wicked associates, he began to entertain notions of putting them in such a posture as might prevent their falling easily into the hands of justice, which many of them within a month or two last past had done.

Full of such projects, and having once more regained his freedom, he took much pains to find out Barton, Marjoram, Berry, Blewit, and Dickenson, in whose company he walked with strange boldness, considering warrants were out against the greatest part of the gang. In the night-time Burnworth stroled about to such little bawdy-houses as he had formerly frequented, and where he yet fancied he might be safe. One evening having wandered from the rest, he was so bold as to go into a house in the Old Bailey, where he heard the servants and successors of Jonathan Wild were in close pursuit of him, and that one of them was in the inner room by himself. Burnworth loaded his pistol under the table, and having primed it, goes with it ready cocked into the room where Jonathan's foreman was, with a quartern of brandy and a glass before him, 'Hark ye,' (says Edward) 'you fellow, who have served your time to a thief-taker, what business might you have with me or my company? Do you think to gain a hundred or two by swearing our lives away? If you do you are much mistaken, but that I may be some judge of your talent that way, I must hear you swear a little on another occasion.' Upon which filling a large glass of brandy, and putting a little gunpowder into it, he clapped it into the fellows hands, and then presenting his pistol to his breast, obliged him to wish most horrid mischiefs upon himself, if ever he attempted to follow him or his companions any more. No sooner had he done this, but Frazier knocking him down, quitted the room, and went to acquaint his companions with his notable adventure; which, as it undoubtedly frightened the new thief-taker, so it highly exalted his reputation for bravery: a thing not only agreeable to Burnworth's vanity, but useful also to his design, which was to advance himself to a sort of absolute authority. His associates were not cunning enough to penetrate his views; but without knowing it, suffered them to take effect, so that instead of robbing as they used to do, as accident directed them, or they received intelligence of any booty, they now submitted themselves to his guidance, and did nothing but as he commanded them.

The morning before the murder of Thomas Ball, Burnworth and Barton, pitch'd upon the house of an old Justice of the Peace in Clerkenwell, to whom they had a particular pique for having formerly committed Burnworth, and proposed it to their companions to break it open that night. They put their design in execution successfully, carrying off some things of real value, and a considerable parcel of what they took to be silver plate; with this they went into the fields above Islington, and from thence to Copenhagen-House, where they spent the greatest part of the day. On their parting the booty, Burnworth perceived what they had taken for silver was nothing more than a gilt metal, at which he in a rage would have thrown it away. Barton opposed it, and said, 'they should be able to sell it for something'; to which Burnworth replied, 'that it was good for nothing but to discover them, and therefore it should not be preserved at any rate.' Upon this they differed, and while they were debating, came Blewit, Berry, Dickenson, Higgs, Wilson, Legee, and Marjoram, who joined the company. Burnworth and Barton agreed to toss up at whose disposal the silver ware should be; they did so, and it fell to Burnworth to dispose of it as he thought fit; upon which he carried it immediately to the New-River-Side, and threw it in there, adding, 'he was sorry he had not the old Justice himself there, to share the same fate'; being really as much out of humour as if the Justice had imposed upon them in a fair sale of the commodity.

They loiter'd up and down the fields 'till towards evening, when they thought they might venture into town, and pass the time in their usual pleasures. While they were thus murdering of time, a comrade of theirs came up puffing and blowing as if ready to break his heart. As soon as he reached them, 'Lads,' (says he,) 'beware of one thing; the constables have been all about Chick-Lane in search of folk of our profession, and if ye venture to the house where we were to have met to-night, 'tis ten to one but we are all taken.' This intelligence occasioned a deep consultation amongst them, what method they had best take: Burnworth exhorted them to keep together, telling them, as they were armed with pistols and daggers, a small force would not venture to attack them. This was approved by all the rest, and when they had made a solemn oath to stand by one another in case of danger, they resolved, as night grew on, to draw towards town, Barton having quitted them and gone home. As they came through Turnmill-Street, they met the keeper of New Prison, from whom Burnworth had escaped about six weeks before. He desired Edward to step cross the way to him, adding, 'that he did not intend to do him any prejudice'. Burnworth replied, 'that he was no way in fear of any injury he was able to do him'. And so concealing a pistol in his hand, he stepped over to him, his companions waiting for him in the street, but the neighbours having some suspicion of the methods they followed, began to gather about them; upon which they called to their companion, to come away, which, after making a low bow to the captain of New-Prison, he did. Finding the people increase they thought it their most adviseable method to retire back into the fields; this they did, keeping very close together, and in order to deter the people from making any attempt, turn'd several times and presented their pistols in their faces, swearing they would murder the first man who came near enough for them to touch him.

As soon as they had dispersed their pursuers, they entered into a fresh consultation, in what manner they should dispose of themselves. Burnworth heard what every one proposed, and said at last 'that he thought the best thing they could do, was to enter the other quarter of the town, and so go directly to the water-side'. They approved his proposal, and accordingly getting down to Black-Fryars, cross'd directly into Southwark. They went afterwards to the musick-house, but did not stay there, retiring at last into St George's-Fields, where their last counsel was held to settle the operation of the night. There Burnworth exerted himself in his proper colours, informing them that there was no less danger of their being apprehended there than about Chick-Lane; for that one Thomas Ball, who kept a gin-shop in the Mint, and who was very well acquainted with most of their persons, had taken it into his head to venture upon Jonathan Wild's employment, and was indefatigable in searching out all their haunts, that he might get a good penny by apprehending them. He added, that but a few nights ago, he himself narrowly missed being caught by him, being obliged to clap a pistol to his face, and threaten to shoot him dead: 'therefore,' continued Burnworth, 'the surest way is to go to this rogue's house, and shoot him dead upon the spot. His death will not only secure us from all fears of his treachery, but it will so terrify others, that no-body will take up the trade of thief-catching in haste; and if it were not for such people, hardly one of our profession in a hundred would see the inside of Newgate.'

Burnworth had scarce made an end of his bloody proposal, before they all testified their assent to it, Higgs only excepted, who seeming to disapprove thereof, they upbraided him with being a coward and a scoundrel, unworthy of being any longer the companion of such brave fellows. When Frazier had sworn them all to stick fast by one another, he put himself at their head, and away they went directly to put their design in execution. Higgs retreating under the favour of the night, being apprehensive that himself might share the fate of Ball, upon the first dislike of him, Burnworth and his party, when they came to Ball's house, and enquired of his wife for him, were informed that he was gone to the next door, a publick-house, and that she would step and call him. Burnworth immediately followed her, and meeting Ball at the door, took him fast by the collar, dragged him into his own house, and began to expostulate with him why he had attempted to take him, and how ungenerous it was to seek to betray his old friends and acquaintance. Ball apprehending their mischievous intentions, addressed himself to Blewit, and beg'd of him to be an intercessor for him, that they would not murder him. But Burnworth with an oath replied, 'he would put it out of the power of Ball ever to do him any farther injury', and thereupon immediately shot him. Having thus done, they all went out of doors again; and that the neighbourhood might suppose the firing the pistol to have been without any ill intention, Blewit fired another in the street over the tops of the houses, saying aloud 'they were got safe into town, and there was no danger of meeting any rogues there'. Ball attempted to get as far as the door, but in vain, for he dropped immediately, and died in a few minutes afterwards.

Having thus executed their barbarous design, they went down from Ball's house directly towards the Faulcon, intending to cross the water back again. By the way they met with Higgs, who was making to the water-side likewise; him they fell upon, and rated for a pusillanimous dog, that would desert them in an affair of such consequence, and then Burnworth proposed to shoot him, which 'tis believed he would have done, had not Marjoram interposed, and pleaded for the sparing his life. From the Faulcon-Stairs they crossed to Pig-Stairs; and there consulting how to spend the evening, they resolved to go to the Boar's-Head tavern in Smithfield, as not being there known, and being at a distance from the water-side, in case any pursuit should be made after them, on account of the murder. At this place they continued till near ten of the clock, when they separated themselves into parties for that night. This murder made them more cautious of appearing in publick; and Blewit, Berry, and Dickenson soon after set out for Harwich, and went over in a packet-boat from thence for Helveot-Sluys.

Higgs also being in fear, shipped himself at Spithead, where he began to be a little at ease; but justice quickly overtook him; for his brother who lived in town, having wrote a letter to him, and given it to a ship-mate of his, this man accidentally fell into company with one Arthur a watchman, of St Sepulchre's parish, and pulling the letter by chance out of his pocket, the watchman saw the direction, and recollected that Higgs was a companion of Frazier's. Upon this he sends word to Mr Delafay, Under Secretary of State, and proper persons were immediately dispatched to Spithead, who seized and brought him up in custody. Wilson, another of his confederates, withdrew about the same time, and preserved himself from being heard of for a considerable time.

Burnworth with some companions continued to carry on their rapacious plunderings, and as they kept pretty well united, and were resolute, they were too strong to be apprehended. Amongst the rest of their pranks, they stopped the chair of the Earl of Harborough in Piccadilly; but the chairmen drawing their poles, and knocking one of the robbers down, the Earl came out of the chair, and after a smart dispute, in which Burnworth shot one of the chairmen in the shoulder, they rais'd their wounded companion, and withdrew. About this time a proclamation was published for the apprehending Burnworth, Blewit, &c. it being justly suppos'd that none but men guilty of these outrages, could be the persons concerned in the murder of Ball. A gentleman who had bought one of these papers, came into an alehouse in White-Cross-Street, and read it publickly. The discourse of the company turning upon the impossibility of the persons concerned making their escape. Marjoram one of the gang who was there, unknown, weighing the thing with himself, retired immediately into the fields, where loitering about till evening, he then stole into Smithfield, and going to a constable, surrendered himself as an accomplice in the murder of Ball, desiring to be carried before the Lord Mayor, that he might put himself in a way of obtaining a pardon, and the reward promised by the proclamation. That night he was confined in Woodstreet compter, his Lordship not being at leisure to examine him.

The next day the noise of his surrender being spread all over the town, many of his companions changed their lodgings, and provided for their safety; but Barton planting himself in the way, as Marjoram was carrying to Goldsmiths Hall, he popped out upon him at once, though the constable had him by the arm, and presenting a pistol to him, said, 'D—n ye I'll kill you.' Marjoram at the sound of his voice duck'd his head, and he immediately firing, the ball graz'd only on his back, without doing him any hurt. The surprize with which they were all struck who were assisting the constable, gave an opportunity to Barton to retire, after his committing such an insult on publick justice, as perhaps was never heard of. Marjoram proceeded, and made a full discovery of all the transactions in which he had been concerned, Legee being taken that night by his directions in White-Cross-Street, and committed to Newgate.

Burnworth was now deprived of his old associates, yet he went on at his old rate by himself; for a few nights after, he broke open the house of Mr Beezely a great distiller, in Clare Market, and took away from thence notes to a very great value, with a quantity of plate, which mistaking for white metal he threw away. One Benjamin Jones picked it up, and was thereupon hanged, being one of the number under sentence, when the condemned-hold was shut up, and the criminals refused to submit to the keepers. Burnworth was particularly described in the proclamation, and three hundred pounds offered to any who would apprehend him; yet so audacious was he to come to a house in Holborn, and laying a pistol down loaded on the table, called for a pint of beer, which he drank and paid for, defying any body to touch him, though they knew him to be the person mentioned in the proclamation.

It happened at this time, that one Christopher Leonard was in prison for some such feats as Burnworth had been guilty of, who lodged at the same time with Leonard's wife and sister; who supposing nothing could so effectually recommend to him the mercy of the Government, as the procuring Frazier to be apprehended; he, accordingly made the proposal, by his wife, to persons in authority, and the project being approved, they appointed a sufficient force to seize him, who were placed at an adjoining alehouse, where the wife of Kit Leonard was to give them the signal. About six of the clock in the evening, on Shrove Tuesday, Kate Leonard and her sister, and Burnworth, being all together, Kate Leonard proposed to fry some pancakes for supper, which the other two approved of; accordingly her sister set about them. Burnworth had put off his surtout coat, in the pocket whereof he had several pistols. There was a little back door which Burnworth usually kept upon the latch, only in order to make his escape, if he should be surprized. This door Kate fastened unperceived by Burnworth, and whilst her sister was frying the pancakes, went to the alehouse for a pot of drink; when having given the men who were there waiting for him the signal, she returned, and entring the house, pretended to lock the door after her, but designedly missed the staple: the door being thus upon the jar only, as she gave the drink to Burnworth, six persons rushed into the room. Burnworth hearing the noise, and fearing his surprize, jump'd up, thinking to have made his escape at the back door, not knowing it to be bolted; but they were upon him before he could get it open, and holding his hands behind him, one of them ty'd them, whilst another, to intimidate him, fired a pistol over his head. Having thus secured him, they immediately carried him before a Justice of Peace, who after a long examination committed him to Newgate. Notwithstanding his confinement in that place, he communicated to his companions, the suspicions he had of Kate Leonard's betraying him, and the danger there was of her detecting some of the rest. They were easily induced to treat her as they had done Ball, and one of them fired a pistol at her, just as she was entring her own house; but that missing, they made two or three other attempts of the same nature, untill the Justices of the Peace placed a guard thereabouts, in order to secure her from being killed, and if possible to seize those who should attempt it, after which they heard no more of these attacks.

In Newgate they confined Burnworth to the condemned-hold, and took what other precautions they thought proper, in order to secure so dangerous a person, who, they were aware, meditated nothing but how to escape. He was in this condition when Barton, Swift &c. were under sentence, and it was shrewdly suspected that he put them upon a new attempt of breaking out, which failed of success. The keepers upon suspicion of his being the projector of this enterprize, removed him into the Bilboa Room, and there loaded him with irons, yet nothing could break the stubbornness of his temper, which urged him continually to force his way thro' all opposition, and regain his liberty, in order to practice more villainies. It is impossible to say how, but by some method or other he had procured saws, files, and other instruments for this purpose. With these he first released himself from his irons, then broke thro' the wall of the room in which he was lodg'd, and got into the Women's Apartment, the window of which being fortified with three tire of iron bars, he forced one of them in a little time. While he was filing the next, one of the women gave the keepers notice, whereupon they came and dragged him back to the condemned hold, and there stapled him down to the ground.

William Blewit, who next to Frazier, was the chief person in the gang, was one of St Giles's breed, his father a porter, and his mother at the time of his execution, selling greens in the same parish. They were both of them unable to give their son education, or otherwise to provide for him, which occasioned his being put out by the parish to a perfumer of gloves; but his temper inclining him to wicked practices, he soon got himself into a gang of young pick-pockets, with whom he practised several years with impunity; but being at last apprehended in the very fact, he was committed to Newgate, convicted the next sessions, and ordered for transportation. Being shipped on board the vessel with other wretches in the same condition, he was quickly let into the secret, of their having provided for an escape. Blewit immediately foresaw abundance of difficulties in their design, and therefore resolved to make a sure use of it for his own advantage, which he did, by communicating all to the captain, who immediately seiz'd their tools, and prevented the loss of his ship.

In return for this service, Blewit obtained his freedom, but before he had been two months in town, somebody seizing him, and committing him to Newgate, at the next sessions he was tried for returning from transportation, and convicted, but pleading the service he had done, in preventing the attempt of the other malefactors, execution was respited till the return of the captain, and on his report the sentence was changed into a new transportation, to what foreign port he would: but he no sooner regain'd his liberty, than he put it to the same use as before, till he got into acquaintance with Burnworth and his gang, who taught him other methods of robbing. He had, to his other crimes, added the marriage of several wives, of which the first had so great a love for him, that upon her visiting him at Newgate, the day before they sat out for Kingston, she fell down dead in the lodge; another of his wives married Emanuel Dickenson, and she survived them both.

His meeting Burnworth that afternoon before Ball's murder was accidental, but the savageness of his temper led him to quick compliance with that wicked proposition. After the commission of that fact, tho' he with his companions went over to Holland, they were so uneasy there, that they were constantly perusing the English news papers, at the coffee-houses in Rotterdam, that they might gain intelligence of what methods had been taken to apprehend the persons concerned in Ball's murther; resolving, on the first news of a proclamation, or other interposition of the state on that occasion, to quit the dominions of the republick. But as Burnworth had been betrayed by the only persons from whom he could hope for assistance, and Higgs seized on board a ship, where he fancied himself secure, so Blewit and his associates, tho' they endeavoured to acquaint themselves with the transactions at London, relating to them, fell also into the hands of justice, when they least expected it.

The proclamation for apprehending them came no sooner into the hands of Mr Finch, the British Resident at the Hague, but he caused an enquiry to be made, whether any such persons as were therein described, had been seen at Rotterdam; and being assured that there had, and that they were lodged at the Hamburgh Arms on the Boom-Keys in that city, he sent away a special messenger to enquire the truth thereof; of which he was no sooner satisfied, than he procured an order from the States General for apprehending them anywhere within the province. By virtue of this order, the messenger, with the assistance of proper officers, apprehended Blewit at the house whither they had been directed; but Dickenson and Berry had left him, and were gone on board a ship, not caring to remain any longer in Holland. They conducted their prisoner to the Stadt-house prison in Rotterdam, and then went to the Brill; where the ship, on board which his companions were, not being cleared out, they surprized them also, and sent them under a strong guard to Rotterdam, where they were put in the same place with their old associate Blewit. We shall now take an opportunity to speak of each of them.

Emanuel Dickenson was the son of a very worthy person. The lad was ever ungovernable in his temper, and being left a child at his father's death, himself, his brother, and several sisters, they unfortunately addicted themselves to evil courses. Emanuel having addicted himself to picking of pockets for a considerable space, at last attempting to snatch a gentleman's hat off in the Strand, he was seized with it in his hand, and committed to Newgate, and at the next sessions convicted, and ordered for transportation; but his mother applying at court for a pardon, and setting forth the merit of his father, procured his discharge; the only use he made of which, was to associate himself with his old companions; who, by degrees, led him into greater villanies, till he was with the rest drawn into the murther of Ball.

Thomas Berry was descended from parents in the most wretched circumstances, who suffered him to idle about the streets, and get into such gangs of thieves, as taught him from his infancy the art of diving. He did not always meet with impunity; for besides getting into the little prisons, and being whip'd several times, he had been thrice in Newgate, and for the last fact ordered for transportation: however, by some means or other, he got away from the ship and returned quickly to his old employment; in which he had not continued long, before falling into the acquaintance of Burnworth it brought him to the commission of murder, and after that with great justice to an ignominious death.

After they were all three secured, the Resident dispatched an account thereof to England, whereupon he received directions for applying to the States-General for leave to send them back. This was readily granted, and six soldiers were ordered to attend them on board, besides the messengers who were sent to fetch them. Captain Samuel Taylor, in the *Delight* sloop, brought them safe to the

Nore, where they were met by two other messengers, who assisted in taking charge of them up the river. In the midst of all the miseries they suffered and the certainty they had of being doom'd to suffer much more as soon as they came on shore, yet they behaved themselves with the greatest gaity imaginable. On their arrival at the Tower, they were put into a boat with the messengers, with three other boats to guard them each filled with a corporal and a file of musqueteers; and in this order they were brought to Westminster; where after being examined before Justice Cholk and Justice Blackerby, they were conducted by a party of foot-guards to Newgate, through a continued lane of spectators, who proclaimed their joy, at seeing these egregious villains in the hands of justice.

On their arrival at Newgate the keepers having put them on each a pair of the heavist irons in the gaol they next did them the honour of conducting them up stairs, to their old friend Edward Burnworth, who congratulated them on their safe arrival, and they condoled with him on his confinement. Being exhorted to apply the little time they had to live in preparing themselves for another world, Burnworth replied, 'if they had any inclination to think of a future state, yet so many persons as were admitted to see them, must needs divert any good thoughts'. But their minds were totally taken up with consulting the most likely means to make their escapes, and all their actions shewed their thoughts were bent only on enlargement, and that they were altogether unmindful of death, or at least careless of the future consequence thereof.

On Wednesday the 30th of March, 1716, Burnworth, Blewit, Berry, Dickenson, Legee and Higgs, were all put into a waggon, hand-cuff'd and chain'd, and carried to Kingston under a guard of the Duke of Bolton's Horse. At their coming out of Newgate they were very merry, charging the Guard to take care that no misfortune happened to them, and calling upon the spectators, as to shew the respect they bore them, by hallowing, and paying them the compliments due to gentlemen of their profession. As they passed along the road, they frequently threw money among the people who followed them, diverting themselves with seeing the others strive for it; and particularly Blewit having thrown out some halfpence amongst the mob, a little boy picked up one of them, and calling out to Blewit, said, 'As sure as you will be condemned at Kingston, so sure will I have your name engraved hereon.' Whereupon Blewit took a shilling out of his pocket, and gave it to the boy, telling him, 'there was something towards defraying the charge of engraving'.

On the 31st of March, the assizes were opened, before the Right Hon. the Lord Chief Justice Raymond, and Mr Justice Denton; and the grand jury having found indictments against the prisoners, they were severally arraigned thereupon, when five of them pleaded not guilty; but Burnworth absolutely refused to plead at all; upon which, after being advised by the judge, not to force the court upon that rigour, his thumbs were ty'd and strain'd with a packthread; which having no effect upon him, the sentence of the press was read to him, and he still continuing contumacious, was carried down to the Stock House, and the press laid upon him. He continued one hour and three minutes, under the weight of three hundred, three quarters, and two pounds, endeavouring to beat out his brains against the floor; during which time, the High-Sheriff himself was present, and frequently exhorted him to plead to the indictment; which at last he consented to no. Being brought up to the court, after a trial which lasted from eight in the morning, till one in the afternoon, on the first day of April, they were all six found guilty of the indictment, and being remanded back to the Stock House, were all chained and stapled down to the floor. Whilst they were under conviction, they diverted themselves with repeating jests and stories of various natures, particularly of the manner of their escapes before out of the hands of justice, and the robberies and offences they had committed; and it being proposed for the satisfaction of the world, for them to leave the particulars of the several robberies by them committed, Burnworth replied, 'that were he to write all the robberies by him committed, an hundred sheets of paper, wrote as close as could be, would not contain them'.

On Monday, the 4th day of April, they were brought up again from the Stock-House, to receive sentence of death. When sentence was passed, they entreated leave for their friends of visit him in the prison, which was granted them by the court, but with a strict injunction to the keeper to be careful over them. After they returned to the prison, they bent their thoughts wholly on making their escape, and for that purpose had procured proper implements for the execution for it. Burnworth's mother being surprized with several files, &c. about her, and the whole plot discovered by Blewit's mother, who was heard to say, 'that she had forgot the opium'. It seems the scheme was to murder the two persons who attended them in the gaol, together with Mr Elliot the turnkey. After they had got out they intended to have fired a stack of bavins adjoining to the prison, and thereby amused the inhabitants while they got clear off. Burnworth's mother was confined for this attempt in his favour and some lesser implements that were sewed up in the waistbands of their breeches being ripped out, all hopes of escape whatsoever were now taken away; yet Burnworth affected to keep up the same spirit with which he hitherto behaved, and talked to one of his guard, of coming in the night in a dark entry, and pulling him by the nose, if he did not see him decently buried.

About ten of the clock on Wednesday morning, (*viz*. April the 6th, 1726) they, together with one Blackburn, who was condemned for robbing on the highway, a fellow grossly ignorant and stupid, were carried out in a cart to their execution, being attended by a company of foot to the gallows. In their passage thither, that audacious carriage in which they had so long persisted, totally forsook them, and they appeared with all that seriousness and devotion, which might be looked for, from persons in their condition. Blewit perceiving one Mr Warwick among the spectators, desired that he might stop to speak to him, which being granted, he threw himself upon his knees, and earnestly entreated his pardon, for having once attempted his life, by presenting a pistol at him, upon suspicion that Mr Warwick had given an information against him. When at the place of execution and tied up, Blewit and Dickenson especially, pray'd with great fervour, and a becoming earnestness, exhorting all the young persons they saw to take warning by them, and not follow such courses as might in time bring them to so terrible an end.

Blewit acknowledged, that for six years he had lived by stealing and pilfering only. He had given all the cloaths he had to his mother, but being informed that he was to be hung in chains, he desired his mother might return them to prevent his being put up in his shirt: he then desired the executioner to tye him up so, that he might be as soon out of his pain as possible: then he set the Penitential Psalm, and repeated the words of it to the other criminals; then they all kissed one another; and, after some private devotions, the cart drew away, and they were turned off. Dickenson died very hard, kicking off one of his shoes, and loosing the other. Their bodies were carried back under the same guard which attended them to their execution. Burnworth and Blewit were afterwards hung up in chains, over-against the sign of the Fighting-Cocks in St George's Fields:

Dickenson and Berry were hung up on Kennington Common; but the Sheriff of Surry had orders to suffer his relations to take down the body of Dickenson after its hanging up one day, which favour was granted on account of his father's service in the army, who was killed at his post, when the Confederate Army besieged Air, in the late war. Legee and Higgs were hung up on Putney-Common, beyond Wandsworth.

THE LIFE OF
CATHERINE
HAYES

C atherine Hall, afterwards Catherine Hayes, was born in the year 1690, at a village on the borders of Warwickshire, within four miles of Birmingham. Her parents were so poor as to receive the assistance of the parish, and so careless of their daughter, that they never gave her the least education. While a girl she discovered marks of so violent and turbulent a temper, that she totally threw off all respect and obedience to her parents, giving a loose to her passions, and gratifying herself in all her vicious inclinations.

About the year 1705, some officers coming into the neighbourhood to recruit, Kate was so much taken with the fellows in red, that she stroled away with them, till they came to a village called Great Ombersley in Warwickshire, where they very ungenerously left her behind them. This elopement of her sparks drove her almost mad, so that she went like a distracted creature about the country, till coming to Mr Hayes's door, his wife in compassion took her in out of charity. The eldest child in the family was John Hayes the deceased, who being then about 21 years of age, found so many charms in this Catherine Hall, that he quickly made proposals to her of marriage. There is no doubt of their being readily enough received, and as they both were sensible how disagreeable a thing it would be to his parents, agreed to keep it secret. They quickly adjusted the measures that were to be taken, in order to their being married at Worcester. Mr John Hayes pretended that he wanted some tools in the way of his trade, *viz.* that of a carpenter, for which it was necessary he should go to Worcester; and under this colour he procured also as much money as was sufficient to defray the expence of the intended wedding.

Catherine having privately quitted the house, and meeting at the appointed place, they accompanied each other to Worcester, where the wedding was soon celebrated. The same day Mrs Catherine Hayes had the fortune to meet with some of her acquaintance, who had dropped her at Ombersley; who understanding where the nuptials were to be solemnized, consulted among themselves how to make a penny of the bridegroom. Accordingly, at evening, just as Mr Hayes was got into bed to his wife, they coming to the house where he lodged, forcibly entered the room, and dragged the bridegroom away, pretending to impress him for her Majesty's Service. This proceeding broke the measures Mr John Hayes had concerted with his wife, to keep their wedding secret; for finding no redemption without a larger sum of money than he was master of, he was necessitated to let his father know of his misfortune. Mr Hayes hearing of his son's adventures, his resentment did not extinguish his affection for him as a father, but he resolved to deliver him from his troubles; and accordingly taking a gentleman in the neighbourhood along with him, he went for Worcester. At their arrival there, they found Mr John Hayes in the hands of the officers, who insisted upon the detaining him for her Majesty's Service; but his father, and the gentleman he brought with him, soon made them sensible of their error, and they were glad to discharge him immediately. But Mrs Catherine, who better approved of a travelling than a settled life, persuaded her husband to enter himself a voluntier, in a regiment then at Worcester, which he did, and went abroad with them, where he continued for some time.

Mr John Hayes being in garrison in the Isle of Wight, and not content with such a lazy, indolent life, sollicited his father to procure his discharge, which at length he was prevailed upon to consent to; but the several journeys he was necessitated to take, and the expences of procuring such discharge, amounted to about sixty pounds. The father then, the better to induce him to settle himself in the country, put him into an estate of ten pounds per annum, but Mr John Hayes representing to his father, that it was not possible for him and his wife to live on that, persuaded his father to let him have also a leasehold of sixteen pounds per annum; upon which he lived during the continuance of the lease.

The characters of Mr John Hayes and his wife were vastly different: he had the repute of a sober honest peaceable man, and a very good husband; the only objection against him was, that he was of too frugal a temper, and rather too indulgent of his wife. She was on all hands allowed to be a very turbulent person, never free from quarrels in the neighbourhood, and fomenting disputes to the disturbance of all her friends. They lived in the country for the space of about six years, until the lease of the last mentioned farm expired; about which time, Mrs Hayes persuaded her husband to leave the country, and come to London.

In the year 1719, upon their arrival in town, they took a house. Part of which they let out in lodgings, and sold sea coal, chandlery ware, &c. whereby they lived in a handsome creditable manner. In this business they picked up money, and Mr Hayes received the yearly rent of the first mentioned estate, tho' in town, and by lending out money in small sums amongst his country people improved the same considerably. She would frequently, in speaking of Mr Hayes, give him the best of characters; tho' to some of her particular cronies, who knew not Mr Hayes's temper, she would exclaim against him, and say, that it was no sin to kill him, and that one time or other she might give him a plot. Afterwards they removed into Tottenham Court-Road, where they lived for some time, following the same business as formerly; from whence about two years afterwards they removed into Tyburn Road, a few doors above where the murther was committed. There they lived about twelve months, Mr Hayes still supporting himself in lending out money upon pledges, and sometimes working at his profession, and in husbandry, till it was computed he had picked up a pretty handsome sum of money. About ten months before the murder, they removed to the house of Mr Whinyard, where the murther was committed, taking lodgings up two pair of stairs. There it was, that Thomas Billings a taylor, who wrought journey work about Monmouth Street, under pretence of being Mrs Hayes's countryman, came to see them. They invited him to lodge with them; he did so, and continued in the house till about six weeks before the death of Mr Hayes. About the same time Thomas Wood, who was a neighbours son in the country, and an intimate acquaintance both of Mr Hayes and his wife, came to town, and pressing being at that time very hot, he was obliged to quit his lodgings, whereupon Mr Hayes very kindly invited him to accept of the conveniences of theirs. Wood accepted the offer, and lay with Billings. In three or four days time Mrs Hayes having taken an oppportunity, opened to him a desire of being rid of her husband, at which Wood, as he very well might, was exceedingly surprized, and demonstrated the baseness as well as cruelty there would be in such an action, if committed by him, who beisdes the general ties of humanity, stood particularly oblig'd to him as his neighbour and his friend. Mrs Hayes in order to hush these scruples, persuaded him that her husband was void of all religion and goodness, an enemy to God, and therefore unworthy of his protection; that he had killed a man in the country, and destroyed two of his and her children, one of which was buried under an apple-tree, the other under a pear-tree, in the county. To these fictitious tales, she added another, which perhaps had the greatest weight, *viz*. that if he were dead, she should be mistress of fifteen hundred pounds, 'And then,' says she, 'you may be master thereof if you will help to get him out of the way, Billings has agreed to it if you'll make a third, and so all may be finished without danger.'

A few days after this, Woods occasions called him out of town: on his return, which was on the first day of March, he found Mr Hayes and his wife, and Billings, very merry together. Amongst other things which passed in conversation, Mr Hayes happened to say, 'that he and another person once drank as much wine between them, as came to a guinea, without either of them being fuddled.' Billings upon this, proposed a wager on these terms, that half a dozen bottles of the best Mountain should be fetched, which if Mr Hayes could drink without being disordered, then Billings should pay for it, but if not, then it should be at the cost of Mr Hayes; who accepting of this proposal, Mrs Hayes and the two men went to the Brawns Head in New Bond-Street to fetch the wine. As they were going thither, she put them in mind of the proposition she made them to murder Mr Hayes, and said they could not have a better opportunity than when he should be intoxicated with liquor; whereupon Wood made answer, that it would be a most inhuman act to murder a man in cool blood, and that too when he was in liquor. Mrs Hayes had recourse to her old arguments, and Billings joining with her, Wood sufferr'd himself to be over-power'd. When they came to the tavern they called for a pint of the best Mountain, and after they had drank it order'd a gallon and a half to be sent home to their lodgings; which was done accordingly, and Mrs Hayes paid ten shillings and six pence for it, which was what it came to. Then they came all back and sat down together to see Mr Hayes drink the wager, and while he swallowed the wine, they called for two three full pots of beer, in order to entertain themselves.

Mr Hayes when he had almost finished his wine, began to grow very merry, singing and dancing about the room, with all the gaity which is natural. But Mrs Hayes fearful of his not having his dose, sent away privately for another bottle, of which having drank some also, it quite finished the work, by depriving him totally of his understanding; however, reeling into the other room, he there threw himself a-cross the bed, and fell fast asleep. No sooner did his wife perceive it, than she came to the two men to go in and do the work; then Billings taking a coal-hatchet in his hand going into the other room, struck Mr Hayes therewith on the back of his head, which blow fractur'd his skull and made him, thro' the agony of the pain, stamp violently upon the ground; insomuch that it alarmed the people who lay in the garret; and Wood fearing the consequence, went in and repeated the blows, tho' that was needless, since the first was mortal of itself, and he already lay quiet. By this time Mrs Springate, whose husband lodged over Mr Hayes's head, on hearing the noise, came down to enquire the reason of it, complaining at the same time, that it so disturbed her family, that they could not rest: Mrs Hayes thereupon told her, 'that her husband had had some company with him, who growing merry with their liquor were a little noisy; but that they were going immediately, and desired she would be easy'. Upon this she went up again for the present, and the three murderers began immediately to consult how to get rid of the body.

The men were in so much terrour and confusion, that they knew not what to do; but the wife of the deceased quickly thought of an expedient in which they all agreed. She said, 'that if the head was cut off, there would not be near so much difficulty in carrying off the body, which could not be known.'

In order to put this design in execution, they got a pail, and she herself carrying the candle, they all entered the room where the deceased lay. Then the woman holding the pail, Billings drew the body by the head over the bed side, that the blood might run the more freely into it; and Wood with his pocket penknife cut it off. As soon as it was severed from the body, and the bleeding was over, they poured the blood down a wooden sink at the window, and after it several pails of water, in order to wash it quite away, that it might not be perceiv'd in the morning; however, their precautions were not altogether effectual, for Springate the next morning found several clods of blood, but not suspecting any thing of the matter, threw them away; neither had they escaped letting some tokens of their cruelty fall upon the floor, stained the wall of the room, and even the ceiling, which it may be supposed happened at the giving the first blow. When they had finished this decollation, they again consulted what was next to be done. Mrs Hayes was for boiling it in a pot, till nothing but the skull remained, which would effectually prevent any body's knowing to whom it belonged; but the two men thinking this too dilatory a method, they resolved to put it in a pail, and go together and throw it in the Thames. Springate hearing a bustling in Mr Hayes's room for some time, and then somebody going down stairs, called again to know who it was, and what was the occasion of it, (it being then about eleven a clock) to which Mrs Hayes answered, 'it was her husband, who was going a journey into the country'.

Billings and Wood being thus gone to dispose of the head, went towards Whitehall, intending to have thrown it into the river there; but the gates being shut up, they were obliged to go forward as far as Mr Macreth's Wharf near the Horse-Ferry at Westminster, where Billings setting down the pail from under his great coat, Woods took up the same with the head therein, and threw it into the dock before the wharf. It was expected the same would have been carried away by the tide, but the water being then ebbing, it was left behind. There were also some lighters lying over-against the dock, and one of the lightermen walking then on board, saw them throw the pail into the dock, but by the obscurity of the night, the distance, and having no suspicion, did not apprehend any thing of the matter. Having thus done, they returned home again to Mrs Hayes's, where they arrived about twelve a-clock, and being let in, found the wife of the deceased had been very busily employed in washing the floor, and scraping the blood off from it, and from the wall, &c. After which they all three went into the fore-Room; Billings and Wood went to bed there, and Mrs Hayes sat by them till morning.

In the morning of the second of March, about the dawning of the day, one Robinson a watchman saw a man's head lying in the dock, and a pail near it: his surprize occasioned his calling some persons to assist in taking up the head, and finding the pail bloody, they conjectured the head had been brought thither in it.

Their suspicions were fully confirmed therein by the lighterman, who saw Billings and Wood throw the same into the dock, as beforementioned. It was now time for Mrs Hayes, Billings, and Wood, to consider how they should dispose of the body: Mrs Hayes and Wood proposed to put it in a box, where it might lay concealed till a convenient opportunity offered for removing it; this being approved of, Mrs Hayes brought a box, but upon their endeavouring to put it in, the box was not big enough to hold it. They had before wrapped it up in a blanket, out of which they took it. Mrs Hayes proposed to cut off the arms and legs, and they again attempted to put it in, but the box would not hold it; then they cut off the thighs, and laying them piece-meal in the box, concealed them till night. In the mean time Mr Hayes's head, which had been found as before, had sufficiently alarmed the town, and information was given to the neighbouring Justices of the Peace. The parish officers did all that was possible towards the discovery of the persons guilty of so horrid an action; they caused the head to be cleaned, the face to be washed from the dirt and blood, and the hair to be combed, and then the head to be set upon a post in publick view in St Margarets church-yard, Westminster, that every body might have free access to see the same, with some of the parish officers to attend, hoping by that means a discovery of the same might be attained. The high-constable of Westminster Liberty, also issued private orders to all the petty constables, watchmen, and other officers of that district, to keep a strict eye on all coaches, carts, &c. passing in the night through their liberty, imagining that the perpetrators of such a horrid fact would endeavour to free themselves of the body, in the same manner as they had done of the head. These orders were executed for some time, with all the secresy imaginable, under various pretences, but insuccessfully; the head also continued to be exposed for some days in the manner before described, which drew a prodigious number of people to see it, but without attaining any discovery of the murderers.

On the second of March in the evening, Catherine Hayes, Thomas Wood, and Thomas Billings, took the body and disjointed members out of the box, and wrapped them up in two blankets, *viz.* the body in one, and the limbs in the other: then Billings and Wood first took up the body, and about nine a clock in the evening carried it by turns into Mary-le-bone Fields, and threw the same into a pond, (which Wood in the daytime had been hunting for) and returning back again about eleven, took up the limbs in the other old blanket, and carried them by turns to the same place, throwing them in also. About twelve a clock the same night, they returned back again, and knocking at the door, were let in by Mary Springate. They went up to bed in Mrs Hayes's fore-room, and Mrs Hayes staid with them all night, sometimes sitting up, and sometimes laying down upon the bed by them. The same day one Bennet, the King's organ-maker's apprentice, going to Westminster to see the head, believed it to be Mr Hayes's, he being intimately acquainted with him, and thereupon went and informed Mrs Hayes, that the head exposed to view in St Margaret's church-yard, was so very like Mr Hayes, that he believed it to be his; upon which Mrs Hayes asserted him that Mr Hayes was very well, and reproved him very sharply for formimg such an opinion, telling him he must be very cautious how he rais'd such false and scandalous reports, for that he might thereby bring himself into a great deal of trouble. This reprimand put a stop to the youth's saying any thing more about it. The same day also Mr Samuel Patrick having been at Westminster to see the head, went from thence to Mr Granger's at the Dog and Dyel in Monmouth Street, where Mr Hayes and his wife were intima-tely acquainted, and told that the head in his opinion was the most like to their countryman Hayes of any he ever saw.

Billings being there then at work, some of the servants replied it could not be his, because there being one of Mrs Hayes's lodgers there they should have heard of it by him if Mr Hayes had been missing, or any accident had happen'd to him; to which Billings made answer that Mr Hayes was alive and well, and that he left him in bed when he came to work in the morning. The third day of March, Mrs Hayes gave Wood a white coat and a pair of leathern breaches of Mr Hayes's, which he carried with him to Greenford, near Harrow on the Hill. Mrs Springate observing Wood carrying these things down stairs bundled up in a white cloath told Mrs Hayes, who replied it was a suit of cloaths he had borrowed of a neighbour, and was going to carry them home again. On the fourth of March, one Mrs Longmore coming to visit Mrs Hayes, enquired how Mr Hayes did, and where he was: Mrs Hayes answered, that he was gone to take a walk, and then enquired what news there was about town. Her visiter told her that most peoples discourse run upon the man's head that had been found at Westminster. Mrs Hayes seemed to wonder very much at the wickedness of the age, and exclaimed vehemently against such barbarous murderers; adding, here is a discourse too in our neighbourhood, of a woman who has been found in the fields, mangled and cut to pieces. 'It may be so' reply'd, Mrs Longmore, 'but I have heard nothing of it.' On the sixth of March, the parish officers considering that it might putrify if it continued longer in the air, agreed with one Mr Westbrook, a surgeon, to have it preserved in spirits. He having accordingly provided a proper glass put it therein, and shewed it to all persons who were desirous of seeing; yet the murther remained still undiscover'd; and notwithstanding the multitude which had seen it, yet none pretended to be directly positive to the face, tho' many agreed in their having seen it before.

In the mean time Mrs Hayes quitted her lodgings, and removed from where the murther was committed to Mr Jones's a disteller in the neighbourhood, with Billings, Wood, and Springate, for whom she paid one quarters rent at her old lodgings. She now employed herself in getting as much of her husbands effects as possible she could; and amongst other papers and securities, finding a bond due to Mr Hayes from John Davis, who had married Mr Hayes's sister, she consulted how to get in that money: to which purpose she sent for one Mr Leonard Myring a barber, and told him, that she knowing him to be her husband's particular friend, and he then being under some misfortunes, thro' which she feared he would not presently return, she knew not how to recover several sums of money that were due to him, unless by sending fictitious letters in his name, to the several persons from whom the same was due Mr Myring considering the consequences of such a proceeding, declining it. But she prevailed upon some other person to write letters in Mr Hayes's name, particularly one to his mother, on the 14th of March, to demand ten pounds of the abovementioned Mr Davis, threatning if he refused, to sue him for it. This letter Mr Hayes's mother received, and acquainting her son-in-law Davis with the contents thereof, he offered to pay the money on sending down the bond, of which she by a letter acquainted Mrs Hayes's on the twenty-second of the same month.

During these transactions, several persons came daily to Mr Westbrook's to see the head. A poor woman at Kingsland, whose husband had been missing the day before it was found, was one amongst them. She at first sight fancied it bore some resemblance to that of her husband, but was not positive enough to swear it; yet her suspicion at first was sufficient to ground a report, which flew about the town in the evening, and some enquiries were made after the body of the person to whom it was suppos'd to belong, but to no purpose. Mrs Hayes in the mean while took all the pains imaginable to propagate a story of Mr Hayes's withdrawing on account of an unlucky blow he had given a person in a quarrel, and which made him apprehensive of a prosecution, through he was then in treaty with the widow in order to make it up. This story she at first told with many injunctions of secresy, to persons who she had good reasons to believe, would tell it again. It happened in the interim, that one Joseph Ashby, who had been an intimate acquaintance of Mr Hayes's, came to see her: she with a great deal of pretended concern, communicated the tale she had framed to him. Mr Ashby asked whether the person he had killed was him to whom the head belonged. She said, 'No; the man who died by Mr Hayes's blow, was buried entire, and Mr Hayes had given, or was about to give, a security to pay the widow fifteen pounds per annum, to hush it up.' Mr Ashby enquired next, 'where Mr Hayes was gone'. She said, 'to Portugal, with three or four foreign gentlemen'; and he thereupon took his leave. But going from thence to Mr Henry Longmore's, cousin to Mr Hayes, he related to him the story Mrs Hayes had told him, and expressed a great deal of dissatisfaction thereat, desiring Mr Longmore to go to her and make the same enquiry as he had done, but without taking notice they had seen one another. Mr Longmore went thereupon directly to Mrs Hayes's, and enquired in a peremptory tone for her husband. She in answer said, 'she suppos'd Mr Ashby had acquainted him with the misfortune which had befallen him.' Mr Longmore replied, 'he had not seen Mr Ashby for a considerable time, and knew nothing of his cousin's misfortune.' He then asked if he was in prison for debt? She answered him, 'No 'twas worse than that.' Mr Longmore again importuning her to know what he had done, to occasion his absconding so, saying, 'I suppose he has not murdered any body?' she replied, 'he had', and beckoning him to come on the stairs, related to him the story as before-mentioned. Mr Longmore being inquisitive which way he was gone, she told him into Herefordshire, and that he had taken four pistols with him for his security, one under each arm, and two in his pockets. Mr Longmore answered ''twould be dangerous for him to travel in that manner, because any person seeing him so armed, might cause him to be apprehended on suspicion of being an highwayman'. She assured him, that once he was apprehended on suspicion of being an highwayman, but that a gentleman who knew him, accidentally came in, and seeing him in custody, passed his word for his appearance, by which he was discharged. Mr Longmore made answer, that it was very improbable he was ever stopped on suspicion of being an highwayman, and discharged upon a man's only passing his word for his appearance. He then demanded which way he was supplied with money for his journey? She told him, she had sowed twenty six guineas into his cloaths, and that he had about him seventeen shillings in new silver. She added, that Springate who lodged there was privy to the whole transaction, for which reason she paid a quarters rent for her at her old lodgings, and the better to maintain what she had averred, called Springate to justify the truth of it. In concluding the discourse, she reflected on the unkind usage of Mr Hayes towards her, which surprised Mr Longmore, more than any thing else she had said, because he had often been a witness to her giving Mr Hayes the character of a most indulgent tender husband.

Mr Longmore then took his leave of her, and returned back to his friend Mr Ashby; when after comparing their several notes together, they judged that Mr Hayes must have had very ill play shewn him; upon which they agreed to go to Mr Eaton a Lifeguardman, who was also an acquaintance of Mr Hayes's which accordingly they did, intending him to have gone to Mrs Hayes also, to have heard what relation she would give him concerning her husband. They went and enquired at several places for him, but he was not then to be found; upon which they went down to Westminster to see the head at Mr Westbrook's. Mr Ashby first went up stairs to look on it, and coming down, told Mr Longmore he really thought it to be Mr Hayes's head; upon which Mr Longmore went up to see it, and after examining it more particularly, confirmed their suspicion. Then they returned to seek out Mr Eaton, and finding him at home, informed him of their proceedings, with the reasons on which their suspicions were grounded, and compelled him to go with them to enquire into the affair. Mr Eaton pressed them to stay dinner with him, which at first they agreed to, but after altering their minds, went all down to Mr Longmore's house, and there renewed their suspicions, not only of Mr Hayes's being murdered, but also that his wife was privy to the same; but in order to be more fully satisfied, they agreed that Mr Eaton should in a day or two's time go and enquire for Mr Hayes, taking no notice of his having seen them. In the mean time Longmore's brother interfered, saying, 'that it seemed apparent to him, that his cousin Hayes had been murdered, and that Mrs Hayes appeared guilty, with Wood and Billings, who, she told him, had drank with him the night before his journey.' He added, moreover, 'that he thought time was not to be delayed, because they might remove from their lodgings upon the least apprehensions of a discovery.'

His opinion prevailed as the most reasonable, and Mr Longmore said, 'they would go about it immediately'. Accordingly to Mr Justice Lambert he immediately applied, and acquainted him with the grounds of their suspicions, and their desire of his granting a warrant for the apprehension of the parties. The Justice, on hearing the story, not only readily complied with their demand, but said also, he would get proper officers to execute it in the evening, about nine o'clock; putting Mrs Hayes, Thomas Wood, Thomas Billings, and Mary Springate, into a special warrant for that purpose. At the hour appointed they met, and Mr Eaton bringing two officers of the guards along with him, they went altogether to the house where Mrs Hayes lodged. They went directly in, and up stairs, at which Mr Jones who kept the house, immediately demanded who and what they were? He was answered, that they were sufficiently authorized in all that they did, desiring him at the same time to bring candles, and he should see on what occasion they came. Light being thereupon brought, they went all up stairs together. Justice Lambert wrapped at Mrs Hayes's door with his cane. She demanded who was there, for that she was in bed, on which she was bid to get up and open the door, or they would break it open. After some little time taken to put on her cloaths, she came and opened it, and as soon as they were in the room, they saw Billings, who was sitting upon her bed-side, without either shoes or stockings on. The Justice ask'd whether he had been in bed with her? She said 'no, but that he sat there to mend his stockings'. 'Why then,' replied Mr Lambert, 'he had very good eyes to see to do it without fire or candle.' Hereupon they seized him too, and leaving persons below to guard them, went up and apprehended Springate; and after an examination in which they would confess nothing, committed Billings to New-Prison, Springate to the Gate-House, and Mrs Hayes to Tothill-Fields-Bridewell.

Mrs Hayes was very assiduous in contriveing such a method of behaviour as might carry the greatest appearance of innocence. She entreated Mr Longmore that she might be admitted to see the head, and Mr Lambert ordered her to have a sight of it as she came from Tothill-Fields-Bridewell to her examination. Accordingly Mr Longmore attending the officers ordered the coach to stop at Mr Westbrook's door, and as soon as she was admitted into the room she threw her self down upon her knees, crying out in great agonies, 'Oh it is my dear husband's head! it is my dear husband's head!' and embracing the glass in her arms, kissed the outside of it several times. Mr Westbrook coming in, told her, that if it was his head she should have a plainer view of it, so taking it out of the glass by the hair he brought it to her: she taking it her arms, kissed it, and seemed in great confusion, withall begging to have a lock of his hair; but Mr Westbrook replied, that he was afraid she had had too much of his blood already; at which she fainted away, and after recovering, was carried to Mr Lambert, to be examined before him and some other Justices of the Peace. While these things were in agitation, one Mr Huddle and his servant walking in Mary-le-bone Fields in the evening espied something lying in one of the ponds, which after they had examined, found to be the legs, thighs, and arms of a man. They being very much surprized at this, determined to search farther; and the next morning getting assistance drained the pond, where to their further astonishment they pulled out the body of a man wrapped up in a blanket, with the news of which, while Mrs Hayes was under examination, Mr Crosby a constable came down to the Justices, not doubting but this was the body of Mr Hayes. Yet tho' she was somewhat confounded at the new discovery made hereby, she could not be prevailed on to make any acknowledgement of her knowing any thing of the fact; whereupon the Justices who examined her, committed her that afternoon to Newgate, the mob attending her thither with as loud acclamations of joy at her commitment, as if they were already convinc'd of her guilt.

Sunday morning following, Thomas Wood came to town from Greenford near Harrow, having heard nothing of the taking up of Mrs Hayes, Billings, or Springate. The first place he went to, was Mrs Hayes's old lodging, where he was answer'd that she was removed to Mr Jones's a distiller, a little farther in the street; thither he went, where the people, knowing him to be suspected of the murther, said Mrs Hayes was gone to the Green Dragon in King-Street, which is Mr Longmore's house, and a man who was there told him moreover that he was going thither and would shew him the way. Wood, being on horseback followed him, and he led him the way to Mr Longmore's house; when Mr Longmore's

327

brother coming to the door, and seeing Wood, immediately seized him, and unhorseing him dragged him in doors, sent for officers and charged them with him on suspicion of the murder. From thence he was carried before Mr Justice Lambert, who asked him many questions in relation to the murder, but he would confess nothing, whereupon he was committed to Tothil-Fields-Bridewell. While he was there he heard the various reports of persons concerning the murder, and judging it impossible to prevent a discovery or evade the proofs that were against him, he resolved to make an ample confession of the whole affair; of which Mr Lambert being acquainted, he, with John Mohun and Thomas Salt, Esqs; two other Justices of the Peace, went to Tothill-Fields-Bridewell, to take his examination, in which he seem'd very ingenious and ample declaring all the particulars before mention'd with this addition, that he had been drawn into the commission thereof partly thro' poverty, and partly thro' her crafty insinuations, who by feeding him with liquors, had spirited him up to the commission of such a piece of barbarity. He farther acknowledged, that ever since the commission of the fact, he had had no peace, but that every day, before he came from Greenford, he was fully persuaded within himself, that he should be seized for the murther when he came to town, notwithstanding which he could not refrain coming, tho' under a kind of certainty of being taken, and dying for the fact.

328

Having thus made a full and ample confession, and signed the same, on the 27th of March, his mittimus was made by Justice Lambert, and he was committed to Newgate, whither he was carried under a guard of a serjeant and eight soldiers, with musquets and bayonets, to keep off the mob, who were so exasperated against the actors of such a piece of barbarity, that without that caution it would have been very difficult to have carried him thither alive.

On Monday the 28th of March, after Mrs Hayes was committed to Newgate, being the day after Wood's apprehension, Joseph Mercer going to see Mrs Hayes, she told him as he was Thomas Billings's friend as well as hers, she desired he would go to him and tell him, 'twas in vain to deny any longer the murder of her husband, for they were equally guilty, and both must die for it. Billings hearing this, and that Wood was apprehended, and had fully confes'd the whole affair, thought it needless to persist any longer in a denial, and therefore the next day, being the 29th of March, he made a full and plain discovery of the whole fact, agreeing with Wood in all the particulars; which confession was made and signed in the presence of Gideon Harvey and Oliver Lambert, Esqs; two of His Majesty's Justices of the Peace, whereupon he was removed to Newgate the same day that Wood was. Wood and Billings acquitting Springate of the aforesaid murder, she was soon discharged from her confinement; but this discovery making a great noise in the town, divers of Mrs Hayes's acquaintance, went to visit her in Newgate, and examin'd into the reasons that induced her to commit the said fact. Her acknowledgement in general was, that Mr Hayes had proved but an indifferent husband, to her; that one night he came home drunk and struck her; that upon complaining to Billings and Wood, they, or one of them, said, such a fellow ought not to live, and that they would murder him for a halfpenny. She took that opportunity to propose her bloody intentions to them, and her willingness that they should do so; that she was acquainted with their design, heard the blow given Mr Hayes by Billings, and then went with Wood to them into the room; that she held the candle while his head was cut off, and in excuse for this bloody fact, said, the Devil was got into them all that made them do it. When she was made sensible that her crime in law was not only murther, but petty treason, she began to shew great concern indeed, making enquiries into the nature of the proof which was necessary to convict, having possessed herself with a notion, that unless it appeared she murthered him with her own hands, it would not touch her life; and therefore she was very angry that either Billings or Wood should acknowledge her guilty of the murther, and subject her to that punishment which of all others she most feared; often repeating it, that it was hard they would not suffer her to be hanged with them.

There are a set of people about Newgate, who get their living by imposing on unhappy criminals, and persuading them that guilt may be covered, and justice evaded, by certain artful contrivances in which they profess themselves masters. Some of these had got access to this unhappy woman, and had instilled into her a notion, that the confession of Wood and Billings could no ways affect her life. This made her vainly imagine, that there was no positive proof against her, and that circumstantials only, would not convict her. For this reason she resolved to put herself upon a trial contrary to her first intentions. Accordingly being arraigned, she pleaded not guilty, and put herself upon her trial. Wood and Billings, both pleaded guilty to the same indictment; at the same time acknowledging their guilt, and desiring to make attonement for the same by the loss of their blood; only praying the court would be graciously pleased to favour them so much as to dispense with their being hanged in chains.

Mrs Hayes having thus put herself upon her trial, the King's Council opened the indictment, setting forth the heiniousness of the fact, the premeditated intentions, and inhuman method of acting it. Then Richard Bromage, Robert Wilkins, Leonard Myring, Joseph Mercer, John Blakesby, Mary Springate and Richard Bows, were called into court; the substance of whose evidence was, that the prisoner being interrogated about the murther, when in Newgate, said, 'the Devil put it into her head; but however, John Hayes was none of the best of husbands, for she had been half starved ever since she was married to him; that she did not in the least repent of any thing she had done, but only drawing those two poor men into this misfortune; that she was six weeks importuning them to do it, that they denied it two or three times, but at last agreed; that she was in the fore room on the same floor when he was killed; that when he was quite dead, she went in and held the candle whilst Wood cut his head off; that it would signify nothing to make a long preamble, she could hold up her hand, and say she was guilty, for nothing could save her, no body could forgive her; that the first occasion of this design to murther him was, because he came home one night and beat her; upon which Billings said, "this fellow deserves to be killed", and Wood, said, "he'd be his butcher for a penny".' Many other circumstances equally with these appeared, and a cloud of witnesses, many of whom, the thing appearing so plain, were sent away unexamined. She herself confessed at the bar, her previous knowledge of their intent, yet foolishly insisted on her innocence, because the fact was not committed by her own hands. The jury without staying long to consider on it, found her guilty, and she was taken from the bar in a very weak and faint condition. On her return to Newgate, she was visited by several persons of her acquaintance, who were so far from doing her any good, that they rather interrupted her in those preparations which became her. One old gentleman indeed, who seemed to have no other motive in coming to see her, took an opportunity of discoursing to her in a suitable and very rational manner. This discourse was taken down, but is too long to insert.

When they were brought up to receive sentence, Wood and Billings renewed their former request to the court, that they might not be hung in chains. Mrs Hayes also made use of her former assertion, that she was not guilty of actually committing the fact, and therefore begged of the court, that she might at least have so much mercy shewn her, as not to be burnt alive. The judges then sentenced the two men, with the other malefactors to be hanged, and Mrs Hayes, as in all cases of petit-treason, to die by fire at a stake; at which she screamed, and being carried back to Newgate, fell into violent agonies. Perhaps no body ever kept their thoughts so long and so closely united in the world, as appeared by the frequent messages she sent to Wood and Billings; and that tenderness which she expressed for both of them, lamenting in the softest terms, her having involved those two poor men in the commission of a fact, for which they were now to lose their lives: in which indeed, they deserved pity, since they were persons of unblemished characters, until misled by her.

As to the sense she had of her own circumstances, there has been scarce any in her state known to behave with so much indifference. She said often, that death was neither grievous nor terrible to her in itself, but was in some degrees shocking from the manner in which she was to die. Her fondness for Billings, hurried her into indecencies of a very extraordinary nature, such as sitting with her hand in his at chapel, leaning upon his shoulder, and refusing upon being reprimanded, to make any amendment in respect of these shocking passages, between her and the murderers of her husband. One of her last expressions was to enquire of the executioner, whether he had hang'd her dear child; and this, as she was going from the sledge to the stake, so strong and lasting were the passions of this woman.

The Friday night before her execution, (being assured she should die on the Monday following) she had procured a bottle of strong poison, designing to have taken the same; but a woman who was in the place with her touching it with her lips, found it burnt them to an extraordinary degree, and spilling a little on her handkerchief, perceived it burnt that also; upon which suspecting her intentions, she broke the viol. On the day of her execution she was at prayers, and received the sacrament in the chapel, where she still shewed her tenderness for Billings. About twelve the prisoners were severally carried to execution: Billings with eight others for various crimes were put into three carts; and Catherine Hayes was drawn upon a sledge. Billings with eight others, after having had some time for their private devotions, were turned off. After which, Catherine Hayes being brought to the stake, was chained thereto with an iron chain, running round her waist, and under her arms, and a rope about her neck, which was drawn thro' a hole in the post; then the faggots, intermixed with light brush, wood, and straw, being piled all round her, the executioner put fire thereto in several places, which immediately blazing out, as soon as it reached her, with her arms she pushed down those that were before her, when she appeared in the middle of the flames as low as her waist.

The executioner got hold of the end of the cord which was round her neck, and pulled it tight, in order to strangle her, but the fire soon reached his hand and burnt it, so that he was obliged to let go again. More faggots were immediately thrown upon her, and in about three or four hours she was reduced to ashes: in the mean time Billings's irons were put upon him as he was hanging on the gallows; after which being cut down, he was carried to the gibbet, about one hundred yards distance, and there hung up in chains.

Mrs Hayes some time before her execution, confidently averred, that Billings was the son both of Mr Hayes and herself; that his father not liking him, he was put out to relations of hers, and took the name of Billings from his god-father: but Mr Hayes's relations confidently deny'd all this, and he himself said he knew nothing more, than that he called a shoemaker, father, in the country, himself being put apprentice to a taylor, with whom he served his time, and then came up to London to work journey-work.

AN ACCOUNT OF
SARAH
MALCOLM

O f the following paper it needs only be said, that it was written by this unfortunate person with her own hand in the press-yard of Newgate, on Tuesday the 6th of March, 1732–3 the day before her suffering. She spent the greatest part of the day in writing it; and when it was finished she read it over several times; being often admonished to be careful to write nothing but what was truth. She then folded it up with her own hands before the Rev. Dr Middleton, Lecturer of St Bride's, and Rowland Ingram, Esq; Keeper of His Majesty's Gaol of Newgate, who both sealed it with their own seals; in which manner she delivered it to the Rev. Mr Piddington, with a desire that it might be published.

After the execution was over, the paper was opened before the Worshipful the Sheriffs of London and Middlesex, Dr Middleton, Mr Peters, Mr Brouncker, and Mr Ingram; and being read, was again sealed up, and produced two nights after, before the Honourable the Masters of the Bench of the Inner and Middle Temples, who read and returned it to the said Reverend person in the manner in which they received it, and in the manner wherein it afterwards appear'd to the world, signed with his name.

March the 6th, 1732–3.

SIR,

You cannot be, nor are not unsensible that there is a just God, before whom we must give an exact Account of all our Actions, at the End of our Lives.

So as my Life is at an End, and I must appear before the All-seeing Judge of Heaven and Earth, to give an Account of mine, so I take that great Judge to witness, that what I here declare is true.

January the 28th, which was Sunday, after my Master was gone to Commons, Mary Tracy came to me, and drank Tea, and then it was I did give my Consent to that unhappy Act of Robbing Mrs Duncomb, but I do declare before the Almighty, before whom I shortly shall appear, I did not know of the Murder.

And on Saturday the 3d of February was the Time appointed, and accordingly they came about 10 a Clock at Night, and Mary Tracey came to Mr Kerrol's Chambers, and I went to Mrs Duncomb's, and on the Stairs I met the Maid, and she did ask me whether I was going to the old Maid, and I answered I was, and as soon as I thought she had got down Stairs, I would have gone in myself, but I thought that I should give some Suspicion, and so I asked which would go in, and James Alexander replied he would, and the Door being left open for the Maid, against her Return, or otherways I was to have knocked at the Door, and after to have let them in, but it being open hindred it; and I gave James Alexander Directions to lie under the Maid's Bed, and desired Mary Tracey and Thomas Alexander to go and stay for me at my Master's Door until my Return, and according they did, and when I came, I desired they would go and stay for me at Mrs Duncomb's Stairs, until my Return, and I went and lighted a Candle, and stirred the Fire in my Master's Chamber, and went again to Mary Tracey and Thomas Alexander, who were on Mrs Duncomb's Stairs, and there we waited until after two a Clock on the Sunday which was the 4th of February, and then I would have gone in, but when Thomas Alexander and Mary Tracey interrupted me, and said if you go in, and they awake, they will know you, and if you stay on the Stairs, it may be that some one will come up and see you; but I made Answer, that no one lives up so high but Madam Duncomb.

And at length it was concluded that Mary Tracey and the other Alexander should go in, and shut the Door, and accordingly they did, and there I remained until between 4 and 5 a Clock, and then they came out, and said, 'Hip', and I came higher up, and they did ask, which way they should shut the Door, and I told them to run the Bolt back, and it would spring into its Place, and accordingly they did, and came down, and having come down, they asked, where they should divide what they had got; I asked how much that was; they said, about three hundred Pounds in Goods and Money, but said they were forced to gag them all.

I desired to know, where they had found it; they said, that fifty Guineas of it was in the old Maid's Pocket in a leathern Purse, besides Silver, that they said was loose; and above an hundred and fifty Pounds in a Drawer, besides the Money that they had out of a Box, and the Tankard and one silver Spoon, and a Ring which was looped with Thread, and one square piece of Plate, one pair of Sheets, and two Pillowbiers and five Shifts; and we did divide all this, near Fig-Tree-Court, as also near Pump-Court; and they did say unto me, besure that you bury the Cole and Plate under Ground, until the Robbery is all over; For if you be seen flush with Cole, you will be suspected; and on Monday, besure, about 3 or 4 a Clock, you come to the Pewter-Platter on Holborn-Bridge.

I being apprehended on the Sunday Night, on the Monday Morning, when I was in the Compter, I happened to see one Bridgewater; he said, he was sorry to see me there, I also was sorry to see him a Brother in Affliction; he desired me to give him a Dram, for he was a great while in Prison, and I threw him a Shilling and a Farthing: And I walking about the Room, I was surprised to hear me called by my Name, and looking about, I observed at the Head of the Bed something move, and I pulled back the Curtain, and there I saw this Bridgewater, and he asked, whether I had sent for any Friends; I told him I had, and not long after he called me again, and said, there was a Friend come to me; and I looked thorough the Hole in the Wall, and asked, whether that was Will Gibbs, and he answered me, yes; and I asked him, how the Alexanders were; he said, they were well; he asked me how I came to be taken, and I told him, my Master having found the Tankard, and some Linen, and he having seen ninety Pounds and sixteen Shillings on the Sunday the 4th of February,

The Execution of Sarah Malcolm *in* Fleet=ſtreet.

but it might through Surprize be forgot, but I had it all. He said, if I would give him some Money, he would get People that would swear that the Tankard was my Mother's according as I would direct; but said I, you must get some one to swear, that I was at their House; he said, it must be a Woman, and he said, she would not go without four Guineas, and the four Men must have two Guineas a piece. So I gave him twelve Guineas, and he said, he and his Friends would be at the Bull's Head in Breadstreet, but when I asked for them, I could not hear of them, and when I came before the Worshipful Alderman Brocas, I was committed to Newgate.

And when I was brought up to the Common Side, I was bid to pull off my Riding-hood, and one Peter Buck a Prisoner observed a Bulk in my Hair to hang down behind, and told one Roger Johnson, that I certainly had Money in my Hair; and Mr Johnson brought me down in a Cellar, and told me, that Peter Buck said, I had Money in my Hair, and bid me take it out, and so I did, and he counted 36 Moidores and eighteen Guineas, and 6 broad Pieces, and 2 of them were 25 Shillings, and 4 were 23 Shilling Pieces, and half a 23 Shillings, and 5 Crowns, and 2 half Crowns, and one Shilling, and he said in the Condemned Hole, he would be cleared and get out of Gaol on that Account.

In the seal'd cover, wherein the foregoing paper was enclos'd, were these words written also with her own hand.

The enclos'd contains six Sides of Paper, which I take Almighty God and my own Conscience to witness, is nothing but the very Truth, as witness my Hand,

SARAH MALCOLM.

When this unhappy malefactor was brought into Fleet-Street, over-against Fetter-Lane End, the place of her execution, on Wednesday the 7th of March, she declared she died in peace with all the world, and earnestly desired to see her master Kerrol; but as she could not, protested that all accusations and aspersions concerning him, were entirely false, and that all confessions, except those delivered as above, were entirely groundless, and likewise solemnly declared that the contents of the foregoing paper were true.

GLOSSARY

accompt (archaic) account

accoutre clothe or equip in something noticeable or impressive

asperse attack or criticise the reputation or integrity of

baggage cheeky or disagreeable woman

bavin stack of firewood

beldam (archaic) old woman

Benefit of Clergy first-time offenders could receive lesser sentences for certain crimes

betty short bar used by thieves to wrench open doors; a jemmy

bilboes iron bar with sliding shackles, formerly used for confining a prisoner's ankles

Boor from boer, Dutch for farmer

burnt in the hand punishment in which the criminal was branded on the thumb

buttock and file (obsolete) common whore and pickpocket

cheat false shirt-front, also known as cheat the devil

clyster enema

compter used variously for counter and a small prison, controlled by a sheriff, especially one for debtors

compting-house (counting house) room used by the accounting and book-keeping departments of a business

contumacious (archaic or Law) stubbornly or wilfully disobedient to authority [especially of a defendant]

cornuto (obsolete) cuckold

Crispin patron saint of shoemakers; see also St Hugh

cully (archaic) man, friend
Cyprian goddess the goddess Venus

dark-lanthorn (dark lantern) lantern with a shutter or panel that can obscure
the light
decollation (archaic) beheading
diascordium herbal medicine, no longer in use, containing among other
ingredients the herb scordium and opium
discipline of the horse-pond punishment through ducking
distich a couplet
diving pickpocketing
doxy (archaic) lover or mistress
drawer (archaic) person who draws beer, etc., in a bar

ell measure of length, equivalent to six hand breadths (about 45 inches)
equipage carriage and horse with attendants

facetious (archaic) witty
flagitious criminal, villainous
foot-pad highwayman operating on foot rather than riding a horse
freebooter pirate or lawless adventurer
fustian thick, hard-wearing twilled cloth

Galen Greek physician, writer and philosopher
gantloop (variant of gauntlet) to undergo the military punishment of receiving
blows while running between two runs of men with sticks, i.e. running the
gauntlet

habiliments (archaic) clothing
hempen widow woman whose husband is hanged
high gammer cook to have sexual intercourse
Hymen Greek god of marriage

imbrue stain
in propria persona in person

journeyman or journey work worker who has finished learning a trade and
is employed by someone rather than working on his own

kine (plural noun, archaic) cows collectively

lacquey (lackey) servant, especially a liveried footman or manservant
lighterman a man operating a flat-bottomed barge used to transfer goods to
   and from ships in harbour

mammon riches or wealth regarded as a source of evil or corruption
mensuration measurement
mercer dealer in textile fabrics, especially silks, velvets and other fine materials
merry andrew (archaic) a clown
mithridate medicine believed to be a universal antidote to or preservative
   against poison and disease
mittimus warrant of commitment to prison or a command to a jailer directing
   him to hold someone in prison
mountebank a person who sold patent medicines in public places
mumpsimus someone who obstinately adheres to old customs or ideas in spite
   of evidence that they are wrong or unreasonable

neat bovine animal
nemine contradicente (archaic) literally with no one contradicting; by consensus
nick and froth landlord

341

ordinary used variously for a judge, a chaplain of a prison, whose job it was to
   minister to those condemned to death, and an inn providing meals at a fixed
   price

pay scot and lot pay in full
perdue hidden, or concealed
periwig highly styled wig, of the type still worn by judges and barristers
peruke wig
petty treason, petit treason the offence of killing a social superior, including a
   wife murdering her husband (based on the assumption that each person in
   society had their appointed place). Those found guilty were burnt at the stake.
pish to express impatience or contempt
pistole any of various gold coins used in Europe or Scotland in the seventeenth
   and eighteenth centuries
pitch and hussel game of tossing a coin and calling Heads or Tails, now called
   pitch and toss

pomatum pomade; a scented ointment or oil applied to the hair

porringer small bowl, typically with a handle, used for soup, stew, etc.

post with haste

precisian (archaic) punctilious observer of rules and forms, especially in the field of religion

pressing the work of the press gang to round up men who were forced to join the army or navy

pro hac vice (Law) for this occasion only

prosecutrix plaintiff

ptisan broth barley broth

put to read his neck verse Latin verse printed in black letter (usually the beginning of Psalm 51) formerly set before a person claiming benefit of clergy, the reading of which he might prove his clerical status and save his neck.

rapine the violent seizure of someone's property

St Hugh patron saint of shoemakers; see also Crispin

sea coal coal that has washed up on a beach. It is jet black and sparkling

sharp'd (archaic from the verb sharp) to cheat or swindle

skip-kennel a lackey or footboy

Socinian member of a Christian sect that rejected many orthodox beliefs, including most notably the divinity of Christ, the Trinity and original sin

sophisters (variant of sophist) teacher of philosophy and rhetoric; a person who reasons with clever but false arguments

spado type of sword

spark (archaic) a lively young man

specie money in the form of coins rather than notes

spunging-house (sponging-house) place (often a tavern) where debtors were kept by a bailiff for twenty-four hours before being lodged in prison, so that their friends might settle the debt

stroller vagrant

surtout gentleman's great coat, similar to a frock coat

talley-man (tally-husband) man with whom a woman cohabits

tapster person who draws and serves alcoholic drinks at a bar

teague (derogatory) an Irishman

throwster person who twists silk fibres into thread

tongue pad great or glib talker

342

tonsor barber

train oil oil obtained from the blubber of a whale (and other sea creatures)

trapann'd (alternative of trepan'd) to trap

Turkish mute on a bashaw the tradition of using mute servants in the Ottoman Empire, as it was believed they would be unable to leak secrets, bashaw being an old-fashioned variant of pasha.

turnkey (archaic) jailer

two-pence wet, and two-pence dry brief act of intercourse with a prostitute, either vaginal (wet) or anal (dry) or masturbation

wen boil or other swelling or growth on the skin

whooper's hide (hooper's hide) blindman's bluff

FURTHER READING

J.M. Beattie, *Policing and Punishment in London, 1660–1750: Urban Crime and the Limits of Terror* (2001).

D. Bentley, *English Criminal Justice in the Nineteenth Century* (1998).

Arne Bialuschewski, 'Daniel Defoe, Nathaniel Mist, and the "General History of the Pyrates"', *The Papers of the Bibliographical Society of America*, Vol. 98, No. 1 (March 2004), pp. 21–38.

David J. Cox, *Crime in England 1688–1815* (2014).

Simon Devereaux and Paul Griffiths, eds, *Penal Practice and Culture, 1500–1900: Punishing the English* (Basingstoke, 2004).

L.B. Faller, *Turned to Account: the forms and functions of criminal biography in late seventeenth- and early eighteenth-century England* (1987).

Philip Gosse, *A Bibliography of the Works of Captain Charles Johnson* (1927).

Douglas Hay ... [et al.], *Albion's Fatal Tree: Crime and Society in Eighteenth-Century England* (1976).

Peter King, *Punishing the Criminal Corpse, 1700–1840: Aggravated Forms of the Death Penalty in England* (2017).

Peter Linebaugh, *The London Hanged: Crime and Civil Society in the Eighteenth Century* (2006).

Frank McLynn, *Crime and Punishment in Eighteenth-Century England* (1989).

Richard McMahon, ed., *Crime, Law and Popular Culture in Europe, 1500–1900* (2008).

John Richetti, *A History of Eighteenth-Century British Literature* (2017).

John J. Richetti, *Popular Fiction Before Richardson: Narrative Patterns, 1700–1739* (1969).

James Sharpe, *A Fiery & Furious People: A History of Violence in England* (2016).

F. Snyder and D. Hay, eds, *Labour, Law and Crime: An Historical Perspective* (1987).

Shelley Tickell, *Shoplifting in Eighteenth-Century England* (2018).

Richard M. Ward, *Print Culture, Crime and Justice in Eighteenth-Century London* (2014).

Tammy Whitlock, 'Wicked Ladies: Provincial Women, Crime and the Eighteenth-Century English Justice System', *The Historian*, Vol. 78, Issue 1 (Spring 2016), pp. 146–147.